ABIDJAN / CÔTE D'IVOIRE ABUJA / NIGERIA
ABABA / ETHIOPIA ALGIERS / ALGERIA ANTANA
ASMARA / ERITREA BAMAKO / MALI BANGUI / CENTRAL AFRICAN REPUBLIC BANJUL / GAMBIA BISSAU / GUINEA-BISSAU BRAZZAVILLE / REPUBLIC OF CONGO BUJUMBURA / BURUNDI CAIRO / EGYPT CONAKRY / GUINEA COTONOU / BENIN DAKAR / SENEGAL DAR ES SALAAM / TANZANIA DJIBOUTI / DJIBOUTI FREETOWN / SIERRA LEONE GABORONE / BOTSWANA HARARE / ZIMBABWE JUBA / SOUTH SUDAN KAMPALA / UGANDA KHARTOUM / SUDAN KIGALI / RWANDA KINSHASA / DEMOCRATIC REPUBLIC OF CONGO LIBREVILLE / GABON LILONGWE / MALAWI LOMÉ / TOGO LUANDA / ANGOLA LUSAKA / ZAMBIA MALABO / EQUATORIAL GUINEA MAPUTO / MOZAMBIQUE MASERU / LESOTHO MBABANE / SWAZILAND MOGADISHU / SOMALIA MONROVIA / LIBERIA MORONI / COMOROS NAIROBI / KENYA N'DJAMENA / CHAD NIAMEY / NIGER NOUAKCHOTT / MAURITANIA OUAGADOUGOU / BURKINA FASO PORT LOUIS / MAURITIUS PRAIA / CAPE VERDE PRETORIA / SOUTH AFRICA RABAT / MOROCCO SÃO TOMÉ / SÃO TOMÉ AND PRÍNCIPE TRIPOLI / LIBYA TUNIS / TUNISIA VICTORIA / SEYCHELLES WINDHOEK / NAMIBIA YAOUNDÉ / CAMEROON

ADJAYE AFRICA ARCHITECTURE

ADJAYE AFRICA ARCHITECTURE

A PHOTOGRAPHIC SURVEY OF METROPOLITAN ARCHITECTURE

EDITED BY PETER ALLISON

This book is dedicated to my father, Mr Affram Adjaye, by whose example I was inspired to love Africa from a very young age.

CONTENTS

FOREWORD

THE MAGHREB

DESERT

THE SAHEL

FOREST

SAVANNA & GRASSLAND

MOUNTAIN & HIGHVELD

ESSAYS

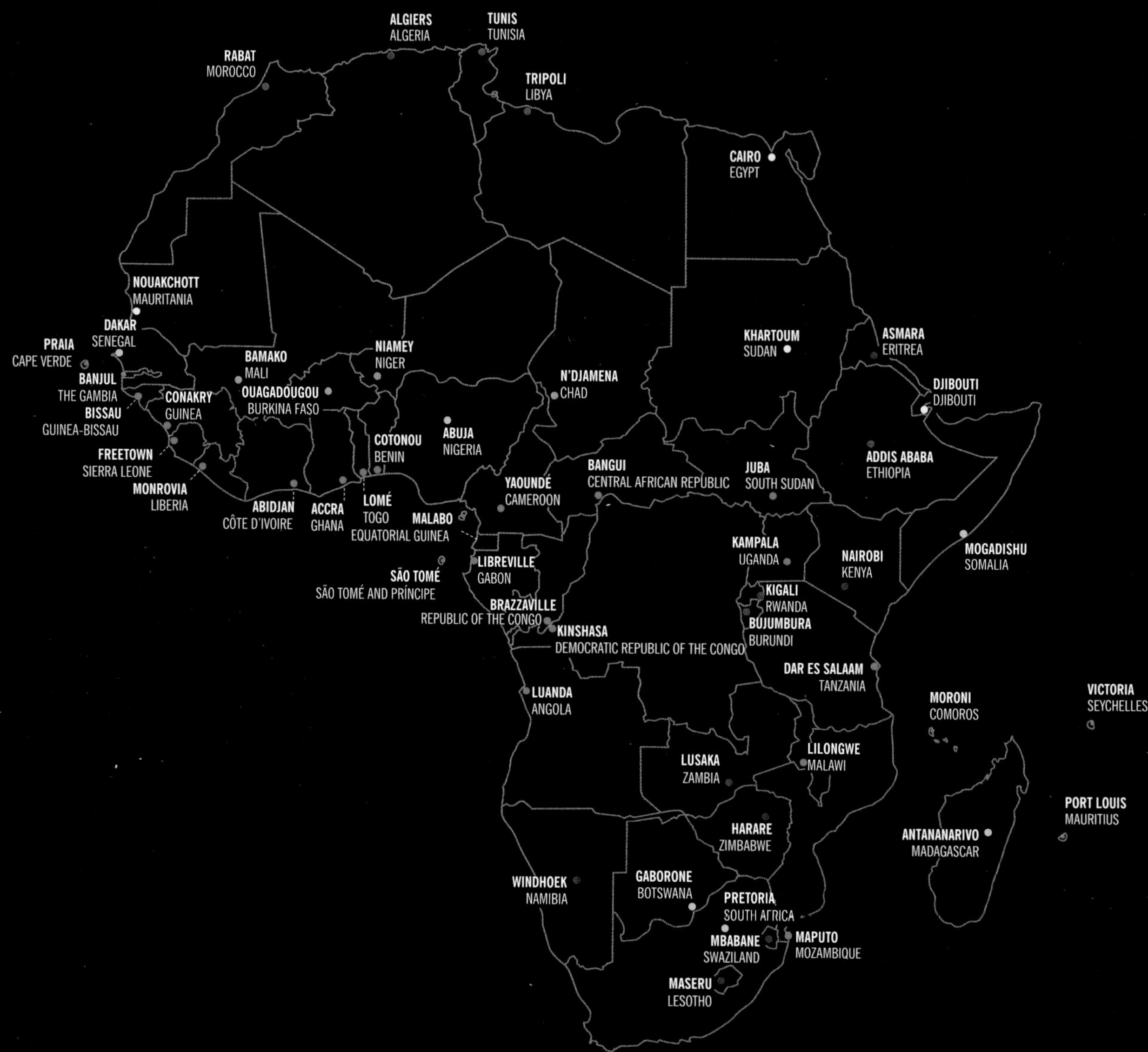
ALGIERS
ALGERIA
TUNIS
TUNISIA
RABAT
MOROCCO
TRIPOLI
LIBYA
CAIRO
EGYPT
NOUAKCHOTT
MAURITANIA
DAKAR
SENEGAL
PRAIA
CAPE VERDE
BANJUL
THE GAMBIA
BISSAU
GUINEA-BISSAU
CONAKRY
GUINEA
FREETOWN
SIERRA LEONE
MONROVIA
LIBERIA
BAMAKO
MALI
OUAGADOUGOU
BURKINA FASO
NIAMEY
NIGER
ABIDJAN
CÔTE D'IVOIRE
ACCRA
GHANA
LOMÉ
TOGO
COTONOU
BENIN
ABUJA
NIGERIA
MALABO
EQUATORIAL GUINEA
N'DJAMENA
CHAD
KHARTOUM
SUDAN
ASMARA
ERITREA
DJIBOUTI
DJIBOUTI
ADDIS ABABA
ETHIOPIA
YAOUNDÉ
CAMEROON
BANGUI
CENTRAL AFRICAN REPUBLIC
JUBA
SOUTH SUDAN
SÃO TOMÉ
SÃO TOMÉ AND PRÍNCIPE
LIBREVILLE
GABON
BRAZZAVILLE
REPUBLIC OF THE CONGO
KINSHASA
DEMOCRATIC REPUBLIC OF THE CONGO
KAMPALA
UGANDA
NAIROBI
KENYA
MOGADISHU
SOMALIA
KIGALI
RWANDA
BUJUMBURA
BURUNDI
DAR ES SALAAM
TANZANIA
LUANDA
ANGOLA
MORONI
COMOROS
VICTORIA
SEYCHELLES
LUSAKA
ZAMBIA
LILONGWE
MALAWI
HARARE
ZIMBABWE
PORT LOUIS
MAURITIUS
ANTANANARIVO
MADAGASCAR
WINDHOEK
NAMIBIA
GABORONE
BOTSWANA
PRETORIA
SOUTH AFRICA
MBABANE
SWAZILAND
MAPUTO
MOZAMBIQUE
MASERU
LESOTHO

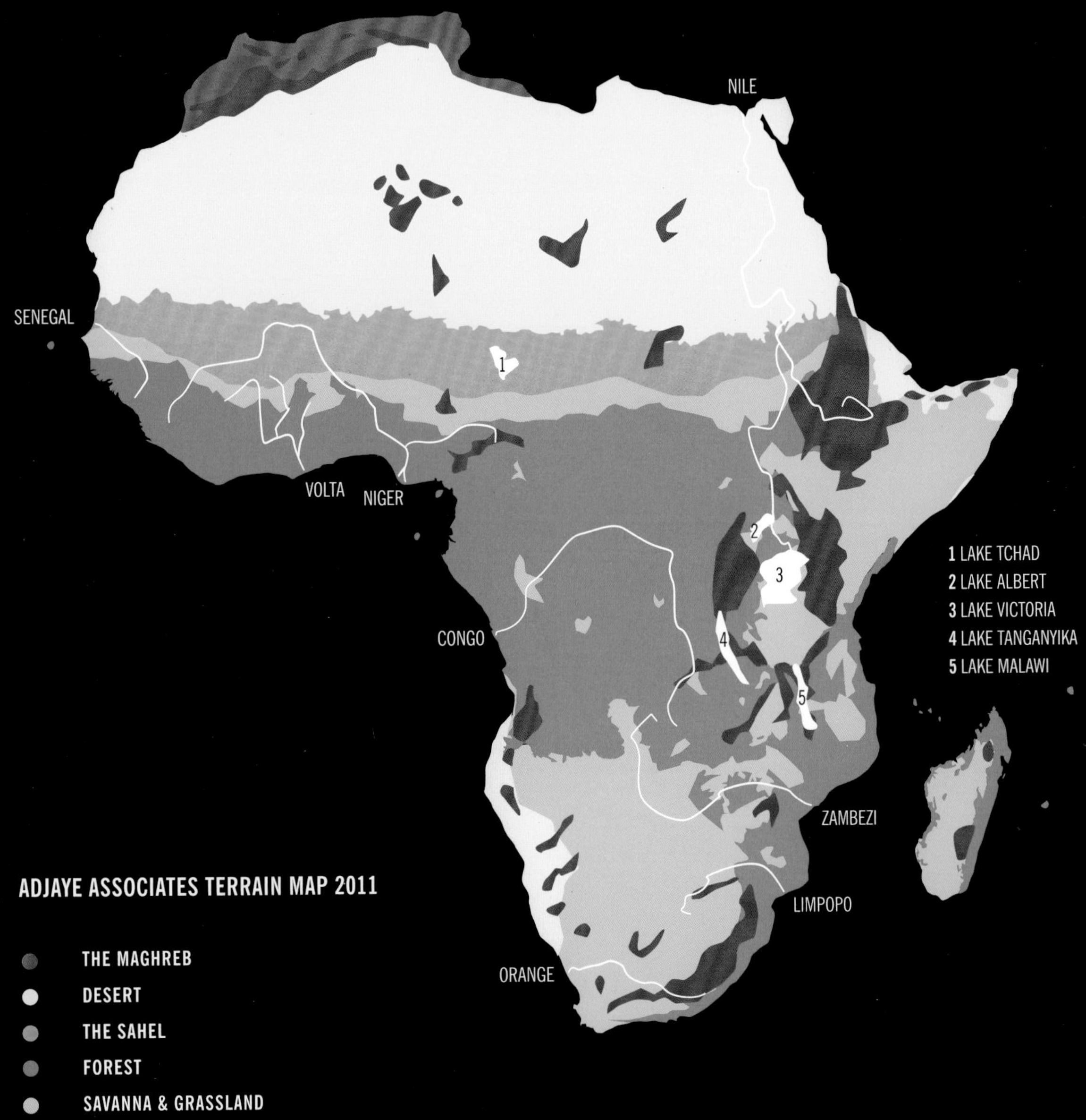
NILE
SENEGAL
VOLTA
NIGER
CONGO
ZAMBEZI
LIMPOPO
ORANGE
1 LAKE TCHAD
2 LAKE ALBERT
3 LAKE VICTORIA
4 LAKE TANGANYIKA
5 LAKE MALAWI
ADJAYE ASSOCIATES TERRAIN MAP 2011
THE MAGHREB
DESERT
THE SAHEL
FOREST
SAVANNA & GRASSLAND
MOUNTAIN & HIGHVELD

grow over the last half-century. But I began with a sense of my hometown as an old place, since my sisters and I learned of its long past as we grew up. One of the city's many nicknames is Oseikrom, which means Osei's town, referring back to Otumfuo Nana Osei Tutu I, Asante's first king, who came to power some four centuries ago. When you want to ask where someone hails from in Asante-Twi, you ask where their *kurom* is, their hometown. And while some come from villages (*kuraase* rather than *kurom*), many of the people of Asante have long lived in great towns, such as Kumasi, Ejisu or Mampong, places that, like the ancient Greek polis, had a form of government in which all the free adult men (but also many of the women) participated.

Though I grew up in an African city, I didn't grow up thinking of the city as new in Africa. Far from it. And for me, as for so many of Africa's people, the continent's name evokes not the forest or the savanna or the desert that so many Europeans and North Americans imagine, but cities such as Accra, Freetown, Lagos, Lomé, Harare, Johannesburg and Tangiers: the cities that have been the sites of my own travels in the continent. Indeed, the urban elite of Asante, people whose families may have lived in Kumasi for centuries, often have something of the disdain for country-folk – village people, *kuraasefoo* – that is carried in the English word 'peasant'. For much of my life, the countryside in Ghana was a place you drove through only to get from one city to another. (I used to tell English friends, when I was a kid, that we grew up with the sounds of lions roaring outside our window, which was true … but only because we lived up the hill from the city zoo!)

So this book surveys some of Africa's great cities, seeing them as connected with a long history that includes the colonial and the postcolonial but begins long before those eras. And while Africa's cities have changed – as all the world's cities have – quite radically in the last half-century, it reveals connections among them that flow from the various geographies and histories they share.

Sometimes, when people are treating Africa as if it were everywhere the same, it is worth remembering Africa's diversity, even if the modern history of the continent has Ludwig Wittgenstein used to insist) does not involve qualities that all relatives have in common: it is rather that I share the shape of nose with my cousin, the colour of my hair with my father, certain distinctive modes of speech with my siblings. So it is with these cities. Each shares much with each of the others, though there is little, save that they are cities, that all of them have in common.

Years ago, when I had finished college, I was living between Kumasi, my home, and the campus of the University of Ghana, where I found my first job. One weekend I was visited by a college friend of mine, who came from across the continent, from the Baganda capital – now Uganda's capital too – Kampala. As we sat on the veranda one evening sipping gin, he told me that Kumasi reminded him very much of his own hometown. Perhaps it was the way the city drifted up and down hillsides, or the colours of the fabrics worn by the women in the street, or the sounds of a bustling urban economy … who knows? It was meant, of course, as a compliment. Nothing kinder to say about a city than that it reminds you of a hometown you love. But that two cities across the continent – old cities, both – set in the hills and surrounded by forests can call to each other is something I already knew to be true.

I am grateful to David Adjaye for these stunning images and for assembling the reflections in the essays that surround them, including his own. And if there is always more to the city than its look – its sounds and smells, the rumble of traffic resonating through your body – I've never seen a more convincing staging of the look of these places and of what is so mesmerizing about the way they strike the eye. One day, I hope, he will take his penetrating eye to Kumasi, too.

THE MAGHREB

This is an area of North Africa that borders the Mediterranean Sea and comprises the northern slopes of the Atlas Mountains and the coastal plain of Morocco, Algeria, Tunisia and Libya. The Atlas extend from southwest to northeast, from Agadir on the Atlantic Ocean to Tunis on the Mediterranean. Their thick rim rises to form a high sill separating the Mediterranean basin from the Sahara to the south, a barrier that hinders, but does not prevent, communication between the two regions. The Maghreb is defined by its climate, which is affected by the Sahara and the Mediterranean Sea and is characterized by hot, dry summers and mild, rainy winters. Annual precipitation exceeds 750 mm in some coastal areas and there is often a drought in the summer months. The Sirocco is a dry and dusty wind that blows from the Sahara and is most common in the autumn and spring. With the arrival of the Sirocco, the shade temperature can rise to more than 40°C and, unable to stand the intense evaporation, some plants die in a matter of hours. The natural vegetation of the Maghreb is characterized as Mediterranean, but there is considerable variation in detail depending on elevation, proximity to the sea, rainfall and temperature. Woodland predominates, with grassland in drier areas, but the natural vegetation has been modified by centuries of agriculture.

THE MAGHREB

Due to its Mediterranean coastline, the Maghreb is quite different from Africa's other geographic regions. It includes four major capitals, each with its own relationship to the Mediterranean or the Atlantic and a unique tradition in terms of city-building and architecture. These are complex cities with layers of history, both distant and recent, that give you a sense of a vast trajectory through different kingdoms and different times. But they also have a strong sense of modernity, a modernity that is still evolving. The origins of these cities lie in their walled medinas: the dense, human-scale environments, with very narrow passageways, whose earliest buildings date back to the Middle Ages. Apart from Algiers, where the geography has had dramatic consequences for construction, the buildings of the medina are never more than two or three storeys high. They are agglomerative organizations that provide an infrastructure for the daily life of the city, where rich and poor occupy similar houses located in different quarters. The Maghreb is the one region in Africa where in the medinas you have a sense of an indigenous typology that has survived the modernization of the cities.

Although there are common elements in their history and built form, each of the four cities is very different. While part of the Mediterranean region, Rabat is the hinge point with the Atlantic coast and has a very distinctive character compared with Tunis or Tripoli. It feels more like a self-contained kingdom and this is reflected in both its historic architecture and its most recent buildings. You are very aware that Rabat is a defensive city on the coast; its ancient walls overlook the waterway that allowed goods and people in and out of the city. The development of the old centre is about the progressive rearrangement of the space available within the confines of the walls, and it embraces the idea of the elevated mound, the protected area where the city's institutions and palaces were built. The French concept of a new city – the colonial overlay – came into play only outside the walls, with the first of the city's suburbs. Despite these developments, Rabat remains a compact and self-contained city in which each of the parts has a strong sense of its geographic location.

Compared with Rabat, Tunis has very extensive suburbs and one of them, Carthage, contains the remains of the Phoenician port. The medina, which is the historic core of the modern city, developed on a site that is close to the coast and a short distance to the west of the ancient harbour. The French constructed the *ville nouvelle* in the area between the medina and the coast, with which it has a formal relationship. Their city is neoclassical in character, with grand boulevards and axes and, as in Rabat, the indigenous and the colonial centres exist side by side as 'twin cities'. The picture has been complicated by the growth of further suburbs but the special relationship between the medina and the French quarter is still at the heart of the city's identity and contributes to the sense that North Africans enjoy of existing simultaneously with their history. Rabat and Tunis also share a way of life that is based on appreciating the pleasures of a particular location. The development and self-image of Algiers and Tripoli, on the other hand, have followed more of a 20th-century socialist agenda, with a French influence in Algiers and an Italian input in Tripoli.

The coastline in Tripoli is flat and the corniche, which runs around the bay, allows you to see the development of the city from the medina in the west to the new city in the east. Visually, they make a compositional whole but as you look across the bay you can see each stage of the city's growth, right through to the latest commercial developments and the new linear parks on the waterfront. Tripoli is also notable for its social housing programme that sought to provide decent homes for all the citizens. This was one of the preoccupations of Gaddafi's government and the city's residential typology is rich and varied. There are examples of terraced housing, which sometimes make reference to the

RABAT / The defensive walls.

TRIPOLI / The Roman arch.

TUNIS / A market in the medina.

TUNIS / A residential street in the French city.

RABAT / The French city.

architecture of the medina, through to the large Soviet-style apartment blocks that are located further inland. With such a high standard of public housing, Libya appeared to be very affluent, especially at the time of my visit.

I was surprised by Tripoli's curious relationship to its Italian heritage, part of which is a very delicate and ornate form of classicism. In the city centre the ancient Roman remains have been celebrated, rather than destroyed, and stand next to a thousand-year-old mosque. The sense of layers of history contributing to the modern city is inescapable and informs the way that the whole city is organized. Once you leave the medina with its ancient walls the city is laid out along grand boulevards framed by buildings in the stripped classicism of the Italian Fascist period. Further from the centre are the areas developed since the 1970s and 1980s, when the city's architecture was enlivened by a Miami-style modernism resulting from the city's oil affluence. The art deco qualities of this latest style resonate with those of the Italian architecture from the interwar years.

Algiers rises steeply from the waterfront and this contributes to the drama of the city and the way it overlooks the sea. It is another twin city in which the ancient medina was the starting point for the building of a substantial *ville nouvelle* when Algeria became a French colony. The French regarded the city as a particularly valuable outpost and this is reflected in the scale on which they transformed the city. They saw Algiers as a place where people would live in the city rather than the suburbs, to best enjoy the magnificent setting. In terms of fabric, it seems like an extension of Haussmann's Paris; it was built with the same grandeur, and the avenues of five- to seven-storey buildings cover a substantial area overlooking the bay. It does not feel like a poor cousin to Paris, but is a unique expression of the architectural potential of the location – as grand a city as the French would have wanted to build anywhere. The axial planning is punctuated by some very fine neoclassical and art deco buildings and this heritage supports the work of later modernists, such as Roland Simounet, who contributed to the tradition of fine villas in the city.

The cities of the Maghreb retain a more complete record of their history than most other African cities. They are cities where you can dive in and immediately understand where you are and where you can go, and I think they have a strong sense of their collective identity. The Maghreb has a long tradition of urbanism that is based on the indigenous precedent of the medina. Although they are rooted in the Mediterranean tradition, medinas are very different from the village architecture that you find in the Greek islands or southern Italy, having a stronger collective dimension to their organization. Due to their historic role as centres of trade, they offer a sense of protection – like citadels – and this seems to have been their overriding inspiration. They are an important reference point for people leading a contemporary life in cities, which is very different from places where the indigenous habitat is rural. These cities are clearly part of world history, as well as the history of Africa.

ALGIERS / An apartment building constructed in stone.

ALGIERS / The French city overlooking the harbour.

TRIPOLI / Stripped classicism from the Italian era.

TRIPOLI / New commercial development.

TRIPOLI / Social housing.

TRIPOLI / Miami-style modernism.

ALGIERS / Looking over the roof terraces of the medina.

ALGIERS / ALGERIA

OVERVIEW

The country and its capital share many aspects of their history with those of neighbouring countries: the Berber inheritance, Phoenician ports, Roman cities, the arrival of Islam with Arab armies, medieval dynastic rule, and so on. But the historic experiences that most affect Algeria today relate to the French conquest, the war of independence in the 1950s and the civil war of the 1990s.

A large French force invaded the country in 1830, sacked Algiers and took control of the most productive land. Although there was serious opposition from a local leader called Emir Abdelkader and from Berbers in the Kabylie area, the country became French. There was little serious discussion of independence until the period before the First World War. After the war many Algerian veterans questioned the future of French rule and the Parti du Peuple Algérien (Algerian People's Party) was founded in 1937. Following an outbreak of violence after the Second World War, in which both Europeans and Muslims died, French nationality and the right to work in France were made available to all Algerians. But the French would not contemplate independence and serious resistance manifested itself in 1954 when the Front de Libération Nationale (National Liberation Front, FLN) announced its intention of securing independence, by attacking targets in Algeria while seeking a political settlement in France. The French took this as a declaration of war and responded in kind. Within two years the FLN had the support of Morocco and Tunisia, as well as President Nasser in Egypt, and had a force of 40,000 on the ground. French forces were given carte blanche on tactics and used torture and the victimization of entire villages. Although the French had secured most of the country by 1959, various armed groups were still active in France and the government entered negotiations with the FLN. A ceasefire came into effect in 1962 and, after a referendum, independence was achieved later that year.

The civil war of the 1990s was the product of the serious divisions that came to the fore after independence. The FLN, the only political party at the time, introduced a socialist programme and had to rebuild the country without the expertise of a previous administration. Public services began to improve but the economy progressively weakened, leading to high unemployment. There were strikes in several cities and the Front Islamique du Salut (Islamic Salvation Front, FIS), founded in 1989, won a landslide victory in the first multiparty elections in 1991. This was not acceptable to the army: they suspended parliament, arrested the leaders of FIS, and appointed a former general to head the government in 1994. In the years that followed, underground Islamic groups were in continuous conflict with government-financed militias. Between 150,000 and 200,000 people are thought to have died before the conflict petered out in 2002. Abdelaziz Bouteflika of the FLN, who won the elections in 1999 and remains in power, addressed the social divisions resulting from the conflict through the Civil Harmony Act and the Charter for Peace and National Reconciliation, which received overwhelming support in a 2005 referendum.

OBSERVATIONS

Algiers is the last city on my journey around the continent. It forms an arc from north to south around a bay and rises steeply up the surrounding hills, giving many buildings a view of the sea. There are no beaches, due to the harbour, but the bay is a popular place for jogging, fishing and long walks.

The medina is perched in the northern half of the city. Its complex network of routes and interlocking roofs has been the inspiration of countless architects, most notably Le Corbusier. The French colonial city is mainly to the south of the medina. The French were keen to bring order to Algiers but their tree-lined boulevards, urban blocks and arcades do respond to the contours of the land.

In the medina the gradients of the lanes are suitable for donkeys to collect the refuse, moving within inches of each door. The roofs are stages for domestic life, with the backdrop of the bay seen from every home. Mornings and the evenings are the time to see this dramatic use of the roofs, which is one of the most amazing urban spectacles I've seen on the continent.

NATIONAL POPULATION

39,667,000

CITY POPULATION

2,594,000

ETHNIC GROUPS

Arab-Berber 99%, European less than 1%

RELIGIONS

Sunni Muslim (official) 99%, Christian and Jewish 1%

LANGUAGES

Arabic (official), French, Berber dialects

GDP

$548.6 billion

AGRICULTURAL PRODUCTS

wheat, barley, oats, grapes, olives, citrus, fruits; sheep, cattle

INDUSTRIES

petroleum, natural gas, light industries, mining, electrical, petrochemical, food processing

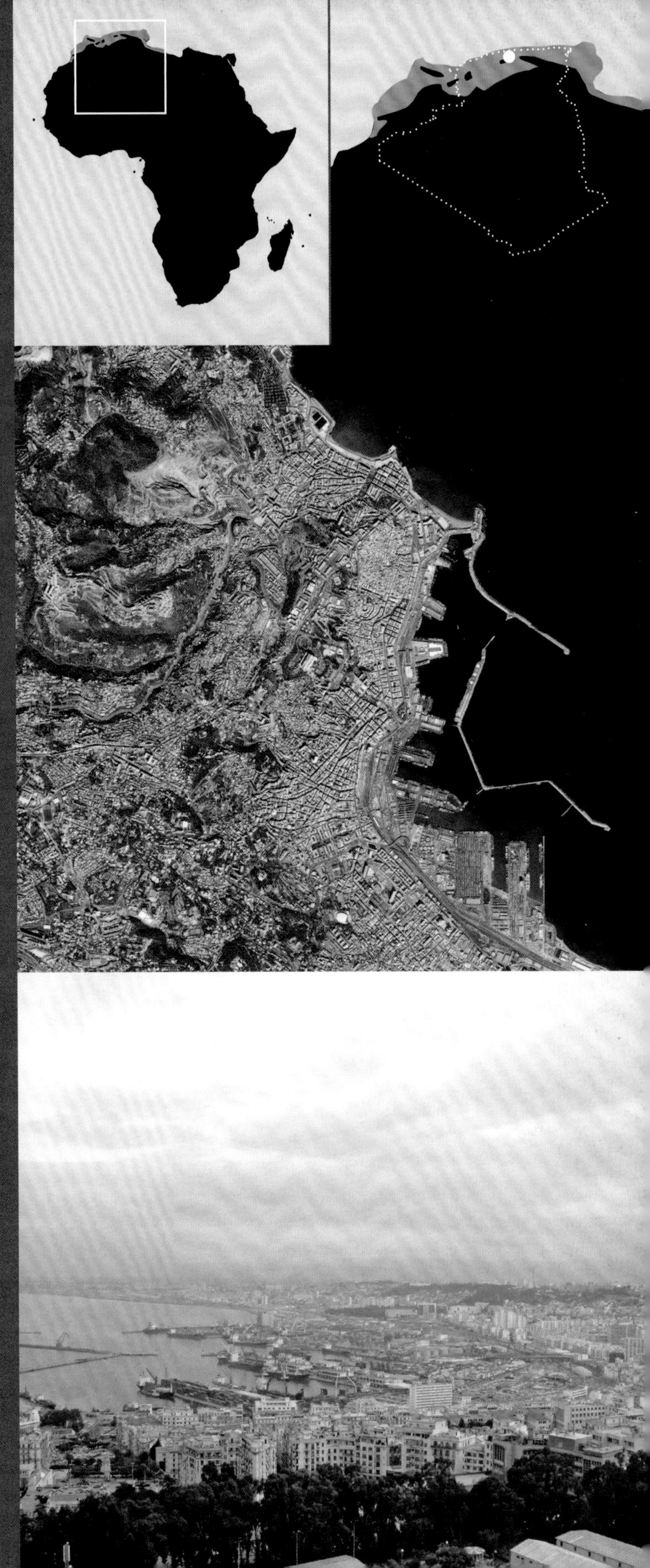

There are Ottoman palaces and administration buildings close to the waterfront, and fine colonial, neoclassical and modernist buildings all over the city. The 'Modern Moorish' style developed by the French was a response to the city's rich heritage. City hall is an austere neoclassical building in light brown stone.

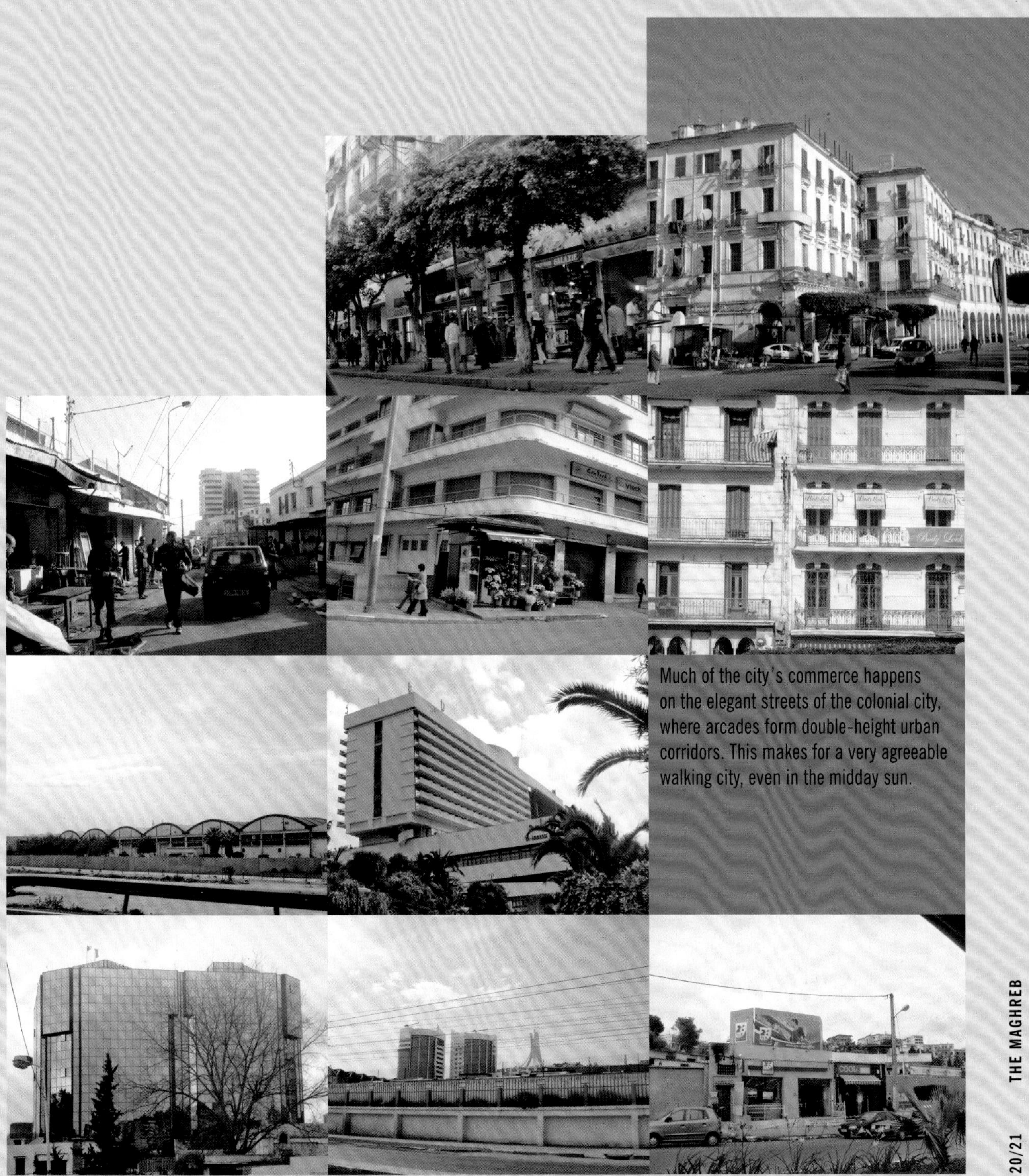

Much of the city's commerce happens on the elegant streets of the colonial city, where arcades form double-height urban corridors. This makes for a very agreeable walking city, even in the midday sun.

ALGIERS / ALGERIA / **MEDINA**

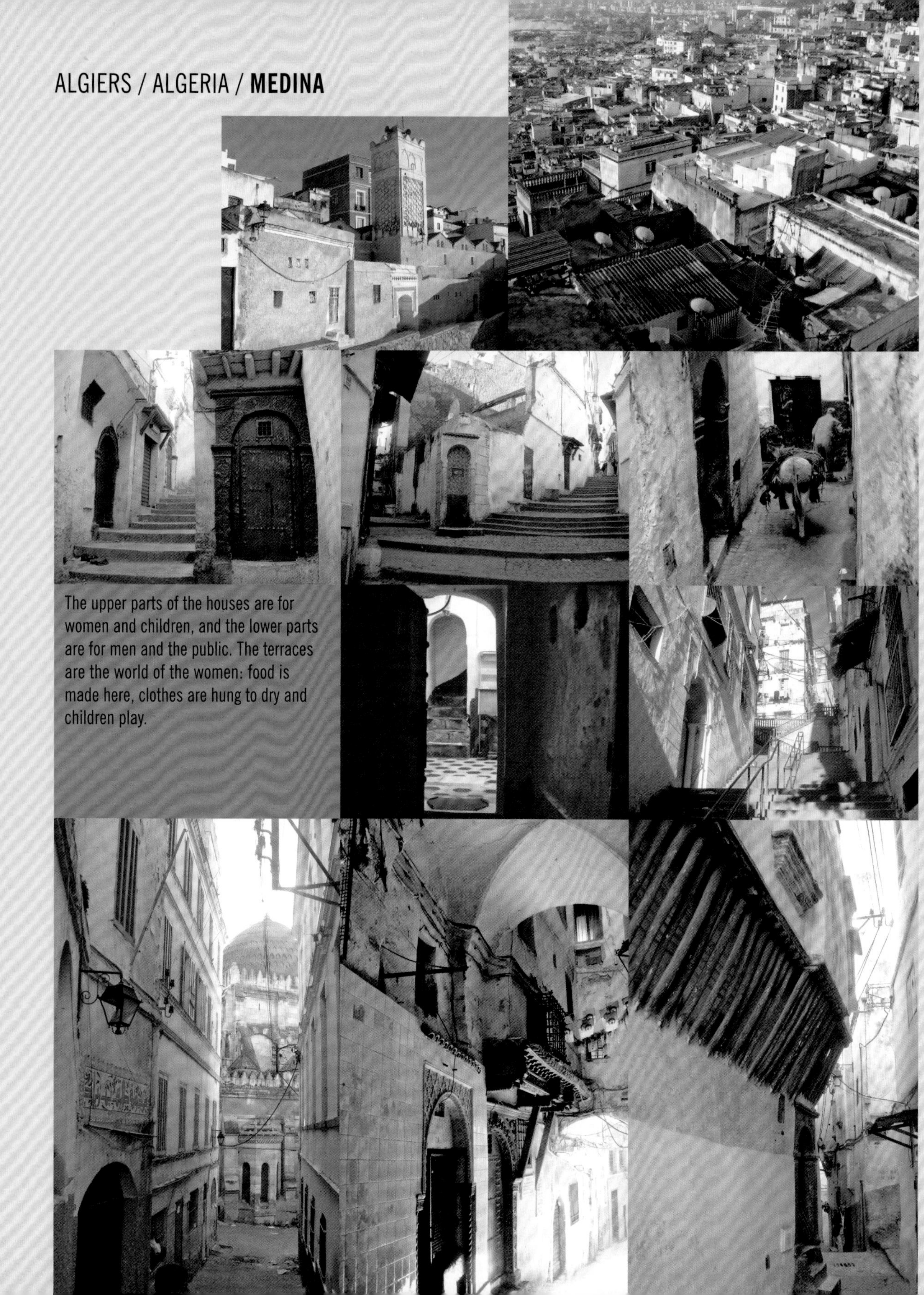

The upper parts of the houses are for women and children, and the lower parts are for men and the public. The terraces are the world of the women: food is made here, clothes are hung to dry and children play.

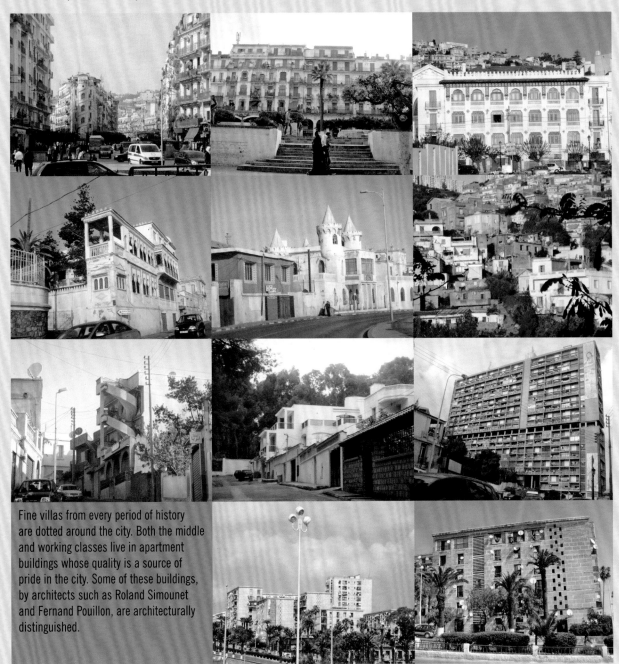

Fine villas from every period of history are dotted around the city. Both the middle and working classes live in apartment buildings whose quality is a source of pride in the city. Some of these buildings, by architects such as Roland Simounet and Fernand Pouillon, are architecturally distinguished.

OVERVIEW

The majority of Moroccans are descended from peoples who migrated from the Middle East, possibly as early as the 10th millennium BCE, and were later known as Berbers. In the 9th century BCE Phoenicians established a number of coastal trading settlements, including Rabat. The Romans defeated the Phoenicians in the Punic Wars and built a new city near modern Meknes, but elsewhere in Morocco the Berbers were able to continue their pastoral or nomadic lives. As on Africa's Mediterranean coast, Arab armies arrived from the east in the 7th century CE and, when the Berbers adopted Islam, they worked together and developed an independent culture that would continue for many centuries. The country was governed by a succession of dynasties, mostly based in Marrakech: the Idrisids from 789 to 985, the Almoravids from 1073 to 1146, the Almohads from 1147 to 1269, the Marinids from 1269 to 1465, the Saadians from 1554 to 1629, and the Alaouites from 1666 to the present. From the 8th to the end of the 15th century, Berber-Arab armies colonized southern Spain, bringing with them a culture that combined knowledge of ancient Greece with an understanding of the latest advances in science. In the 19th century Morocco's independence was threatened by a growing appreciation of its strategic significance, although an international conference in 1880 agreed that the territorial integrity of the country should be maintained. But the French were not discouraged and, as a result of the Treaty of Fes in 1912, most of Morocco became a French protectorate. Rabat became the capital and the non-French areas were controlled by Spain.

The French began to make improvements to the infrastructure and built new towns for their settlers but soon met serious resistance. In 1921 Abdelkrim Khattabi led a revolt of Berbers in the Rif region of northeast Morocco, which was suppressed in 1926, and the Istiqlal (Independence Party) was founded in 1934. In the Second World War Morocco was aligned with the Vichy government until the arrival of Allied troops in 1942, when the Istiqlal demanded immediate independence. They continued to gather support in the unsettled years after the war, much to the frustration of the French. When the party was banned in 1953, Sultan Mohammed V supported the public demonstrations and the French exiled him to Madagascar. His absence inspired increasingly violent clashes and in 1955 all the French residents of the village of Oued Zem were massacred. French and Spanish forces withdrew a year later and Mohammed V returned from exile to take the throne of Morocco in 1957, the year after its independence. After his unexpected death in 1961, he was succeeded by his son, Hassan II, who survived two assassination attempts to reign for thirty-eight years. With the power to appoint the prime minister and cabinet, he presided over a multiparty chamber of deputies and was particularly successful in handling the country's international interests. His son, Mohammed VI, ascended to the throne in 1999 and has taken steps to modernize the country, introducing equal rights for women and, in a reverse of his father's policy, giving greater support to the Berber language and culture. The 2011 election was won by a moderate Islamist party, the Justice and Development Party led by Abdelilah Benkirane.

OBSERVATIONS

Rabat enjoys an elevated position overlooking the coast and developed in stages. The oldest mosque, in the Kasbah des Oudayas, was constructed in the 12th century. The medina, which is located at the mouth of a small river, took its present form in the 17th century and the French developed the *ville nouvelle* to the south in the first part of the 20th century.

The suburbs are full of villas in myriad styles, from modernist to mock-Arab. The good thing is that most of them have opulent gardens, which spill over their walls and transform the streets into green thoroughfares. The poor housing is denser but retains continuity with the rest of the city.

NATIONAL POPULATION

34,378,000

CITY POPULATION

1,967,000

ETHNIC GROUPS

Arab-Berber 99%, other 1%

RELIGIONS

Sunni Muslim (official) 99%, other 1% (includes Christian and Jewish)

LANGUAGES

Arabic (official), Berber dialects, French

GDP

$259.2 billion

AGRICULTURAL PRODUCTS

barley, wheat, citrus fruits, grapes, vegetables, olives; livestock; wine

INDUSTRIES

automotive parts, mining (phosphate), aerospace, food processing, leather goods, textiles, construction, energy, tourism

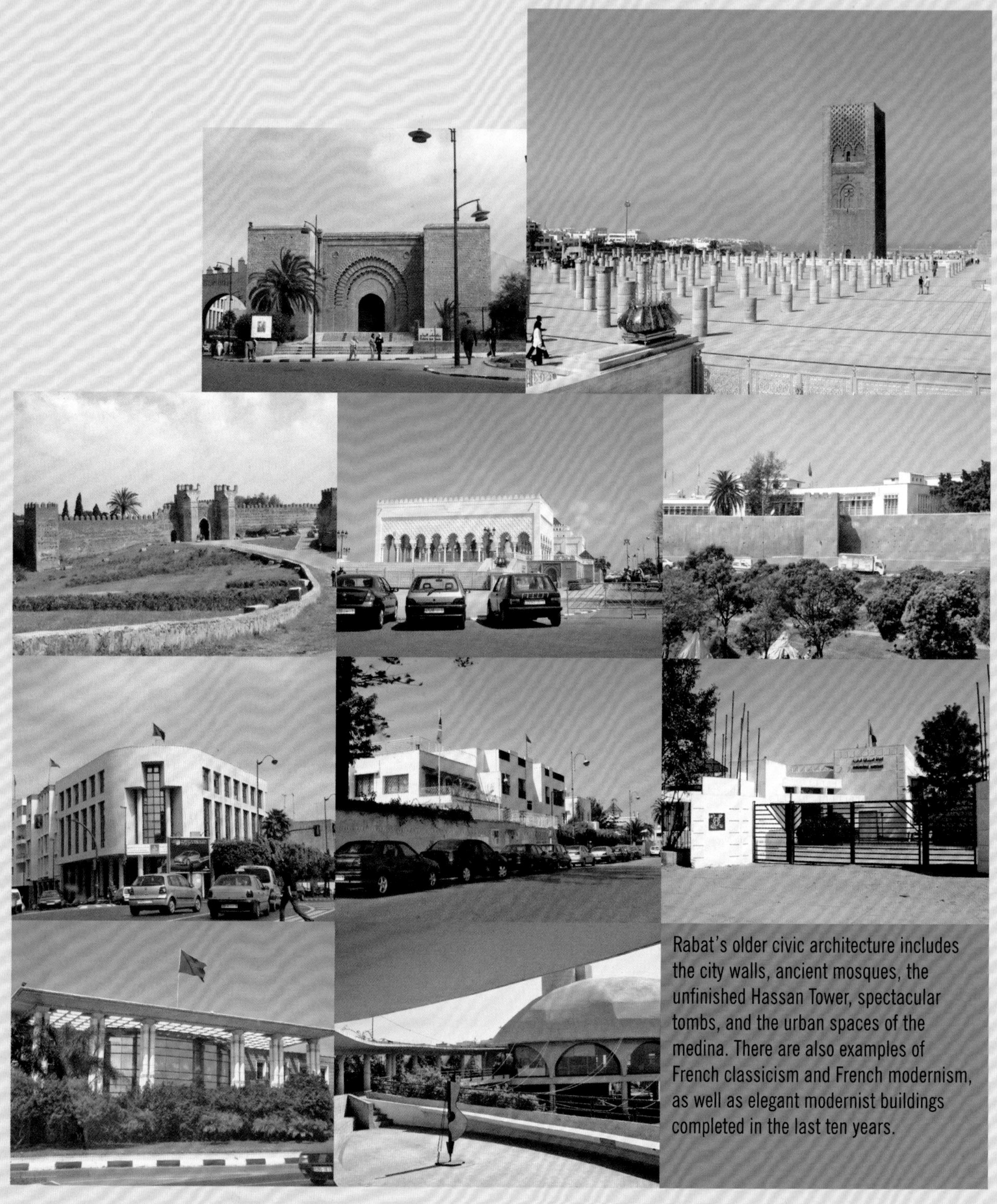

Rabat's older civic architecture includes the city walls, ancient mosques, the unfinished Hassan Tower, spectacular tombs, and the urban spaces of the medina. There are also examples of French classicism and French modernism, as well as elegant modernist buildings completed in the last ten years.

The main commercial area is in the *ville nouvelle*. Older buildings and recent mid-rise blocks have office accommodation above the shops. A limited amount of informal trading takes place in tented structures on the edge of the city.

Marjane مرجان
BOULANGERIE - PATISS

Examples of residential architecture range from the beautiful small palaces of the medina to the freestanding villas in more recent suburbs. The styles may be eclectic but there is a general aspiration to live in a white villa with an abundant garden.

TRIPOLI / LIBYA

OVERVIEW

Tripoli was founded by the Phoenicians around 700 BCE. Their base in the western Mediterranean was at Carthage, in modern Tunisia, and they traded with the Berbers who controlled the trans-Saharan trade routes. Starting in 635 BCE, the Greeks founded five ports to the east of Carthage, in what is now Libya, but they came under control of the Ptolemaic Empire, based in Alexandria, after the death of Alexander the Great in 323 BCE. When Rome destroyed Carthage, Libya's western and eastern regions became separate Roman provinces. The Vandals' sack of Rome in 455 CE undermined the Roman presence in North Africa and there was little resistance when the Arab army, which had previously invaded Egypt, arrived in Tripoli in 643. As Islam replaced Christianity, Arab men married Berber women and the country was ruled by a succession of local dynasties. Tripolitania, the region around Tripoli, became part of the Ottoman Empire in the 16th century, but Ottoman influence was curtailed in the 18th century when cavalry officer Ahmed Karamanli seized power and declared independence. The Karamanli dynasty increased the wealth of Tripolitania by developing trade links in the Mediterranean and North Africa, before the Ottomans returned to power in 1835.

Taking advantage of the Ottomans' weakness, Italy invaded in 1911 and had taken control of most of the country, which it named Italian North Africa, by the end of the First World War. Resistance continued in the eastern state of Cyrenaica until 1931, when the Italians renamed the country Libya and moved quickly to improve the infrastructure and build model settlements for over 100,000 of its settlers. With the outbreak of the Second World War, the nationalists declared their support for the Allies and, when Italy attacked the British in Egypt, they worked with the British to expel the Italians from Libya. After the war the question of sovereignty was referred to the General Assembly of the United Nations and as a result the Emir of Cyrenaica, Idris Senussi, became king of an independent Libya in 1951. Most of the population were subsistence farmers but the economy was to change irrevocably with the discovery of oil at the end of the decade. As Libya became a major oil producer, there was a growing frustration with the government's failure to manage the changes it brought, such as an exodus from the land. But there was no warning of the military coup in 1969. With little resistance, a number of junior officers under Muammar Gaddafi occupied key positions throughout the country and the king abdicated. Gaddafi had become politically active in the army and was highly critical when the Idris government did nothing to assist Egypt when it was defeated by Israel in 1967. Following Nasser's example, he set up a radical socialist government and pursued a variety of non-aligned policies. As a result of his support for several terrorist organizations, Tripoli and Benghazi were bombed by the US in 1986 and economic sanctions were imposed in 1992. As the economy declined, Gaddafi took steps to reconcile his position with world opinion and sanctions were lifted. He was captured and killed by rebels in the civil war that followed the arrival of the Arab Spring in 2011. An interim government organized elections in 2014 but the results were disputed by the losing party, resulting in continuing instability.

OBSERVATIONS

In the old town the souks, or markets, stand on plateaus that enjoy cool breezes and magnificent sea views. The colonial town combines tree-lined streets with art deco and modernist architecture of the Mussolini era. Its lanes and family cul-de-sacs are still intact, showing how important the extended family is to Libyan society.

The main square is called Green Square after Libya's national colour and stands next to the old fort. From there, the city's main streets radiate outwards to the south. It is an extremely simple and satisfying plan. This square, which is the genesis of the city, is next to the old town so its Libyan identity is unmistakable.

The first prominent high-rise is affectionately referred to as 'the five bottles' – but they are upside down. Before the fall of Gaddafi, Tripoli was in a building boom and on a trajectory to a vivid future.

NATIONAL POPULATION

6,278,000

CITY POPULATION

1,126,000

ETHNIC GROUPS

Berber and Arab 97%, other 3% (includes Greeks, Maltese, Italians, Egyptians, Pakistanis, Turks, Indians and Tunisians)

RELIGIONS

Muslim (official; virtually all Sunni) 96.6%, Christian 2.7%, Buddhist 0.3%, other/ unspecified 0.4%

LANGUAGES

Arabic (official), Italian, English, Berber

GDP

$97.94 billion

AGRICULTURAL PRODUCTS

wheat, barley, olives, dates, citrus, vegetables, peanuts, soybeans; cattle

INDUSTRIES

petroleum, petrochemicals, aluminium, iron and steel, food processing, textiles, handicrafts, cement

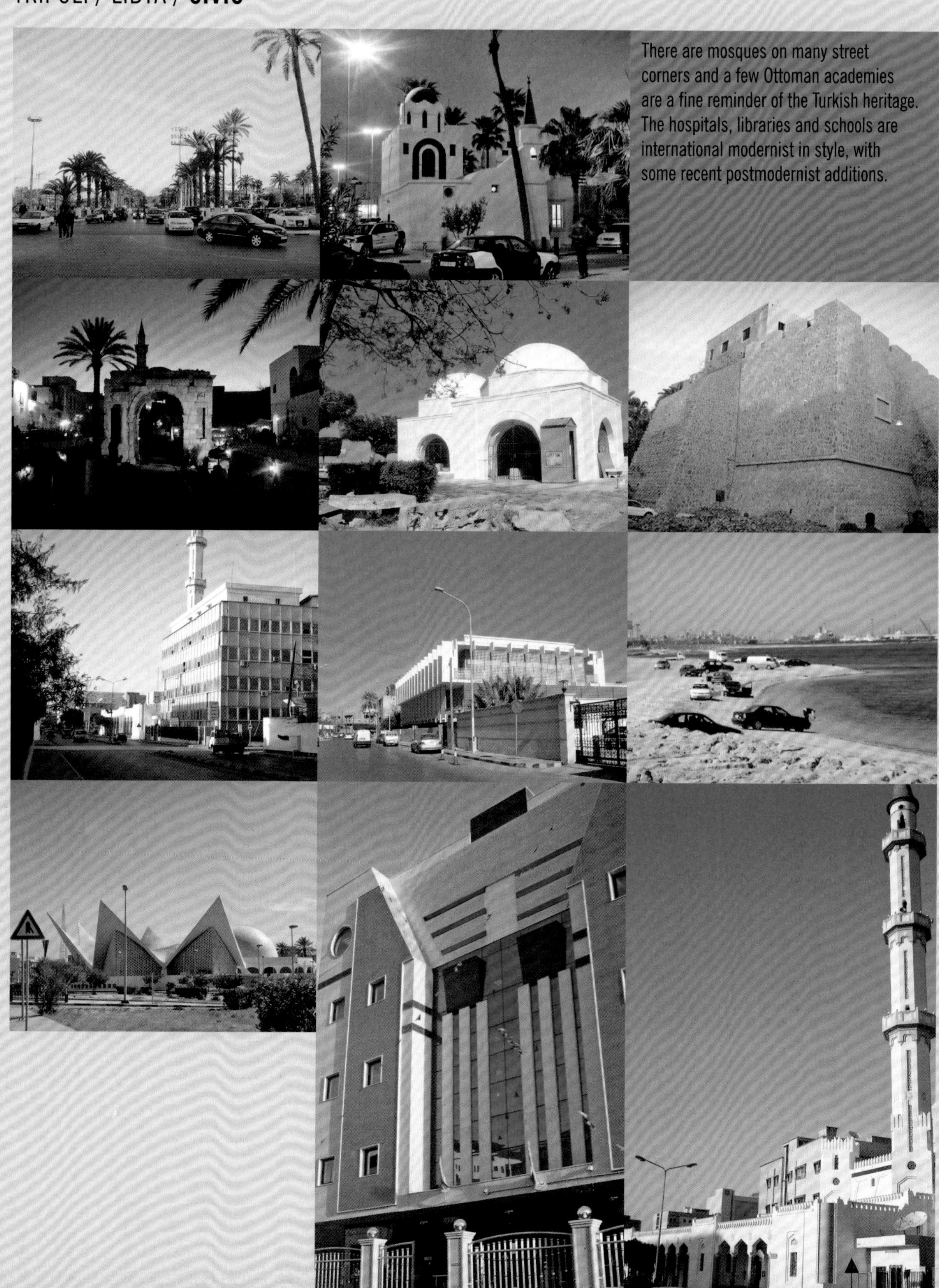

There are mosques on many street corners and a few Ottoman academies are a fine reminder of the Turkish heritage. The hospitals, libraries and schools are international modernist in style, with some recent postmodernist additions.

The arcaded spaces in the souks make outdoor rooms for the city, with shops and cafes in the cool shade. The new commercial city is dominated by the oil industry, which is state-run, and recent buildings are postmodern in style.

TRIPOLI / LIBYA / **RESIDENTIAL**

The middle classes occupy apartment blocks, with amenities at their base, which were developed as an idea of urban density. There are no shanty towns in Tripoli. Gaddafi demolished them and built Soviet-style housing.

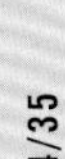

OVERVIEW

Although Stone Age remains have been found in Kelibia, most Tunisians trace their roots to the migrations from Arabia that began perhaps as early as the 10th millennium BCE. The Berbers, as they were later called, developed trade routes across the Sahara. In the 9th century BCE these became of interest to the Phoenicians who, from a base in Tyre in Lebanon, maintained a trading empire that extended to the Atlantic coast of Morocco. The Phoenicians founded Carthage in 814 BCE as their capital in the western Mediterranean. Their gradual demise began when they lost control of Sicily to the Greeks, and continued in the Punic Wars, which resulted in the Romans destroying Carthage in 146 BCE. The Romans returned to Carthage in 44 BCE, when they recognized the country's potential for producing grain. As Roman power declined, the Vandals invaded North Africa from Spain, stopping in Carthage before sacking Rome in 455 CE. When Arab armies invaded in the 7th century, the Berbers converted to Islam and the country was ruled by a succession of local dynasties: the Aghlabids in the 9th century, the Fatimids in the 10th, the Zirids from the 10th to the 12th century, the Almohads, and finally the Hafsids from the 13th to the 16th century. By this stage the Ottoman Turks had begun to control the Mediterranean and Tunisia became part of the Ottoman Empire in 1754.

Early in the 19th century several European countries and the US persuaded Tunisia to ban pirates operating on the coast and to outlaw slavery in 1846, both of which contributed to a weakening of the economy. Having already occupied Algeria, the French invaded Tunisia in 1881. Although power remained in Tunisian hands for ceremonial purposes, the French effectively ran the country and took possession of some of the most productive land. When the first nationalist party, the Destour Party, was organized in 1920, the French immediately took steps to suppress its activities. In 1934 Habib Bourguiba founded the Neo-Destour Party and it succeeded in gathering support, despite hostility from the French. In the Second World War Tunisia was initially allied to the Vichy regime but, when the Allies liberated the country in 1943, the Free French stepped in to suppress the nationalist movement and he went into exile in Cairo. After a failed attempt to reach agreement in 1951, further negotiations led to Tunisian independence in 1956 with Bourguiba as prime minister. In the following year the last dynastic head of the country was deposed and he was made president. He pursued socialist policies with the intention of modernizing the country. His attempts to curtail the influence of religious leaders inevitably led to Islamic opposition but they were excluded when the first multiparty elections were announced in 1981. Bourguiba's anti-Islamic policies put him at odds with the people, and his prime minister, Zine El-Abidine Ben Ali, took power in a bloodless coup in 1987. Many of his policies were similar to those of his predecessor and appeared to undermine human rights. Ben Ali remained in power until the mass demonstrations that marked the start of the Arab Spring in January 2011. A government of national unity was formed later that year and Beji Caid Essebsi was elected president in 2014.

OBSERVATIONS

Tunis is a real surprise. It is made up of five boroughs, of which the first is the medina, close to the port and lagoon. It is a dramatic and varied city, and includes the ancient port of Carthage.

The large and active medina, the medieval city, is one of the great Arab inventions of urban living. Comprising a network of lanes and three-storey buildings, it feels remarkably human in scale and atmosphere. Some of the lanes run through souks or into small squares in front of public buildings. The striking thing is to see the medina in full use, by government workers and clerics, shoppers and tourists.

The French built the first suburb outside the medina, centred on what is now Avenue Habib Bourguiba, which is lined with mature trees and pavement cafes. As the suburbs have developed, commerce has sprung up in different neighbourhoods, resulting in a network city with multiple centres and a range of lifestyles. With the construction of more apartment buildings, the density of the suburbs is increasing but there is good access to open space.

NATIONAL POPULATION

11,254,000

CITY POPULATION

1,993,000

ETHNIC GROUPS

Arab 98%, European 1%, other 1%

RELIGIONS

Sunni Muslim (official) 99%, other 1% (includes Christian and Jewish)

LANGUAGES

Arabic (official), French, Berber

GDP

$124.7 billion

AGRICULTURAL PRODUCTS

olives, olive oil, grain, tomatoes, citrus fruit, sugar beets, dates, almonds; beef, dairy products

INDUSTRIES

petroleum, mining (phosphate, iron ore), tourism, textiles, footwear, agribusiness, beverages

The architecture is very symbolic and ranges from the vernacular forms of the medina, articulated with towers and generous porches, to the neoclassical and art deco buildings in the *ville nouvelle*. Larger open spaces, some with stadiums, relieve the density.

The buildings of all periods are used for commerce: ancient souks, neoclassical and art deco blocks, and later modernist developments. Even the most recent examples are integrated with the fabric of the city.

The wealthier neighbourhoods have detached villas with lush gardens and bustling commercial areas. The poor areas make a stark contrast, with incomplete houses, half-finished streets and impoverished shops, but this is still better than comparable housing in other African cities.

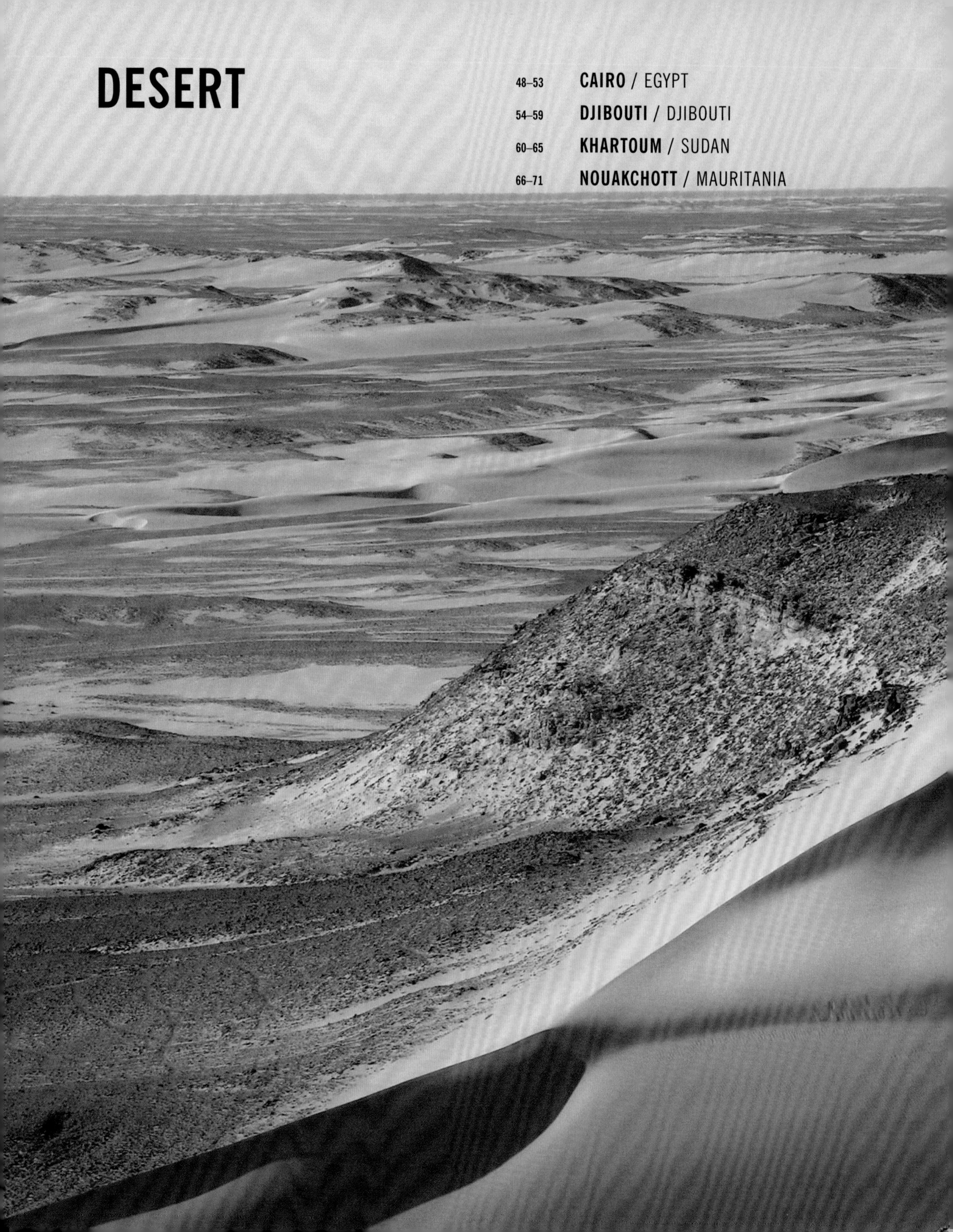

DESERT

Deserts and their extended margins account for two-fifths of the total land area of the African continent. They occur between 15 and 30 degrees latitude, on either side of the equator, and comprise the Sahara, the Kalahari and the Namib deserts. The annual precipitation is up to 250 mm but the timing is often unpredictable and its effects are minimized by the high daytime temperatures, reaching 38–40°C, and strong winds, which combine to produce high levels of evaporation. These conditions desiccate the land and make plant life unsustainable. In neighbouring areas, annual precipitation of 250–400 mm produces a semidesert environment. The Sahara has one of the lowest species densities in the world, and sustained vegetation covers only the higher ground and oases. Moisture is uncommon and the subterranean water is often highly saline but, where it is suitable for irrigation, settlements have grown up in the desert. In Egypt and Sudan alluvium deposits provide a basis for productive agriculture along the Nile. Other land may permit light grazing but this runs the risk of exacerbating the desertification. Surface materials in deserts include bedrock, areas of shingle and boulders, and shifting sand, the last accounting for ten per cent of the area of the Sahara.

DESERT

These four capitals are in locations that distort what you might expect from desert cities; two are on rivers and two on the coast. In many respects the cities of the Sahel, where water is scarce, are closer to what I would otherwise expect in the desert. Nouakchott on the Atlantic coast, Cairo and Khartoum on the Nile, and Djibouti on the Gulf of Aden, are highly developed cities. They represent sophisticated ideas of urbanism and they all have a vibrant civic and communal life, which gives a specific quality to each city. They have precise bucolic aspects, with either the sea or a river for their main respite.

Cairo is, of course, one of the densest and most metropolitan cities in Africa. It is a city of hybrid styles organized around the old fortified area at its heart. One of the first extensions, the neoclassical city, anticipates the megadensity that occurs in the modernist suburbs as they pull away from the historic city. The concentration of these suburbs is established in the ring of development outside the central area, where the residential architecture creates a cooler ground plane that allows the life of the city to extend in all directions without interruption. It activates the city in a way that you do not see in the Sahel, for instance. The life that is lived on the ground plane in Cairo is extremely striking. There is trade everywhere and the compactness of the urban fabric gives shade. The buildings are linked by a web of activity that covers a wide area and terminates at the river's edge. The compactness of the neoclassical city provided a blueprint for Cairo's burgeoning suburbs; the density is not imposed but grows out of the way people live. This is the basis for the lifestyle modernism and the supermodernism that you now see on the periphery of Cairo.

Comparing Cairo to the other desert city located on a river, Khartoum has a civic quarter that looks across the Blue Nile, just before it joins the White Nile. The university and the administrative departments are also based here, so the public face of the city addresses the river and the commercial and residential areas spread outwards from it. The business area has recently begun to attract glazed towers that depend on technology to make them habitable. Their effect on the city as a whole is similar to that of the towers in the Sahel cities, which model the light and mark the position of the city on an extensive land mass. The ones in Khartoum act as symbols of modernity that update the imagery of the lush river architecture that dominates the rest of the city. Such towers are no more out of place here than they are in Houston, Texas. On the other hand, Khartoum is the city with the greatest concentration of mosque towers that I have seen anywhere on the continent. They come in every possible form, from highly ornate to the simplest articulations and contemporary expressions that are extremely original. And these towers, which are generic to the city, have a relationship to the new habitable towers; they punctuate the horizontal and the general scale of the city.

I was particularly surprised by Khartoum's modernist villas. They have cubist-like geometry and are always coloured, never white. Their architecture is based on the use of a continuous render finish, with apertures of different sizes that penetrate the interior, although the openings are often quite small because of the heat. There are always articulating elements, such as profiles and frames, that make a relationship between the proportions of the volume and the various openings. In many respects, the style of the villas is reminiscent of the cellular architecture of walls and courts found in the Sahel and is very consistent throughout the residential areas of the city. Unfortunately, the mud bricks that are used to construct these villas are hidden from view by the rendered finish. Overall, Khartoum is a modernist zoned city; hardly anyone lives in the civic quarter, which is surrounded by commerce, and then there are the suburbs. It is a three-tier city that is the complete opposite of Cairo.

Moving on to the two coastal cities, Nouakchott is the one city in this group that most expresses the desert, even though it is located close to the sea. It is more temperate than if it were in the interior but it nevertheless embodies a strong sense of an abstract and simple geometry that pervades the local

CAIRO / High-density housing.

NOUAKCHOTT / Tent structures creating shade.

KHARTOUM / A glazed tower.

CAIRO / A shopping street in the neoclassical city.

KHARTOUM / The lush river architecture.

culture. Mauritania expresses reduced elegance, with very little ornamentation, and the architecture takes a lead from that. The light is extremely harsh; this is one of the few cities where you absolutely have to wear sunglasses, otherwise you cannot see. In terms of its built fabric, the city orientates itself away from the sea, but in the evenings the life of the city moves to the beach. After the fishermen have finished for the day and come in, the citizens leave their work and go to the seafront. Every day there is a migration to the ocean and what is interesting is that, whereas in some Muslim countries there is a strong separation between men and women, in Nouakchott the whole family goes to the beach to swim and eat, before going home to sleep. It is something really powerful that you sometimes see in cities, this migration to the edge, and then the return.

Ornamental detail has little place in the city; only form and bold geometry stand out in the landscape. This can be seen in the latest housing, which is about primary and secondary cubic forms becoming the identity of the city. Even the colours are not very strong. The strength of the sun quickly bleaches them and there is an overriding atmosphere – a soft atmosphere – throughout the city which is very distinctive. In the powerful light the dome form is very comfortable; it is modelled by the light but its softness is easy on the eye. The mosque in Nouakchott, with multiple domes, celebrates this with great elegance; it represents an architecture of domes, cubes and half-rounds – all very simple but powerful when repeated. Similar shapes can be seen in the city's housing, whose simple volumes are punctuated by apertures, balconies and niches. You get a strong sense of visual continuity extending from the civic buildings through to the residential areas. You feel that you are part of a larger agglomeration where each building contributes to the identity of the whole place.

Djibouti is an intriguing city on the northeast coast of Africa that faces Yemen. It is an important port, which serves Ethiopia and has always been a relatively wealthy trading city. It has absorbed many influxes from the Middle East but the old city is organized on a neoclassical grid, with major and minor streets, squares and open spaces. The civic architecture is on the main boulevards and, although the city is on the coast, it does not address itself to the sea. This is partly because the port has traditionally occupied much of the coastal area; it is only recently that there have been suburban developments that have started to engage with the waterfront. In the heart of the city, you have no idea that you are near the sea. You are in an urban grid that is so beautifully organized that it establishes a continuous public realm across the ground plane. The grain of the old town is defined by two- to three-storey residential and three- to four-storey commercial architecture, but the planning of the streets and the height-to-width proportion give a particular quality to the way in which the city is used in a very hot climate. One side of the street is basically always in the shade. The city has a mixed population that occupies different quarters, though they are no longer as clear-cut as they were in the past. In this respect, this is an unusually accommodating form of urbanism, a low city that is also very public. In some ways, it is like an oasis: in a harsh environment, it offers protection to all who go there.

Beyond the grid of the old town, the new developments adopt a form of coastal architecture – villa architecture with terraces and balconies that look towards the view. They are cubic in nature and not overly ornamented, although you do see more complex articulations in the wealthy areas. The architecture of the poor is based on a terraced cubic typology, with low external walls for privacy. Djibouti is not a big city but it is important because of its strategic location. It is a true metropolis, despite its limited size – very intense and very international. Before Dubai became what it is today, Djibouti was its equivalent in that region; it was the metropolitan place where all the different nations could meet and trade. Djibouti sees itself as the softer, more classical version of contemporary Dubai.

KHARTOUM / A brick villa before the application of a plaster finish.

DJIBOUTI / Colonnades and loggias for shade.

KHARTOUM / A brick villa with plaster finish.

DJIBOUTI / Villa-style housing.

NOUAKCHOTT / New housing with primary and secondary cubic forms.

NOUAKCHOTT / The mosque with multiple domes.

OVERVIEW

Cultivation of the Lower Nile had begun by the 7th millennium BCE and the first of the country's ancient dynasties was established around 3100 BCE. The rule of the pharaohs ended in 332 BCE, when Alexander the Great invaded the country. After his death his general, Ptolemy, became head of a Greek-speaking kingdom that lasted three centuries. The Romans invaded Egypt in 31 BCE and introduced Christianity early in the 1st millennium CE. By the 4th century Christianity was the official religion of the Byzantine Empire, the successor to the Roman Empire in Constantinople (now Istanbul) and earlier religions were banned. Arab armies attacked the Persian and Byzantine empires in the 7th century and took control of North Africa from the Indian Ocean to the Atlantic. Egypt remained a Muslim province for two centuries and it was during this period that Cairo was founded. From the 15th to the early 19th centuries the eastern Mediterranean was controlled by the Ottomans, a Turkish sultanate. By this time the Egyptians were beginning to press for independence, before Napoleon invaded the country as part of his campaign against the British.

The Ottomans drove Napoleon out of the country in 1801 but one of their officers, Muhammad Ali, then declared himself ruler of an autonomous Egypt. Both he and his successors were committed to modernizing the country and under their direction it became a major regional power. When the completion of the Suez Canal in 1869 bankrupted the country, the principal creditors, Britain and France, took financial control of the country and this led to political instability. The situation was formalized when Egypt became a British protectorate from 1914 until 1922, and the British remained in effective control of the country until after the Second World War. During this period opposition to the British came from several quarters: the Wafd Party founded in 1919, the Muslim Brotherhood founded in 1928, and the Free Officers Movement in the army in the 1940s. The Free Officers were involved in the 1952 coup that led to the abolition of the monarchy. The first president was quickly replaced by Gamal Abdel Nasser. He negotiated the withdrawal of the remaining British troops in 1956 and restructured the economy on a socialist basis. His most serious defeat came in 1967, when Israel launched a surprise attack against Egypt, Jordan and Syria, and annexed the Sinai Peninsula. Nasser was succeeded by Anwar el-Sadat in 1970 and, with Syria, he launched a successful offensive against Israel in 1973. Sinai was returned in 1979 but Islamic extremists assassinated Sadat in 1981. His successor was Hosni Mubarak who remained in power to win the first presidential elections in 2005. Following the example of the Tunisian Revolution, Tahrir Square was occupied in 2011 and Mubarak was removed by the military. A similar fate awaited Mohamed Morsi and the Muslim Brotherhood who won the succeeding election. A new constitution was approved in 2014 and Abdel Fattah el-Sisi was elected president.

OBSERVATIONS

As the largest city in Africa and the largest in the Arab world, Cairo is the crossroads of Arabic and African culture. It is split in two by the River Nile but due to its vast size the two halves now read as one. Although predominantly Arab, Cairo still feels distinctly African.

Old Cairo is defined by its ramparts and Moorish architecture. Then there is the old colonial centre whose impressive six- or seven-storey blocks are now largely used for commercial purposes. The new city edges and the riverfront are as vital as the central areas, with restaurants and hotels enjoying the vista of the Nile.

The Moorish architecture of the old city emulates the life of its people and gives expression to their culture. The souks are woven into the fabric of this area and beautiful lanes, with projecting screens that give you an insight into the life of the city, lead you to shops that must have existed for centuries.

Many of the wealthy houses are in the new suburbs, with their better roads and infrastructure. They take the form of walled villas on plots that are not very large. Styles range from modernist to Riviera and mock rural. The old quarter still has some grand houses, displaying the Moorish style of high walls on the outside and courtyards articulating their interior.

NATIONAL POPULATION

91,508,000

CITY POPULATION

18,772,000

ETHNIC GROUPS

Egyptian 99.6%, other 0.4%

RELIGIONS

Muslim (mostly Sunni) 90%, Christian (majority Coptic Orthodox, other Christians include Armenian Apostolic, Catholic, Maronite, Orthodox and Anglican) 10%

LANGUAGES

Arabic (official), English and French widely understood by educated classes

GDP

$946.6 billion

AGRICULTURAL PRODUCTS

cotton, rice, corn, wheat, beans, fruits, vegetables; cattle, water buffalo, sheep, goats

INDUSTRIES

textiles, food processing, tourism, chemicals, pharmaceuticals, hydrocarbons, construction, cement, metals, light manufacting

The old city, with its ramparts, narrow lanes and Moorish architecture, has a particularly intimate character. Recent public buildings are postmodern in style, with Arabic motifs. Many public buildings from the colonial period have been converted to cultural uses, such as the Museum of Egyptian Antiquities.

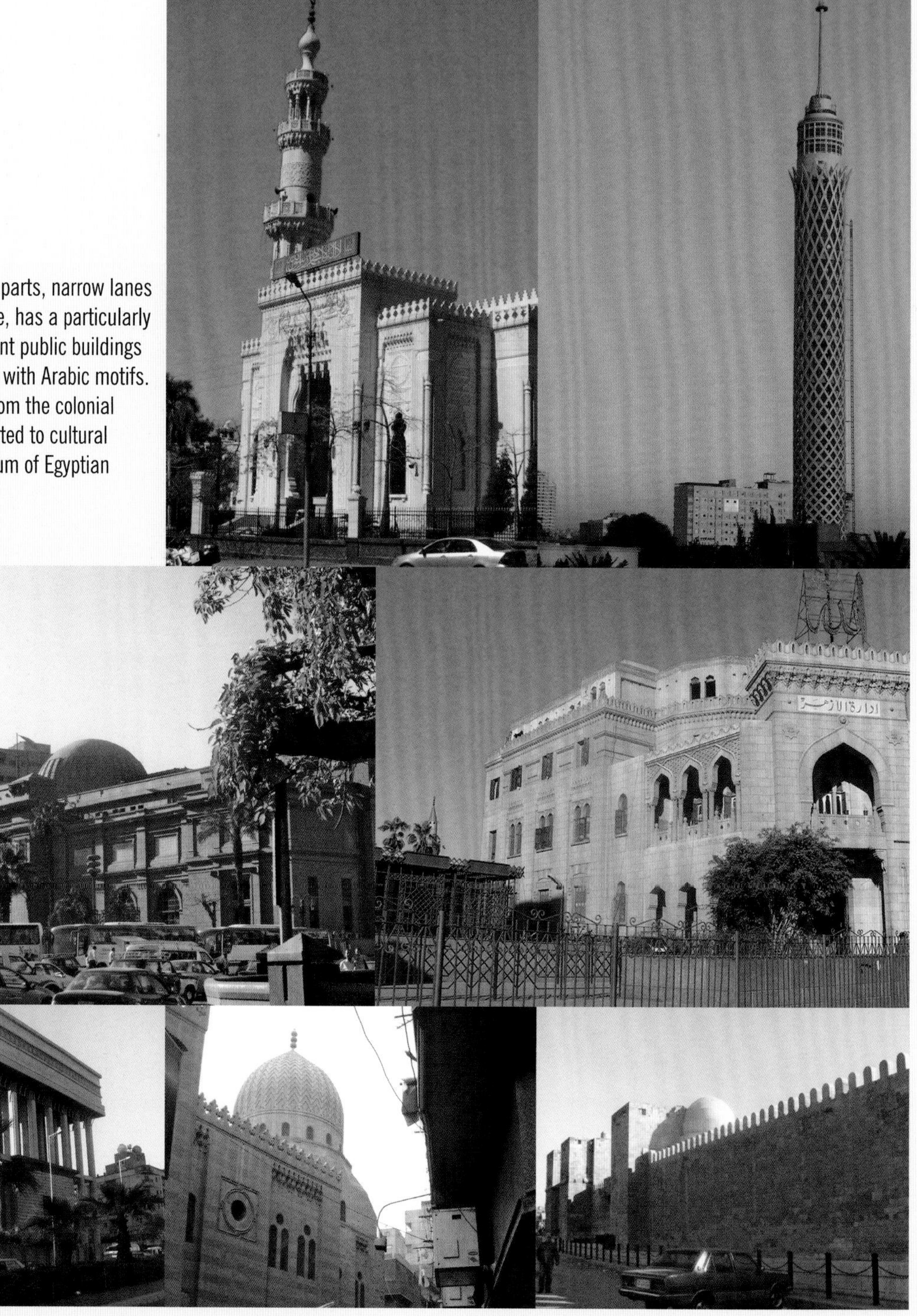

CAIRO / EGYPT / **COMMERCIAL**

From the souks of the old city to the department stores on the colonial boulevards and the street markets found in most neighbourhoods, commercial activity permeates the city.

CAIRO / EGYPT / **COMMERCIAL**

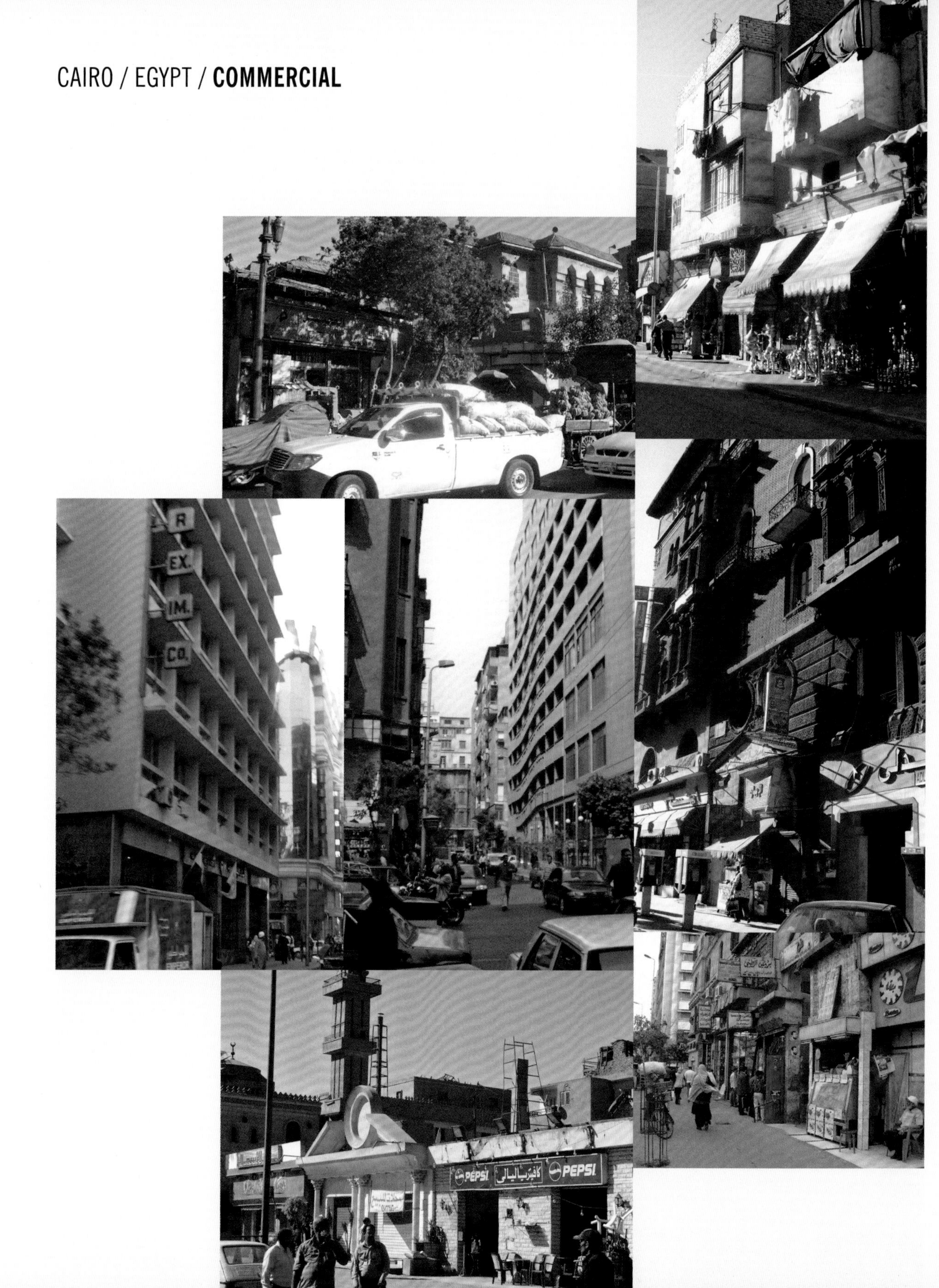

CAIRO / EGYPT / **RESIDENTIAL**

Although single-family houses can be found in the suburbs, and occasionally in the old city, most of the population live in apartment buildings. Clusters of such buildings, reached off narrow lanes, support tight urban communities.

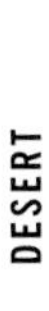

DJIBOUTI / DJIBOUTI

OVERVIEW

The land occupied by Djibouti is a northerly extension of the East African Rift Valley and is mainly desert with a small number of lakes and oases. At the beginning of the 1st millennium CE it was part of the Aksumite Kingdom, which controlled the area of modern Eritrea and southern Arabia from a capital in the north of Ethiopia. Christianity was introduced during this period but it was superseded by Islam, the religion of Arab traders, in the 9th century. In the latter part of the 19th century the French were keen to match the British presence on the Red Sea and made an agreement with the Afar sultans of two towns on the Gulf of Tadjoura, giving them access to the interior. They began the construction of the city of Djibouti in 1888, which was to be the capital of French Somaliland, as the country was then called. The economic role of the city was underpinned by an agreement between France and Ethiopia that it would be the port for Ethiopia's trade with the rest of the world, an arrangement that was reinforced by the completion of the railway from Addis Ababa to Djibouti in 1917.

The country's population is made up of Issas, who also live in neighbouring Somalia, Afars and a smaller number of Arabs and Europeans. Tension between the main ethnic groups became evident in the 1940s, when the Issas supported reunification of British, French and Italian Somaliland and the Afars were keen to remain a French colony. These differences played a significant part in later discussions around independence. In a 1958 referendum on whether Djibouti should become part of an independent Somalia, the Afars combined with resident Europeans to win the vote for staying in France, with the Issas voting the other way. Further votes in 1967 and 1977 were decided on similar lines. The result in 1967 also favoured continuing the link with France but the name of the country was changed from French Somaliland to the French Territory of the Afars and Issas. In 1977 the result was decisively in favour of giving up the French connection and Hassan Gouled Apitdon became the first president. Despite independence, ethnic tension continued to be an issue until the country's first multiparty elections in 1999. Because of its strategic location at the meeting of several continents, Djibouti City has taken on a dominant position in the country's economy. During the period of the 1990 Gulf War the French had a military base in the country and the United States made use of its naval facilities. The development of the port has been supported by Saudi Arabia and Kuwait, and Ethiopia has maintained its import and export trade. Following the second Gulf War, when the US made further use of the port, modernization has continued with the intention of providing the most up-to-date facilities in the region. The elections in 1999 were won by the current president, Ismaïl Omar Guelleh. Despite its relative isolation, Djibouti City supports a lively cosmopolitan culture that combines African, Arabic and European influences.

OBSERVATIONS

The city and country of Djibouti have become important transit points in the region. The city is a metropolitan melting pot of East African countries and an attraction for tourists. You find Ethiopians and Sudanese in the city, as well as Yemenis and Saudi Arabians. When you drive out of the city, the landscape is breathtaking.

Djibouti is a hybrid city in the sense that the French colonial city, laid out on a regular grid, is inhabited in a completely African way. The built fabric is highly permeable with a continuous blurring of inside and outside spaces. The streets in the core are arcaded, which is important in the middle of the day.

The European architecture of the old city works well as a vertical Arab city, with grain and goods on the ground floor and living quarters above. The basements are used for the nightlife, which is prolific! It is cooler then, and the perfect time to chew qat leaves. A great feature of the city is the money-changing neighbourhood that is entirely run by the women. There are no men to be found, only old and colourfully dressed Djibouti women with sacks of money, all vying to trade your dollars or euros.

NATIONAL POPULATION

888,000

CITY POPULATION

529,000

ETHNIC GROUPS

Somali 60%, Afar 35%, other 5% (includes French, Arab, Ethiopian and Italian)

RELIGIONS

Muslim 94%, Christian 6%

LANGUAGES

French (official), Arabic (official), Somali, Afar

GDP

$2.88 billion

AGRICULTURAL PRODUCTS

fruits, vegetables; goats, sheep, camels, animal hides

INDUSTRIES

construction, agricultural processing, shipping

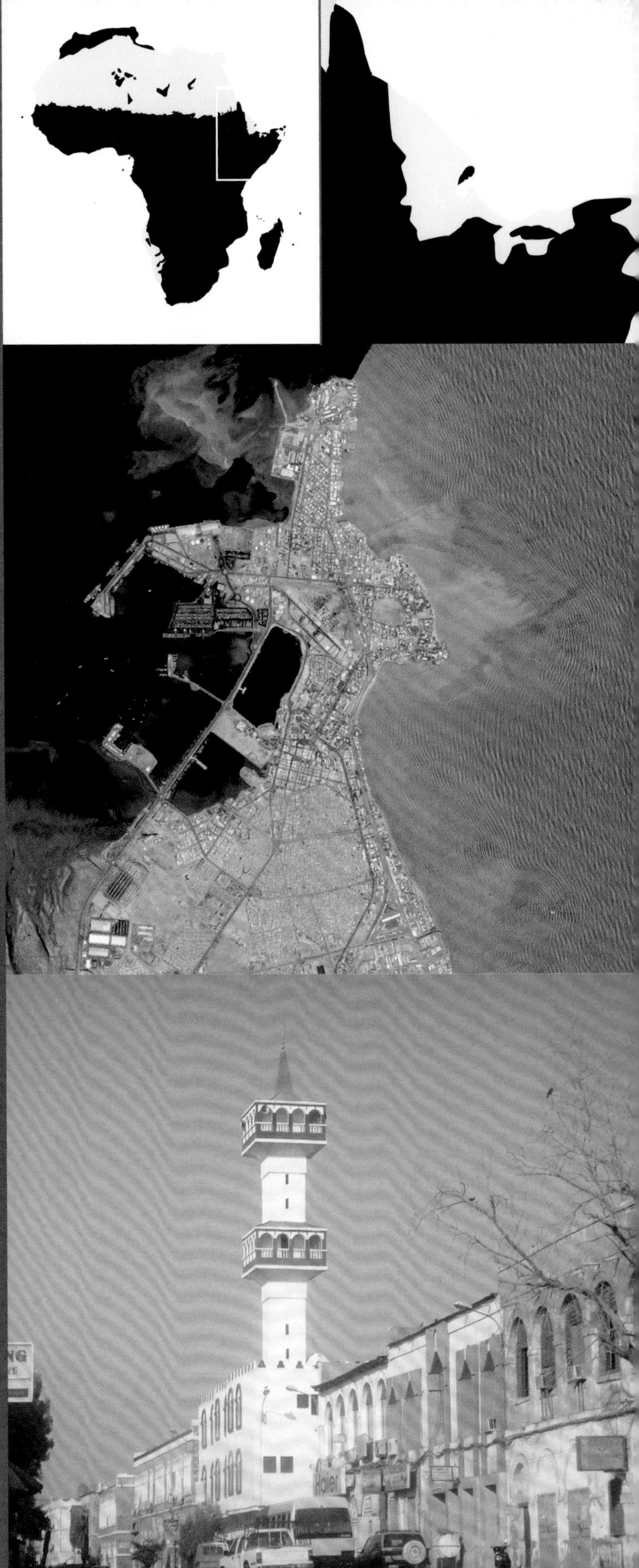

There are two main squares in the old city, and one has little awareness of the sea. Civic buildings, such as government departments and embassies, are found on or near these squares, with more recent public buildings on the periphery of the old city.

It is interesting to see the Christian cathedral and Ethiopian Coptic chapels holding pride of place along the main avenue. The main mosque is beside an old city gate. Outside the old city one is immediately aware of the sea.

DJIBOUTI / DJIBOUTI / **COMMERCIAL**

Much of Djibouti's trade is done in the old city. Although it looks French, it is basically an Arab trading city. Informal trade occurs on almost every street corner, with stalls and stands that blur the distinction between inside and outside.

The rich have moved towards the coast with its beaches and the cool breeze. Their mansions are protected by fences and tall walls. The middle class and the poor occupy the inland suburbs, where there are also Somali refugee camps.

KHARTOUM / SUDAN

OVERVIEW

Sudan's history is closely connected with that of Egypt. From the time of the First Dynasty (3100–2900 BCE), the land through which the Upper Nile and its tributaries run, then known as Nubia, was a source of slaves and natural materials for its northern neighbour. At other times Nubia was in the ascendant and supported an independent civilization. This relationship continued until the Romans subjugated Egypt in the 1st century BCE and both countries fell into decline. In the middle of the 1st millennium CE Nubia became Christian and only gradually converted to Islam, with the first Muslim king being crowned in 1323. In the succeeding period the Funj people occupied the country from the south and remained in power until the 18th century. The ready availability of slaves was seized on by the Egyptian outpost of the Ottoman Empire, whose leader, Muhammad Ali, invaded Sudan in 1821. Under the new regime, Khartoum developed one of the largest slave markets ever known, a situation that began to change only when Ali's grandson, known as Ismail the Magnificent, appointed the British officer Charles Gordon to be governor of Sudan. After the British dislodged Ismail in 1879 they reappointed Gordon as governor, but he was killed in Khartoum in the aftermath of a siege in 1885. The British returned to Sudan in 1895, decimated the army that was responsible for the siege, and the country was incorporated in the Anglo-Egyptian Condominium. When Egypt became independent in 1922, the Sudanese were motivated to liberate their country but the British dragged their feet and the Republic of Sudan only saw the light of day in 1956.

Shortly before independence, the shooting of strikers provoked an army-led rebellion in the south and to escape reprisals the rebels fled to Uganda. Together with militias inside Sudan, their aim was independence for the south of the country and, having occupied large areas, they set up an independent administration. In 1972 a new government under Jaafar Nimeiry negotiated a peace agreement that gave regional autonomy to the south and initiated programmes intended to develop the country's natural resources. The level of borrowing involved led to serious problems in the economy and in the resulting backlash Sharia law was introduced throughout the country and the south lost its autonomy. With strikes in the north and guerrilla warfare in the south, Nimeiry was removed from power in a coup in 1985 and the government attempted to regain control in the south by encouraging the Baggara Arabs to carry out armed raids there. In 1989 a further coup brought an Islamic government to power, which began to take back areas of the south from rebel control in the early 1990s. Between 2002 and 2004 lengthy discussions resulted in the cessation of north–south hostilities and the re-establishment of a regional assembly. But these events were overtaken by a rebellion in Darfur, where the Sudan Liberation Army and the Justice and Equality Movement sought redress for the historic neglect from which the area suffered. In response, the government supported Arab militias, the Janjaweed, to suppress the opposition, and used the air force to bomb villages. Following a referendum in 2011, South Sudan finally gained independence but conflict has continued in two of Sudan's southern states, resulting in over a million displaced people. In 2009 the International Criminal Court charged the president, Omar al-Bashir, with war crimes in Darfur. He was reelected in 2015.

OBSERVATIONS

The oldest part of Khartoum stands at the confluence of the White Nile and the Blue Nile. The colonial city, with its civic buildings and the commercial core, faces the Blue Nile and is bounded by the White Nile to the west. Then there are the barrios and ever-developing suburbs that make up greater Khartoum.

Each part of the city has a distinct quality and, though centrally planned, the sense of distinct settlements within the whole has been maintained and is appreciated by the citizens. They also have the gift of the Nile, where people fish and take riverboats.

The homes of the poor are usually made from mud brick and stand one storey high, forming human-scaled terraces and urban blocks. The cubic form of this housing is very striking in the sun, and the brick has the tone of the earth from which it has been made. Since life happens in the shade, Khartoum starts the day early because by noon in the summer the sun can be punishing.

NATIONAL POPULATION

40,235,000

CITY POPULATION

5,129,000

ETHNIC GROUPS

Sudanese Arab 70%, Fur, Beja, Nuba, Fallata

RELIGIONS

Sunni Muslim, small Christian minority

LANGUAGES

Arabic (official), English (official), Nubian, Ta Bedawie, Fur, diverse dialects of Nilotic, Nilo-Hamitic, Sudanic languages

GDP

$160.2 billion

AGRICULTURAL PRODUCTS

cotton, groundnuts (peanuts), sorghum, millet, wheat, gum arabic, sugarcane, cassava (manioc, tapioca), mangos, papaya, bananas, sweet potatoes, sesame; sheep, livestock

INDUSTRIES

oil, cotton ginning, textiles, cement, edible oils, sugar, soap distilling, shoes, petroleum refining, pharmaceuticals, armaments, automobile/light truck assembly

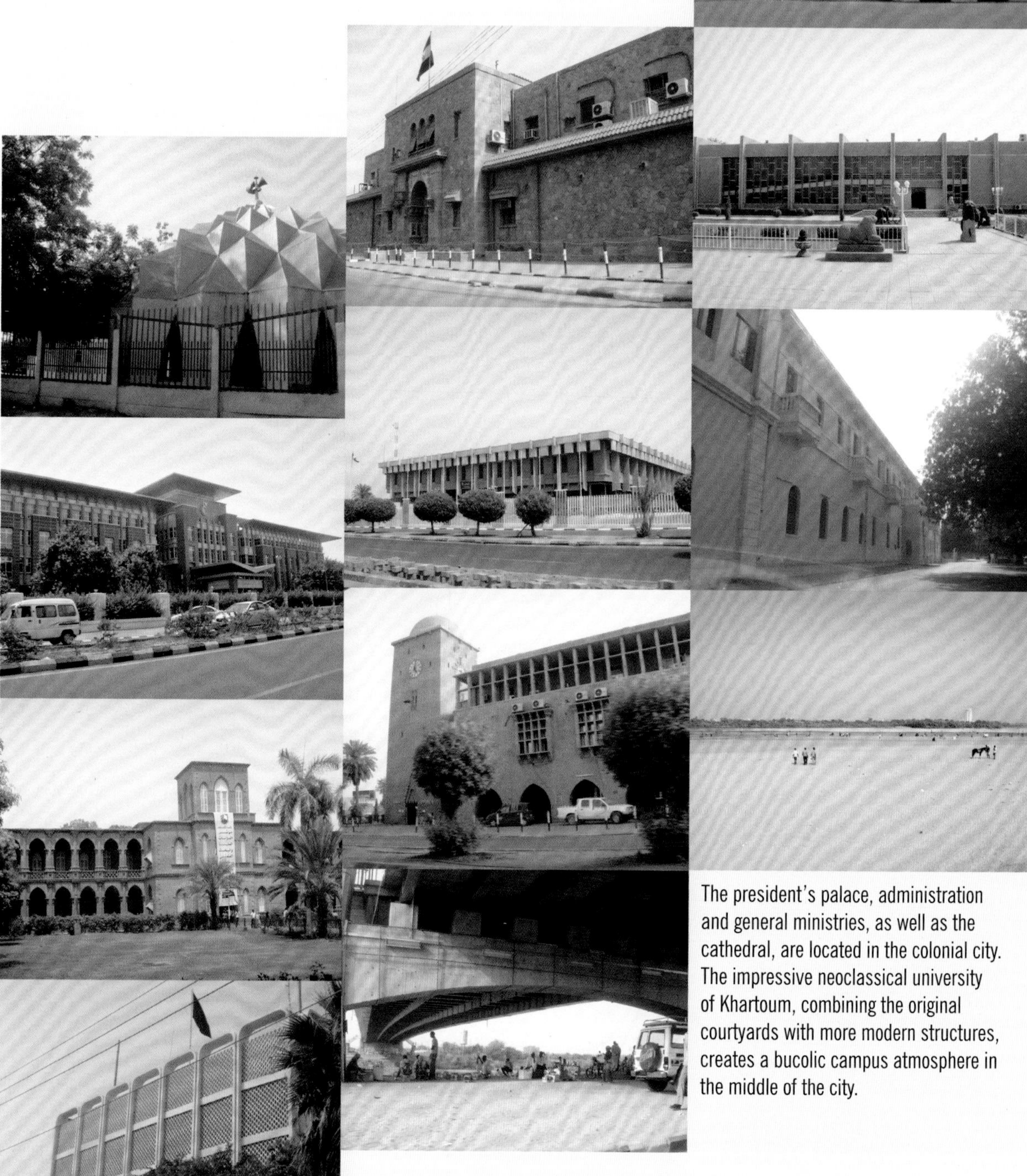

The president's palace, administration and general ministries, as well as the cathedral, are located in the colonial city. The impressive neoclassical university of Khartoum, combining the original courtyards with more modern structures, creates a bucolic campus atmosphere in the middle of the city.

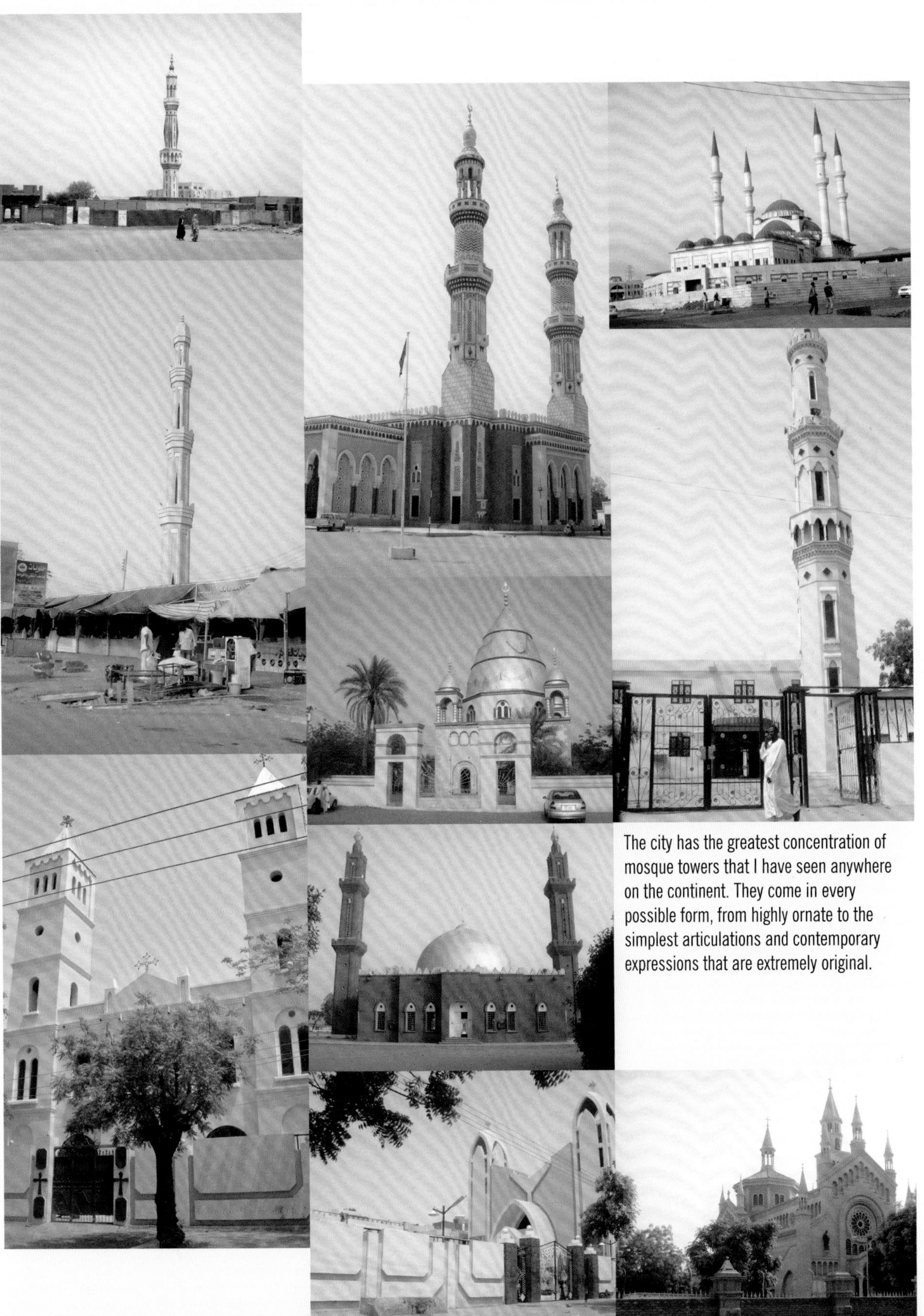

The city has the greatest concentration of mosque towers that I have seen anywhere on the continent. They come in every possible form, from highly ornate to the simplest articulations and contemporary expressions that are extremely original.

The city has as many forms of commercial architecture as there are districts, from the old souks of Omdurman, just across the river, to the light-hearted shops and cafes in the centre. With an increasing number of higher buildings, the city now has a skyline.

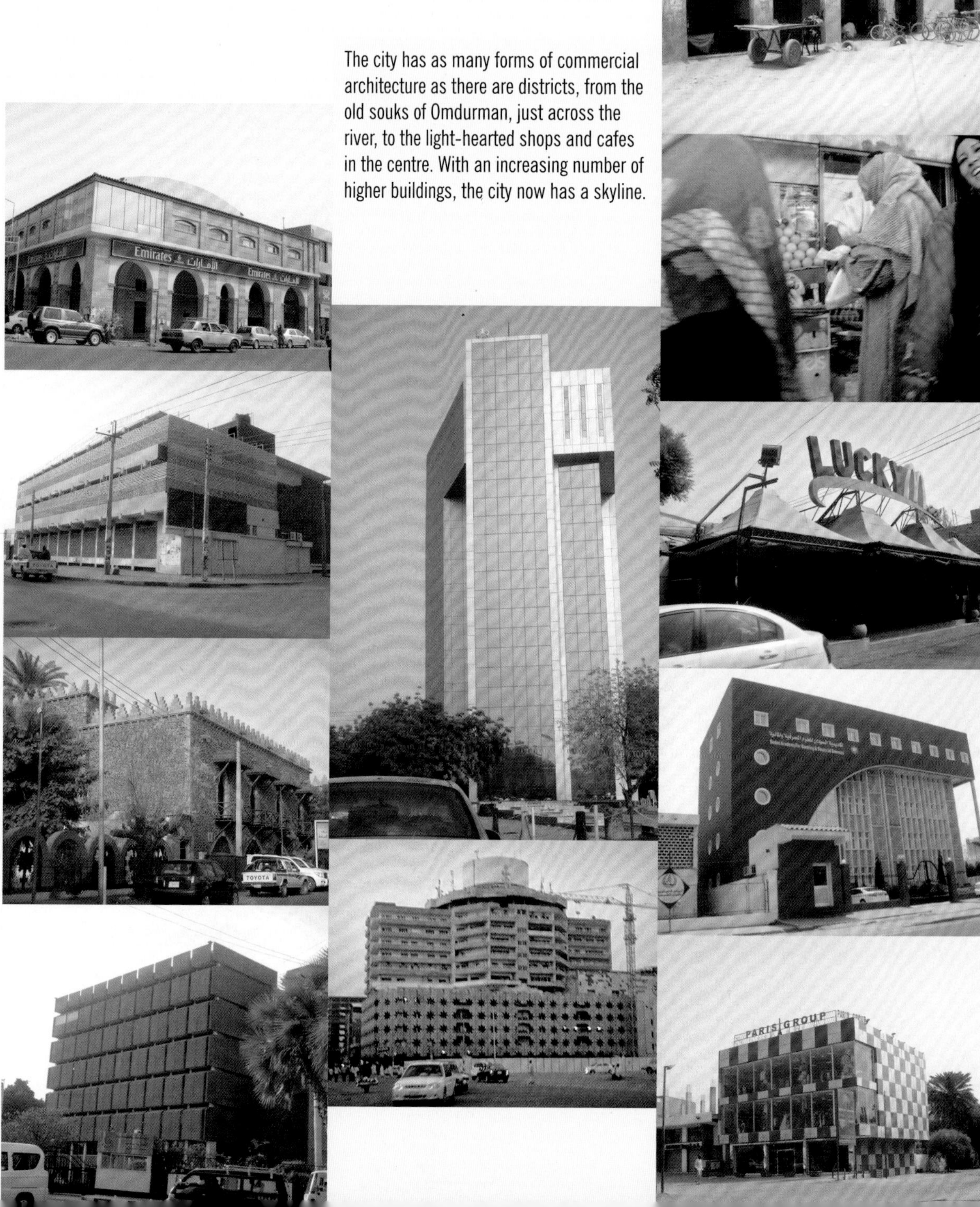

KHARTOUM / SUDAN / **RESIDENTIAL**

There is a typology that has led the city into a building frenzy. Old properties in the centre are being torn down and replaced with large multistorey apartment blocks. They are used as hostels and rental apartments for visitors to the city.

NOUAKCHOTT / MAURITANIA

OVERVIEW

The history of Mauritania begins in the 3rd century when the Berbers established trade routes that connected West Africa with Mediterranean North Africa. The shipment of gold, ivory, salt, silver and slaves generated considerable wealth and led to the development of the Empire of Ghana, which had its capital at Koumbi Saleh in the southeast of modern Mauritania. By the 7th century Islam had been introduced from the north, but south of the Sahara it was often combined with local beliefs. The Empire of Ghana was therefore less united than it might have been and in the 11th century it was destroyed by the Almoravids from their base in Marrakech. Six centuries later, in 1674, the area that would become Mauritania came under Arab control and the language of the invaders, Hassaniya, was adopted by the Berber population. By this stage, European ships sailing up and down the west coast of Africa had begun to undermine the previous monopoly of the trans-Saharan trade routes. With the advent of colonialism, the French established strategic bases in Mauritania to protect their dominant position in West Africa. But they were slow to explore the interior, claiming the country as a colony only in 1904. It took a further thirty years to control the Moors in the north and after that the country was isolated from many of the developments that led to independence in other parts of Africa.

Mauritania's first political party, the Union Progressiste Mauritanienne (Mauritanian Progressive Union), was founded in 1957 and won most of the seats in the next election. When independence was declared in 1960, Moktar Ould Daddah became the first president of the Islamic republic and decided to build a new capital at Nouakchott. The new government joined the Arab League and at a later stage declared Hassaniya and French to be the official languages – all schoolchildren being required to study Hassaniya. These policies alienated the predominantly black African population in the south of the country. In the 1970s Mauritania made an agreement with Morocco to subdivide the former Spanish colony of Western Sahara but this was fiercely resisted by the Polisario Front, a guerrilla movement based in Western Sahara. Following a coup in 1978 Mauritania's new military government gave up all claims to the Western Sahara. The military's choice of leader was Colonel Maaouya Ould Sid'Ahmed Taya whose plans to improve the economy and reestablish democratic government were undermined by his repressive attitude to the south of the country. After street battles between Moors and black Africans in 1989, 70,000 black Africans were expelled to Senegal. In the 1990s Taya attempted to moderate his position and permitted the organization of opposition parties. But when he was reelected as president in 1992 ballot rigging was widely suspected, and a new tax on bread led to riots in 1995, giving Taya a pretext for jailing his opponents. After further riots in 2003, Taya's regime was terminated by a coup in 2005 that would bring Sidi Ould Cheikh Abdallahi to power as the country's first elected president in 2007. The leader of a military coup, Mohamed Ould Abdel Aziz, won the elections in 2009 and 2014.

OBSERVATIONS

The small capital of a large country, Nouakchott is a planned city with the administrative functions of the state in the centre, surrounded by commercial and residential areas. The civic architecture is modern with Islamic or French motifs.

The main mosque is plain, noble and elegant; the Saudi mosque is adorned, elaborate and dust coloured, and the Moroccan mosque has a tall geometric tower, clad in tile. One has a strong sense of the Muslim world asserting its relationship with the country.

Most houses present a blank wall to the street, with discreet openings for vehicles and people. The upper floor has access to roof terraces and more open views. Government-subsidized housing is built as large homogenous estates.

Although it is situated on the Atlantic, the city stretches into the Sahara Desert. The fish market is on the coast and the white sand beaches are regularly invaded by the residents who come to cool down from the harsh midday sun.

NATIONAL POPULATION

4,068,000

CITY POPULATION

968,000

ETHNIC GROUPS

black Moors 40%, white Moors 30%, black Africans (Halpulaar, Soninke, Wolof and Bamara ethnic groups) 30%

RELIGIONS

Muslim 100%

LANGUAGES

Arabic (official and national), Pulaar, Soninke, Wolof (all national languages), French, Hassaniya

GDP

$15.62 billion

AGRICULTURAL PRODUCTS

dates, millet, sorghum, rice, corn; cattle, sheep

INDUSTRIES

fish processing, oil production, mining (iron ore, gold, copper)

The centre turns its back on the ocean. Modernism, with Arabic or French influence, is the predominant style of the government buildings that cluster around the president's palace. The grand mosque is also in this area.

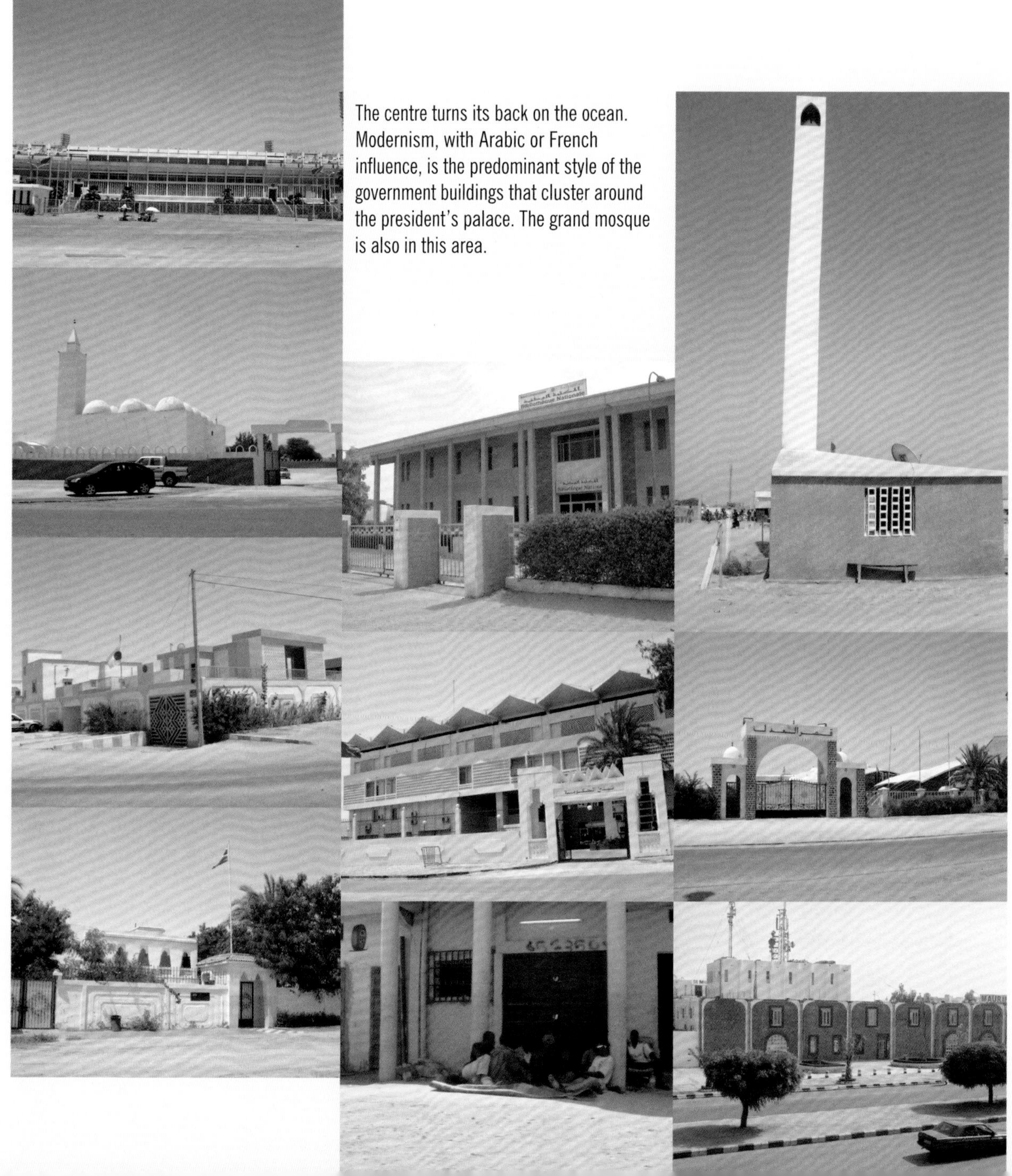

NOUAKCHOTT / MAURITANIA / **COMMERCIAL**

Apart from markets and two shopping malls, commerce takes the form of shops on the main roads through residential areas. These appear to be driven by local needs and form clusters in various locations.

HOTEL

NOUAKCHOTT / MAURITANIA / **RESIDENTIAL**

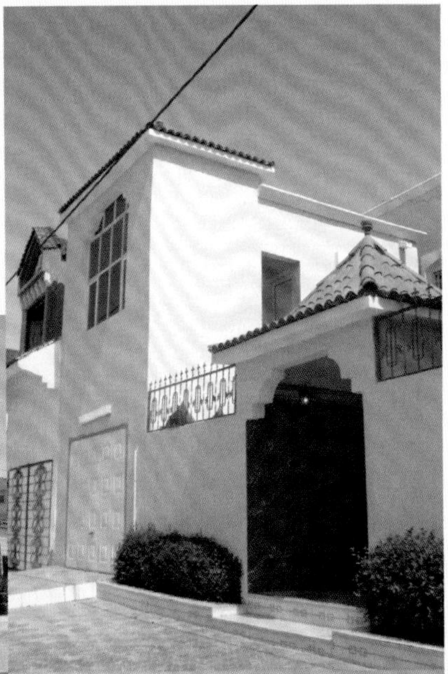

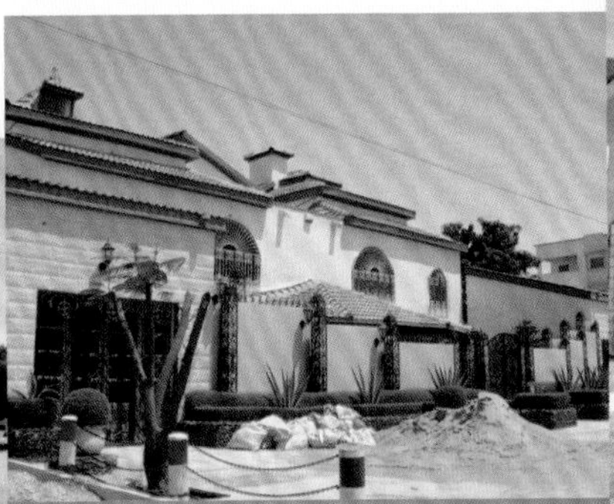

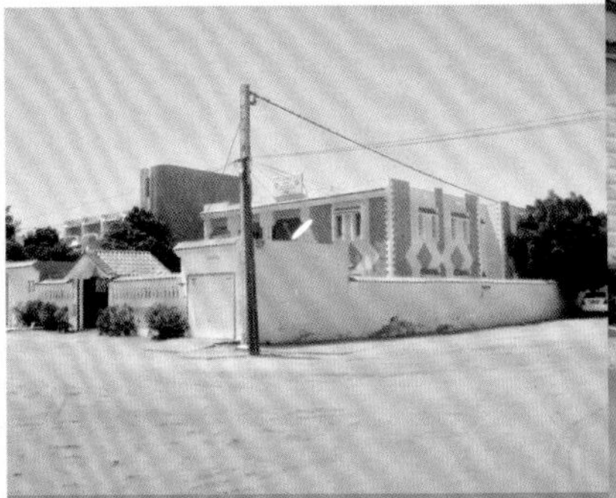

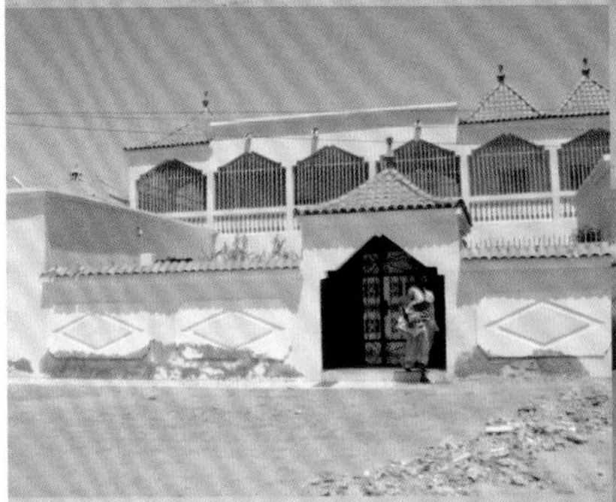

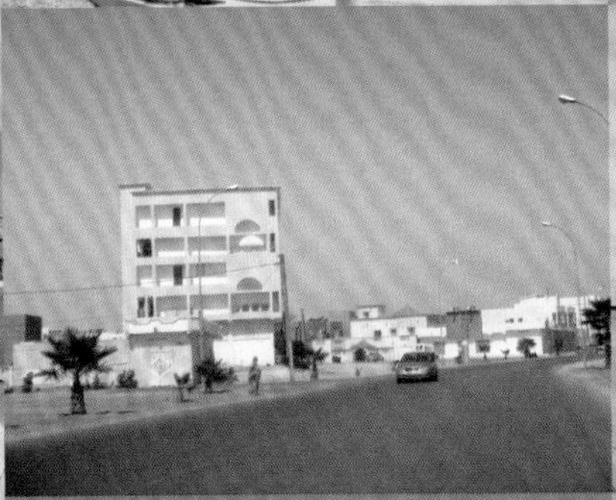

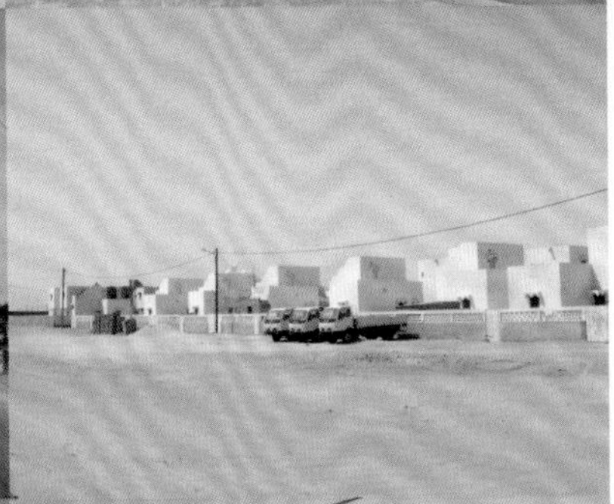

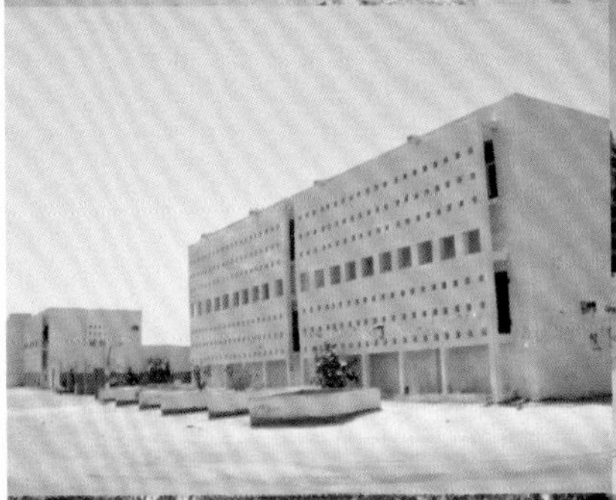

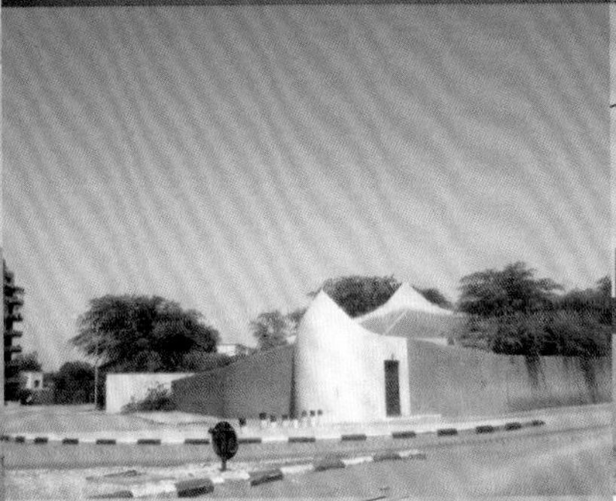

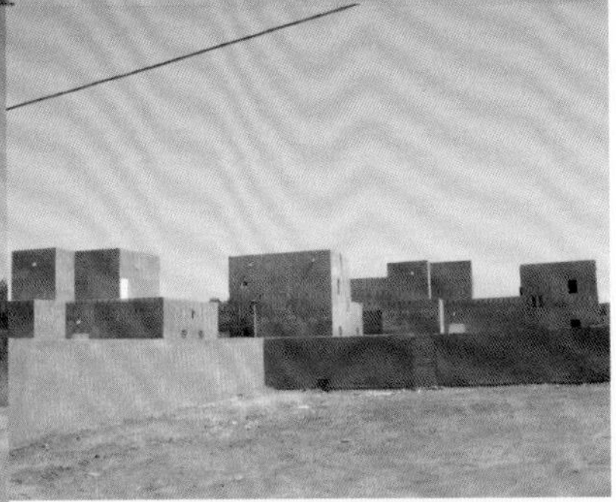

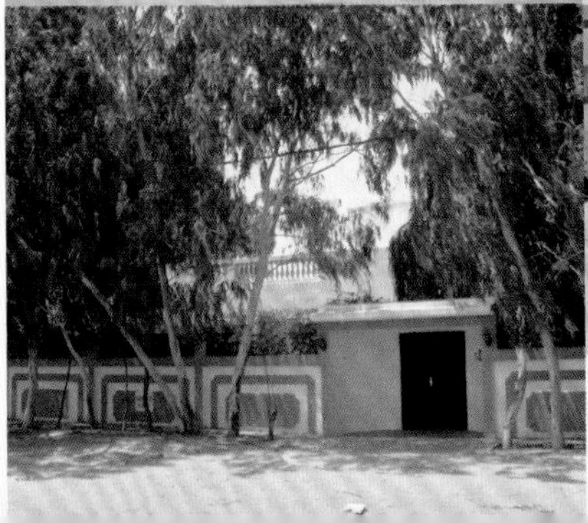

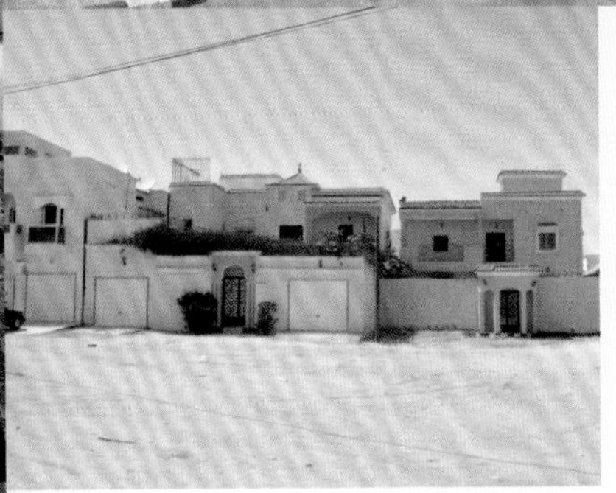

Wealthy housing is of the compound and villa type, with Arabic decoration. Apartment buildings are normally three or four storeys high, and more of them are being built. Low-cost housing is state built and organized in quarters.

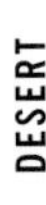

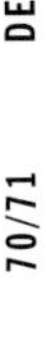

THE SAHEL

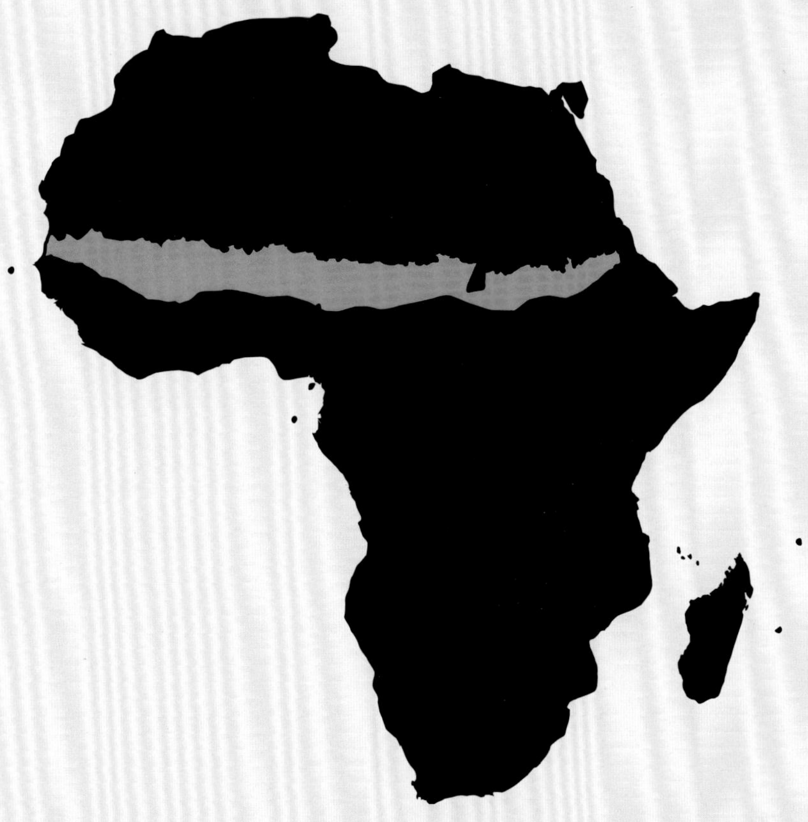

This is a semiarid region that forms a continuous band, of variable width, from the Red Sea to the Atlantic Ocean, where it includes the Cape Verde islands. It is a transitional zone between the Sahara Desert to the north and the belt of more humid savannas and scrublands to the south. *Sahel* means 'shore', which describes the position of this area along the southern edge of the desolate sea of sand and rock that is the Sahara. The Sahel is subject to strong variations in rainfall and temperature. At least seven months of the year are dry, and there is normally 200–600 mm of rainfall a year, which falls mostly between June and September. Rainfall is generally higher in the south and lower towards the Sahara. High temperatures are in the range 33–36°C, with lows of 18–21°C. The vegetation consists of grassland and scrub that have adapted to the strong seasonal variations; they are verdant in the wet season and scorched at other times. The Sahel previously supported a wide range of grazing animals, but many of these have been displaced by human activity. In the second half of the 20th century the Sahel was increasingly afflicted by soil erosion and desertification as a growing population made increasing demands on the fragile ecology.

THE SAHEL

When I visited the four cities of the Sahel, I was struck by the sense of civic life operating in each one of them. There is a very clear layering of the relationship with the countryside and of how the city engages with its hinterland. Because the landscape is flat and is on the threshold between vegetation and desert, the domestic architecture is generally horizontal – a cellular, atria-like architecture – while civic buildings are more concerned with emphatic vertical symbols. The architecture of Islam, with its domes and minarets, plays a significant role here but there is a more general symbolism that relates to a tradition of marking the distinction between desert and built environment. The sense of materiality in these cities is based on the sand and stone and, where there is vegetation, it is encouraged as a way of providing shade and moderating the climate. It can also take on ornamental qualities – framing certain buildings, for instance – but that is not its primary function.

The Sahel cities are close to being desert cities and their architecture is a response to the strength of the light, which flattens everything. There is a kind of invisibility that happens here due to the light and that flattening is something that the local architecture starts to work against. The dramatic monuments that you find in Ouagadougou are a response to this condition: the cluster of towers comprising Cinema City (the location of the city's film archive), the cultural centre in the form of the Eiffel Tower in concrete, and so on. There is also a use of certain types of volume to give geometry and form to the light, to shape the light and act as a counter to the luminosity of the sky. This explains the boldness of the forms employed – the cylinders and cubes. They represent an absolute desire to see geometry expressed in light. Unlike Mediterranean architecture, which is about reflecting the light, it concerns the use of light to reveal form in an environment that normally renders it as an indistinct plane. These bold forms, with their strong silhouettes, allow you to see things in viewing conditions that are otherwise very difficult. This is the compelling idea in the public architecture of the Sahel. If you look at a recent building, such as the National Bank in Bamako, a concrete-framed tower that has been clad in mud bricks, it attempts – successfully, I think – to give definition to the light by means of the deep vertical reveals that have been cut into the external walls. There is no sign of conventional layering in the detailing of this architecture, the step-by-step change of scale that you normally expect when you approach a building. It operates purely as a monument in the landscape. The water towers are part of this; their importance to the city is acknowledged in the sculptural forms that are visible from all directions. Monuments of this kind articulate the central areas of these cities and influence the arrangements between them at ground level.

Like fragments from a previous era, the Sahel cities contain some strong colonial buildings that continue to make an important contribution to the larger environment. These buildings started to develop a dry, tropical architecture that could take its place between the forest and the desert. It is an architecture of colonnades and porticoes, rather than interior space; one that starts to talk about moderating the harshness of the heat and giving some respite from the humidity. This is especially clear in the civic buildings of Bamako, and in the shopping buildings where the goods are displayed in a shaded area in front of an enclosed storage space. There is a very interesting mercantile component to the Sahel cities: the way in which produce and goods are thrust into the public realm. The notion of trade is closely related to display and, to be effective, the display needs to be excessive.

At close quarters, some public buildings use a decorative pattern to articulate the facade. Contrary to the modernist programme, they often use a geometry that contrasts with that of the building itself and is somewhat symbolic. It is about engaging with people and, if you look at the traditional artefacts from here, which I have been able to do, there is a geometric expression that is understood as the

OUAGADOUGOU / The cultural centre with a vertical emphasis.

N'DJAMENA / The horizontal domestic architecture.

BAMAKO / The National Bank building.

OUAGADOUGOU / A mosque with bold forms.

NIAMEY / A water tower.

OUAGADOUGOU / Cinema City.

cultural trope of the region. The decorative geometries that figure on the facades of buildings make reference to these artefacts and are a celebration of this sense of ornament. Sometimes the markings are expressed and brought through as figure-ground patterns, like oversized letters, or there may be strong profiles of the type that you see in the tower of the market building in Bamako, which also has an artefact quality to it. You can make connections with Islamic architecture and to the traditions of the local Berber people; it is a truly cosmopolitan architecture.

In the Sahel it is the architecture of the poor that most expresses the horizontality of the landscape. This architecture is about walls that enclose individual spaces – cells – and define perimeters. The thresholds are never experienced visually, except as simple apertures. When you are welcomed through the outer wall, you start to realize that the building is made up of a series of volumes that form deeper and more private spaces, depending on the size of the house. Residences in the Sahel do not normally articulate themselves as singular dwellings but as clusters or groups; this seems to be the operating standard. You see this even more clearly in the shanty towns and the informal housing, whose fabric forms a continuous urban plate articulated according to people's need for privacy.

In middle-class housing the cellular architecture remains the dominant typology but it always sits within the site boundaries of each property. It is still the expression of volume that is seen as authentic and indigenous to the area. When you travel through the Sahel, this wall and volumetric architecture is the vernacular architecture of the landscape. It is very powerful to see – an architecture that is solely about the landscape where it was created.

N'DJAMENA / An architecture of colonnades and porticoes.

BAMAKO / A shop with a shaded area in front of the storage space.

BAMAKO / The tower of the market building.

NIAMEY / A building with a patterned facade.

OUAGADOUGOU / New residential architecture.

NIAMEY / Residential architecture with simple apertures.

BAMAKO / MALI

OVERVIEW

There is evidence that the north of the country was occupied in 50,000 BCE, farming was established by 5,000 BCE and the use of iron had begun by 500 BCE. Its position on the main trade route across the Sahara supported the growth of three separate empires, spanning a period of a thousand years and starting in the 6th century CE. The Empire of Ghana included much of Mali and Senegal, and declined in the 11th century. The Empire of Mali, with an important centre at Timbuktu, covered a larger area than the present country and lasted until the 14th century. It was followed by the Songhai Empire, based on the Niger River, which was overrun by Moroccan mercenaries in the 16th century. In the following centuries Islam became the predominant religion as a result of jihad-inspired invasions from the north and west. By this time European traders had arrived on the coast of West Africa and by the 19th century the French had moved into Mali. In the context of French West Africa, Mali was less prosperous than Senegal and Côte d'Ivoire. The French were mainly interested in growing cotton and rice but did complete some major infrastructure projects, such as the Dakar to Bamako railway and an extensive irrigation project near Ségou.

Since independence in 1960 politics and government have been through a lengthy development. Modibo Keïta, the first president, was committed to state socialism but the deteriorating economy undermined his position and he was deposed in a military coup in 1968. His successor was an army officer, Moussa Traoré, who survived several attempted coups and ruled until 1991. The socialist policies of his predecessor were dropped and the government became increasingly repressive. Elections in 1979 and 1985 confirmed Traoré's position as president and leader of the Democratic Union of the Malian People, the only political party permitted. Opposition to the government increased in the late 1980s, driven in part by austerity measures associated with support from the IMF. When non-violent protests in 1991 were violently suppressed, the army intervened to set up an interim government under General Amadou Toumani Touré in 1991. He stepped down a year later, having organized multiparty elections won by Alpha Oumar Konaré and the Alliance for Democracy in Mali, who initiated a programme of modernization. His position was undermined by a major devaluation of the currency and perceived irregularities in the elections of 1997 but after reelection he established a government of national unity to continue the programme of reform. Under the presidencies of Konaré and Touré, who succeeded him in 2002, Mali was politically stable and attempted to diversify its agriculture-based economy. Following the government's encouragement of multinational companies, Mali is now Africa's third biggest exporter of gold. Touré was deposed in 2012 and, following an international intervention to drive Islamic militants from the country's northern states, Ibrahim Boubacar Keïta won the elections in 2013.

OBSERVATIONS

The city is teeming with activity. There are donkeys and goats in most areas and markets on every street corner. The quarter system has been overrun with people establishing commerce wherever they can. This ranges from formal to the informal set-ups that serve the poor who cannot afford to live in the city.

Life is lived outdoors and most activities are on public view. It is hot so the sense of privacy is a matter of degrees. Things erupt and subside in this teeming melting pot of people and the city market introduces density at an incredible scale. Everything is on show from the artisan making instruments to women making food. The poor quarter is laid out in a series of boulevards, and lanes that break down the blocks into courtyards. The courts are family yards.

Although this might seem like a chaotic city, what is on display is the trading nature of the Arab and West African. The colonial city is simply a backdrop for the real city. This is a culture that does not need many monuments in order to function. Culture comes into being by the collision of people and the agent for this is trade and commerce.

NATIONAL POPULATION

17,600,000

CITY POPULATION

2,515,000

ETHNIC GROUPS

Manding (Bambara, Malinke) 52%, Fulani (Peul) 11%, Saracole 7%, Songhai 7%, Tuareg and Moor 5%, Mianka 4%, other 14%

RELIGIONS

Muslim 94.8%, Christian 2.4%, animist 2%, none 0.5%, unspecified 0.3%

LANGUAGES

French (official), Bambara 46.3%, Peul/foulfoulbe 9.4%, Dogon 7.2%, Maraka/soninke 6.4%, Malinke 5.6%, Sonrhai/djerma 5.6%, Minianka 4.3%, Tamacheq 3.5%, Senoufo 2.6%, unspecified 0.6%, other 8.5%

GDP

$27.5 billion

AGRICULTURAL PRODUCTS

cotton, millet, rice, corn, vegetables, peanuts; cattle, sheep, goats

INDUSTRIES

food processing, construction, mining (phosphate, gold)

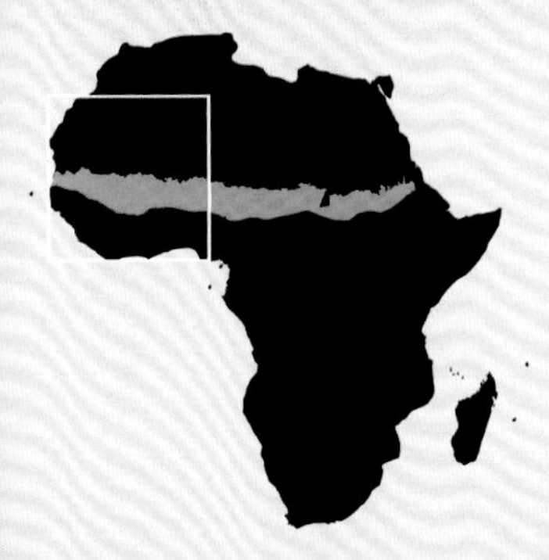

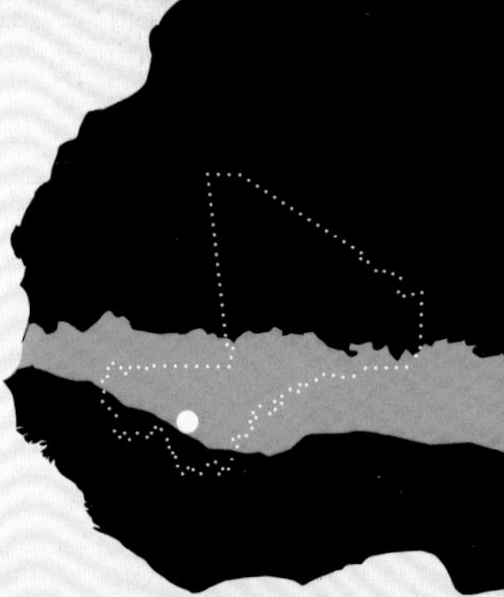

The buildings of the central area are from the turn of the 20th century, and the character of the city is that of a green garden. A few contemporary buildings break this rule, such as the new bank building on the River Niger.

CHEMIN DE FER DE DAKAR AU NIGER
MUSEE
HOTEL DE VILLE

Rural life and the city collide in a dynamic mix that can be disconcerting for someone from a Western city, but this is the buzz of an African city. With mopeds and cars, the atmosphere can get a little heady in terms of pollution.

BAMAKO / MALI / **RESIDENTIAL**

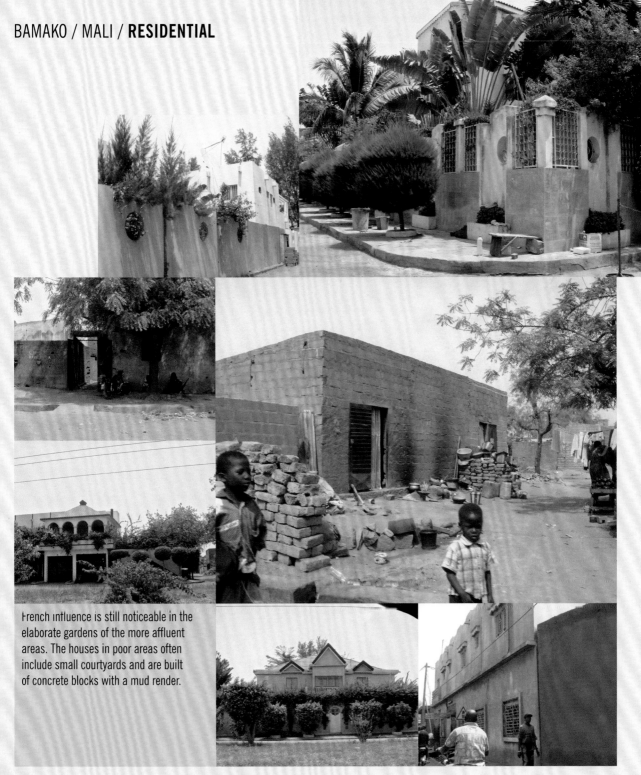

French influence is still noticeable in the elaborate gardens of the more affluent areas. The houses in poor areas often include small courtyards and are built of concrete blocks with a mud render.

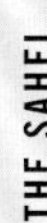

N'DJAMENA / CHAD

OVERVIEW

Chad has a long history; there are prehistoric rock paintings in the north of the country and the Sao people had developed an urban culture before the time of Christ. By the end of the 1st millennium CE, several empires derived their wealth from the trans-Saharan trade routes. The Kanem–Bornu Empire around Lake Chad was the most enduring and the trade connection brought Islam to the area. During the 14th century, Kanem–Bornu domination was undermined when the Arabic-speaking Bulala, Bagirmi and Wadai peoples migrated from the north and east. The country's boundaries are the result of an agreement between France and Britain in 1898, and France began to occupy Chad in 1900, when their forces defeated the Bornu people close to N'Djamena. Resistance in other areas continued until 1914, especially in the far north and east. French rule brought few benefits. Some of the population were forced to work on the construction of the Congo–Ocean Railway, when they had no railway in their own country and only a primitive road system. The education system was the worst in French West Africa and the economy remained weak and underdeveloped. The country's settlement pattern is the result of climate and topography: the northern desert is mainly occupied by people of Arab descent who live as nomadic herders, and the savanna in the south is cultivated by black Africans who are Christians and animists. Agriculture is most productive in the southwest where various cash crops are grown.

The movement towards independence began in 1946 with the founding of the Parti Progressiste Tchadien (Chadian Progressive Party, PPT), which became the dominant party in the mid 1950s. By the time of independence in 1960 a labour leader, François Tombalbaye, had formed a breakaway coalition between his branch of the PPT and the Muslim population in the north, and succeeded in becoming president. As it became clear that his presidency was becoming a repressive dictatorship, a guerrilla-based opposition movement developed in the north of the country. Following Tombalbaye's assassination in 1975, another southerner, General Félix Malloum, formed an uneasy alliance with a northern leader, Hissène Habré. The distrust between them erupted in serious violence in N'Djamena in 1979, resulting in many civilian deaths. In the resulting power vacuum, Libyan troops occupied the capital. They were driven out by French forces who supported Habré when he seized power in 1982. In 1987 his military advisor, Idriss Déby, succeeded in driving the Libyans out of the country, only to be accused by Habré of planning a coup in 1989. Déby left the country and returned with a private army in 1990. Having occupied N'Djamena, he assumed the presidency the following year and won the elections in 1996. Despite doubts about the fairness of these and later elections, and several uprisings and attempted coups, Déby has remained in power since then. Chad became an oil exporter in 2004 but this has done little to improve the lives of the population and the instability caused by rebel groups in Sudan has created an internal refugee problem. N'Djamena's population is expanding rapidly as more people leave the land.

OBSERVATIONS

This is a Sahel city where the temperatures reach the mid 40s in the summer. It stands on the north bank of the River Chari but turns away from it, with streets spreading outwards from the Place de la Libération. To the west is a colonial area around the circular Place de l'Etoile, with embassies and wealthy residences on the streets that radiate out from it.

The commercial area is to the east, with the central market, grand mosque, stadium and playing fields. To the north of the mosque is a dense residential quarter and further residential areas are clustered to the east and further north, where the city has expanded in the past decade. Most of the city's buildings are no more than three storeys high, which is good news for the nearby airport.

Life is led in the streets, which are wide and at times leafy, providing cool shade from the harsh sun. The public spaces are quite symbolic and for official ceremonies, and most of the roundabouts have structures commemorating some aspect of Chad's life and history. The banks of the river are generally used by local farmers for growing crops.

NATIONAL POPULATION

14,037,000

CITY POPULATION

1,260,000

ETHNIC GROUPS

Sara 27.7%, Arab 12.3%, Mayo-Kebbi 11.5%, Kanem-Bornou 9%, Ouaddai 8.7%, Hadjarai 6.7%, Tandjile 6.5%, Gorane 6.3%, Fitri-Batha 4.7%, unspecified 0.2%, other 6.4%

RELIGIONS

Muslim 53.1%, Catholic 20.1%, Protestant 14.2%, animist 7.3%, atheist 3.1%, unspecified 1.7%, other 0.5%

LANGUAGES

French (official), Arabic (official), Sara (in south), more than 120 different languages and dialects

GDP

$29.64 billion

AGRICULTURAL PRODUCTS

cotton, sorghum, millet, peanuts, sesame, corn, rice, potatoes, onions, cassava (manioc, tapioca); cattle, sheep, goats, camels

INDUSTRIES

oil, cotton textiles, brewing, natron (sodium carbonate), soap, cigarettes, construction materials

N’DJAMENA / CHAD / **CIVIC**

The government buildings are either modernist, with canopies and *brises-soleil*, or inspired by the Sahel. The president’s postmodern palace and the cathedral stand on two sides of the Place de la Libération. The smaller mosques are often quite modest and lack minarets.

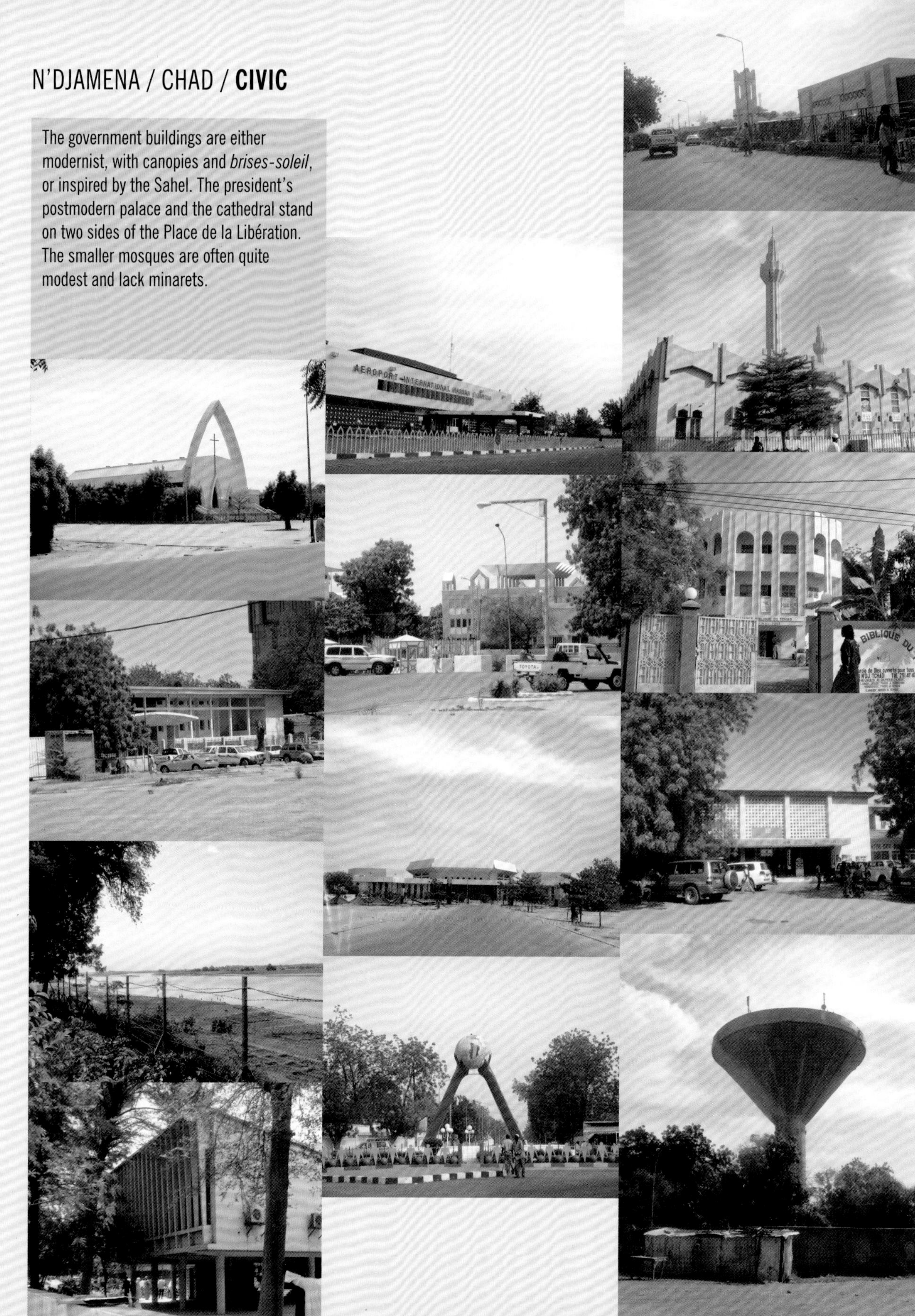

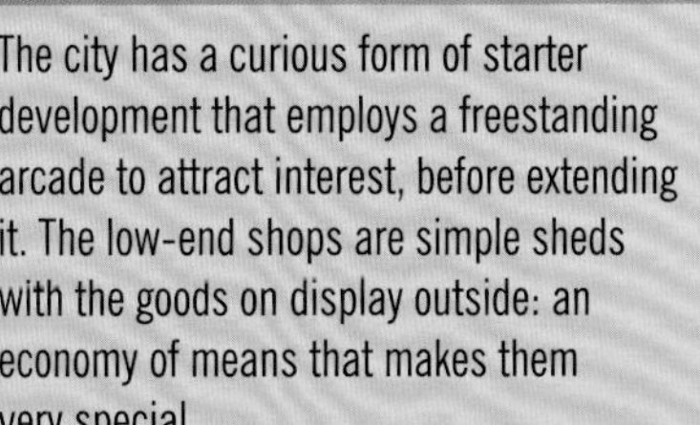

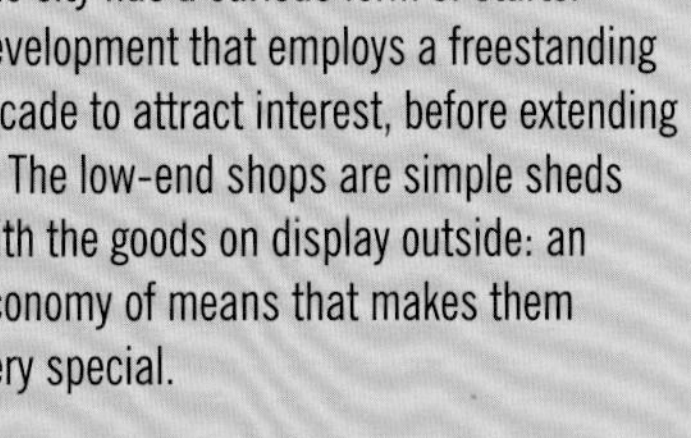

The city has a curious form of starter development that employs a freestanding arcade to attract interest, before extending it. The low-end shops are simple sheds with the goods on display outside: an economy of means that makes them very special.

Like other Sahel cities, the houses of the poor are sometimes made of baked mud. It has a beautiful texture that is specific to the city. With tin, timber and straw, it contributes to a family of materials for the architecture of poverty.

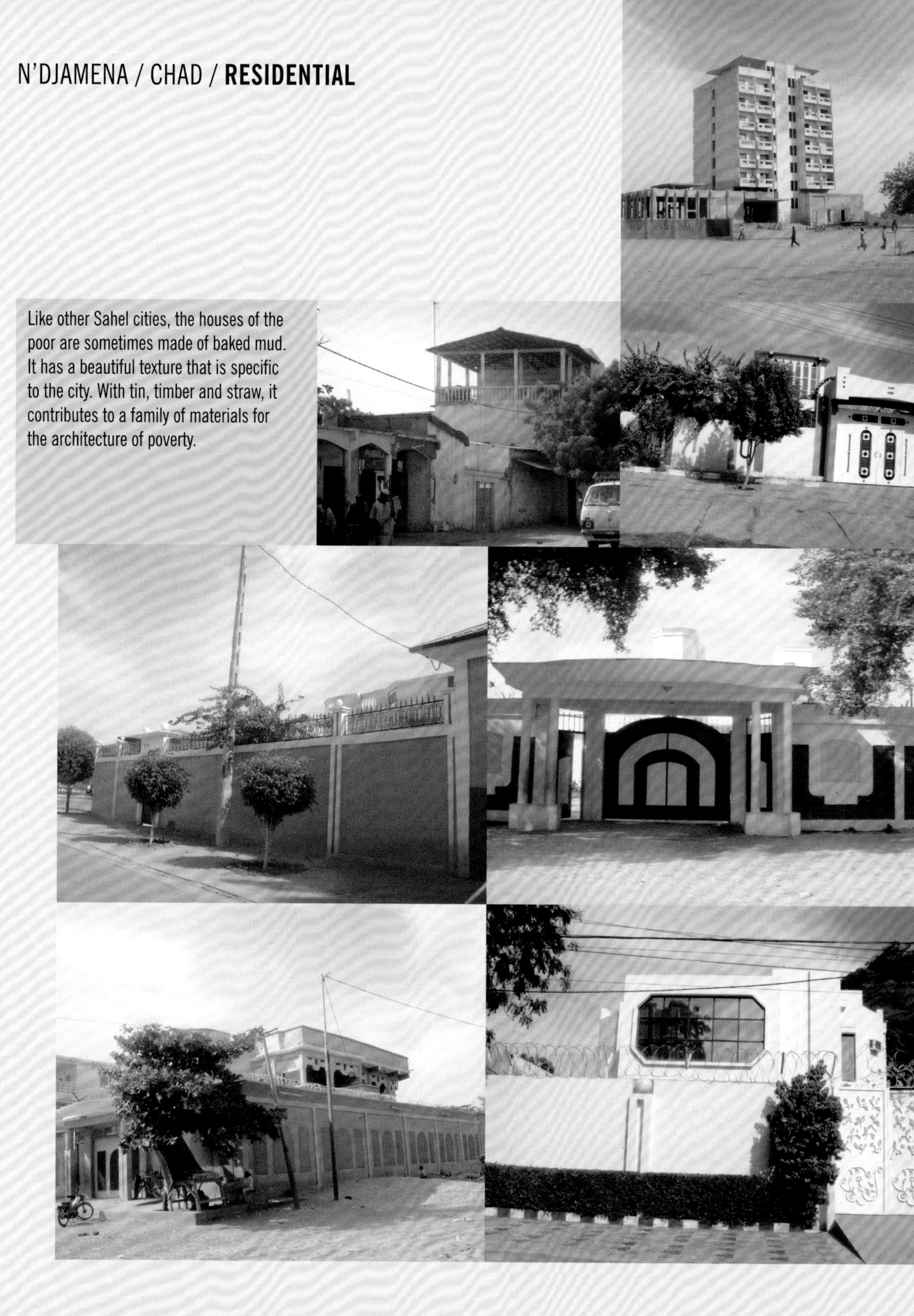

NIAMEY / NIGER

OVERVIEW

The people of Niger benefited from the wealth associated with the trans-Saharan trade routes and this wealth contributed to the development of several empires. The Kanem–Bornu Empire developed around Lake Chad between the 10th and 13th centuries; western Niger was part of the Islamic Empire of Mali in the 14th and 15th centuries, before it was taken over by the Empire of Songhai in the 16th century. As trade on the continent's west coast increased, the overland routes became less important and the amount of gold being traded in Agadez fell dramatically. This loss was partially compensated by an increase in the trading of the salt that the Tuareg people mined in remote oases. When the French arrived towards the end of the 19th century they were surprised by the level of resistance they encountered and employed their military strength to subjugate the south of the country. In the north the Tuareg revolts ended with the siege of Agadez in 1916–17 but by this time the French were in effective control of the country.

In 1958, faced with de Gaulle's alternative options for the future, self-government within a union of France's former colonies or immediate independence, many of the referendum votes for independence went missing and France was able to claim that there was majority support for staying within a union. After the party that had campaigned for independence was banned, Hamani Diori of the Parti Progressiste Nigérien (Nigerian Progressive Party) was the only presidential candidate after independence in 1960. He became head of a single-party state whose repressive policies inspired several unsuccessful coups during the 1960s. The position deteriorated during the Sahel drought of 1968–74 and Seyni Kountché removed Diori in a violent coup, installing himself as head of a military government. Kountché benefited from the increase in the price of uranium between 1974 and 1979, after it had been discovered in the Air Mountains in 1968. A later drop in the price of uranium was followed by the drought in 1983 when the River Niger dried up. Kountché survived these difficulties but died in 1987. His successor, Ali Saibou, was at odds with the democratic movement in other parts of West Africa. Public unrest was expressed in strikes and demonstrations in 1990 and the following year security forces killed several people at a demonstration at Niamey University. The resulting outcry pressured Saibou into arranging a national conference in 1991, which installed a provisional government prior to multiparty elections in 1993. Mahamane Ousmane of the Hausa people was the winner but his democratic government was curtailed by a military coup in 1996, led by Ibrahim Baré Maïnassara who won the following election but was assassinated in 1999. The leader of the coup organized democratic elections by the end of the year and the winner, Mamadou Tandja, formed a coalition government with Ousmane. The movement towards democracy was sustained by the first local government elections in 2004, when Tandja won the presidential elections. After serious unrest in Tuareg areas in the north of the country in 2007–9, he was deposed in 2010. Issoufou Mohamadou of the Nigerien Party for Democracy and Socialism won the elections in 2011.

OBSERVATIONS

Niamey is a planned modernist city on the north bank of the River Niger. The centre is a network of diagonal roads, making urban blocks and quarters. Beyond the centre, the poorer quarters make a striking double image, as the countryside invades the plan so that it is neither town nor country.

The mosques and churches are quite different. There are many small mosques on street corners, allowing people to pray in close proximity to their home or workplace. The churches are more hidden and support outreach work in schools and hospitals.

The single-storey structures that line most of the commercial streets outside the centre are usually brightly coloured. The informal architecture is very parasitic in the way it occupies wide pavements, street corners, and the shaded areas beneath trees. There is usually a roof of some light material and then it is all about product display.

The more wealthy residents live in the centre of the city. The architecture is very Muslim, with discreet access from the main roads into lanes, and then walled compounds. Houses are usually single-storey with access to rooftops. It is rare to see any ostentation. The only clues are the Jeeps and Mercedes coming and going.

NATIONAL POPULATION

19,899,000

CITY POPULATION

1,090,000

ETHNIC GROUPS

Haoussa 55.4%, Djerma Sonrai 21%, Tuareg 9.3%, Peuhl 8.5%, Kanouri Manga 4.7%, other 1.1%

RELIGIONS

Muslim 80%, other (includes indigenous beliefs and Christian) 20%

LANGUAGES

French (official), Hausa, Djerma

GDP

$18 billion

AGRICULTURAL PRODUCTS

cowpeas, cotton, peanuts, millet, sorghum, cassava (manioc, tapioca), rice; cattle, sheep, goats, camels, donkeys, horses, poultry

INDUSTRIES

mining (uranium), petroleum, cement, brick, soap, textiles, food processing, chemicals, slaughterhouses

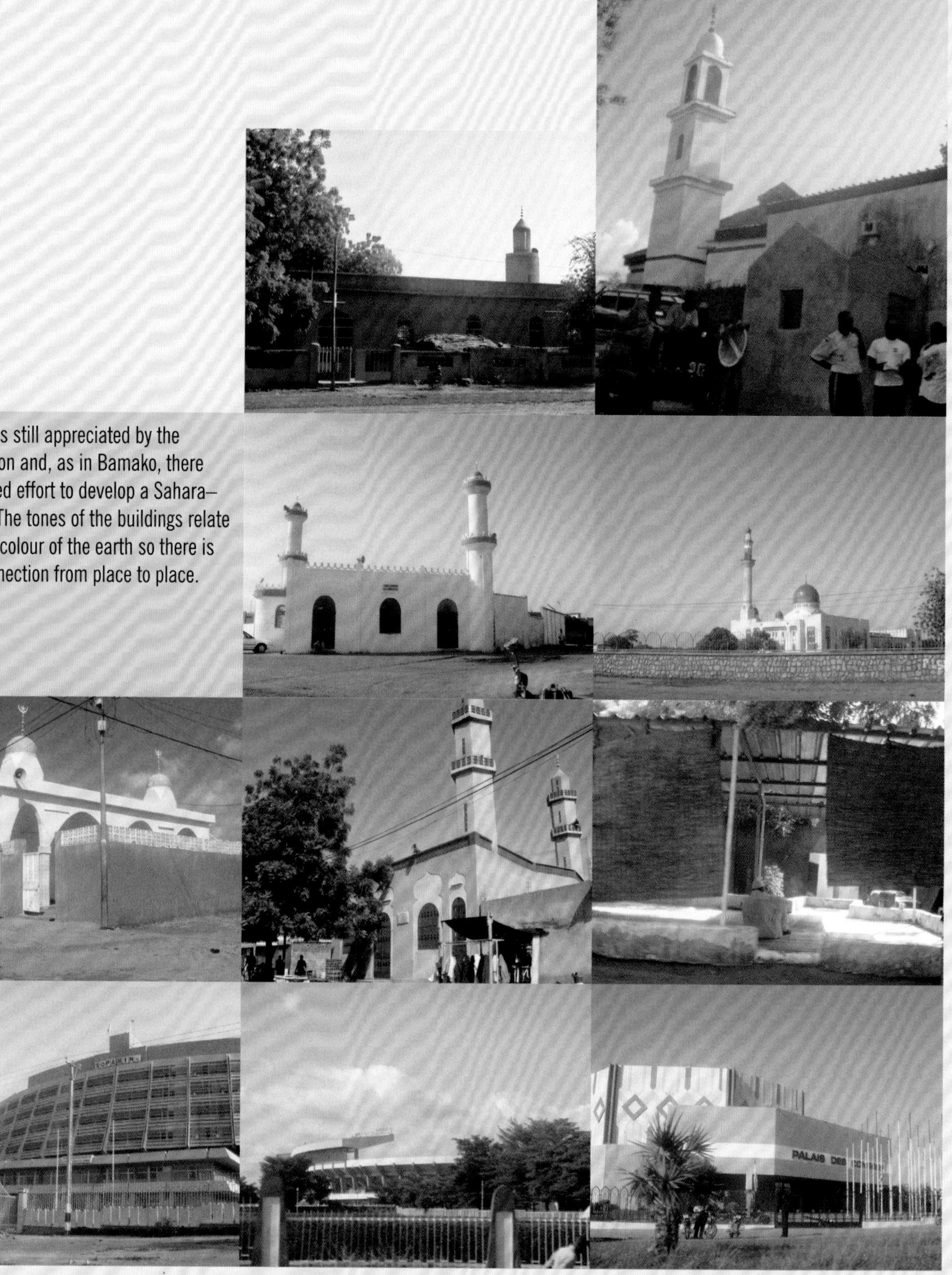

Modernism is still appreciated by the administration and, as in Bamako, there is a concerted effort to develop a Sahara–Niger style. The tones of the buildings relate to the dusty colour of the earth so there is an easy connection from place to place.

PALAIS DE JUSTICE
PALAIS DE JUSTICE
MoneyGram

NIAMEY / NIGER / **COMMERCIAL**

The commercial architecture ranges from towers for major banks and commercial concerns, to Lebanese and West African chop houses and the teeming markets. Informal market structures colonize strategic locations throughout the city.

Most houses are of the compound type. In poor areas, the countryside seems to invade the city, creating an in-between place of earth, mud, straw, wood, concrete and render.

OUAGADOUGOU / BURKINA FASO

OVERVIEW

The earliest traceable inhabitants of Burkina Faso are thought to have arrived in the 13th century, though there is evidence of much earlier settlements. Mossi tribespeople migrated into the area from the Niger River in the 14th century. Three further Mossi kingdoms were founded, each supporting a highly developed form of government, and armies that regularly attacked the Muslim population of Mali. Due to its history and prestige, Ouagadougou was selected as the permanent home of the Mossi king in the 17th century. In 1884–5 the area became part of French West Africa but was neglected by its new masters. After the Mossi kingdoms had been broken up, a separate colony, Upper Volta, was established in 1919, which in 1932 was divided between Côte d'Ivoire, Mali and Niger. Ouagadougou developed around the imperial palace, and expanded during the colonial period and after the railway from Abidjan was completed in 1954.

When independence was declared in 1960 the immediate effects were disappointing, as the economy declined and the first president, Maurice Yaméogo, banned all opposition. After demonstrations in 1966 the military seized power and the former president was jailed. In a pattern that continued for many years, there was a return to civilian rule in 1970, followed by a further coup in 1974. A powerful trade union movement constituted the main opposition and, after serious strikes in 1975, the government was pressed into holding a general election in 1978. Of the three coups which followed, the one led by Thomas Sankara in 1982 was the most notable. As leader of the People's Salvation Council, he pursued radical and effective self-help policies and renamed the country Burkina Faso, meaning 'country of honest people'. Under him there were substantial improvements in the provision of healthcare and education and a drive against the misuse of public funds. Although he was popular with ordinary people, Sankara's policies were not supported by other political groups or by countries like France that had interests in Burkina Faso. After leading the country into a five-day war with Mali in 1985, he was deposed by his previous collaborator Captain Blaise Compaoré in 1987. Compaoré, an in-law of Félix Houphouët-Boigny of Côte d'Ivoire, was elected president in 1991 but he was the only candidate and the leader of the opposition was killed a short time later. Despite a constitutional amendment in 2000 that was intended to limit presidential tenure to two terms, Compaoré only stepped down in 2014 shortly before he died. The 2015 election was won by Roch Marc Christian Kaboré who in 2014 had set up a new party, the People's Movement for Progress. Sankara remains an inspiration and is officially commemorated on 15 October, the date of his assassination. The Mossis now make up the greater part of Burkina Faso's population and have a significant presence in the capital, where the government consults their emperor, the Moro-Naba of Ouagadougou, on all major issues.

OBSERVATIONS

The atmosphere is immediately very pleasant with a sense of ease. The city is dusty so that the predominant colours are browns and beiges. It is a low city, mostly two storeys, with the exception of the public and commercial buildings.

Everyone in the city cycles – men, women and children! It is a great surprise, as I have not seen that in any other African city to date. If people are not cycling, they use motorbikes, keeping congestion to a minimum.

The main market is a concrete acropolis, reached by steps at the corners. A network of stalls makes up the building blocks. The commercial quarter is built of three-storey buildings, with loggias that shade the customers and support a convivial street life.

The nouveau riche live in a new part of the city, a grid of plots with houses in walled gardens. Their appearance is a free-for-all of ideas from Las Vegas chic to fanciful ideas about modernity and Africanism. As most of the houses are incomplete, the high fences and security predominate, like a prison quarter.

The poor live in a separate quarter. The atmosphere is lively as they have their own commercial core. The houses are of mud and block and tend to be the colour of the earth. There is a uniform quality of walls and apertures, and an additional layer of commerce that is protected by more modern materials, such as corrugated sheeting.

NATIONAL POPULATION

18,106,000

CITY POPULATION

2,741,000

ETHNIC GROUPS

Mossi 52.5%, Fulani 8.4%, Gurma 6.8%, Bobo 4.8%, Gurunsi 4.5%, Senufo 4.4%, Bissa 3.9%, Lobi 2.5%, Dagara 2.4%, Tuareg/Bella 1.9%, Dioula 0.8%, other/unspecified 7.1%

RELIGIONS

Muslim 60.5%, Catholic 19%, animist 15.3%, Protestant 4.2%, other 0.6%, none 0.4%

LANGUAGES

French (official), native African languages belonging to Sudanic family spoken by 90% of the population

GDP

$29.42 billion

AGRICULTURAL PRODUCTS

cotton, peanuts, shea nuts, sesame, sorghum, millet, corn, rice; livestock

INDUSTRIES

cotton lint, beverages, agricultural processing, soap, cigarettes, textiles, mining (gold)

This is very much a grid city, divided into quarters. The civic and administrative functions in the central area are surrounded by the market and commercial quarters, and the mosque, church, public gardens and stadium on the edge of the centre.

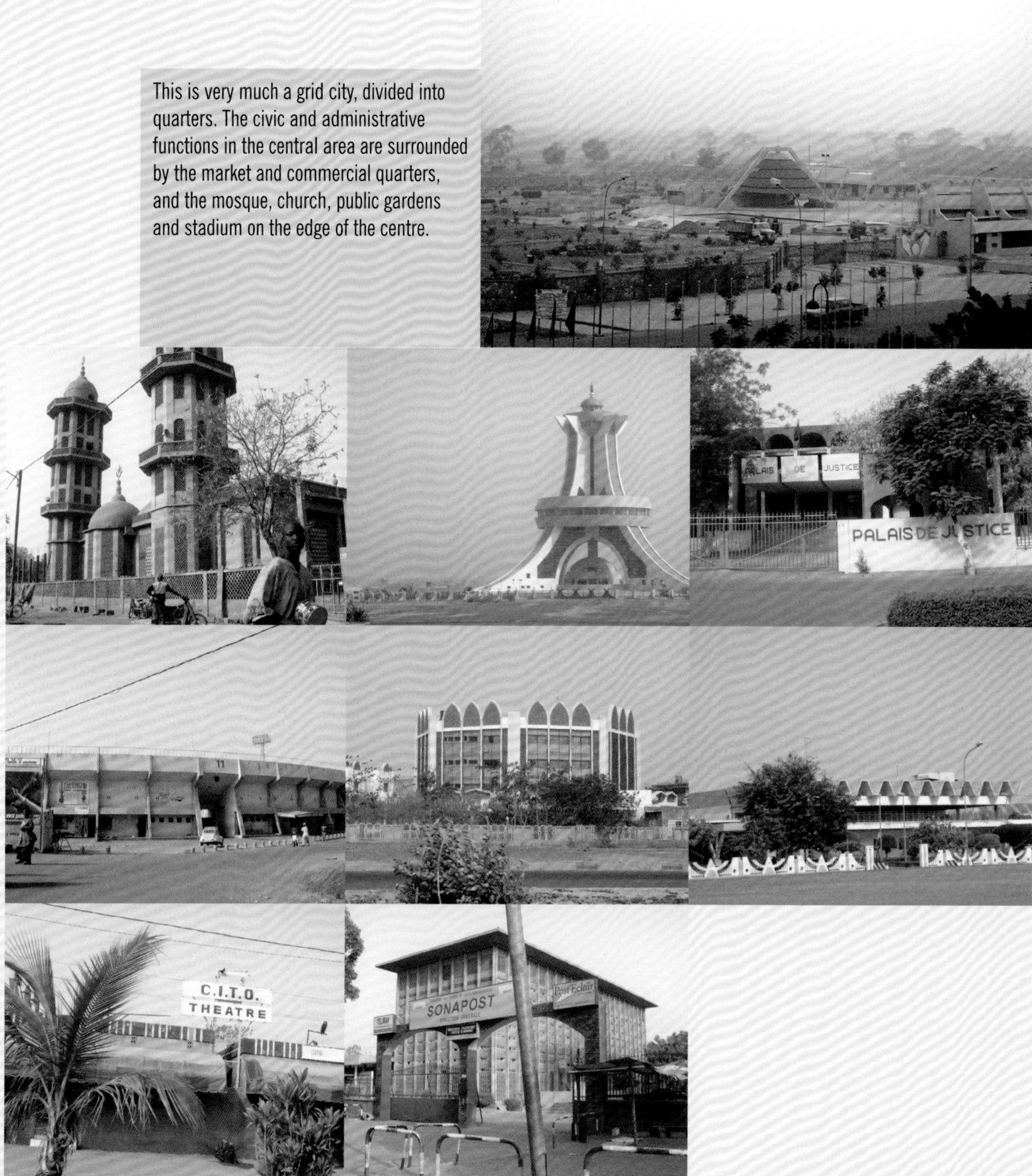

OUAGADOUGOU / BURKINA FASO / **COMMERCIAL**

The banks and large businesses have built the only high-rise buildings in the city, which combine African and futurist motifs. Since most of the public and commercial buildings are constructed in concrete, the architecture has a handmade quality.

OUAGADOUGOU / BURKINA FASO / **COMMERCIAL**

OUAGADOUGOU / BURKINA FASO / **RESIDENTIAL**

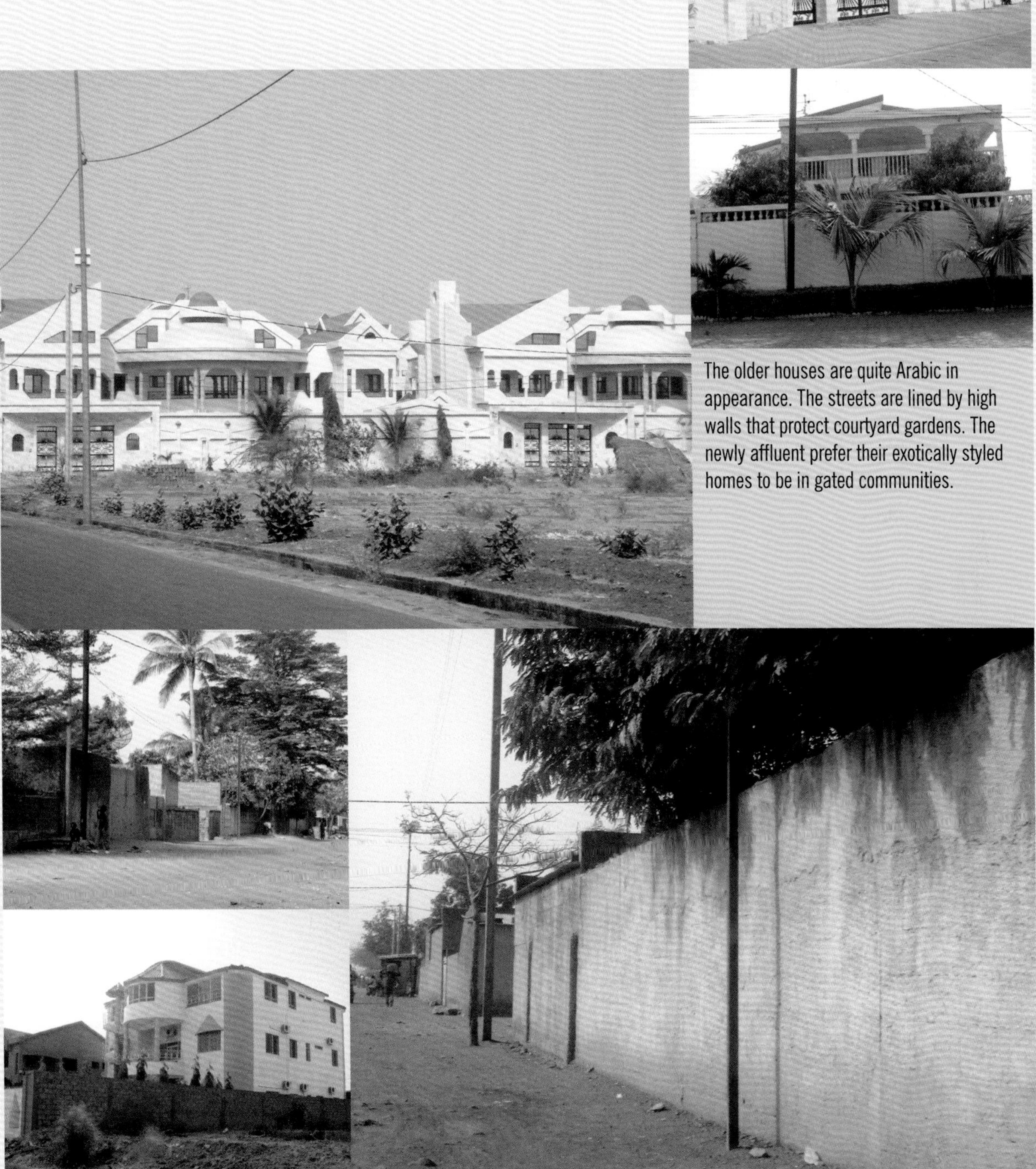

The older houses are quite Arabic in appearance. The streets are lined by high walls that protect courtyard gardens. The newly affluent prefer their exotically styled homes to be in gated communities.

FOREST

Tropical rainforest is one of the oldest types of vegetation to have survived and is found in an area that extends from Guinea in the north to the basin of the River Congo in the south. The topography of this area is very varied, from coastal plains to higher ground crossed by deep valleys, and to the east are the temperate forest and mountain pastures of the East African highlands. The climate in the rainforest has high humidity and little seasonal variation. Temperatures are typically 30°C by day and 20°C at night. The combination of high rainfall with high temperature and humidity encourages the growth of a dense evergreen forest, where different species of trees grow to different heights; above the thick undergrowth the canopy is formed by trees that may be 60 metres tall. The remaining rainforest provides a habitat in which primitive plants and animals have survived; supporting a rich variety of species, it is a model of biodiversity. Historically the forest has provided food and material support for the indigenous people who live there. In many cases this did not involve destruction of the natural environment but in some areas there is a history of burning the forest, which is then replaced by savanna. During the last century this process gathered pace and resulted in the complete destruction of large areas of forest. Many of the continent's cities are in this zone.

FOREST

Forest is the largest of the geographic regions, both in terms of the number of cities and the diversity of cultures it covers. It includes coastal and inland areas and, due to its size, there is a wide range of expression. I shall be looking at different aspects of the Forest cities as we move through the discussion. After considering the region in general, I will look at three cities whose characteristics can be found in many other Forest cities. As colonialism has played a major role in the history of this part of Africa, I will then discuss the defining characteristics of the three main types of colonial city – Portuguese, British and French – before concluding with a look at the four cities that were developed for freed slaves.

Forest is where the wetlands are, where the tropical rains dominate the climate. There is an architecture of fertility in this area, an architecture that has to deal with the climate and at the same time is responsive to the specific conditions in different places. The roof architecture of Freetown is a good example of the language of form that is necessary to deal with the heavy rains. You can also see it in the architecture of Monrovia where you have overhanging roofs everywhere; if you go there in the rain, you understand why certain forms and details are used in such a consistent way. Because of the incredible rains, the architecture of Accra is dominated by big roofs that protect the other building elements from the worst of the weather. Being in the middle of the Indian Ocean, the Seychelles are also liable to torrential rain – not continuously but on a regular basis – and the architecture is completely conditioned by that. This readiness to respond to the constant risk of inundation is what I mean about the fertility of the architecture.

The humidity and the rainfall impart an atmosphere that is as powerful as that of the sunshine in the Sahel. It is just as severe and you really feel it; there is a thickness to the humidity that is a feature of the entire Forest region – you simply cannot escape it. The cities of the Mountain & Highveld and Savanna & Grassland regions are the most moderate, the ones where you can do almost anything. But in the Forest region everything is growing all the time and there is always moisture in the air, even at the height of summer. This evergreen environment, where things are in continual decay because of the onslaught of all this moisture, is the setting of the distinctly African city, and is why so much of the life of the city is lived externally. Luanda is one of the few tropical cities whose centre is developing a modernist life of 'interiority', as I call it – an environment that is controlled by technology. But this is only a small part of Luanda; in most of the city, the experience is still to do with this tropical intensity. Desert and Forest are both primary articulations: Desert articulates the architecture more directly but in Forest the atmosphere is all-pervasive and casts a more subtle influence over all aspects of the environment, even in a forward-looking place like Abidjan.

The culture of the Forest region attaches considerable importance to markets and trading in regional produce, so the celebration of the mercantile aspect of the city is all-encompassing. Markets are also important in the Desert and Sahel regions, but they are more concerned with the exchange of goods. In the Forest, it is really about market activities being part of daily life, so that people from the city always get produce from the land. Seeing these things, you understand the role of the family unit and how the relationship between the countryside and the city is working. The Forest region is where the blurring of the countryside and the city is most complete. The countryside is very close and the villages are dotted around the cities, making it easy for people to commute between the two worlds, and you often find farms and plantations in the middle of the city.

This connection is reflected in the markets: Accra is organized around the idea of produce and its delivery from the farms, and you have truckloads of fruit and vegetables just tipped on the ground. I found this almost everywhere. In a landlocked city like Lilongwe, the market is the most important

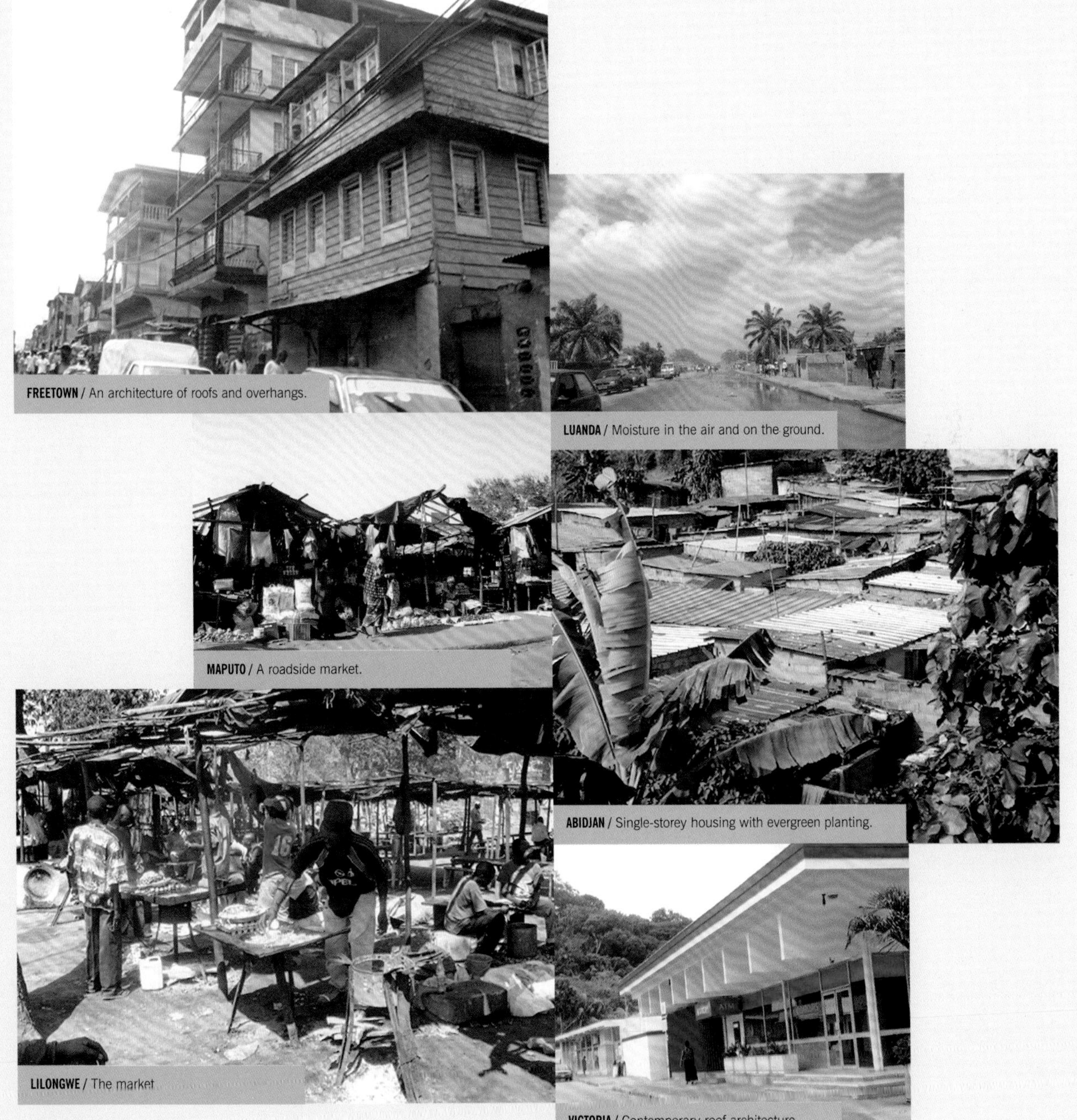

FREETOWN / An architecture of roofs and overhangs.

LUANDA / Moisture in the air and on the ground.

MAPUTO / A roadside market.

ABIDJAN / Single-storey housing with evergreen planting.

LILONGWE / The market.

VICTORIA / Contemporary roof architecture.

place. It is where all the life is and everybody goes there; it is in a focal position and has an identity of its own. The commercial and political centres are elsewhere, and are internal rather than external. The understanding that the produce of the land, the organization of the community, and the architecture that supports them, are part of the daily life of the city is important to this region. The reason you see people on the streets at different times of day is food – it is all about going to the right place to find certain things.

Colonialism is a defining characteristic in all the Forest cities. You sense a different colonial presence in each of the geographic regions, and their influences define the civic architecture in the majority of capitals. African cities work through the colonial to their current identity, and every one of the cities that I visited included this experience. There were expressions of Frenchness, Belgianness or Portugueseness as integral parts of the current identity. The culture of the African city is basically hybridized and the African citizen sees himself – reads himself – through his local condition, his ethnic group, which is his history, and through his colonial experience, which is his modernity. That period brought modernity to Africa and a greater awareness of the outside world. There was never at any point just one thing that formed its history; the experience was always laminated and layered, and I found this throughout the continent. People do not operate within a single or a double consciousness, but a quadruple consciousness, and the colonial is only one articulation among several. The majority of current administrations, because they still have relationships with their previous colonizers, express their identities through a colonial image. The connections are still there. They have not been cut off, but reformed, and the countries concerned are still trading or political partners. In Accra, for instance, the judicial system is very much influenced by English courts – they still wear wigs, it is just like the Old Bailey in London.

Bissau's architecture has exactly this type of multiple identity, where you can see both the colonial expression and specific references to the local cultural heritage. In Bissau there is a classical Portuguese influence – it sets up emphatic vistas and avenues – but the residential architecture, sitting within the Portuguese plan, is primarily a response to the climate, making shade from the sun and being able to get rid of water as fast as possible. The commercial architecture takes on the same motifs, but adds to them with projecting eyebrows over the windows, to stop water penetration, and balconies that create the maximum amount of shade. So the city provides a very clear demonstration of this type of simultaneous articulation of different histories. The humidity is articulated by the indoor–outdoor zones that are a prominent part of the residential architecture. These threshold spaces, porches and balconies, are the places where you live.

Kampala is an inland city and the architecture and planning respond to the garden-like nature of the site and the low hills that define different parts of the city. The sense of orientation in Kampala is unique in that the hills always give you an idea where you are. The articulation of the city is understood through the way in which you look at the different hills, so they provide the plan for constructing moments. You have really long views and the key image shows the mosque on top of a hill. The cathedral, with its twin towers and Victorian brick details, is also very prominent, as is the Sikh temple, standing in its own neighbourhood. What is so lovely about Kampala is that you find streets with impressive public buildings and residential streets where you scarcely see any buildings, just a lush landscape with the buildings in retreat. There are very few vertical emphases and those are either religious buildings or office buildings that have recently appeared. The architecture strives to deal with the horizontality of the land, the way in which you create shade, and extension and a relationship to the next site by layering things. You can see this in some of the commercial areas and the way in which the architecture makes things continuous. All the buildings on the main commercial avenue, and on most of the other streets, have projecting balconies and overhangs that define the public zone on the ground plane. In the residential areas there are many places where you could be in an agrarian community, rather than a relatively dense city.

ACCRA / Oranges dumped on the ground.

ABIDJAN / A colonial portico.

KAMPALA / The cathedral.

BISSAU / A colonial street.

LILONGWE / The location of the market.

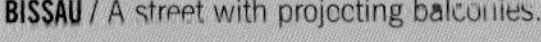

BISSAU / A street with projecting balconies.

BISSAU / An architecture that combines indigenous roofs and colonial detail.

Brazzaville was a wealthy city and remains an important banking centre. It is small by comparison with its neighbour Kinshasa, standing on the other side of the River Congo. But some of the most emphatic objects on the Congo – including the highest building in central Africa – are found here. The urban fabric is well conceived, with some fine vistas, and garden-city thinking is combined with modernist buildings from several periods. The art deco architecture is particularly strong and it is interesting to see how it responded to the context and became a local style with its own personality. Of the classic modernist buildings, the city hall is exceptionally fine: an elegant composition in two parts, with a beautiful staircase that leads to the main hall. It is very impressive to see how the colonial infrastructure has been reinforced by the postindependence architecture.

PORTUGUESE CITIES

The Portuguese cities are all located on the coastal edges of Africa. Over time Luanda and Maputo developed into major centres, whereas the island settlements and Bissau remained more like outposts. Portugal was continuously involved in Africa for 500–600 years – longer than other colonial powers – and you find what I refer to as 'deep planning' in their urbanism and architecture. Generations of Portuguese settled on the continent and contributed to the growth and the wealth of the cities. The continuous narrative of Portuguese architecture in Europe, as it moves from its classical roots to a modernist tradition, has its direct equivalent in Africa – nuanced by environmental and strategic considerations but pursued with a similar rigour. This is what you find in Luanda and Maputo: architecture and urbanism that have developed gradually over a long period of time and have real depth to them. In São Tomé, Praia and Bissau, on the other hand, you have settlements for the relatively small populations that were left to manage the plantations. They are miniature cities, where many of the buildings are quaint and picturesque.

All the Portuguese settlements were sited for strategic reasons, each with a specific orientation and a particular view towards the ocean. But they are also cities that enjoy the bucolic qualities of their location. Luanda is on a protected bay, with fresh breezes and a sense of lightness and well-being. The city rises behind it, but the scale and density of development are controlled so that the humidity and heat are not overwhelming. The centre of Maputo and many of its recreational facilities are located on the coast, but the residential areas have developed on the hillsides overlooking it, where they can take full advantage of the landscape. In the smaller cities the strategic nature of their siting is clear but they are still very enjoyable places to spend time in, and this aspect of the Portuguese cities is reflected in their planning. Although they made use of grids to occupy and develop the land, they were never relentless, but loose enough to adapt to the rise and fall of the ground or the line of the coast. There is a comfortable balance between the demands of development and the underlying character of the place. This kind of sensitivity is apparent in Maputo, where the layout and architecture of the downtown area have a loose formality, whereas the residential roads on the nearby hills have a gentle organic character.

The civic and commercial architecture in these cities is generally restrained but can be somewhat mannerist in detail. It has grain and repetition but retains the ability to take on a decorative quality – what I refer to as mannerist or rococo – in places that have special significance. These baroque styles were not particularly forward-looking but combined a sense of order with an ability to celebrate time and place when required. You do not leave Portuguese architecture remembering the emphatic artefact qualities of the buildings, but they do give you a definite feeling for the grain of the city. You find this in the most recent buildings here – and it is very much how Lisbon is made. In the African context, the Portuguese also took steps to adapt their buildings to the humidity and high temperatures. There is a Louisiana element to their architecture: a use of deep porches and verandas that create shade while being open to the breezes. Such features are an important part of the work of the Portuguese-

MAPUTO / A landscaped square in the downtown area.

BRAZZAVILLE / City hall.

LUANDA / Portuguese urbanism.

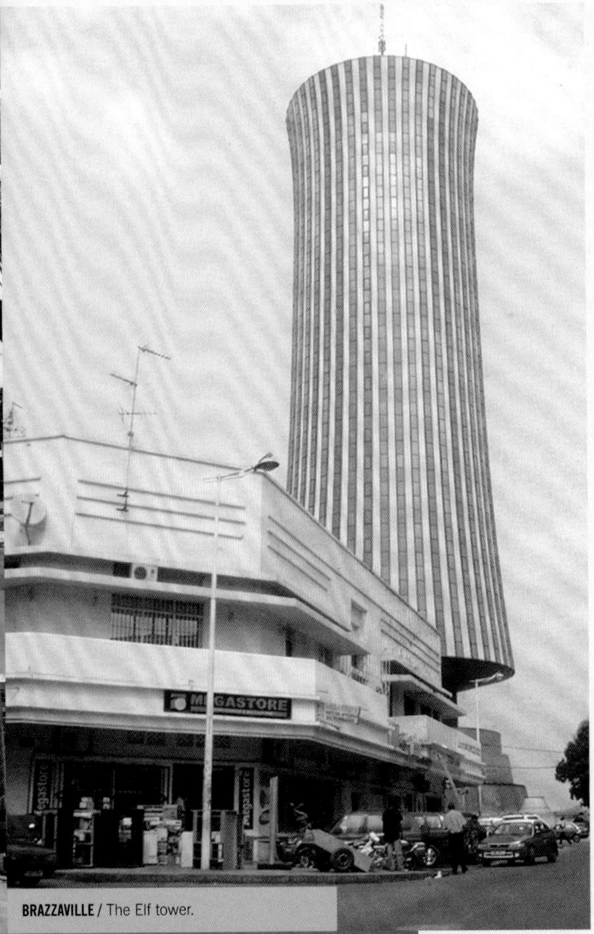

BRAZZAVILLE / The Elf tower.

SÃO TOMÉ / Outpost architecture.

SÃO TOMÉ / A mannerist facade.

Mozambique architect Amâncio Guedes. After independence in 1974, Portuguese cities had a difficult time until the last ten years, which have been more prosperous. Before that, the lack of skills in the general population had had a devastating economic effect that, in Angola and Mozambique, was magnified by civil war. All the cities suffered serious neglect following the Portuguese withdrawal and the consequences of this neglect are still visible in Bissau, where the process of renewal has only recently begun. Within the past few years Portugal has reengaged with its former colonies because in a globalized age they represent the largest Portuguese-speaking population, apart from South America. There has been some Portuguese involvement in modernizing the cities but their original infrastructure and buildings were so well planned and constructed that it has been possible to return them to full use within a relatively short period. Both Luanda and Maputo have been through a period of considerable stress but have managed to regenerate quickly, which is a testament to their colonial builders.

BRITISH CITIES

For the British cities in the Forest region, I would say that the overriding organizational idea was the garden city. The idea was to start living in this extensive landscape, accepting what it had to offer by adopting an open-ended settlement pattern. I think this is why it is still so difficult to get an overall sense of the structure of the British cities. There are almost no emphatic moments, such as powerful vistas that reveal the scale and structure of the city. Even in Jamestown, which is the old colonial settlement in Accra, you really would not know that this was the centre of the British administration – except for the lighthouse. The Britishness has a very soft presence there, as it does in the Seychelles. In the downtown area of Victoria, the colonial architecture establishes the urban grain but there is no overriding system and it lacks focus. The British idea was to make a settlement, rather than a city: a cultural settlement in the landscape.

As a counter-argument to this lack of formality, it is clear that there is a more engaged relationship between the British architecture and the landscape, and an intention to enjoy it, rather than to employ artificial systems that work against it. The British were the most ecological in terms of their relationship with nature. You feel the sense of a garden in all the British cities, and this is also true of the postindependence development of Lilongwe. Typically, you have a cultivated garden in a very lush setting, and then you discover the architecture. This remains the dominant image of these cities, even when they have become denser due to later developments. You do not leave the British cities thinking too much about architecture, except for Dar es Salaam with its art deco quarter. That happens to be in a densely gridded area of the city and you are struck by the architecture, in the same way that that the seafront buildings in Miami just hit you. But this area is not very British; it is one dramatic moment within the city as a whole and, as soon as you leave that area, you are back in the slumber of a suburban garden.

If you take a British city like Accra, the weird thing is that it is organized in a similar way to the borough system in London. In a British city, you have no way of understanding where things are unless you know how its administration is organized. In Accra it is difficult to sense where the centre is because it is a network of different places that are connected by roadways – very much like London. There are symbolic spaces but they are not very emphatic. This is reflected in current discussions in Accra and Kampala about the organization of their central areas in relation to an overall increase in density. The intention is not to construct more powercentric monuments but to create satellites of density within the existing fabric. As each of the dispersed nodes takes on a separate identity, the weblike structure of these cities should become more legible.

When Kwame Nkrumah was president of Ghana his monuments began to articulate the centre of Accra by establishing identifiable places for major institutions and public events. Next to the Black Star monument he created a formal space for military displays and the pageantry of the city. The space is overlooked by the Independence Arch that, in a rather French manner, suggests that this

MAPUTO / A perforated screen.

VICTORIA / The urban grain responds to the place but lacks focus.

ACCRA / Jamestown, the site of the colonial administration.

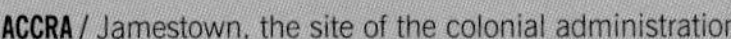

DAR ES SALAAM / A mixed-use building in the art deco quarter.

KAMPALA / A view of the central area.

is the most noble destination in the city. He was also responsible for the construction of a cluster of judicial buildings, including an emphatic court space and a new library. In all of these projects Nkrumah intended to create much stronger artefacts than anything that had been seen previously: ones that would have symbolic significance in the life of the city. I am convinced that he intended to link the various parts of the city under a bigger idea and, if he had succeeded, the city would now be very different. But I can imagine Accra before Nkrumah being an even softer environment than it is today, with its discrete village-like neighbourhoods.

FRENCH CITIES

Compared with the British, the French were prepared to make more dramatic compositions of their cities and buildings. You encounter stand-alone buildings that talk about some part of the civic culture, some ambition of nation-building – or the advantages of a particular commercial enterprise – in a way that you do not see in other colonial cities. These buildings were very forward-looking and they did not compromise their modernism. They are full expressions, launching into a brave new future, but they are absolutely not about France: they are talking about the place where they stand. In this respect, some of the things that are starting to be concerns in Europe were previously tested in Africa.

You sense the nature of the infrastructure as soon as you arrive in a French city. The overall organization makes it clear where the centre is, where the grand boulevards are, and where the instruments of the city can be found. There is a civic area, a commercial area, and the routes out to the various suburbs. This is a consistent trope in all of the French cities and it gives a strong sense of order to each of them. You can see it in Yaoundé, with its grand boulevards, and even in Bangui, this little town in the middle of the continent. The distinction between the centre and the suburbs is clear; their identity is not blurred, as it would be in a British city. Each *quartier* of the French system has a distinct identity, so that you always know where you are in the bigger picture. In this way French cities are relatively open to visitors. The stranger is immediately given clues to the organization; he is not required to work it all out before he can find his way. You have to explore the British city, whereas the French lays itself out for you, and the Portuguese is easily readable without being as emphatic as the French.

The architecture of the French cities makes powerful statements about the role of the institutions within it. If you make a formal plan, you need strong buildings to centre the axes, otherwise it is a meaningless gesture. The French were consistent in following this approach and because it was so integral to the way in which these cities were built, it has carried on to the present. You can see it in Dakar and Abidjan, for instance. Abidjan has a cluster of buildings on a central rise; that is where all the new towers are located, making it easier to understand where you are. In Kinshasa all roads lead to the grand boulevard, which is named after the revolution, and that is where most of the new buildings are located. In Lomé, the grand boulevard is on the waterfront and the city is a rectangle on the African coast, punctuated by key moments: the president's palace, a beautiful conference centre, bank buildings, and public monuments on the main roundabouts. Considering that Togo is a small country, the object nature of these buildings is impressive.

In the Francophone countries you find a wider range of modernist building types in play than in the British cities. There are more apartment buildings and there is a longer history of living at higher densities. Modernity and having a home are more about living in a great apartment building rather than living in a house. You have arrived if you live in an apartment building in town, whereas in British cities like Accra it is important to have a house. The French imported more of the apparatus of their architecture for building their cities than the British, who imported an architecture of detached villas but not much more. You see this especially clearly in a city like Algiers, in the Maghreb, where it is clear that the French intended to make a city that was complete in every respect.

ABIDJAN / A suburban landscape.

ACCRA / The law courts building.

ACCRA / The Black Star monument.

ABIDJAN / A mixed-use building with triangular section.

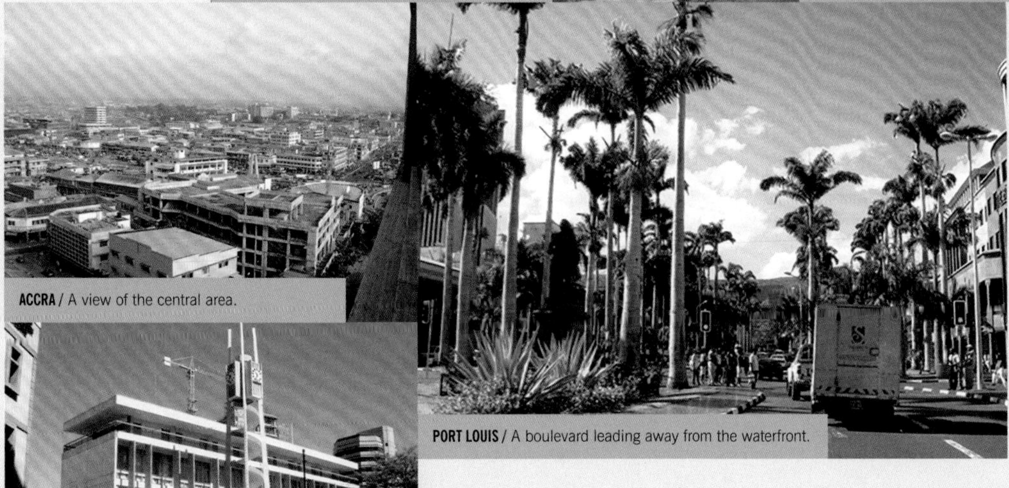

ACCRA / A view of the central area.

PORT LOUIS / A boulevard leading away from the waterfront.

PORT LOUIS / Uncompromised modernism.

CITIES FOR FREED SLAVES

These cities were idealistic and forward-looking communities where, nevertheless, it was considered better to be a freed slave, or from the family of a freed slave, than to be an African who had not had this experience. This produced a social and political hierarchy that persisted into the 20th century. The architecture of these cities reflects a similar tendency to look outwards to the rest of the world, and you can still feel this in a place like Libreville, where they think they are more French than the French. Malabo was founded by the Portuguese in the 18th century, before it was taken over by the British to resettle freed slaves in the 19th century. From its colonial origins, it has developed into a forceful composition, with a clear relationship between the centre and the suburbs, from which you can see the twin towers of the cathedral. The styles employed in its buildings are a mix of the German and the Dutch, right through to the grandest of French and British – it is a real potpourri of aspirations.

All of the cities for freed slaves are in the Forest region. Freetown was the first to be founded in 1808, followed by Monrovia and Malabo in the 1820s, and Libreville in 1849. There is a similarity between Freetown's architecture and that of Monrovia. In Freetown the grain of the city and its relationship to the sea developed from the earlier British settlement. Although the public architecture is quietly impressive, there are no outstanding buildings and, as the city has developed, it has become ever more closely integrated with its coastal landscape. Much of Monrovia also has a distinctly British quality. There is a boulevard along the coast that terminates at the top of a small hill, where the government buildings are. This part of the city is set in the landscape and the effect of its architecture is very diffuse. That changes in the area of the old town, at the end of the peninsula, where you have stores and warehouse buildings with residences above. The gridded streets below are protected from both the sun and the heavy rain by large projecting balconies.

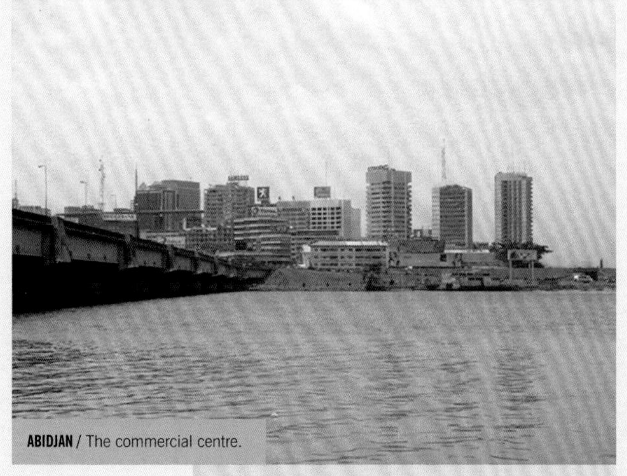

ABIDJAN / The commercial centre.

MALABO / Buildings in the grandest of colonial styles.

LOMÉ / A public monument on a traffic island.

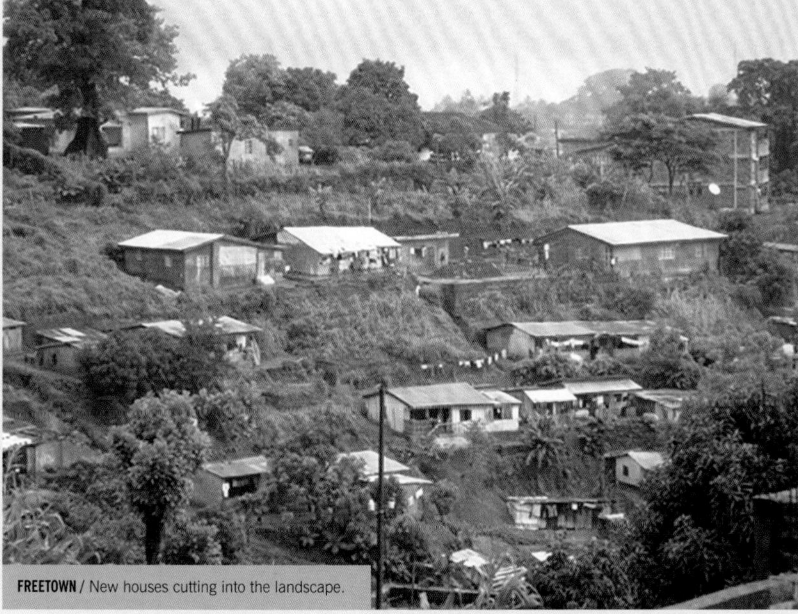

FREETOWN / New houses cutting into the landscape.

ABIDJAN / An apartment building.

ABIDJAN / CÔTE D'IVOIRE

OVERVIEW

This area was settled by people of different ethnic groups migrating from the surrounding countries in the 17th to the 19th centuries. Though the trade in slaves had little impact on Côte d'Ivoire, the establishment of agreements with France on general trade in the 1840s met armed opposition from Malinké and Baoulé forces as they began to occupy the interior. The French were interested in promoting the production of cocoa, coffee and palm oil, and encouraged the settlement of their farmers and operated a forced-labour system. Grand-Bassam followed by Bingerville were the French capitals. Abidjan is situated on the Ébrié Lagoon and became a major port when the French completed a canal between the lagoon and the ocean in 1951.

The 20th century was dominated by Félix Houphouët-Boigny. He was the son of a chief and studied medicine in Dakar before taking up cocoa farming. In 1944 he founded a trade union that opposed colonial farming policies and encouraged indigenous plantation owners to recruit immigrant workers rather than support forced labour. In the following year he converted the union into a political party and the French abolished forced labour. Houphouët-Boigny became the country's first president and was keen to maintain an alliance with the French. His policy of promoting agriculture rather than industry stimulated the economy and the country became a successful exporter of coffee, cocoa, pineapples and palm oil. This period of continuous growth was only ended by the effects of droughts and the world recession in the 1980s. In 1990, strikes and civil unrest forced presidential elections that were contested by several parties for the first time. Houphouët-Boigny was still in power when he died at the age of 88 in 1993.

The new president was Henri Konan Bédié and his initial success at the polls was marred by the effects of the 'parenthood clause' that required that both parents of a presidential candidate should be Ivorians. The anti-immigrant sentiment enshrined in the clause led to widespread discrimination against foreign Muslim workers and Muslims living in the north of the country, regardless of whether they were immigrants. Bédié was deposed in a military coup in 1999 but the new leader, General Robert Guéï, continued with the discriminatory policies, provoking a growing opposition movement. In the elections in 2000 he had his main opponent disqualified on the grounds that the candidate's mother was not from Côte d'Ivoire. The winner of the election was Laurent Gbagbo, but his period in office was marked by serious violence. In the wake of a failed coup in 2002, rebel troops from the north took over much of the country. In 2007 Gbagbo offered the leader of the rebels the position of prime minister and they agreed to reunite the country and hold elections, which took place in 2010. After taking power several months late due to Gbagbo's refusal to stand down, Alassane Dramane Ouattara has worked to rebuild the country and was reelected in 2015. Yamoussoukro has been the official capital since 1983 but Abidjan is the major city.

OBSERVATIONS

For an African city, Abidjan is very modern, a city of grids. The Ébrié Lagoon divides the centre into two main areas, Le Plateau and Treichville. It is a very beautiful setting.

There seems to be an equal split between churches and mosques. The mosques are mainly in the poorer neighbourhoods and near markets, and the churches are in the other residential areas.

In Abidjan the mutation of African life and the modernist city have no parallel. The schizophrenia about urban life found in other cities is largely absent here and the use of the city is distinctly African.

Fashion, with a strong link to the textiles of different ethnic groups, is an important component of people's lives, and the citizens of Abidjan effortlessly straddle the divide between modernity and their ethnic roots.

NATIONAL POPULATION

22,702,000

CITY POPULATION

4,860,000

ETHNIC GROUPS

Akan 32.1%, Voltaique or Gur 15%, Northern Mande 12.4%, Krou 9.8%, Southern Mande 9%, other 21.2% (includes European and Lebanese descent), unspecified 0.5%

RELIGIONS

Muslim 40.2%, Catholic 19.4%, Evangelical 19.3%, Methodist 2.5%, other Christian 4.5%, animist or no religion 12.8%, other religion/ unspecified 1.3%

LANGUAGES

French (official), 60 native dialects, Dioula most widely spoken

GDP

$71.67 billion

AGRICULTURAL PRODUCTS

coffee, cocoa beans, bananas, palm kernels, corn, rice, cassava (manioc, tapioca), sweet potatoes, sugar, cotton, rubber; timber

INDUSTRIES

foodstuffs, beverages, wood products, oil refining, truck and bus assembly, textiles, fertilizer, building materials, electricity, ship construction and repair

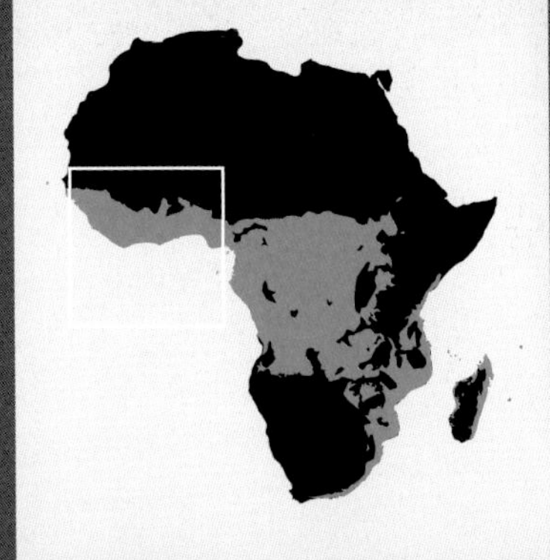

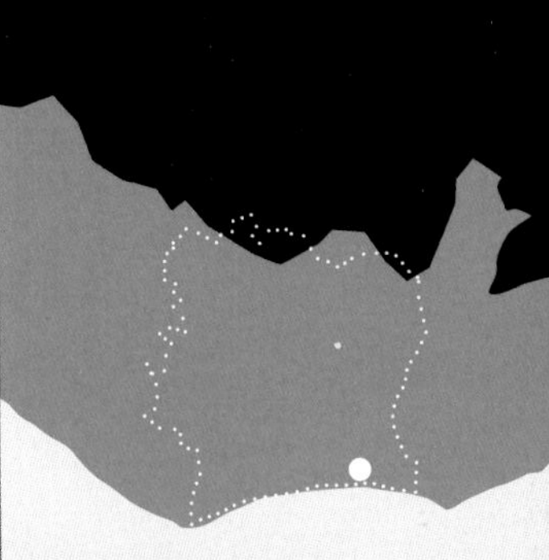

ABIDJAN / CÔTE D'IVOIRE / **CIVIC**

The French infrastructure provides a basis for the African's sense of public life. There are speakers' corners, parks and grand boulevards that magnify the perception of the city. Abidjan fulfils an image of the modern African city.

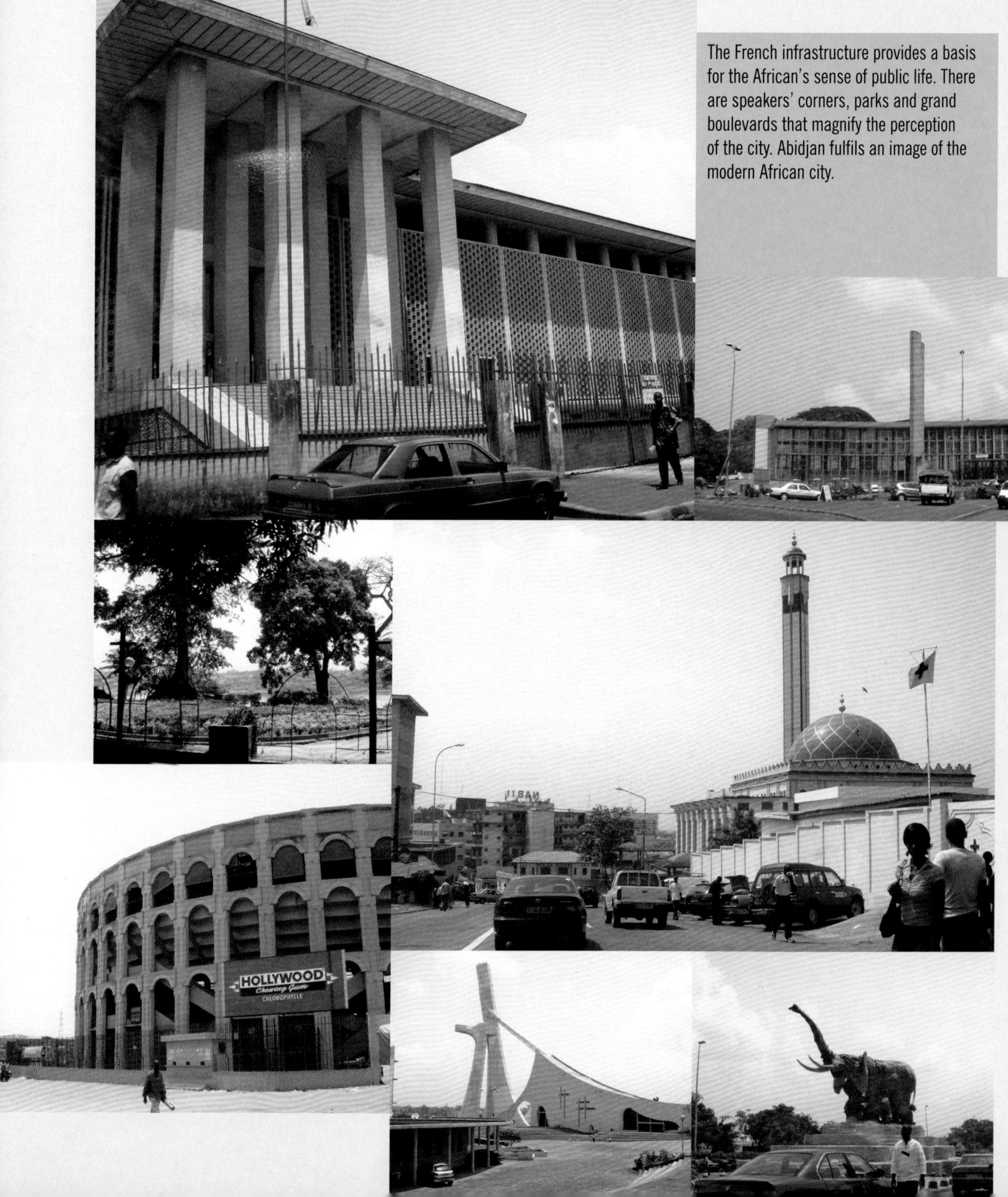

ABIDJAN / CÔTE D'IVOIRE / **COMMERCIAL**

A cluster of sculptural high-rise buildings in Le Plateau forms the new business centre. The largest market is in Treichville and almost anything can be purchased there.

TELEPHONE

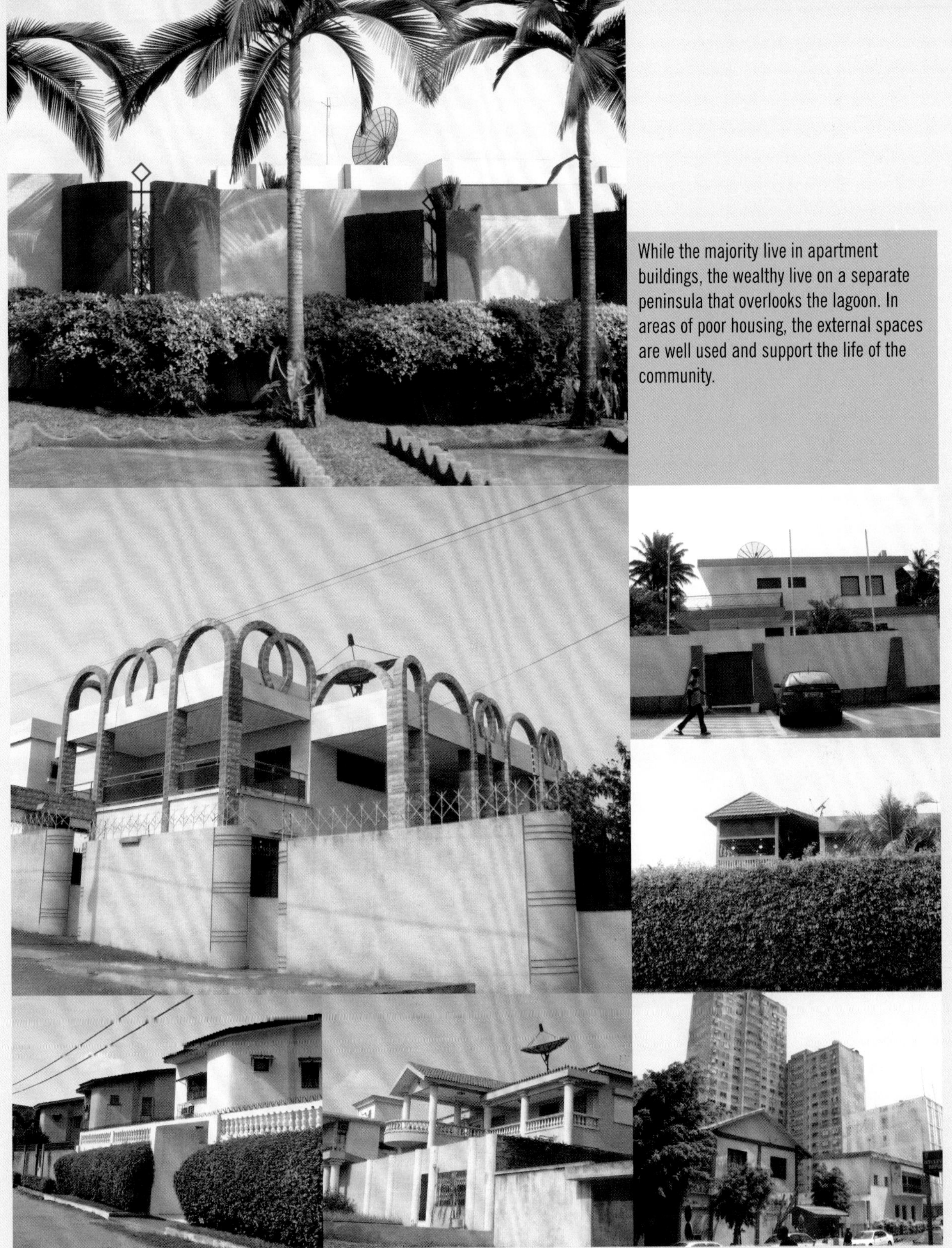

While the majority live in apartment buildings, the wealthy live on a separate peninsula that overlooks the lagoon. In areas of poor housing, the external spaces are well used and support the life of the community.

ACCRA / GHANA

OVERVIEW

Occupied since 4000 BCE, this area was subject to migration from the north and east. By the 13th century several kingdoms had developed of which the Ashanti was the most powerful. They controlled the trade routes to the sea and in the 18th century this brought them into conflict with coastal people and European traders. From the 16th century, the trade in gold and ivory was replaced by the slave trade involving the Dutch, British and Danes. Britain was the dominant force when slavery was abolished, and was then drawn into a series of wars with the Ashanti. Their capital, Kumasi, was occupied in 1896 and its leader was sent into exile. The British established a protectorate that included most of the future country. Based on the export of cocoa and gold, the Gold Coast, as it was then called, had one of the most successful economies in colonial Africa. The movement towards independence began in the 1920s but progress was slow until Kwame Nkrumah broke away from the leading political party to found the Convention People's Party (CPP). He called a national strike in 1950 and was immediately imprisoned by the British. But the CPP won the general election in 1951 and Nkrumah was released from prison to form the government. Ghana was the first West African country to gain independence, on 6 March 1957.

The political situation after independence was complicated by the difficulty of reconciling regional and factional interests and the government attempted to exert control by pursuing repressive policies. Nkrumah preferred to keep himself out of internal issues and, as his international standing increased, he sought financial backing for major investment projects, such as the damming of the Volta River. He was deposed in a military coup in 1966 and went into exile in Guinea. After his death in 1972 the country's international loans became a serious problem due to the difficulty of meeting the repayments. The deteriorating economic situation resulted in hyperinflation and serious food shortages and, after several governments had failed to control the situation, the Armed Forces Revolutionary Council (AFRC) under Jerry Rawlings took power in 1979. The AFRC handed control to a civilian government but this was not successful and Rawlings returned to power in 1982. He embarked on a period of economic reform that reassured the World Bank and the International Monetary Fund. In contrast to the period after Nkrumah's death, they were happy to extend their support. The economy began to flourish and Rawlings introduced a new constitution in 1992 that lifted the previous ban on political parties. Although the 1990s were a period of stability when economic growth was maintained, it did not always translate into improvements in social services. After eight years of Rawlings's National Democratic Congress, the New Patriotic Party (NPP), under John Kufuor, won the 2000 election. The NPP has had to proceed cautiously since then due to remaining weaknesses in the economy. In the past, cocoa and gold were the main exports but now there are several initiatives to diversify agricultural production and the number of minerals that are mined. John Atta Mills won the presidential election in 2008 but died in office in 2012. His deputy John Dramani Mahama won the election to replace him. From its early days as a group of small villages, Accra has developed into an extensive patchwork of contrasting environments.

OBSERVATIONS

Accra has been transformed from its colonial past into a West African metropolitan city. To mark this change, President Nkrumah commissioned a series of striking tropical-modernist buildings, including the main library, Flagstaff House and trade centres.

The vibrant street life of the centre continues in newer commercial areas, such as the one around Oxford Street, but this cannot be said for most shopping malls. Except for the amount of traffic they generate, the malls are insular and do not have a porous relationship with the rest of the city.

Although Jamestown, the original colonial settlement, and Kwame Nkrumah Memorial Park, where his tomb is located, are situated on the coastal strip, the modern city turns its back on the ocean and forms a web of local centres.

NATIONAL POPULATION

27,410,000

CITY POPULATION

2,277,000

ETHNIC GROUPS

Akan 47.5%, Mole-Dagbon 16.6%, Ewe 13.9%, Ga-Dangme 7.4%, Gurma 5.7%, Guan 3.7%, Grusi 2.5%, Mande 1.1%, other 1.6%

RELIGIONS

Christian 71.2% (Pentecostal/Charismatic 28.3%, Protestant 18.4%, Catholic 13.1%, other 11.4%), Muslim 17.6%, traditional 5.2%, other 0.8%, none 5.2%

LANGUAGES

Asante 16%, Ewe 14%, Fante 11.6%, Boron (Brong) 4.9%, Dagomba 4.4%, Dangme 4.2%, Dagarte (Dagaba) 3.9%, Kokomba 3.5%, Akyem 3.2%, Ga 3.1%, other 31.2% (includes English (official))

GDP

$108.5 billion

AGRICULTURAL PRODUCTS

cocoa, rice, cassava (manioc, tapioca), peanuts, corn, shea nuts, bananas; timber

INDUSTRIES

mining, lumbering, light manufacturing, aluminium smelting, food processing, cement, small commercial ship building, petroleum

AD 1957

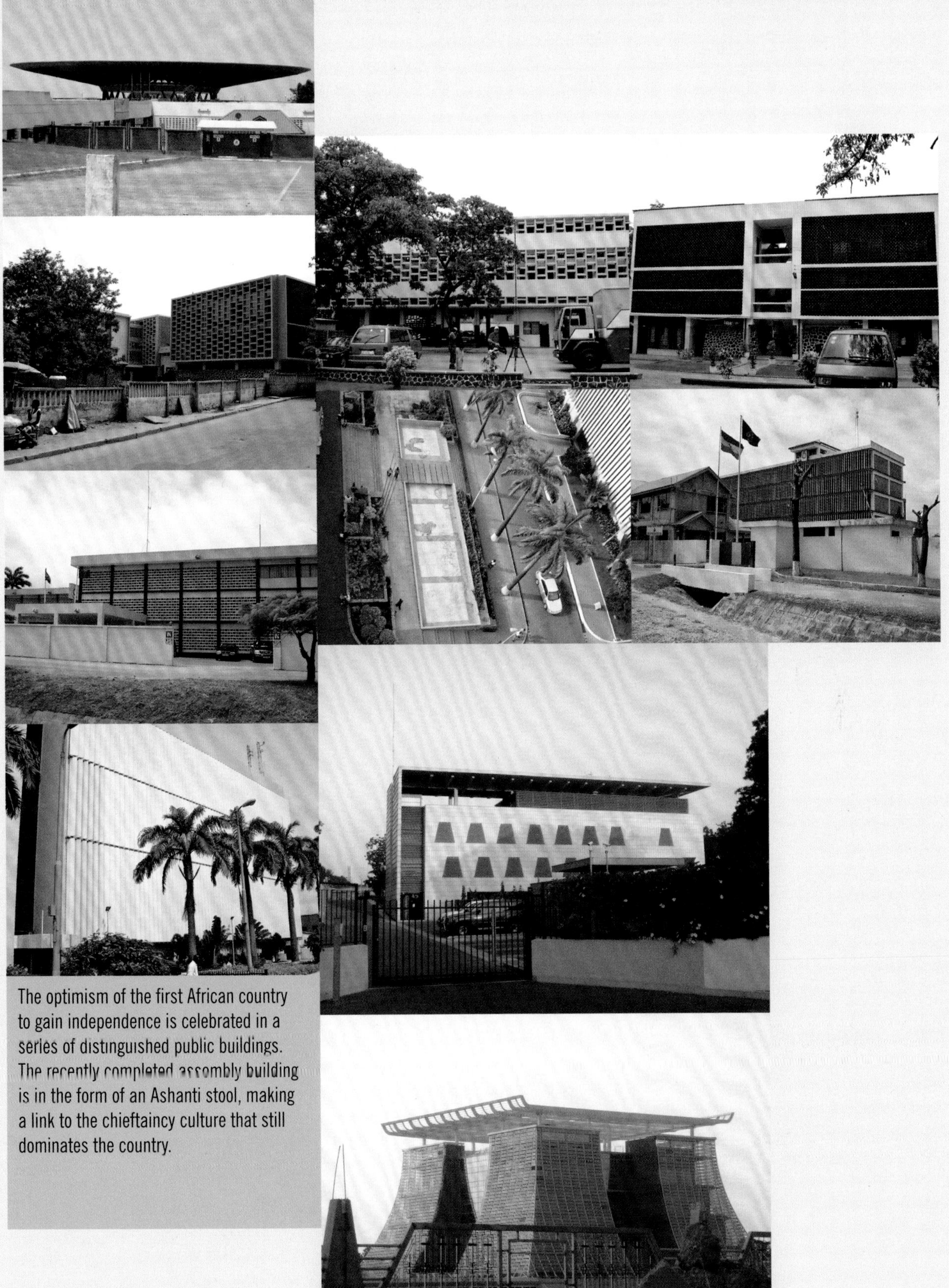

The optimism of the first African country to gain independence is celebrated in a series of distinguished public buildings. The recently completed assembly building is in the form of an Ashanti stool, making a link to the chieftaincy culture that still dominates the country.

ACCRA / GHANA / **COMMERCIAL**

The commercial centre has gradually moved inland from the original colonial settlement, and the latest developments are close to the airport. Makola market, where the formal and the informal economies overlap, is largely run by women.

Historic settlements include an area of colonial villas built on small lots, and an early garden suburb where the planting is now mature. Recent suburbs are more commercial in character, and areas of informal housing are found on the edges of the city and on the coast.

BANGUI / CENTRAL AFRICAN REPUBLIC

OVERVIEW

The boundaries of the Central African Republic correspond closely with the area occupied by Ubangi-speaking groups whose culture was well established in the 1st millennium BCE. By the middle of the 1st millennium CE they were joined by Zande-speaking Bantu who had migrated from West Africa. But the position of the country in the centre of Africa's landmass attracted both Arab and European slave traders, and the population was depleted. The French arrived in 1880 and their intention to colonize the country was recognized by other colonial powers at the Berlin convention in 1894. In order to promote economic development, the French divided the country between twenty-seven European companies who, in exchange for an annual payment and fifteen per cent of the profits, were free to exploit the natural resources of their portion of the country. Coffee, cotton, rubber and tobacco were cultivated in large plantations that were worked by forced labour. Local people were antagonized by this brutal system and resistance to the French occupation continued into the 1920s, by which time most of the concessions had stopped trading due to poor profits.

Conditions did not improve and after the Second World War Barthélemy Boganda founded the Mouvement pour l'Evolution Sociale de l'Afrique Noire (Movement for the Social Evolution of Black Africa, MESAN). Following Boganda's early death, David Dacko assumed leadership of MESAN and became the first president after independence in 1960. His government combined repression with favouritism and in 1965 he was deposed by Jean-Bédel Bokassa whose thirteen-year rule climaxed in 1977 with his coronation as Emperor Bokassa I of the Central African Empire. During his years in power all opposition was violently suppressed and he squandered huge sums of money. After his coronation the French withdrew financial support and, when the Emperor was on a visit to Libya, they provided military assistance for a coup that saw Dacko return to power in 1979. But his leadership skills had not improved and in 1981 he was ousted by André Kolingba at the head of a military government. A slow transition to civilian rule culminated in multiparty elections in 1993 that were won by Ange-Félix Patassé, a former minister in Bokassa's government. Patassé's years in power were marred by deep-seated financial problems and, when the government was unable to pay public employees or the armed forces in 1996, the military took the lead in an anti-government uprising. After fighting in Bangui and other areas, order was restored a year later and Patassé won the elections in 1998 and 1999. An unsuccessful coup in 2002 led to a civil war in which the forces of François Bozizé were able to take over large areas of the country. The government forces were augmented by troops from the Democratic Republic of the Congo who terrorized and looted the indigenous population. Thousands of people fled the country before Bozizé was able to occupy Bangui, when Patassé was visiting Niger. Although Bozizé won the elections in 2005 and 2011, parts of the country remained outside his control. In 2013 a short-lived coalition with the rebels resulted in the rebels taking power and Bozizé leaving the country. After a period with Catherine Samba-Panza as interim president, the 2016 election was won by Faustin-Archange Touadéra. The French founded Bangui and named it after the nearby rapids on the Oubangui River.

OBSERVATIONS

On the north bank of the Oubangui River, Bangui is a relatively small town arranged on the French system, with nine *quartiers*. Looking across the city, one sees the fine silhouette of the Democratic Republic of the Congo.

Signs of fishing and farming are visible throughout the city and along the river. Bangui is not too crowded so the *quartiers* do not blur in terms of use, and you see distinct neighbourhoods and zones. Because of its location in the centre of Africa, Bangui attracts immigrants from the surrounding countries, creating a melting pot of Afro culture. The cosmopolitan zones, where immigrants settle, are on the water fringes where the city's best buzz is found.

Roundabouts are a feature of the city and the main roads start from the principal one. It is a fancy roundabout with pedimented arches marking major roads and a fountain in the form of a globe. Important events in the country's history, as well as presidents and national heroes, are commemorated on other roundabouts.

NATIONAL POPULATION

4,900,000

CITY POPULATION

794,000

ETHNIC GROUPS

Baya 33%, Banda 27%, Mandjia 13%, Sara 10%, Mboum 7%, M'Baka 4%, Yakoma 4%, other 2%

RELIGIONS

indigenous beliefs 35%, Protestant 25%, Roman Catholic 25%, Muslim 15%; note: animistic beliefs and practices strongly influence the Christian majority

LANGUAGES

French (official), Sangho (lingua franca and national language), tribal languages

GDP

$2.87 billion

AGRICULTURAL PRODUCTS

cotton, coffee, tobacco, cassava (manioc, tapioca), yams, millet, corn, bananas; timber

INDUSTRIES

mining (gold and diamonds), logging, brewing, sugar refining

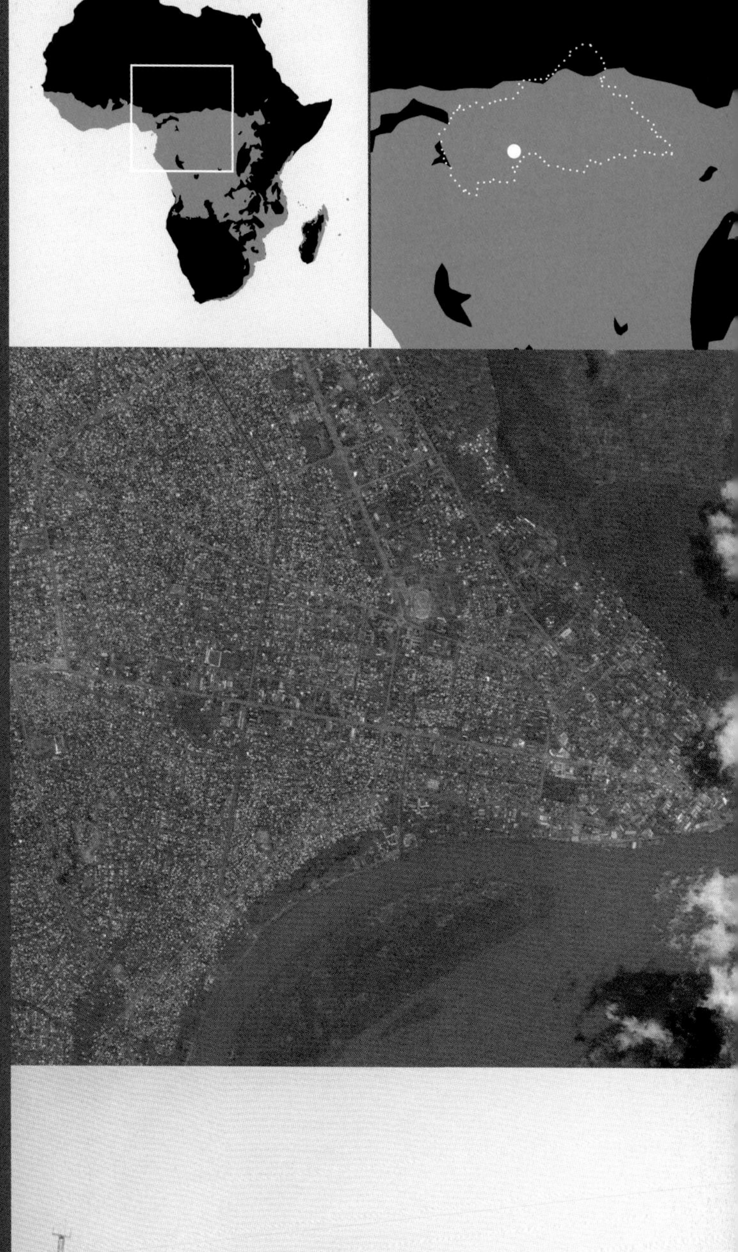

BANGUI / CENTRAL AFRICAN REPUBLIC / **CIVIC**

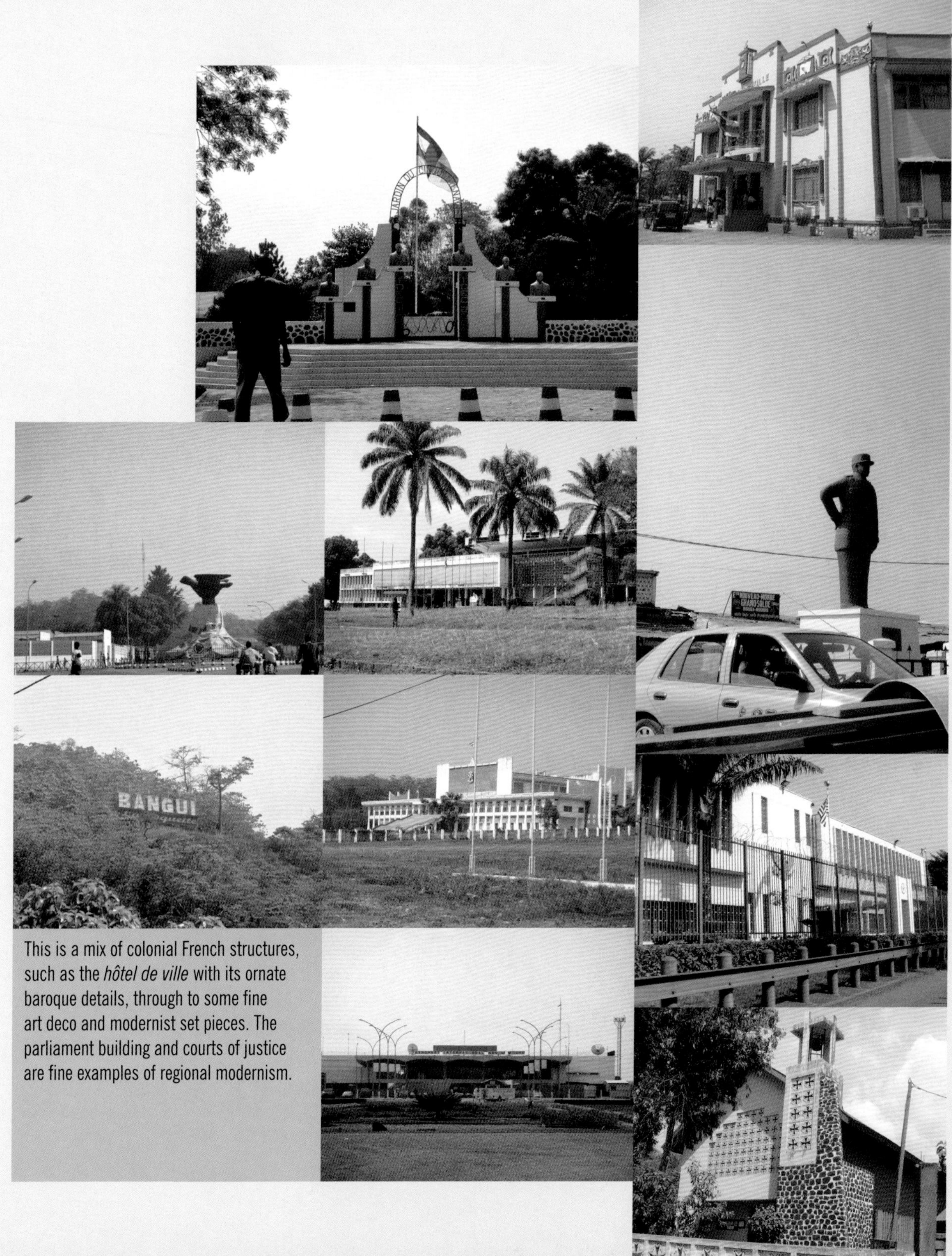

This is a mix of colonial French structures, such as the *hôtel de ville* with its ornate baroque details, through to some fine art deco and modernist set pieces. The parliament building and courts of justice are fine examples of regional modernism.

Allianz
Imprimerie Centrafricaine

The art deco buildings around the main roundabout were designed to provide a sense of townscape in this area, giving it a metaphysical aura – like a painting. There is a wide variety of building types from the last 100 years.

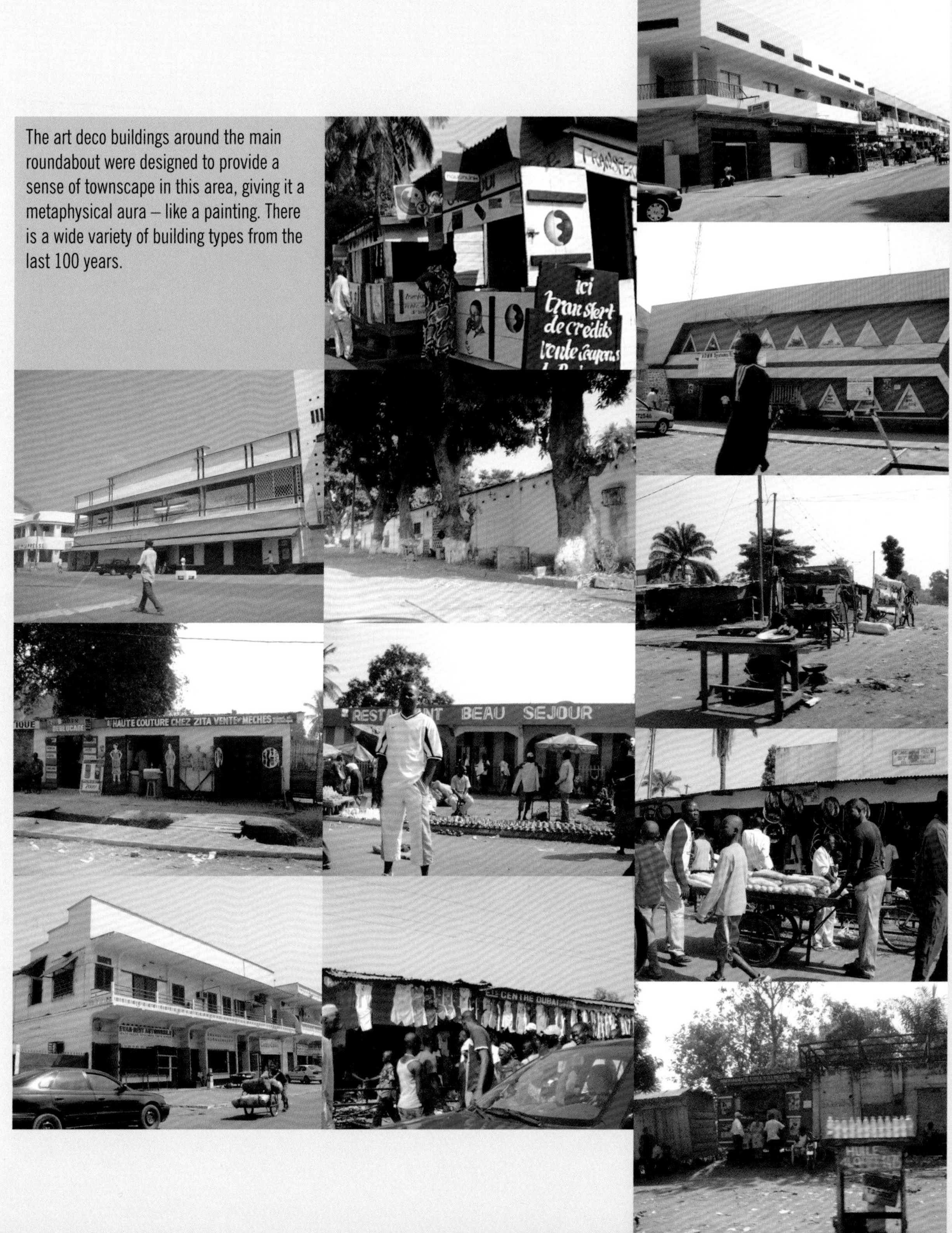

Whether in villas or apartment buildings, the wealthy detach themselves from the city in compounds, and the middle-class areas are quite entrepreneurial, with shops integrated into the residential facade. The infrastructure is well organized in all areas.

BANJUL / THE GAMBIA

OVERVIEW

The remains of stone circles and burial mounds suggest that this area has been inhabited for more than 1,500 years. In the 13th century CE, it was part of the Empire of Mali that extended from the Atlantic coast to the area now occupied by Niger. When the Empire of Songhai superseded the Empire of Mali in the 15th century, the Malinké people moved to the River Gambia. Bringing Islam with them, they became known as the Mandinka. Although the Portuguese had explored the coast by 1455, they were displaced by the British and French, who competed for the area's trade in the 17th and 18th centuries. Britain took control of the River Gambia in 1783 and Fort James, their base on an island 17 miles from the coast, became a major centre for the shipment of slaves. This situation changed abruptly in 1807 when Britain abolished slavery and began to intercept the slave ships of other countries, returning the slaves to Africa via Fort James. As part of this campaign, they established a second base at the mouth of the river; originally known as Bathurst, it was destined to become the future capital. The Gambia was administered from Sierra Leone until it became a colony in its own right in 1888. In the following years Britain's input scarcely extended beyond encouraging the cultivation of groundnuts for export and the country remained a quiet backwater. In 1960, following developments elsewhere, the country's first political party, the People's Progressive Party, was founded by Dawda Jawara and, despite uncertainty about its future viability, the country became independent in 1965. Jawara was president and Bathurst was renamed Banjul (the Mandinka word for 'bamboo' and the original name of the island at the mouth of the River Gambia).

The Gambia became a republic in 1970 but rumblings of discontent came to a head in 1981, when there was a short-lived military coup. In line with a mutual defence agreement, the Senegal army quickly removed the rebels. In the same period, a fall in the price of groundnuts and a reduction in agricultural subsidies created hardship in rural areas. But Jawara retained popular support and was reelected for a sixth term in 1992. Throughout his years in power there had been muted criticism of his government but the military coup of 1994 was not anticipated. Its leader was Lieutenant Yahya Jammeh and the new government was to be under the direction of the Armed Forces Provisional Ruling Council (AFPRC). In the light of this development, the country began to lose international aid and the tourist trade went into decline. Jammeh responded by calling an election in 1996 that was won by the successor to the AFPRC, now known as the Alliance for Patriotic Reorientation and Construction. Jammeh himself became president and promptly embarked on a number of ambitious projects to improve the country's infrastructure and public services. Despite some human rights issues, Jammeh remains in power.

OBSERVATIONS

Banjul is a small port with British roots. As you approach the city off the main road, you pass large sheds for light industry and distribution, then beaches and the cemetery, before reaching Independence Arch. Beyond it, you pass shops and hotels until you arrive at the parade ground that marks the centre of the city.

There is a satisfying mix of colonial, art deco and modernist buildings in the central area. The civic buildings are relatively low and do not impose themselves. Compared with other places they have a gentle presence. The religious buildings are either Victorian-looking churches or late Islamic mosques, with the main mosque in the high Saudi style.

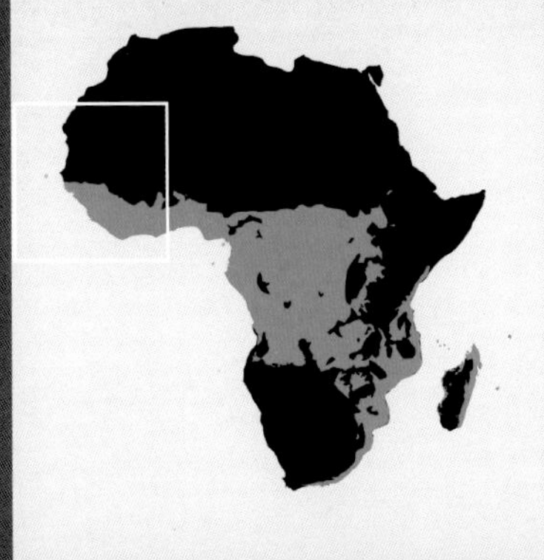
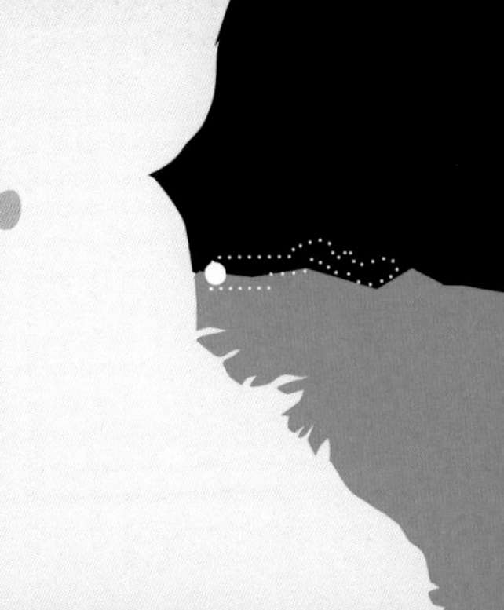

NATIONAL POPULATION

1,991,000

CITY POPULATION

504,000

ETHNIC GROUPS

Mandinka/Jahanka 33.8%, Fula/Tukulur/Lorobo 22.1%, Wolof 12.2%, Jola/Karoninka 10.9%, Serahuleh 7%, Serere 3.2%, Manjago 2.1%, Bambara 1%, Creole/Aku Marabout 0.8%, other 0.9%, non-Gambian 5.2%, unspecified 0.8%

RELIGIONS

Muslim 95.7%, Christian 4.2%, none/unspecified 0.1%

LANGUAGES

English (official), Mandinka, Wolof, Fula, other indigenous vernaculars

GDP

$3.09 billion

AGRICULTURAL PRODUCTS

rice, millet, sorghum, peanuts, corn, sesame, cassava (manioc, tapioca), palm kernels; cattle, sheep, goats

INDUSTRIES

processing peanuts, fish and hides, tourism, beverages, agricultural machinery assembly, woodworking, metalworking, clothing

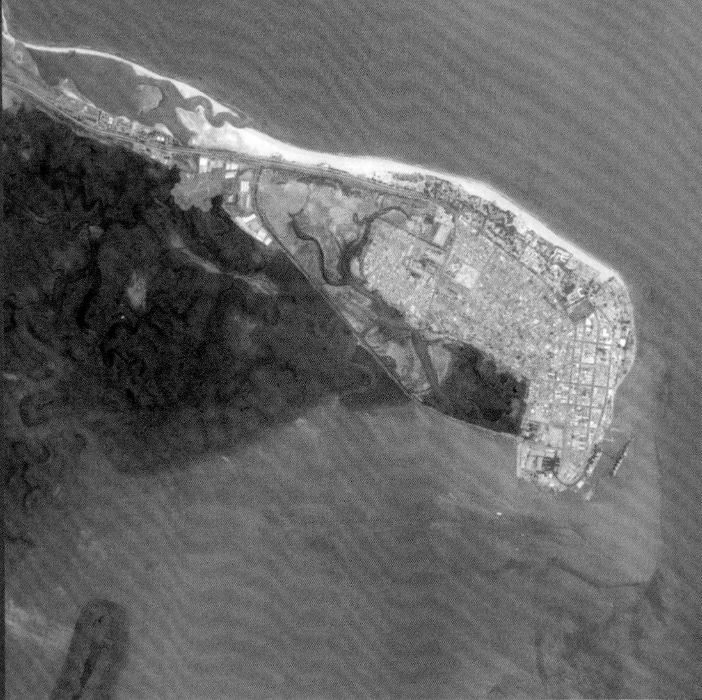

Independence Arch, a postmodernist monument on a traffic island, forms a gateway to the government and administrative area, where many of the buildings are hidden in walled compounds. Other public buildings are modest in scale and integrated with their neighbours.

NESCAFÉ
NESCAFÉ
NAM SA SOULA TELECENTRE
LOCAL INT. CALLS & FAX SERVICES
Standard Chartered

The scale of the commercial buildings is limited but, with their assertive appearance, they are beginning to transform the streets of the colonial city. In the suburbs, there is strip-type development down many of the main roads.

BANJUL / THE GAMBIA / **RESIDENTIAL**

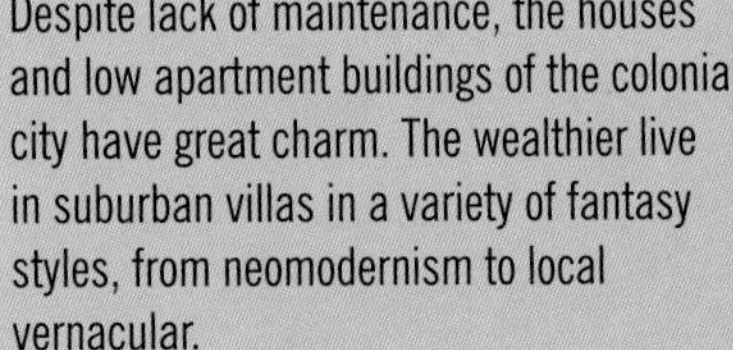

Despite lack of maintenance, the houses and low apartment buildings of the colonial city have great charm. The wealthier live in suburban villas in a variety of fantasy styles, from neomodernism to local vernacular.

BISSAU / GUINEA-BISSAU

OVERVIEW

From the 13th to the 15th centuries this area was part of the Empire of Mali that extended from the Atlantic coast to present-day Niger. When the Portuguese explored the coast in the 1450s they were attracted by the number of rivers giving access to the interior and established trading stations for the shipment of gold, ivory and slaves. With increased competition from other European powers, the Portuguese would be dislodged from other stretches of the Atlantic coast but they were able to retain their foothold in Guinea-Bissau. Following the abolition of the slave trade in the 19th century, Portugal came under economic pressure to occupy the interior of the country and take advantage of the groundnut trade. But its policies were exploitative and it had little to offer the local people. This situation was made worse by the demands of its right-wing dictator, António Salazar, when he assumed power in 1926. He wished to strengthen the colonial identity of Portuguese possessions so he was reluctant to recognize the independence movement that affected much of Africa in the 1950s and 1960s. As a result, the liberation of Guinea-Bissau took considerably longer than that of other countries. Amílcar Cabral founded the Partido Africano da Independência da Guiné e Cabo Verde (African Party for the Independence of Guinea and Cape Verde, PAIGC) in 1956 and it began a campaign of armed resistance in 1961. In just over five years PAIGC was able to liberate half of the country and, due to its repressive policies, Portugal began to lose international support. Cabral was assassinated in 1973 but by that stage the PAIGC had organized elections in the liberated areas and had declared independence. Eighty governments had recognized the new government before Salazar was deposed in 1974.

The first president was Luíz Cabral, Amilcar's half-brother, and his government faced serious problems caused in part by the struggle for independence. Following a coup in 1980, João Vieira assumed the presidency but continued with the socialist policies of his predecessor, supported by military aid from the USSR and non-military aid from the West. After a failed coup in 1985, Vieira realized that socialism had done little to improve the country's economic prospects and decided to sell off many of the state's assets. The 1990s were slightly more prosperous but the quality of public services remained poor. Doubts about the government surfaced in a strike of public workers in 1997 against the misuse of foreign aid. This was followed by a successful coup led by General Ansumane Mané. The situation became more complicated when Senegal and Guinea sent troops to defend Vieira and the troops that were loyal to him. As the two sides attacked each other in the vicinity of Bissau, innocent civilians were killed and many people were made homeless. By 1999 Mané's army had taken control of the city and asked the president of the national assembly to become the interim president. There were elections at the end of the year but, after two further coups, Vieira won the presidential elections in 2005. Following the murder of the chief of staff of the army, Vieira was assassinated in 2009 and Malam Bacai Sanhá won the following elections. He died in 2012 and a military coup prevented the election to replace him from taking place. Following international mediation, a transitional government organized a free election in 2014, won by José Mário Vaz. The remains of colonial Bissau are dominated by the Portuguese fort, which is still used for military purposes, and the ruins of the presidential palace.

OBSERVATIONS

The centre is no more than three storeys high and many of the buildings have projecting balconies that are protected by overhanging roofs: an arrangement that creates intimate streetscapes. Although it does not have a grand scale, the city has an active life and things are not always as they seem. This sense of a double life, of certain things being hidden, makes it all the more intriguing.

The new civic buildings are outside the city centre, where suburbs have sprung up around a new road and power infrastructure. Like the central bank, these buildings are postmodern in style – very symbolic but with little relationship to place.

The residential area immediately next to the centre consists largely of bungalows with large pyramidal roofs and front porches. This is something one finds in poorer neighbourhoods: village architecture intermingling with garden-suburb bungalows.

NATIONAL POPULATION

1,844,000

CITY POPULATION

492,000

ETHNIC GROUPS

Fula 28.5%, Balanta 22.5%, Mandinga 14.7%, Papel 9.1%, Manjaco 8.3%, Beafada 3.5%, Mancanha 3.1%, Bijago 2.1%, Felupe 1.7%, Mansoanca 1.4%, Balanta Mane 1%, other 1.8%, none 2.3%

RELIGIONS

Muslim 45.1%, Christian 22.1%, animist 14.9%, none 2%, unspecified 15.9%

LANGUAGES

Crioulo 90.4%, Portuguese (official) 27.1%, French 5.1%, English 2.9%, other 2.4%

GDP

$2.53 billion

AGRICULTURAL PRODUCTS

rice, corn, beans, cassava (manioc, tapioca), cashew nuts, peanuts, palm kernels, cotton; timber; fish

INDUSTRIES

agricultural product processing, beer, soft drinks

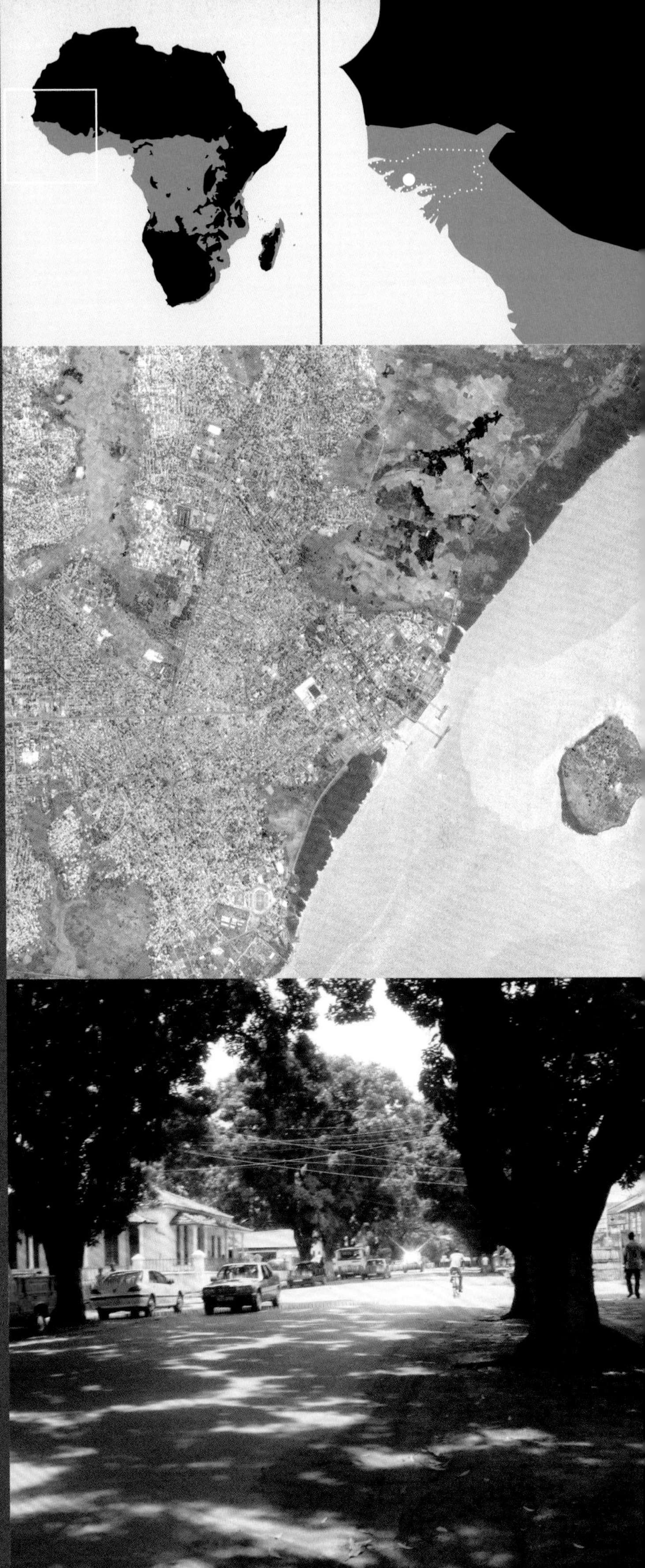

Bissau combines colonial and modernist cities. There are pastel-coloured and tile-roofed buildings on the shaded streets in the old quarter, and an area for new developments between here and the airport.

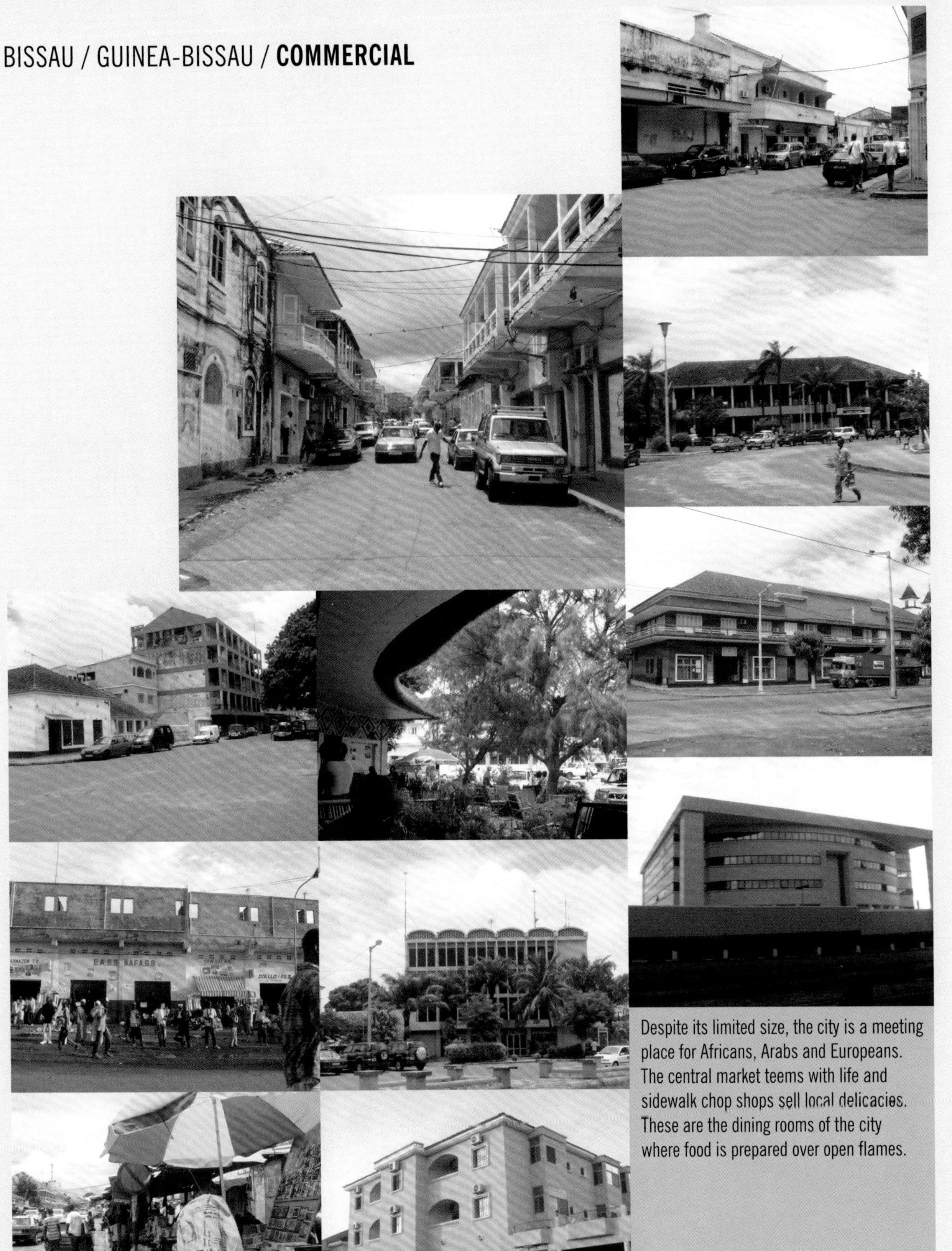

Despite its limited size, the city is a meeting place for Africans, Arabs and Europeans. The central market teems with life and sidewalk chop shops sell local delicacies. These are the dining rooms of the city where food is prepared over open flames.

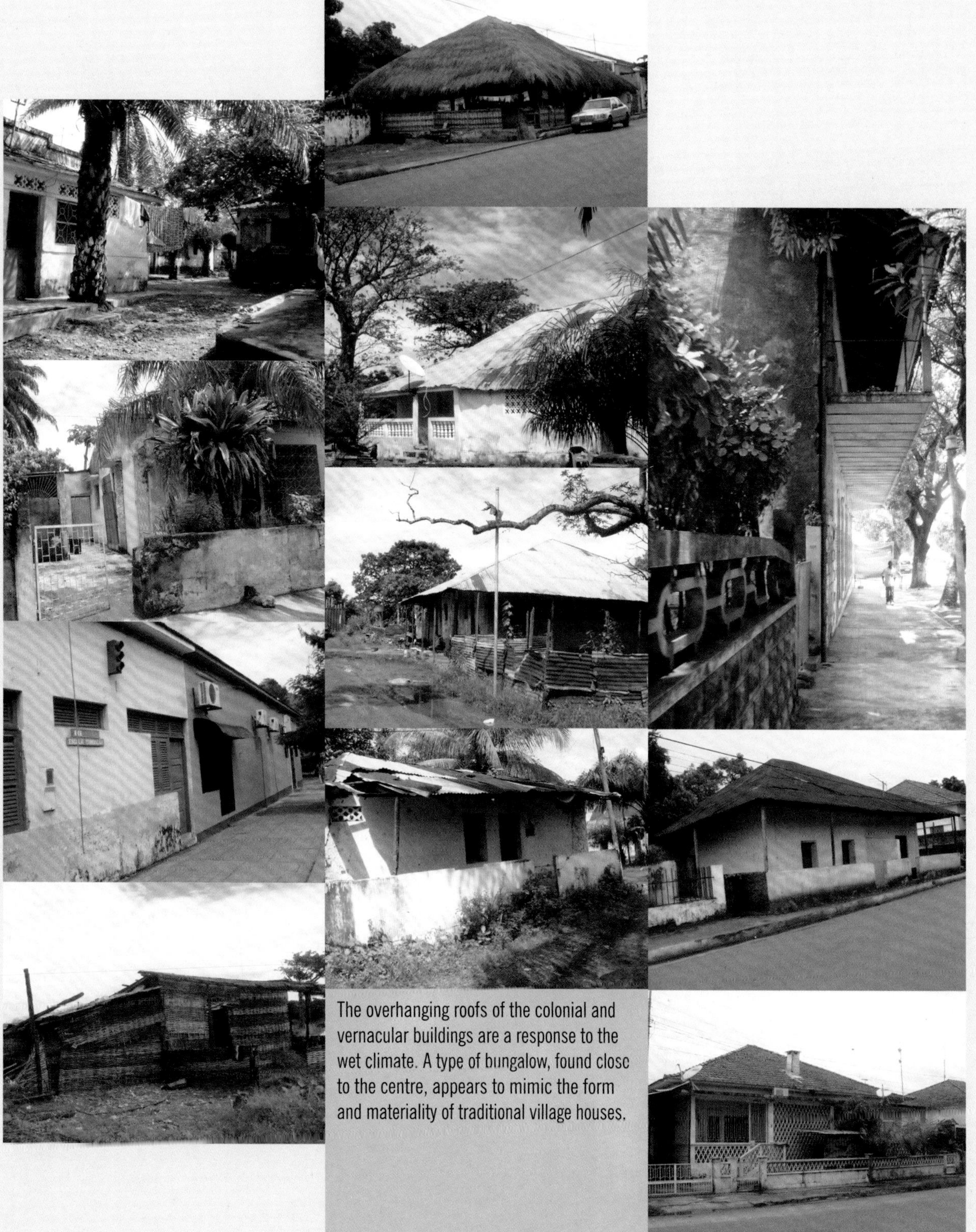

The overhanging roofs of the colonial and vernacular buildings are a response to the wet climate. A type of bungalow, found close to the centre, appears to mimic the form and materiality of traditional village houses.

BRAZZAVILLE / REPUBLIC OF THE CONGO

OVERVIEW

During its early history, the country was part of a larger trading area that consisted of several Bantu kingdoms. The Loango Kingdom developed between the 12th and 14th centuries and had a capital at Loango, to the east of modern Pointe Noire, and a base at the mouth of the River Congo, which was then known as the River Nzadi. Although powerful in its own right, the Loango Kingdom was a vassal state to the Kongo Kingdom, which was located in the area that is now the Democratic Republic of the Congo. In 1482 the Portuguese navigator Diogo Cão explored the mouth of the River Congo and took the first steps to make contact with local people, contact that would lead to the growth of the slave trade in this area. Colonization of the interior was largely initiated by Pierre de Brazza, an Italian who took French nationality and, with the support of the French navy, established Brazzaville as a trading post in 1880 and signed treaties with local leaders that ceded the west bank of the River Congo to France. Apart from ivory and tropical hardwoods, the French were interested in harvesting rubber from trees in the forest and treated local people with great cruelty in order to pressurize them into locating the trees and taking their sap. But they took little responsibility for the practical or social development of the country, apart from constructing a railway from Brazzaville to Pointe Noire on the Atlantic coast between 1924 and 1934.

Independence in 1960 was followed by several short-lived governments. The first president was deposed in 1963 and the National Council of the Revolution, which replaced him, only survived until 1968, when a military coup brought Marien Ngouabi to power. With political associates from the north of the country, he presided over Africa's first Marxist state, the People's Republic of the Congo. The shift in power from the once-dominant south created new tensions and Ngouabi was assassinated in 1977. An interim military government was followed, two years later, by that of Denis Sassou Nguesso and his Congolese Workers Party. A former Marxist, his socialism was more flexible and, following the collapse of Soviet communism and increasing unrest at home, he agreed to hold multiparty elections in 1992. The country's name had already been changed back to Republic of the Congo and the successful candidate was Pascal Lissouba, who was committed to restoring the historical dominance of the south. Unfortunately, each of the parties represented in the election had a strong following in different parts of the country, and many activists were armed. When, in protest at the distribution of seats in the new parliament, Sassou Nguesso withdrew his party from government, his supporters expressed their disappointment in a series of anti-government demonstrations. As government forces increasingly clashed with opposition groups the antagonism between the various parties finally degenerated into civil war in 1994. With assistance from Angola and Democratic Republic of the Congo, Sassou Nguesso's forces were able to gain the upper hand, and he resumed the presidency in 1997 and remains in power. After sporadic fighting had continued for several more years, an uneasy peace was declared in 2003. The country's turbulent history has taken its toll on the fabric of the capital, which is now in the middle of a rebuilding programme.

OBSERVATIONS

Heading into the city, two main boulevards lead south towards the river. They are connected by an east–west boulevard, where the parliament, law courts and a conference centre stand next to a vast expanse of tarmac, which is used as a parade ground by the military.

Avenue du Maréchal Foch is lined with local government buildings, banks and commerce, and although it is only one block from the river, it turns its back on it. Across the river, the profile of Kinshasa is clearly visible and seeing the two capitals together lays open the tragedy of the Congo's past.

To the west of the centre, there is an area of informal markets that has a West African character, while the rest of the city has a French feel, with many intriguing colonial and modernist buildings. The wealthy live in the centre, leaving the suburbs for the middle classes and the poor. The suburbs are also where the famed Congolese nightlife is to be found.

NATIONAL POPULATION

4,620,000

CITY POPULATION

1,888,000

ETHNIC GROUPS

Kongo 48%, Sangha 20%, Teke 17%, M'Bochi 12%, Europeans and other 3%

RELIGIONS

Roman Catholic 33.1%, Awakening Churches/ Christian Revival 22.3%, Protestant 19.9%, Salutiste 2.2%, Muslim 1.6%, Kimbanguiste 1.5%, other 8.1%, none 11.3%

LANGUAGES

French (official), Lingala and Monokutuba (lingua franca trade languages), many local languages and dialects (of which Kikongo is the most widespread)

GDP

$28.36 billion

AGRICULTURAL PRODUCTS

cassava (manioc, tapioca), sugar, rice, corn, peanuts, vegetables, coffee, cocoa; forest products

INDUSTRIES

petroleum extraction, cement, lumber, brewing, sugar, palm oil, soap, flour, cigarettes

HOTEL DE VILLE
LA POSTE

Often dilapidated, these buildings are slowly being brought back to full use. City hall has touches of Terragni, constructed of white marble with fine *brises-soleil*. More recent administrative buildings have a tendency towards White House pastiche, a 90-degree turn from the city's modernist legacy.

BRAZZAVILLE / REPUBLIC OF THE CONGO / **COMMERCIAL**

This is quite special, particularly the sweeping, white-painted, modernist compositions on the main thoroughfares. The buildings of the 1970s and 1980s culminate in the Elf Tower, the highest building in the Congo, an elegant column-like structure that balances on a slender post at its base.

The wealthy live on the hills around the cathedral. In the suburbs, where most people live, the small plots are fully occupied by the houses that stand on them, leaving very little external space. The homes of the poor are normally approached through a small compound, and are often unfinished.

CONAKRY / GUINEA

OVERVIEW

Rock paintings on the Fouta Djallon plateau date from 30,000 years ago and, by the beginning of the 1st millennium BCE, several ethnic groups had settled in the northwest of the future country. After the fall of the Empire of Ghana in the 13th century CE the Malinké people settled the north, and by the 14th century the entire country was part of the Empire of Mali. During the 15th century the Portuguese explored the coast but did not journey inland. At this time the Peul people migrated into the north of the country, which in the 19th century became a French colony. The early stages of the French occupation were resisted by Samori Touré but, after his arrest in 1898, his followers gave up their struggle. In 1956 Sékou Touré, a descendant of Samori, organized an alliance of African trade unions and led the campaign for independence. In 1958 General de Gaulle suggested that French colonies could be part of a Franco-African organization but Touré opted for immediate independence. De Gaulle retaliated by withdrawing the French administration and many French left the country with large amounts of capital, which precipitated a crisis in the country's economy. In desperation, Touré sought assistance from the former USSR and, although this connection was not maintained, he pursued revolutionary socialist policies during the 1960s. Unfortunately, they were seriously counterproductive and many people left the country.

Touré favoured his fellow Malinké in all major appointments and had a repressive attitude towards his political opponents. In 1976 he accused the Peul population of supporting an earlier Portuguese-led invasion that had been unsuccessful, and many Peul felt compelled to leave. Touré's death in 1984 was followed by a military coup, Diarra Traoré became prime minister and Lansana Conté was president. They introduced austerity measures to secure support from the IMF and in 1991 a new constitution encouraged the development of multiparty democracy. But the elections in 1993 were highly suspect and those in 1998 were marred by the jailing of members of the opposition and subsequently their leader, Alpha Condé. Conté actually won on both occasions but political tensions increased and in 2000 there were armed raids by rebels based in Sierra Leone and Liberia. The refugees living in camps close to the border were suspected of being involved and the camps were either closed or deliberately targeted. Despite serious unrest, a referendum on the constitution in 2001 removed the two-term limit on the presidency and extended the length of each term from five to seven years, creating the possibility of Conté being president for life. He won the 2005 elections, despite making only one public appearance due to ill health. Meanwhile, Condé had returned from exile in France and joined other leaders in the Front Républicain pour l'Alternance Démocratique (Republican Front for a Democratic Alternative) in calling for Conté to resign for the benefit of the country. When Conté died in 2008, a coup brought Moussa Camara to power but, following an attempt on his life, he was replaced by Sékouba Konaté as head of a military junta. The election he organized in 2010 was won by Alpha Condé, who was reelected in 2015. Conakry came to prominence as a French port that was linked to the interior by a railway to Kankan in Upper Guinea.

OBSERVATIONS

Conakry was originally Christian but is now largely Muslim. The geography of the city is quite beautiful and the colonial settlement was based on a grid of streets, on flat land surrounded by water. The climate is good and the city is full of mature trees.

Most of the city is low and horizontal; only a few high-rise residential buildings break the skyline. Extensions to the old town, known as Conakry 2 and Conakry 3, are the site of recent public buildings, new residential developments, markets and business, which benefit from the looser infrastructure in these areas.

The main mosque is very grand and dominates the skyline in Conakry 2. There are many smaller mosques, which articulate the neighbourhoods. Churches are few and far between, although the bell-tower of the cathedral dominates the old town.

The housing of the most needy is extremely informal, and is often located on the fringes of earlier bungalow developments. The informal housing is usually one room deep, with family life taking place outside, either directly on the street or modestly screened.

NATIONAL POPULATION

12,609,000

CITY POPULATION

1,936,000

ETHNIC GROUPS

Fulani (Peul) 33.9%, Malinke 31.1%, Soussou 19.1%, Guerze 6%, Kissi 4.7%, Toma 2.6%, other 2.6%

RELIGIONS

Muslim 85%, Christian 8%, animist/other/none 7%

LANGUAGES

French (official); note: each ethnic group has its own language

GDP

$15.13 billion

AGRICULTURAL PRODUCTS

rice, coffee, pineapples, palm kernels, cocoa, cassava (manioc, tapioca), bananas, sweet potatoes; cattle, sheep, goats; timber

INDUSTRIES

mining (bauxite, gold, diamonds, iron ore), light manufacturing, agricultural processing

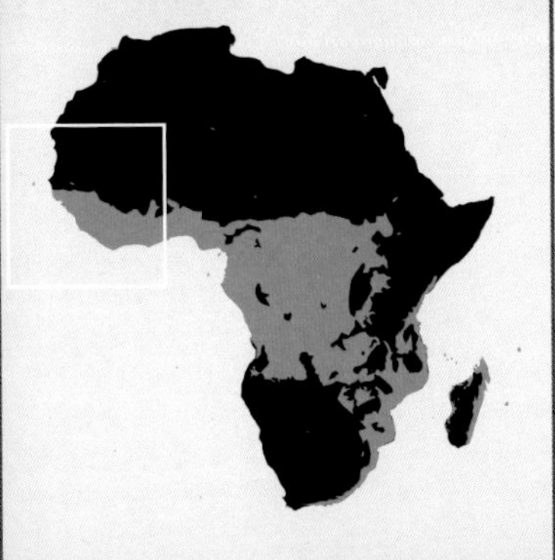

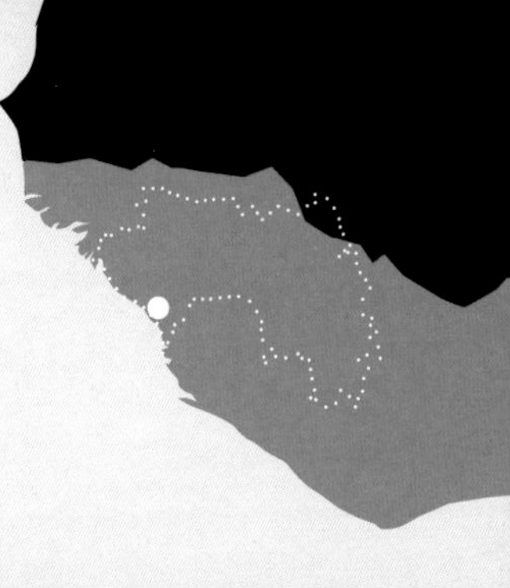

There are few public spaces and they are mainly in the old town, situated at the end of the peninsula. Newer public buildings, such as the main mosque and the parliament, in tropical modernist style, are located in an extension to the colonial city.

The life of the city is found on the wide pavements of the commercial area. The stalls of the informal traders create hybridized sinuous streetscapes, with people shopping, resting and socializing in these in-between spaces.

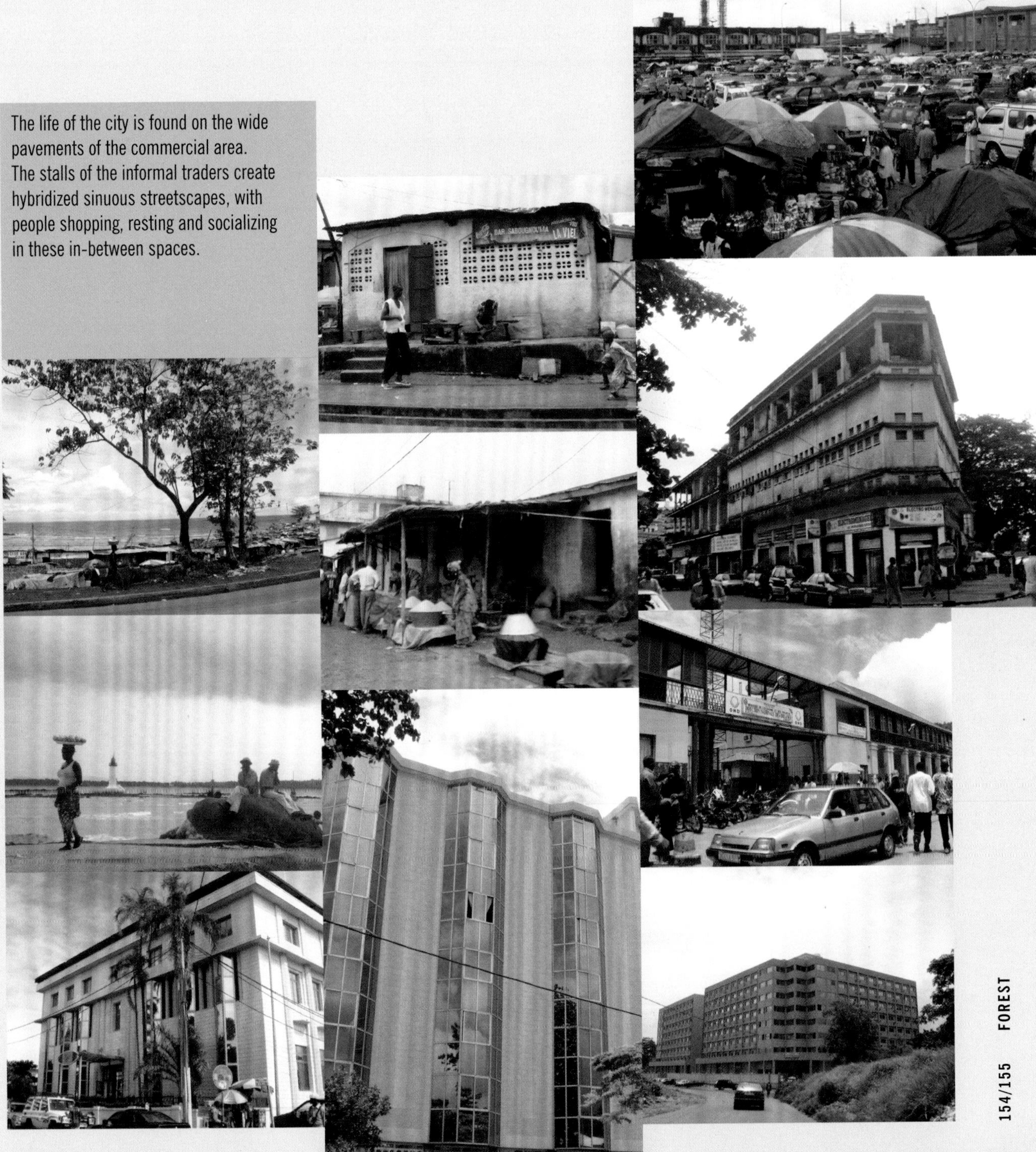

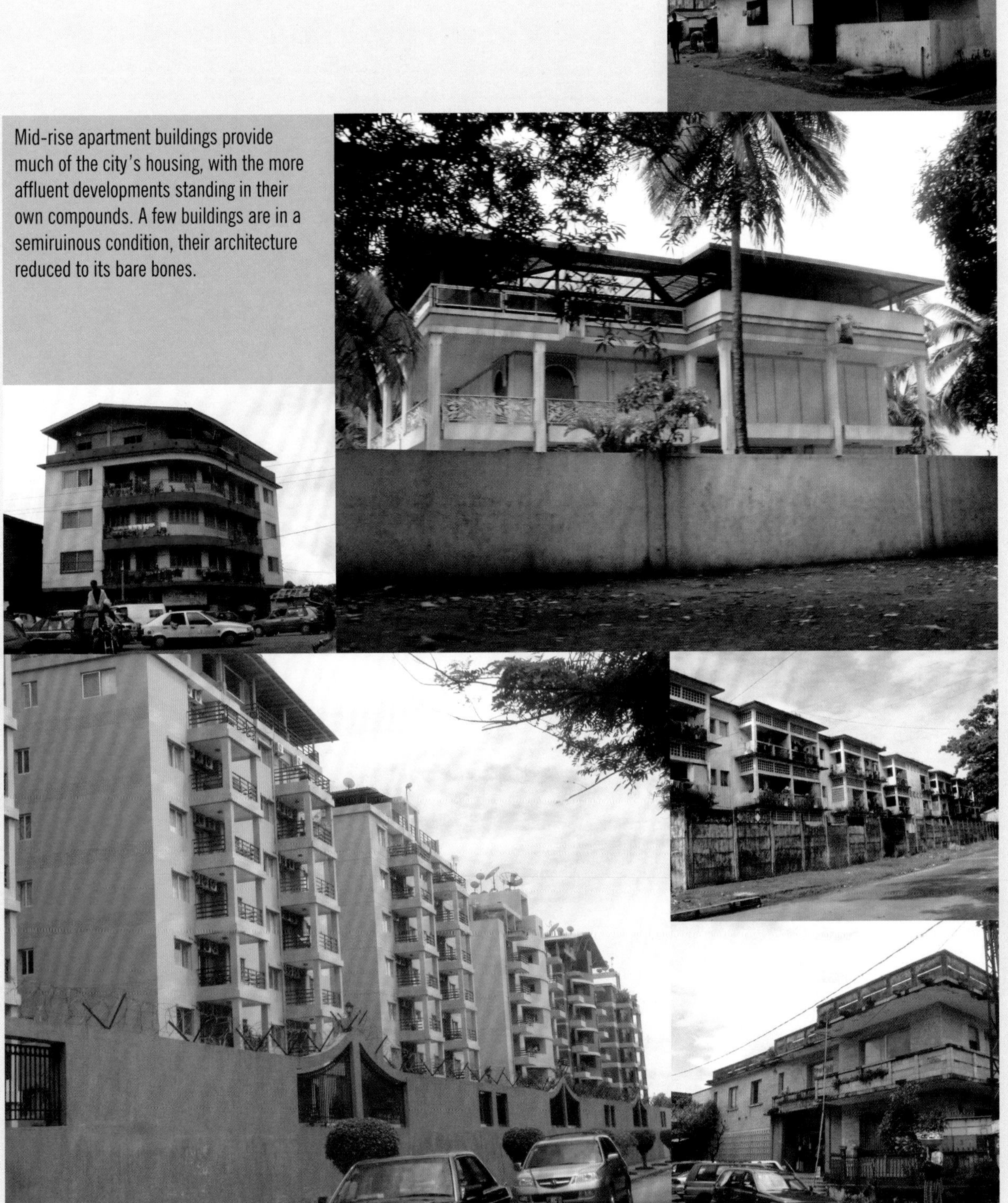

Mid-rise apartment buildings provide much of the city's housing, with the more affluent developments standing in their own compounds. A few buildings are in a semiruinous condition, their architecture reduced to its bare bones.

COTONOU / BENIN

OVERVIEW

In the 17th century the future Benin was occupied by many small kingdoms that were often in conflict over the land that they occupied. Of these, the Dahomey Kingdom was especially successful and came to dominate its neighbours. The country became known to European powers and the Portuguese, English, French and Dutch established separate trading posts on the coast. This was to prove a fateful combination as in the following years the Dahomey kings exchanged slaves from other ethnic groups for the guns that they used to raid the surrounding areas. It is estimated that, for over 100 years, about 10,000 slaves per year were shipped from the Dahomey to the Caribbean and the Americas. In the 19th century, with the end of the slave trade, the kingdom became a French colony and, recognizing the ability of the people, the French developed an education system that led to many Dahomeyans working in the colonial administrations of other countries in French West Africa. When many French colonies became independent in 1960 they began to deport their Dahomeyan immigrants. Back home and without work, they contributed to a general air of political instability. Having seen the ease with which it was done in neighbouring Togo, the army organized its first coup three years after independence – and several more in the next ten years.

A decisive break in this pattern took place when Mathieu Kérékou seized power in 1972 to launch a military dictatorship that would survive for nearly twenty years. To underline the significance of his accession, he changed the name of the country to Benin and broadcast his intentions on the radio. Politically, he was committed to restructuring the country on socialist principles and entered alliances with the USSR, China and North Korea. Agriculture was reorganized on a collective basis, manufacturing and public services were nationalized, and all workers joined a single trade union. These changes did not lead to an improvement in the economy but to the exact opposite: inflation, rising unemployment and wages left unpaid. Against this background there was growing tension between the president, who was from near Natitingou in the north, and the Yoruba who lived in the south. After a number of unsuccessful coups and under financial pressure from the French, a general strike led Kérékou to renounce his socialist programme. At a conference to discuss a new constitution in 1989, the delegates made him the head of the army and set up a new government under Nicéphore Soglo. Although Soglo won the elections in 1991, his particular brand of austerity and favouritism soon became unpopular and Kérékou returned to power in the 1996 elections. In 2001 the opposition withdrew from the elections, giving him a second term that ended in 2006. Kérékou was in power for thirty-three years and, towards the end of this period, Benin had become one of the more stable democracies in Africa. The current president is Yayi Boni, a former head of the West African Development Bank. Although Porto-Novo is the official capital, Cotonou remains the country's most important city.

OBSERVATIONS

Cotonou is situated on the southern tip of the country, where an inlet connects Lake Nokoué to the sea. Lagos, its metropolitan neighbour, is 75 miles to the east. The city has a large port and its layout is orientated towards the waterfront.

The plan of the city is dominated by a grid of boulevards, where monuments on the roundabouts celebrate symbolic events in the country's history. The boulevards are lined with formal and informal commerce and support the public life of the city. On their pavements, stalls and shopfronts form pedestrian corridors that are shielded from the intense traffic.

The city is animated by the large number of people who ride motorcycles. Collectively they emit a huge amount of noise and a great deal of pollution, resulting in a hazy atmosphere. There is a lot of energy but it is quite dislocating.

NATIONAL POPULATION

10,880,000

CITY POPULATION

682,000

ETHNIC GROUPS

Fon 39.2%, Adja 15.2%, Yoruba 12.3%, Bariba 9.2%, Peulh 7%, Ottamari 6.1%, Yoa-Lokpa 4%, Dendi 2.5%, other 1.6% (includes Europeans), unspecified 2.9%

RELIGIONS

Catholic 27.1%, Muslim 24.4%, Vodoun 17.3%, Protestant 10.4% (Celestial 5%, Methodist 3.2%, other Protestant 2.2%), other traditional religions 6%, other Christian 5.3%, other 1.9%, none 6.5%, unspecified 1.1%

LANGUAGES

French (official), Fon, Yoruba, tribal languages

GDP

$19.86 billion

AGRICULTURAL PRODUCTS

cotton, corn, cassava (manioc, tapioca), yams, beans, palm oil, peanuts, cashews; livestock

INDUSTRIES

textiles, food processing, construction materials, cement

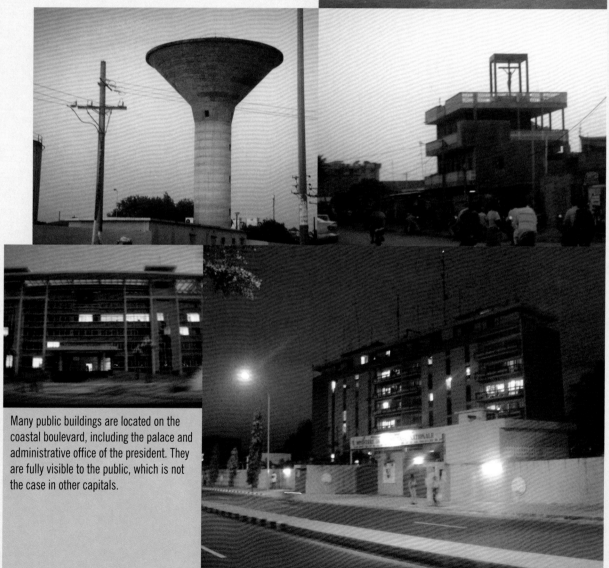

Many public buildings are located on the coastal boulevard, including the palace and administrative office of the president. They are fully visible to the public, which is not the case in other capitals.

COTONOU / BENIN / **COMMERCIAL**

There is a wide mix of examples, from the neomodernism of the 1960s, through to the fantasy styles of the present. Some of the new bank buildings attempt to express an African corporate image.

COTONOU / BENIN / **RESIDENTIAL**

The most fashionable address is the area where the president lives. The middle classes live in apartment buildings or in the suburbs, and many of the poor live in informal compounds on land that lies between the main thoroughfares.

DAR ES SALAAM / TANZANIA

OVERVIEW

The oldest remains in the country are hominid footprints found in the Olduvai Gorge that are over three million years old. A series of later migrations concluded with an influx of Bantu speakers, around 1000 BCE, who remain the dominant ethnolinguistic group in the area. The coast was explored by traders from Arabia and Persia, resulting in a string of well-established coastal settlements by the 13–15th centuries CE. Following an agreement between Britain and Germany in 1890, Tanganyika and Burundi were designated German East Africa, and the Zanzibar archipelago became a British protectorate. After the First World War the British assumed control of Tanganyika but the focus of their interest remained in Kenya. The move towards independence had begun in 1905, with the Maji Maji rebellion that followed the establishment of a series of cotton plantations along the railway line from Dar es Salaam to Morogoro. Based on forced labour, the conditions in the plantations were extremely harsh and the resistance movement that they provoked spread through the south of the country, as a general reaction to the oppression of colonialism. Germany suppressed this uprising by destroying crops and killing over 100,000 people in two years. There were two main responses to these brutal events: a growing belief in the need for independence and, on the German side, a slight liberalization of attitude.

Throughout the colonial period, agriculture was organized on the basis of farming cooperatives. By 1950 there were over 400 of them and they were represented by the Tanganyika Africa Association (TAA), located in Dar es Salaam, and became a major force in the independence movement. When Julius Nyerere became president of the TAA in 1953, he transformed it into an openly political organization, the Tanganyika (later Tanzania) African National Union (TANU) that stood for 'freedom and unity'. After TANU electoral successes in 1958 and 1959, Britain agreed to independence under Nyerere. This was declared in 1961 and a year later the country became a republic with Nyerere as president. Following political unrest on the island of Zanzibar it was united with Tanganyika in 1964 and the country was renamed Tanzania. In 1977 Nyerere amalgamated TANU and the leading Zanzibar party to form Chama Cha Mapinduzi (Party of the Revolution, CCM). The CCM has dominated Tanzanian politics ever since.

Nyerere's government inherited a country that had been economically neglected and, due to the limitations of the education system, there was a serious shortage of relevant expertise. This situation was addressed in the Arusha Declaration of 1967, which stated that the country should be run on socialist principles and each village would be managed on a traditional basis and function as an agricultural collective. Between 1973 and 1978 a large proportion of the population was resettled into 7,000 of these villages but the planned improvement in agricultural output did not materialize. Nyerere was reelected in 1980 but handed power to Ali Hassan Mwinyi in 1985. He began to introduce economic reforms but, with the collapse of socialism in Eastern Europe, Tanzania was under pressure to seek support from Western nations who were more sympathetic to countries with democratic governments. Opposition parties were legalized in 1992 and the first open election was held in 1995. After disputed elections in 2000, several demonstrators were killed in Zanzibar, and the elections of 2005 chose Jakaya Kikwete who was reelected in 2010. The 2015 election was won by John Pombe Magufuli of the CCM. Dar es Salaam became the colonial capital in 1891 and remained the country's most important city after the government was relocated in Dodoma in 1973.

OBSERVATIONS

Dar es Salaam, 'haven of peace', is a potpourri of African, Arab and Indian influences and is the place where I was born. The earliest settlement took place in what is now the downtown area and overlooked a large natural harbour. Since then the city has expanded inland and several miles along the coast.

This was a German colony before the English arrived here. As a result, it has an eclectic mix of styles that contributes to the basic character of the city. Many buildings, whether colonial, modernist or postmodernist, are painted in bright colours.

NATIONAL POPULATION

53,470,000

CITY POPULATION

5,116,000

ETHNIC GROUPS

mainland – African 99% (95% Bantu consisting of over 130 tribes), other 1% (Asian, European and Arab); Zanzibar – Arab, African, mixed Arab and African

RELIGIONS

mainland – Christian 30%, Muslim 35%, indigenous beliefs 35%; Zanzibar – Muslim 99%, other 1%

LANGUAGES

Kiswahili or Swahili (official), Kiunguja (name for Swahili in Zanzibar), English (official), Arabic (widely spoken in Zanzibar), local languages

GDP

$128.2 billion

AGRICULTURAL PRODUCTS

coffee, sisal, tea, cotton, pyrethrum (insecticide made from chrysanthemums), cashew nuts, tobacco, cloves, corn, wheat, cassava (manioc, tapioca), bananas, fruits, vegetables; cattle, sheep, goats

INDUSTRIES

agricultural processing (sugar, beer, cigarettes, sisal twine), mining (diamond, gold, iron ore), salt, soda ash, cement, oil refining, shoes, apparel, wood products, fertilizer

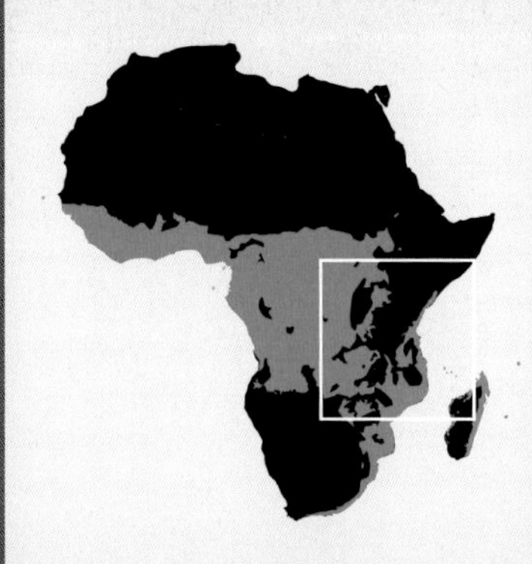

There are churches, mosques and Hindu and Sikh temples dotting the skyline and giving a focus to the city's neighbourhoods. The president's palace and various embassies are situated on the coast but, since 1973, many government departments have moved to Dodoma.

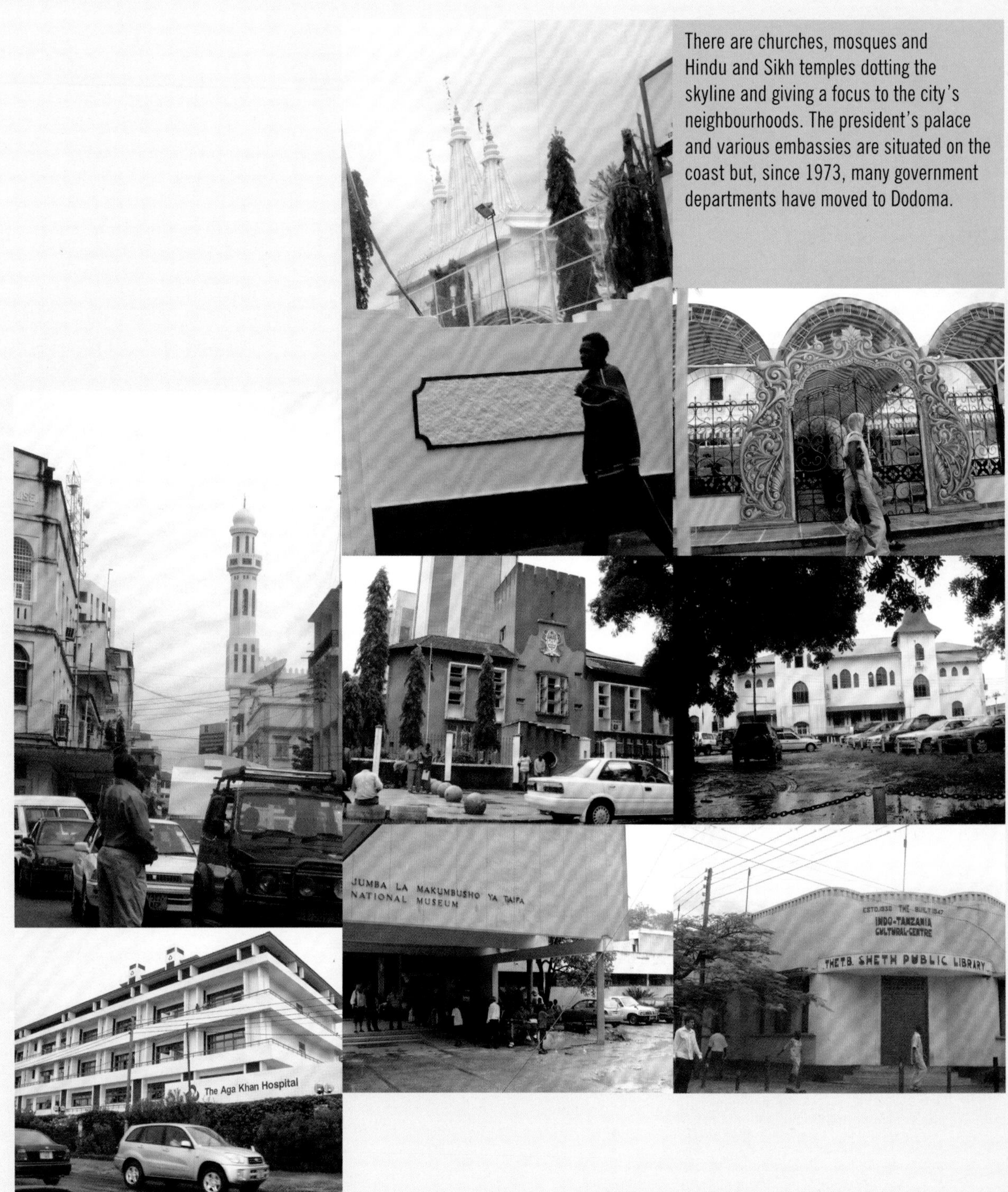

Downtown is a mix of colonial-period buildings, with a human scale and a variety of occupants, and larger structures from the 1960s to the present. As the city has always been relatively prosperous, there are buildings from most periods and styles.

DAR ES SALAAM / TANZANIA / **RESIDENTIAL**

The city's coastal location permeates its residential architecture. Whether villa or apartment, loggias and balconies address the view and welcome the breeze. The poorer housing is denser, consisting of row houses and linear blocks.

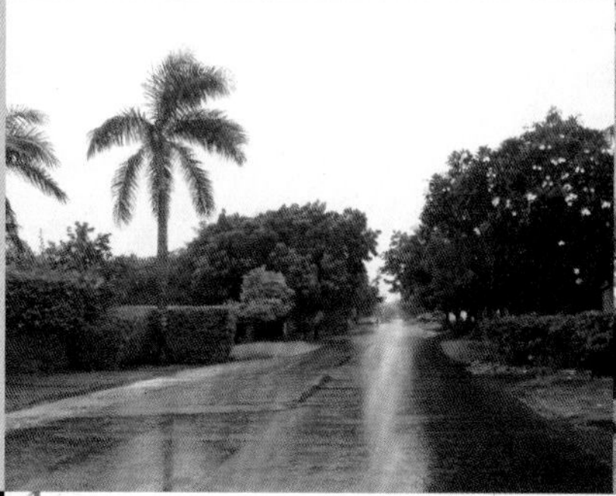
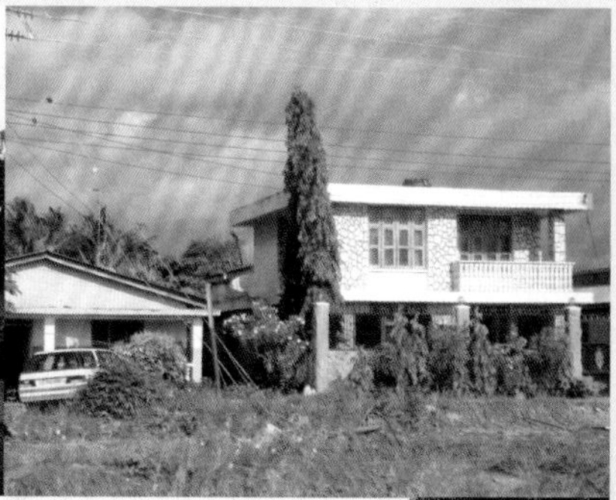
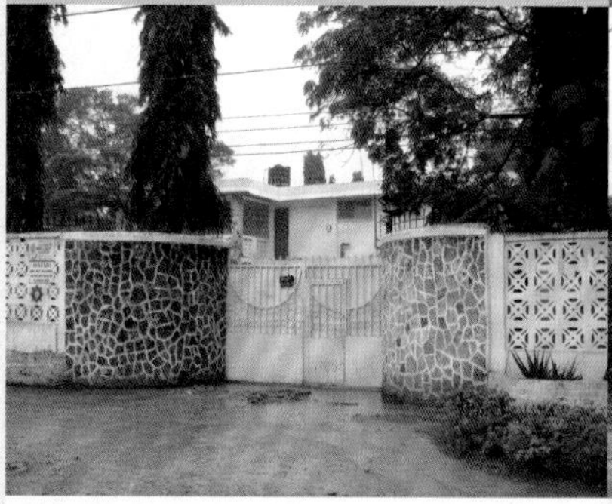
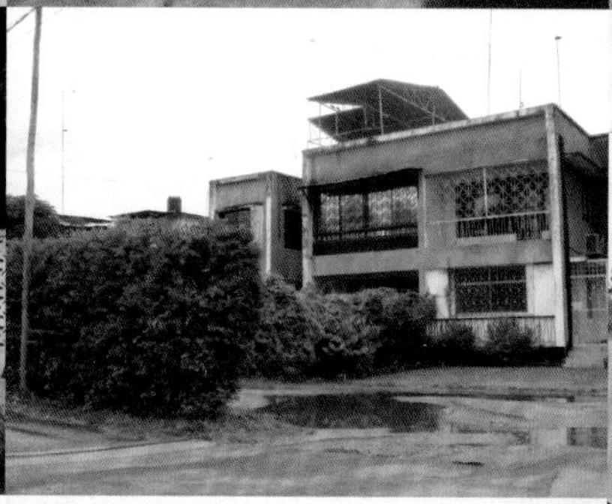
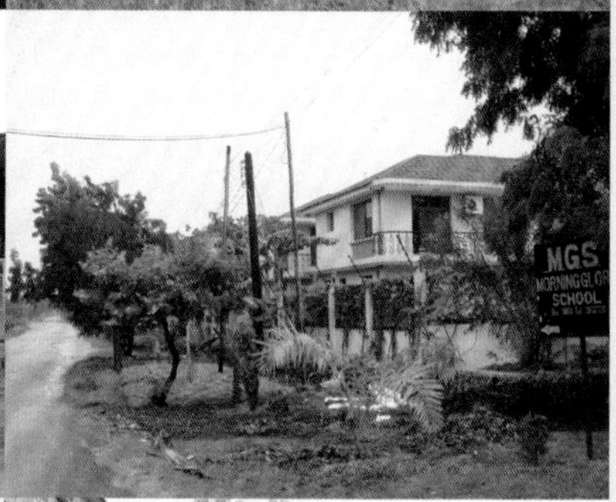

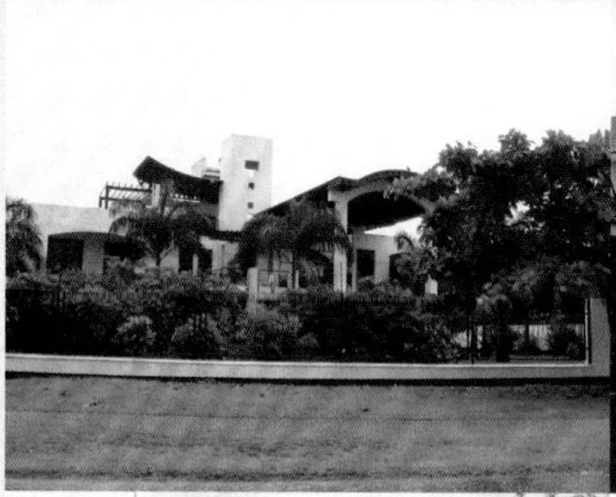
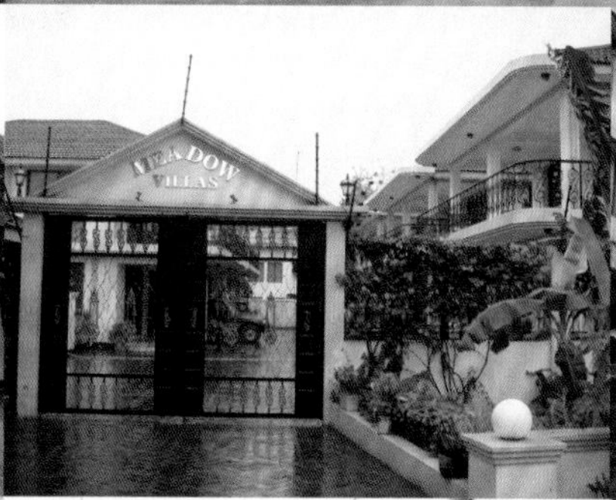
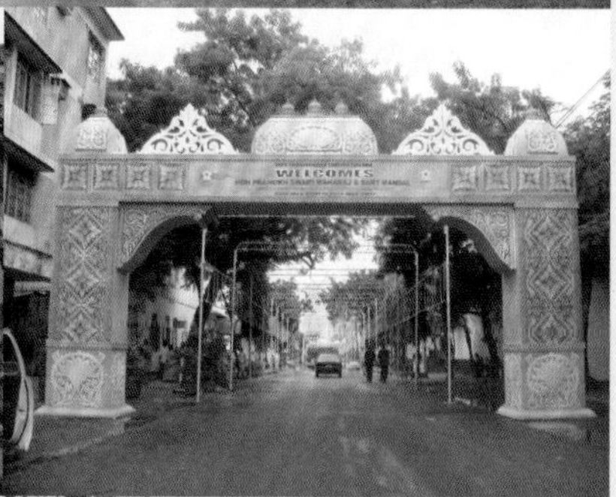

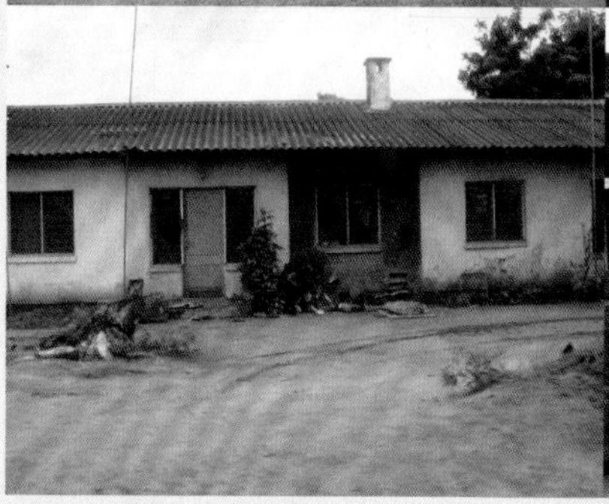
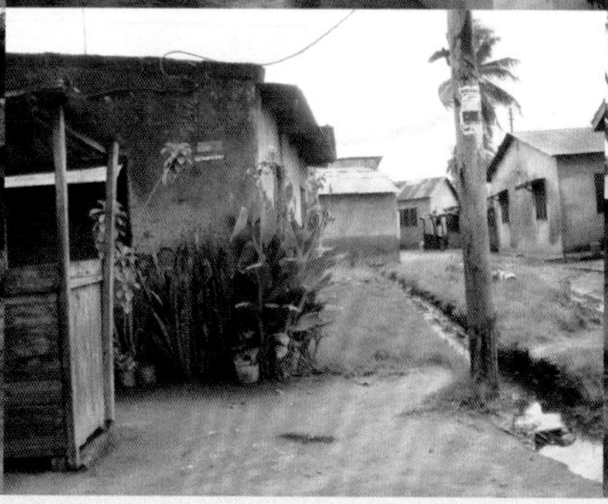
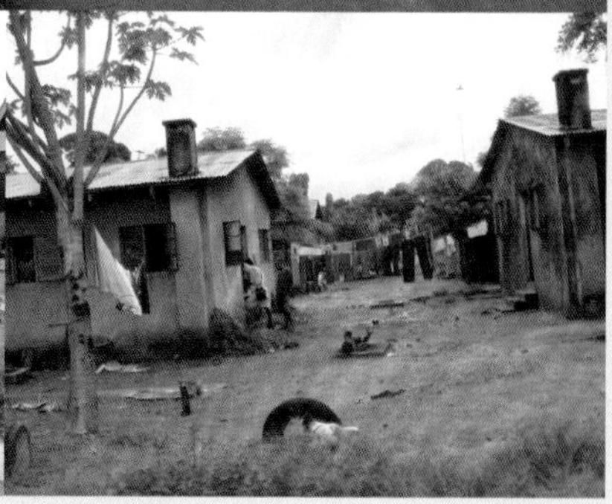

FREETOWN / SIERRA LEONE

OVERVIEW

The Limba, Sherbro and Temne peoples were early inhabitants of the area, long before the Portuguese explored the coast in the 15th century and Sir Francis Drake landed in the 16th century, during his voyage round the world. As the British became more involved in the slave trade in the 18th century, they assumed control of Sierra Leone. This had repercussions in the American War of Independence in the 1770s, when many slaves had the opportunity to gain their freedom by fighting for Britain. After the war thousands of freed slaves moved to London where they lived in poverty. In response to this situation, a group of philanthropists purchased land at the mouth of the Sierra Leone River for the ex-slaves to establish a 'Province of Freedom', which was the origin of Freetown. Britain made Freetown a colony in 1808 and it provided a base from which the British navy intercepted the slave ships of other countries. Freetown therefore became a major centre both for returning slaves and for inhabitants of the interior who wished to avoid being taken into slavery in the first place. By the middle of the century over a hundred ethnic groups were living in the colony. As nonindigenous blacks, they were known as Krios and were often given positions within the British administration. The situation continued until 1924 when arrangements were put in place for a legislative council whose composition recognized the ethnic make-up of the whole country.

At the time of independence in 1961, there were two main political parties. The Sierra Leone People's Party (SLPP) was the party of the Mende, the dominant ethnic group in the south. The All People's Congress (APC), led by the trade unionist Siaka Stevens, represented the Temne and Limba of the north. With the support of the Krios, the SLPP's leader, Milton Margai, became the first prime minister. On the death of his brother in 1964 Albert Margai took over and started to replace Krios in the administration with Mende, causing the Krios to move their support to the APC who won the election in 1967. This set a pattern that was to continue for over thirty years, with coups and countercoups alternating power between the major parties. Stability was further undermined by the civil war in Liberia in 1989, when armed rebels of the Revolutionary United Front (RUF) occupied eastern areas of Sierra Leone, causing a civil war in that country which lasted until 2002. After winning the elections for the SLPP in 1996, Ahmed Tejan Kabbah attempted to negotiate with the RUF but his efforts were overtaken by a coup in 1997, led by officers who were sympathetic to the RUF. Kabbah fled to Guinea and guerrilla warfare swept through the country. In 1998 a Nigerian-led peace force reasserted some control and reinstated Kabbah, before the RUF made a final assault on Freetown, destroying much of the city and killing thousands of people. After the battle the government signed the Lomé Peace Agreement with the RUF in 1999 and their leader, Foday Sankoh, became the vice president. But the RUF failed to keep the agreement and Sankoh was arrested for planning a coup. The disarming of the RUF was completed in 2002 and Kabbah was reelected. Since then, there has been only one unsuccessful coup, and a war-crimes court and a truth and reconciliation commission are continuing their work. Ernest Bai Koroma won the election in 2007 and remains in power. The country is recovering from the effects of the Ebola outbreak in 2014.

OBSERVATIONS

Greater Freetown occupies a line of hills where the Sierra Leone River meets the sea. It is made up of a series of independent neighbourhoods that have grown together over time. With winding roads and coastal bridges, it has the feeling of a seaside hill town.

The tops of the hills have been occupied by wealthy residencies and embassies, and the centre is marked by an extraordinary cotton tree that now stands on a traffic island. The churches are modest Victorian-looking buildings and the mosques are modern, with all their energy expressed in the towers.

In the downtown area, colonial villas have been subdivided so that several families can occupy them. The poorer areas are near the coast, where the informal houses are built from recycled materials. Served by schools and markets, they are vibrant neighbourhoods.

NATIONAL POPULATION

6,453,000

CITY POPULATION

1,007,000

ETHNIC GROUPS

Temne 35%, Mende 31%, Limba 8%, Kono 5%, Kriole 2% (descendants of freed slaves; also known as Krio) Mandringo 2%, Loko 2%, other 15% (includes refugees from Liberia, and small numbers of Europeans, Lebanese, Pakistanis and Indians)

RELIGIONS

Muslim 60%, Christian 10%, indigenous beliefs 30%

LANGUAGES

English (official), Mende, Temne, Krio (English-based Creole, spoken by the descendants of freed Jamaican slaves who were settled in the Freetown area, a lingua franca and a first language for 10% of the population but understood by 95%)

GDP

$12.8 billion

AGRICULTURAL PRODUCTS

rice, coffee, cocoa, palm kernels, palm oil, peanuts; poultry, cattle, sheep, pigs; fish

INDUSTRIES

mining (diamonds, iron ore, rutile, bauxite), small-scale manufacturing (beverages, textiles, cigarettes, footwear), petroleum refining, small commercial ship repair

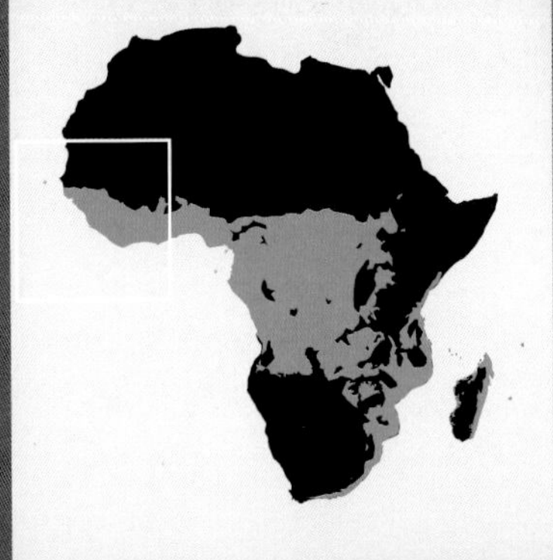

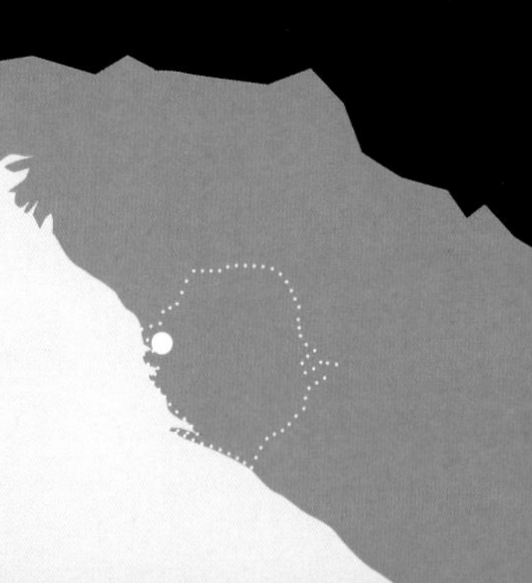

The architecture ranges from the colonial Supreme Court to the modernist parliament and administration buildings. They are located on Tower Hill and enjoy views across Victoria Park to the ocean.

LE VILLAGE
CAR CENTRE LTD.
zain
celtel
ROKEL COMMERCIAL BANK (SIERRA LEONE) LIMITED
GATE
Opened!

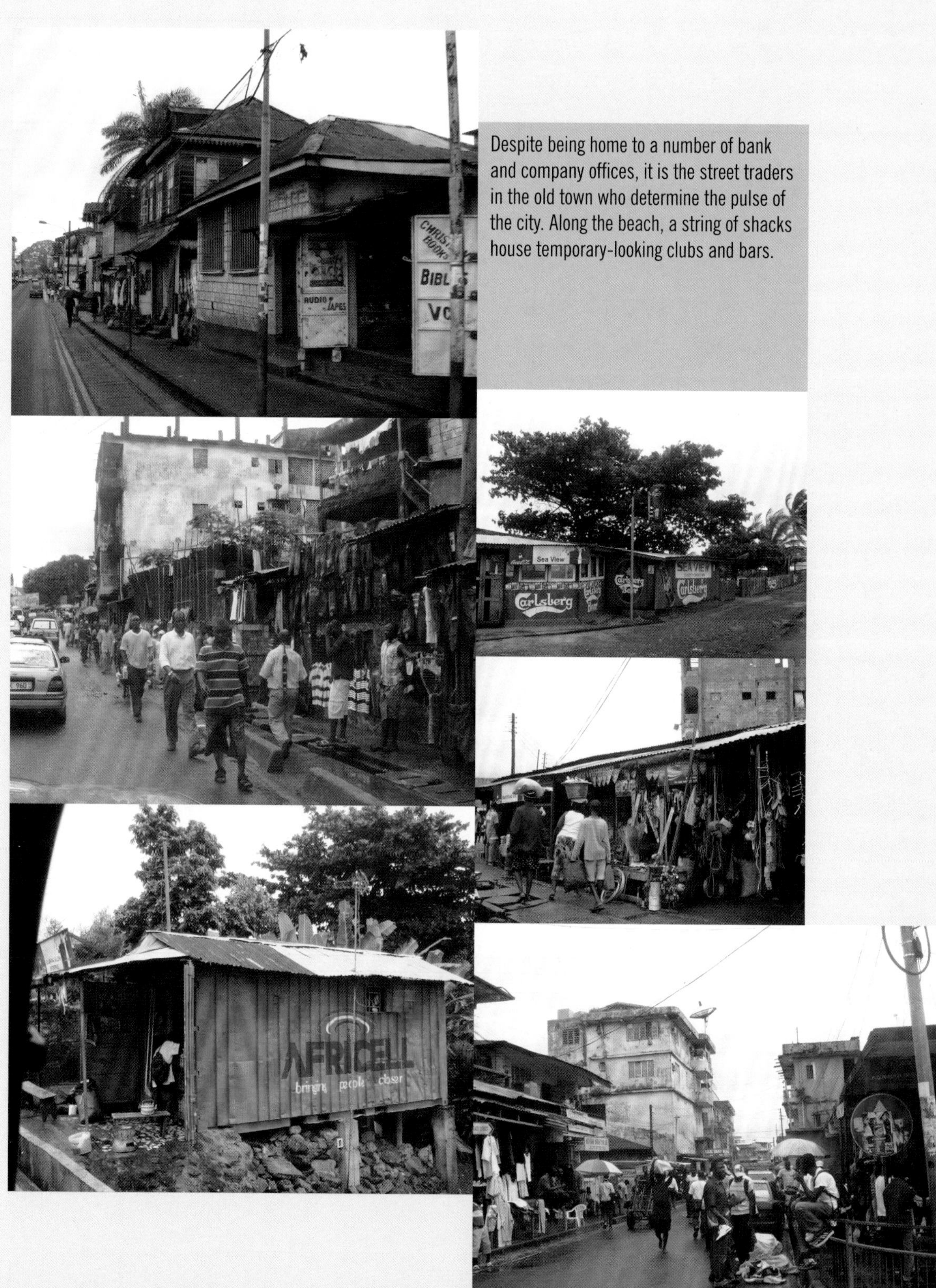

Despite being home to a number of bank and company offices, it is the street traders in the old town who determine the pulse of the city. Along the beach, a string of shacks house temporary-looking clubs and bars.

The colonial city, where newer buildings imitate their older neighbours, has the highest residential density. Away from the centre, a scattering of formal and informal settlements covers the hillsides.

JUBA / SOUTH SUDAN

OVERVIEW

The territories that became Sudan and South Sudan have always had different identities. Most of modern Sudan is desert and the major source of water is the Nile, with the Blue Nile and the White Nile meeting in Khartoum. Situated to the north, Sudan was historically closer to Arab trading routes and Islam started to displace early Christianity by the end of the 1st millennium. The landscape of South Sudan, on the other hand, includes areas of forest and savanna and the main river is the White Nile. To the north of Juba it flows through one of the largest wetlands areas in the world, known as the Sudd. Ethnic groups such as the Dinka and the Shilluk are thought to have arrived here in the first half of the 2nd millennium, to raise cattle and cultivate crops. Until the middle of the 19th century the Sudd wetlands were an effective barrier to Western exploration of the interior, a situation that began to change in the early 1840s, when there were two German expeditions to discover the source of the White Nile. They were quickly followed by ivory traders who were prepared to venture deep into the interior. Throughout this period the area was ruled from Cairo as an extension of the Ottoman Empire and, with the opening of trade routes to the south, the ethnic groups who lived there became a source of slaves, to be sold in Khartoum. Anti-slavery missionaries introduced Christianity to the same groups. From 1879, when the British ousted the Ottoman ruler Ismail the Magnificent and appointed Charles Gordon as governor of Khartoum, both the north and the south were subject to British involvement. Following a revolt that resulted in Gordon's death, a British-Egyptian force reasserted control and in 1899–1954 the whole area was subject to joint rule in an arrangement known as the Anglo-Egyptian Condominium.

The Sudan that gained full independence in 1956 included both the southern and the northern territories but there were few benefits for the south. A military coup in 1958 brought General Abboud to power and he pursued pro-Arab policies that antagonized the southern states. Their opposition was expressed by the Sudan African Nationalist Union based in Kampala and by rebel forces, known as the Anyanya, who took control of large areas of the south. The causes of this conflict were only addressed when Jaafur Nimeiri took power in a further coup in 1969. His negotiations led to the Addis Ababa Agreement of 1972, which ended the civil war and led to the setting up of a regional government for the southern states. But the optimism of the following years was short-lived, as a change of heart in the north led to the suspension of the regional government and the introduction of Sharia law throughout the country. As the rebels in the south began to reorganize, they were joined by a new group, the Sudan People's Liberation Movement/Army led by John Garang. Civil war returned in 1983 and, with the national government in disarray and growing conflict between the rebel groups themselves, it continued until 2003. Under the Machakos Protocol, which ended hostilities, Khartoum agreed that Sharia would only apply in the north and that there would be a referendum on independence for the south. The southern states were also free to set up a parallel government in 2005, which took full control of South Sudan following the positive vote for independence in 2011.

The first years of the new state have been difficult. Some ethnic groups do not trust the government to act in their interest, which has led to conflict with government forces and between the groups. With different ethnic supporters, President Salva Kiir Mayardit accused his then deputy, Riek Macher, of planning a coup in 2013. On the economy, oil exports have been hit by disagreements with Sudan over the cost of using their pipelines, which has had serious economic consequences. Juba was first settled in 1922, close to the historic trading station of Gondokoro.

OBSERVATIONS

Juba is in the very early stages of its formation as a capital, as I discovered when I visited in 2012. It is in the middle of building boom but the basic infrastructure is not in place and many institutions are in temporary buildings. Due to the intensity of the situation, direct comparisons with the other capitals are not yet possible.

NATIONAL POPULATION

12,340,000

CITY POPULATION

321,000

ETHNIC GROUPS

Dinka 35.8%, Nuer 15.6%, Shilluk, Azande, Bari, Kakwa, Kuku, Murle, Mandari, Didinga, Ndogo, Bviri, Lndi, Anuak, Bongo, Lango, Dungotona, Acholi

RELIGIONS

animist, Christian

LANGUAGES

English (official), Arabic, regional languages include Dinka, Nuer, Bari, Zande, Shilluk

GDP

$23.5 billion

AGRICULTURAL PRODUCTS

sorghum, maize, rice, millet, wheat, gum arabic, sugarcane, mangoes, papayas, bananas, sweet potatoes, sunflower seeds, cotton, sesame seeds, cassava (manioc, tapioca), beans, peanuts; cattle, sheep

INDUSTRIES

crude oil

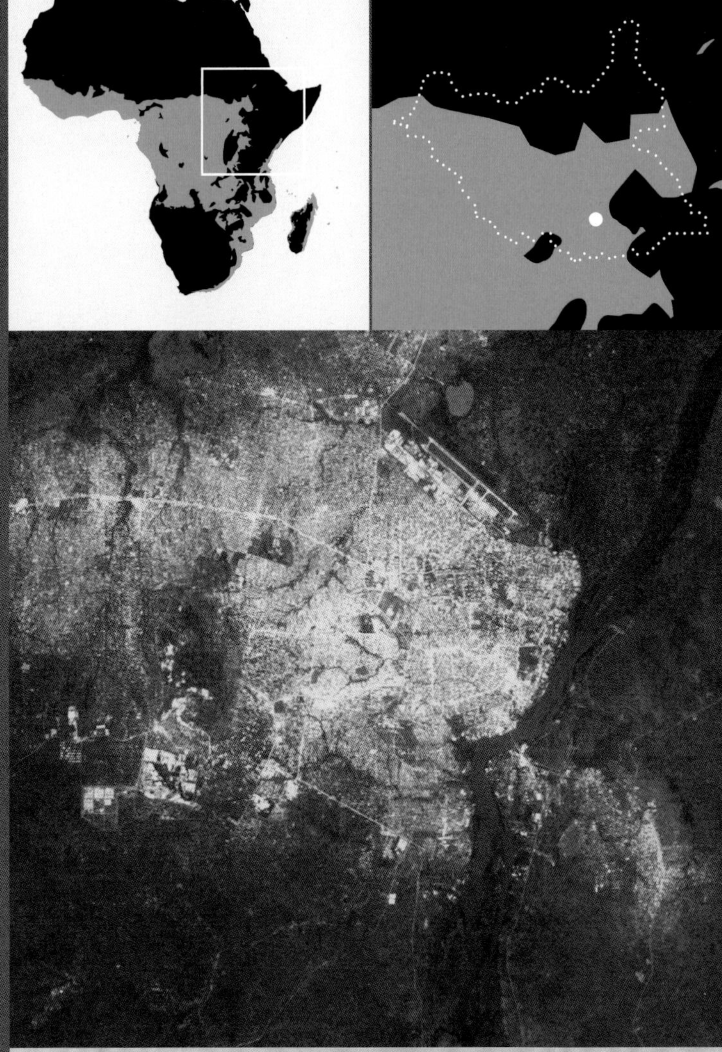

KAMPALA / UGANDA

OVERVIEW

Uganda shares an exceptionally long history with other countries in East Africa, the area from which man's earliest ancestors gradually moved into Asia. There is evidence of *Homo sapiens* having lived here 100,000 years ago and the roots of the current population go back at least 10,000 years. Since then migrants have arrived from the north and west and, with the imposition of national boundaries by colonial powers, the population of each country included people from several ethnic groups. Following an agreement with Germany in 1890, Uganda became a British colony and they favoured Buganda people for positions in their administration and the Lango people as military personnel, an arrangement that led to a lingering sense of resentment on both sides. Instead of seeing their land expropriated, as happened elsewhere, indigenous farmers were encouraged to grow crops and sell them for export through local cooperatives. Partly for this reason, nationalist resistance developed later than in other countries and there was a relatively smooth transition to independence in 1962.

The first prime minister was Milton Obote, leader of the Uganda People's Congress, and the president was Edward Mutesa II, the *kabaka* or king of the Buganda people. By 1966 it was clear that Obote did not intend sharing power and he ordered his chief of staff, Idi Amin, to take action against Mutesa who went into exile in London. With Obote assuming presidential powers, the situation gradually deteriorated. When a substantial sum of money and armaments went missing, Amin was questioned and asked to resign but instead he staged a successful coup while Obote was out of the country in 1971. Amin outlawed all political organizations and the army was empowered to shoot anyone suspected of opposition, which led to the deaths of over 300,000 people. He also took action against Uganda's Asian population who in 1972 were given ninety days to leave the country with minimal possessions. As the country slipped further into chaos, Amin sought financial support from Colonel Gaddafi of Libya to launch an invasion of Tanzania in 1978. With limited resources, it was difficult for Tanzania to organize a counterattack but when it came in 1979 the Ugandan army fled and Amin went into exile in Libya. Against a background of shortages and unrest, a general election and return to civilian rule took place in 1981. Obote was the newly returned victor but his government proved as unsatisfactory as its predecessors, with positions and favours going to some ethnic groups and not others. Once again the country descended into violence along ethnic lines and Obote was deposed in an army coup led by Tito Okello in 1985.

He in turn was soon under pressure from Yoweri Museveni, leader of the National Resistance Army (NRA), who wanted anyone who had been involved in earlier atrocities to go on trial. The NRA took overall control of Kampala in 1986, Okello's army fled and Museveni has since presided over a more settled period in Uganda's history, despite the 'unofficial' invasion of Rwanda in 1990 and the continuing violence of the sectarian Lord's Resistance Army in the north of the country. Following a referendum in 2005, the constitution was amended to legalize opposition parties and delimit presidential terms. Kampala was ravaged by the armed conflict in the 1980s but since then there has been a programme of renovation and improvement.

OBSERVATIONS

Kampala is near Lake Victoria and has a great climate. It is an East African powerhouse of intellectuals and commerce. Like Rome, it is sited on seven hills, with the centre on Nakasero Hill. With its windmill-powered streetlights, Kampala Road is the main high street, bustling with life and commerce.

The grand mosque is on Old Kampala Hill, making an impressive sight when seen from the centre. The university is on Katanga Hill, and the Kasubi Tombs are on Kasubi Hill. This is the sacred site where the Bugandan kings are buried.

Many people live in shanty towns around the capital. Like Kibera in Nairobi, they consist of single-storey interlocking bungalows, whose roofs make small courtyards and spaces that are protected from the harsh sun. They are constructed from mud brick or concrete block, with corrugated iron sheeting for the roof.

NATIONAL POPULATION

39,032,000

CITY POPULATION

1,936,000

ETHNIC GROUPS

Baganda 16.9%, Banyankole 9.5%, Basoga 8.4%, Bakiga 6.9%, Iteso 6.4%, Langi 6.1%, Acholi 4.7%, Bagisu 4.6%, Lugbara 4.2%, Bunyoro 2.7%, other 29.6%

RELIGIONS

Protestant 42% (Anglican 35.9%, Pentecostal 4.6%, Seventh Day Adventist 1.5%), Roman Catholic 41.9%, Muslim 12.1%, other 3.1%, none 0.9%

LANGUAGES

English (official), Ganda or Luganda, other Niger-Congo languages, Nilo-Saharan languages, Swahili, Arabic

GDP

$75.08 billion

AGRICULTURAL PRODUCTS

coffee, tea, cotton, tobacco, cassava (manioc, tapioca), potatoes, corn, millet, pulses, cut flowers; beef, goat meat, milk, poultry

INDUSTRIES

sugar, brewing, tobacco, cotton textiles, cement, steel production

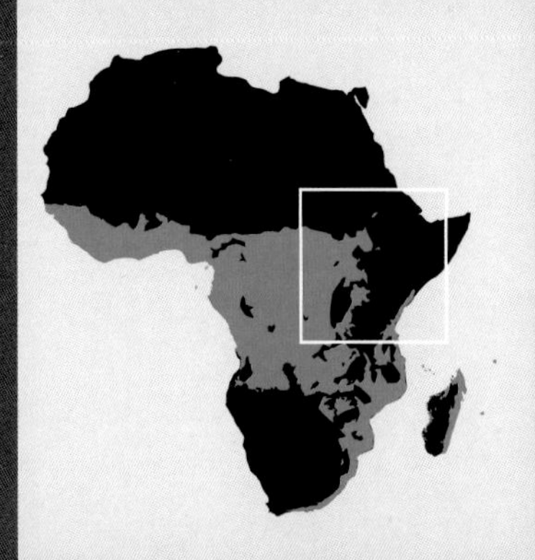

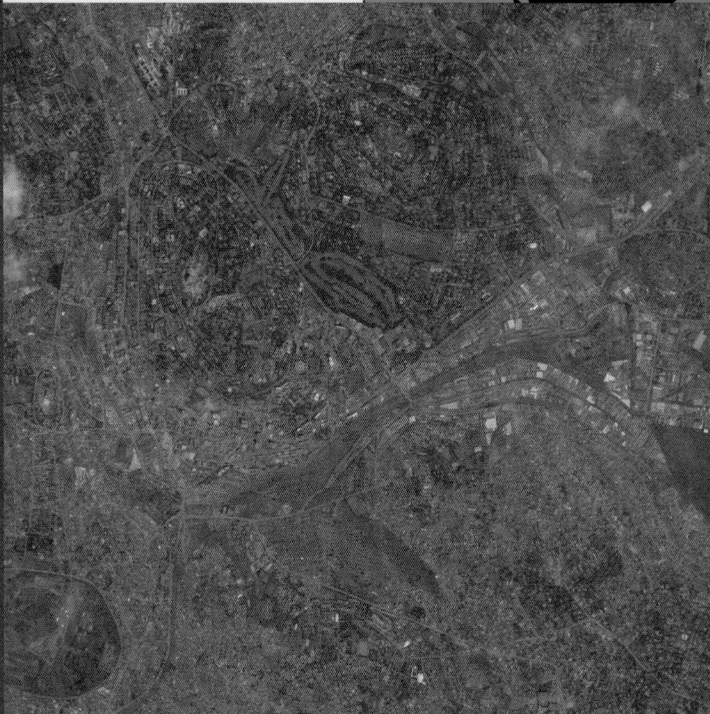

International
Medical

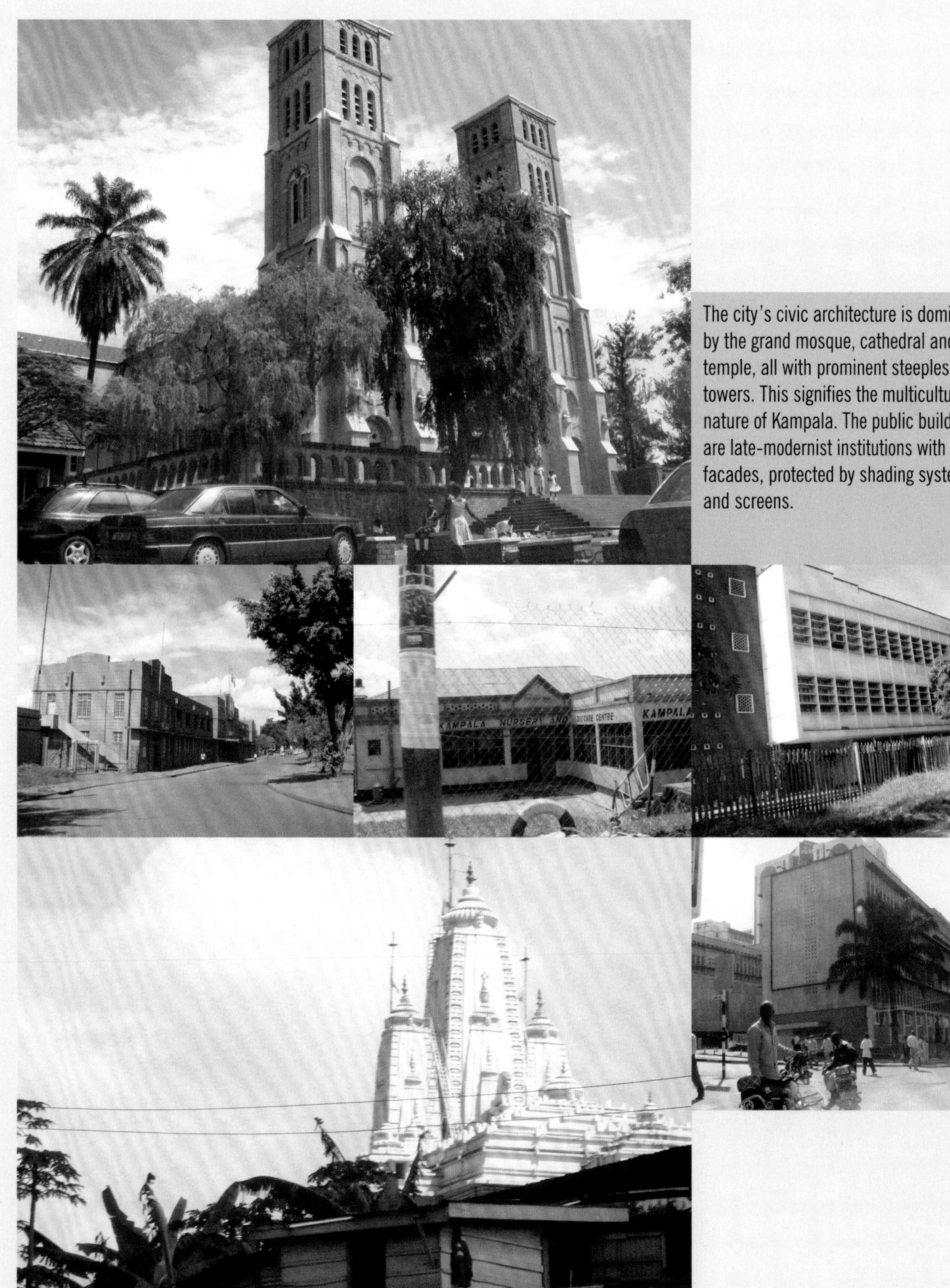

The city's civic architecture is dominated by the grand mosque, cathedral and sikh temple, all with prominent steeples and towers. This signifies the multicultural nature of Kampala. The public buildings are late-modernist institutions with austere facades, protected by shading systems and screens.

Kampala was an important city after independence and, with the refurbishment of its colonial heritage and new commercial buildings, it is attempting to recapture the progressive spirit of that time. Tables and awnings are used for informal trading.

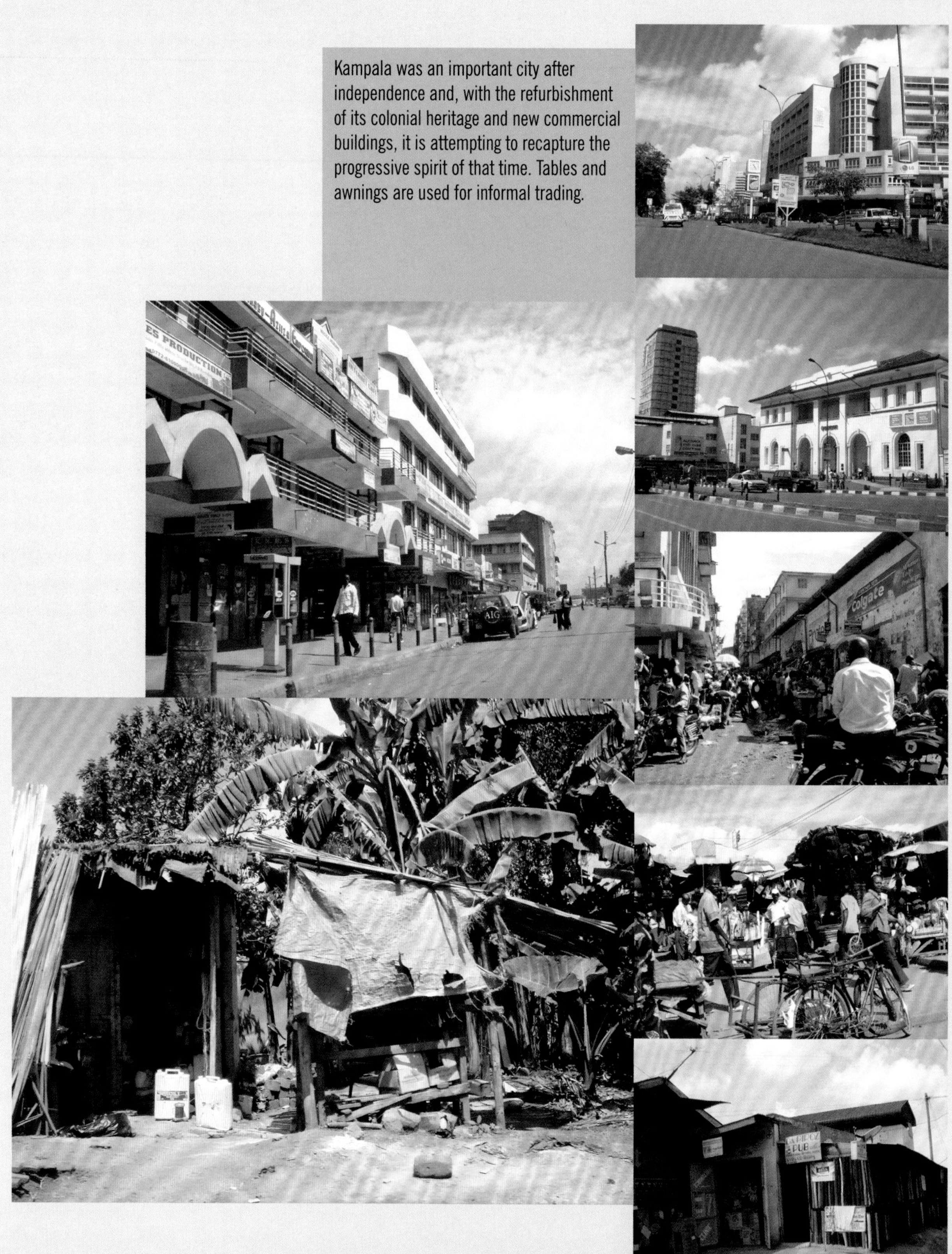

People live in houses and apartment buildings, or shantytowns that resemble village architecture that has been built from industrial materials. The wealthy homes, often with unfinished external walls, are separated from the centre by Centenary Park and the golf course.

KINSHASA / DEMOCRATIC REPUBLIC OF THE CONGO

OVERVIEW

The Democratic Republic of the Congo is home to many ethnic groups, of whom the Kongo are the most numerous. They came to prominence when the Kongo Kingdom controlled the lands to the north and south of the Congo River, and held sway over the surrounding kingdoms from the 12th to the 16th centuries. After Diogo Cão had explored the mouth of the Congo River, the Portuguese made contact with the leader of the Kongo and were able to buy slaves for their farms on the island of São Tomé. As the slave trade increased, it undermined the older kingdoms and they fell into disarray. But the greatest tragedy occurred in the 19th century, when King Léopold II of Belgium decided to acquire an empire and commissioned Henry Morton Stanley, the Welsh explorer, to visit the Congo valley and sign treaties with local leaders that would give control of their land to a holding company. Léopold and his partners were primarily interested in commercial exploitation and they systematically abused local people. This caused an international outcry and in 1908 a commission of enquiry paid Léopold 50 million francs to hand over his interests to the Belgian state.

Despite discussion of independence in the 1950s, Belgium did little to prepare the country for an orderly hand over and left abruptly in 1960, creating an immediate power vacuum. Patrice Lumumba, leader of the Mouvement National Congolais (Congolese National Movement), was the first prime minister and Joseph Kasa-Vubu was made president. Two weeks after independence an army mutiny spread across the country and caused political chaos. Lumumba was captured, transferred to the secessionist state of Katanga and executed. Following a major intervention by a United Nations peacekeeping force, Moise Tshombe won the elections in 1965. His time in power was limited due to an army coup at the end of the year which overthrew Kasa-Vubu and brought Joseph Mobutu to power. Mobutu used the army to suppress dissent and proceeded to rename places and institutions in order to obliterate all traces of the colonial past (he renamed the country Zaire). As in other countries, the stranglehold of one man and his army was thrown into question by the end of the Cold War and gave Western countries the opportunity to link financial aid to the possibility of democratic government. Multiparty elections were scheduled for 1991 but had to be suspended due to riots in Kinshasa by unpaid soldiers. Although some reforms did take place, Mobutu's days were numbered when he supported the Hutu side during the 1994 genocide in Rwanda and, in doing so, antagonized the Tutsis in his own country. Supported by Rwandan and Ugandan troops, the Tutsis marched on Kinshasa in 1996. As Mobutu fled the country, he was replaced by the leader of the rebels, Laurent Kabila. After his rise to power, Kabila turned against the Tutsis and led the country into a civil war that he would have lost if he had not received assistance from Angola and Zimbabwe. The war was effectively ended when Kabila was assassinated in 2001 and succeeded by his son. Joseph Kabila moved quickly to set up a transitional government and, despite ongoing conflicts with various rebel groups, he won the elections in 2006 and 2011. As the colonial capital, Kinshasa was known as Léopoldville when it was founded by Stanley in 1881.

OBSERVATIONS

The third largest city in Africa, and capital of a vast jewel of a country, was the home of my favourite resistance leader after Nkrumah, Patrice Lumumba. Its organization is based on the French system of *quartiers*, of which there are twenty-four – where the larger numbers designate areas for future development.

The city is set on the floor of the valley and connects the banks of the river on either side of a bend. The main axis is the north–south Boulevard Lumumba, which provides a trajectory into the city. It connects the airport to the centre, where it intersects with the Boulevard du 30 Juin, which commemorates independence. Brazzaville, capital of the Republic of the Congo, stands on the other side of the river.

In the centre, the crossings of the boulevards are often the location of public buildings, such as the central post office, the main stadium and the parliament building. They serve to articulate the layout of the city and, together with a few corporate and residential towers, dominate an otherwise horizontal skyline.

NATIONAL POPULATION

77,267,000

CITY POPULATION

11,587,000

ETHNIC GROUPS

Mongo, Luba, Kongo (all Bantu) and the Mangbetu-Azande (Hamitic) 45%, over 200 ethnic groups (of which the majority are Bantu)

RELIGIONS

Roman Catholic 50%, Protestant 20%, Kimbanguist 10%, Muslim 10%, other 10%

LANGUAGES

French (official), Lingala (a lingua franca trade language), Kingwana (a dialect of Kiswahili or Swahili), Kikongo, Tshiluba

GDP

$57.78 billion

AGRICULTURAL PRODUCTS

coffee, sugar, palm oil, rubber, tea, quinine, cassava (manioc, tapioca), bananas, plantains, peanuts, root crops, corn, fruits; wood products

INDUSTRIES

mining (copper, cobalt, gold, diamonds, coltan, zinc, tin, tungsten), mineral processing, consumer products (textiles, footwear, cigarettes, processed foods and beverages), timber, cement, commercial ship repair

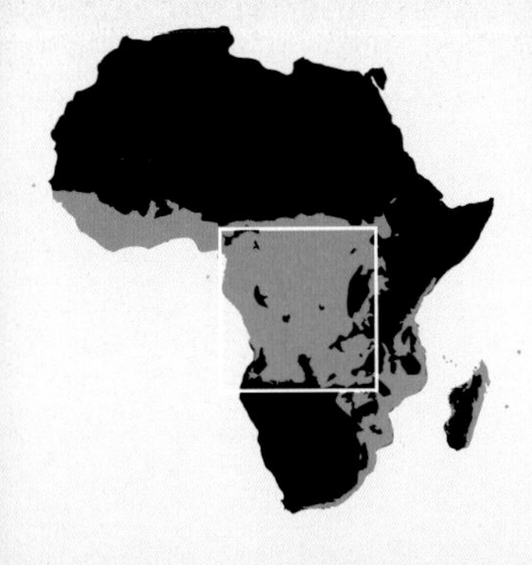

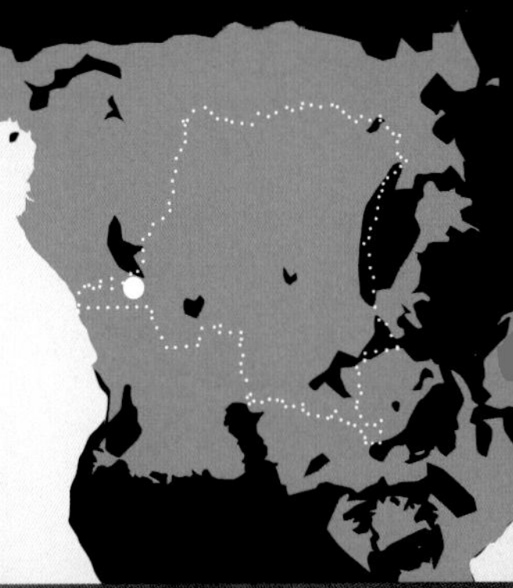

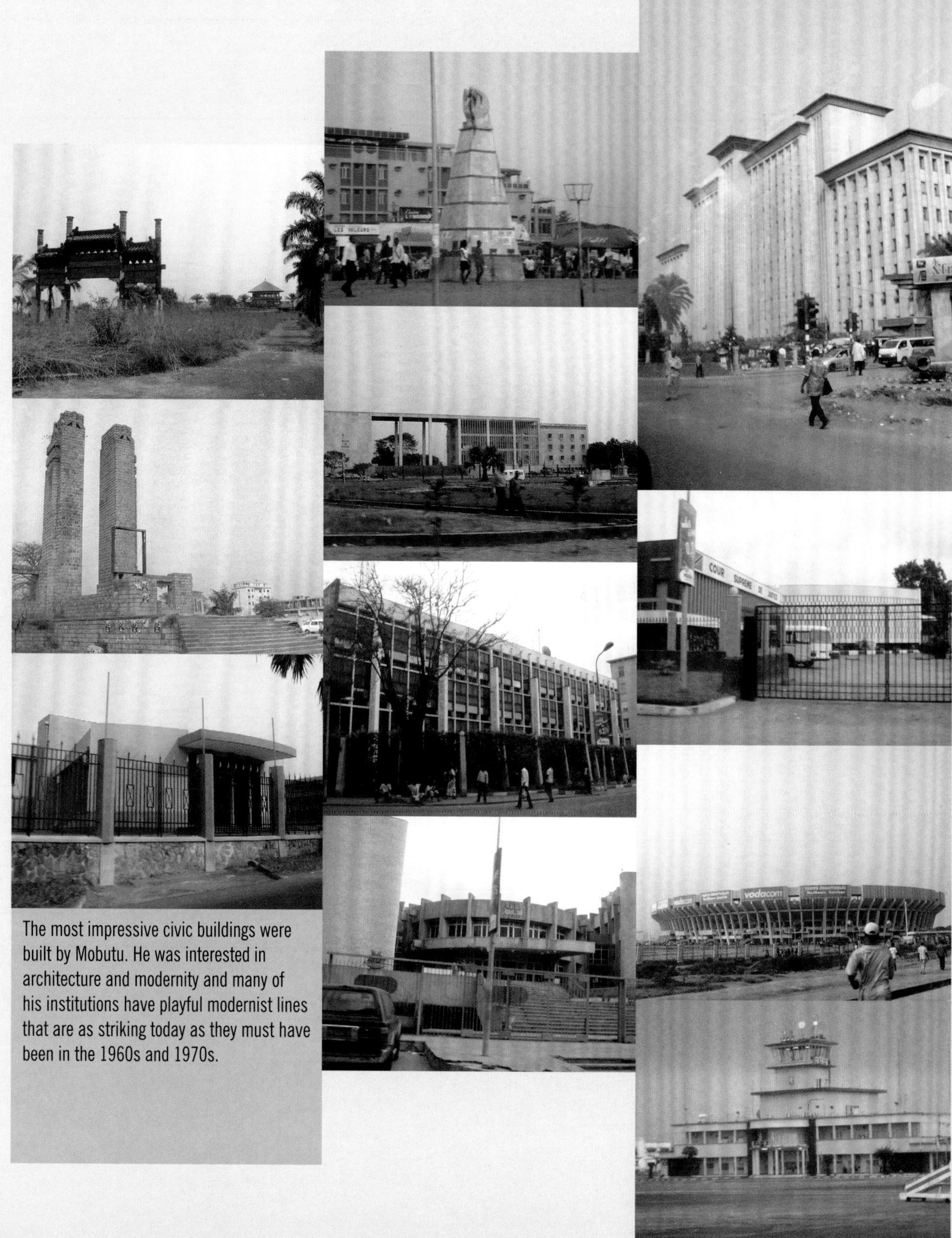

The most impressive civic buildings were built by Mobutu. He was interested in architecture and modernity and many of his institutions have playful modernist lines that are as striking today as they must have been in the 1960s and 1970s.

KINSHASA / DEMOCRATIC REPUBLIC OF THE CONGO / **UNIVERSITY**

The university is a further example of Mobutu's commitment to architecture. Set in the hills, with excellent views of the city, it is a tropical paradise devoted to study. This modernism is distinctly Belgian, concentrating on weight, order, rhythm, and sometimes employing extremely long lines.

Despite the large scale of the city, many of the commercial buildings are quite modest in their intentions. The best street is in the Matonge area, with its large diaspora of West Africans. Here you see lively signage and graphics amid the hustle and bustle of commerce, loud music and haggling.

KINSHASA / DEMOCRATIC REPUBLIC OF THE CONGO / **RESIDENTIAL**

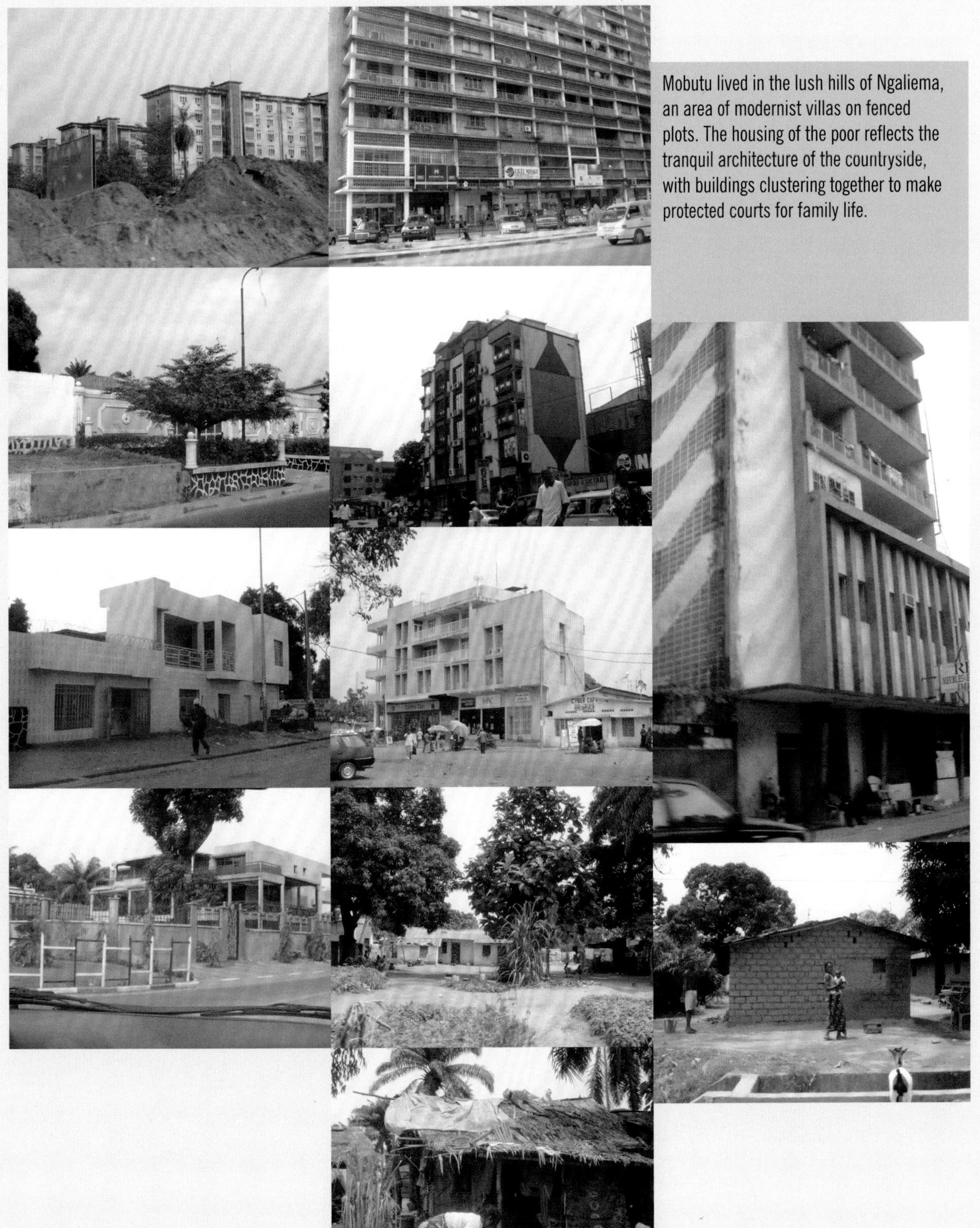

Mobutu lived in the lush hills of Ngaliema, an area of modernist villas on fenced plots. The housing of the poor reflects the tranquil architecture of the countryside, with buildings clustering together to make protected courts for family life.

LIBREVILLE / GABON

OVERVIEW

The valley of the Ogooué River has been inhabited for over 9,000 years but the Pygmies, who arrived from central Africa in the 12th century CE, have lived in the country longer than any other people who live there. At a later date they were partially displaced by Bantu, and by Fang people who invaded the southwest of Gabon. The first Europeans to arrive were the Portuguese. They explored the coast in 1474, and in the following centuries the British, Dutch and French purchased slaves here without venturing into the interior. In an effort to prevent further trading in slaves, the French established a base on the Ogooué estuary in 1839 and ten years later Libreville was founded as a settlement for freed slaves. French interests in Gabon were recognized at the Berlin conference in 1884. The country was incorporated into the French Congo, with Pierre de Brazza as the first governor, before becoming part of French Equatorial Africa in 1910. As the colonial apparatus fell into place, the Gabonese expressed their resentment in local rebellions and attacks on the French, which were gradually suppressed over the next twenty years. For their part, the French sold concessions to harvest rubber by forced labour but business did not prosper and there was little investment in the country's infrastructure.

Since independence in 1960, the history of Gabon has been dominated by El Hadj Omar Bongo who became president in 1967, following the death of the first president, Léon M'ba. Born in 1935, Bongo was a member of the Mouvement Socialiste Africain (African Socialist Movement) and once in power, he founded the Parti Democratique Gabonais (Gabon Democratic Party) as the basis for a single-party state that survived for twenty-two years. This arrangement was not without its critics; the Mouvement de Redressement National (Movement for National Renewal), for instance, claimed that the interests of some ethnic groups were being repeatedly overlooked. Bongo's ambition was to build a uniquely prosperous African state and this was brought within reach by the discovery of oil in the 1970s. But the strength of the economy was undermined by increased imports and by Bongo's commitment to projects that consumed large amounts of capital, such as the construction of the Transgabonais Railway between Libreville and Franceville completed in 1987. As the economy went into decline, the demonstrations against Bongo's government became increasingly forceful and in 1989 he agreed to the introduction of a multiparty system. Despite continuing opposition from the Parti Gabonais du Progrès (Gabon Progressive Party), Bongo remained in power to become the longest-serving leader in Africa. Following the low turnout of voters in the 2001 elections and suspicions of irregularities in the poll, he included members of the opposition in the new government and committed himself to eradicate corruption and poverty. In line with Africa Union policies, he has also taken steps to strengthen the country's economic independence from France. When Bongo died in 2009, his son Ali Ben Bongo won the following elections and assumed the presidency. From a modest start, Libreville now stretches a considerable distance along the north coast of the Gabon Estuary. Its population expanded rapidly when people were attracted by the developing oil industry: from 31,000 at independence, it has reached 707,000.

OBSERVATIONS

Gabon is a Francophone country and Libreville is a French-African riviera city with long beaches. It is organized along the waterfront with a series of perpendicular boulevards stretching into the interior, where the commercial and government centres are located. The buildings range in style from the classic modernism of the senate, the regional contextualism of some government offices, the late 1970s verticality of the finance building, through to the postmodernism of the state television building.

Libreville is a modern city with good infrastructure, including ATMs and internet access, buildings of widely different quality, and houses and apartment blocks that enjoy spectacular views of the Atlantic. Because of the ocean and the beaches, there are no parks in the city.

Given the relatively small size of the city, the contrast between poor and wealthy is more marked than one would expect. There is very little colonial architecture left and most of the buildings are from the 1960s or later. The few remaining examples of commercial and civic modernism set a clear aspiration for later projects.

NATIONAL POPULATION

1,725,000

CITY POPULATION

707,000

ETHNIC GROUPS

Bantu tribes (including four major tribal groupings: Fang, Bapounou, Nzebi, Obamba) 91%, other Africans and European (including French and persons of dual nationality) 9%

RELIGIONS

Catholic 41.9%, Protestant 13.7%, other Christian 32.4%, Muslim 6.4%, animist 0.3%, other 0.3%, none/unspecified 5%

LANGUAGES

French (official), Fang, Myene, Nzebi, Bapounou/Eschira, Bandjabi

GDP

$32.91 billion

AGRICULTURAL PRODUCTS

cocoa, coffee, sugar, palm oil, rubber; cattle; okoume (a tropical softwood); fish

INDUSTRIES

petroleum extraction and refining, mining (manganese, gold), chemicals, ship repair, food and beverages, textiles, plywood, cement

LIBREVILLE / GABON / **CIVIC**

The civic architecture of the city is very grand and somewhat imperial. The presidential palace is a modern, finely proportioned building with gold windows. The 1970s cathedral occupies an elevated site overlooking the ocean, while the main mosque is closely integrated with its surroundings.

There are four main types of commercial architecture: headquarters buildings on the main boulevards, retail units at the base of apartment buildings, new retail sheds on peripheral sites, and informal stalls and markets that can be found throughout the city.

LIBREVILLE / GABON / **RESIDENTIAL**

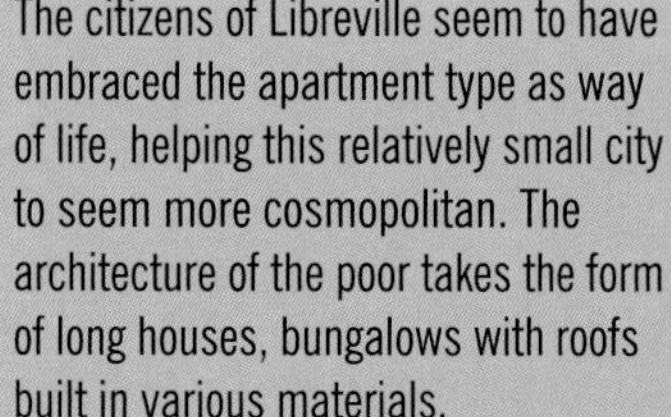

The citizens of Libreville seem to have embraced the apartment type as way of life, helping this relatively small city to seem more cosmopolitan. The architecture of the poor takes the form of long houses, bungalows with roofs built in various materials.

LILONGWE / MALAWI

OVERVIEW

After the San people, or Bushmen, had been displaced by Bantu tribes, the Maravi people established a powerful kingdom in the south of what is now Malawi in the late 15th century. The first Europeans to arrive were the Portuguese in the 16th century, taking advantage of the already extensive slave trade. Demand for slaves increased dramatically at the end of the 18th century and Yao people, who had migrated from Mozambique, collaborated with Swahili Arab traders to capture people from other ethnic groups. The Zulu took over the south of the country in the 19th century but it was the Scottish explorer and missionary David Livingstone who would have the most significant impact on the country. With the aim of introducing Christianity and undermining the local slave trade, he founded the Universities Mission to Central Africa and, having reached Lake Malawi in 1861, he returned there with seven missionaries. Trading companies such as the African Lakes Corporation also countered the activities of the slave traders. In 1891 the British Central African Protectorate was extended to include the area west of Lake Malawi and became the colony of Nyasaland in 1907. The slave trade was eliminated and the conflict between different ethnic groups was brought to an end. But as European settlers took over the land an increasing number of Africans were displaced and many of them migrated to what are now Zambia and Zimbabwe.

One of the first opponents of colonialism was John Chilembwe who spoke out against the conscription of Africans into the British army in the First World War. In 1915, with the intention of starting an uprising, he and his supporters killed an estate manager but their actions were quickly suppressed and Chilembwe was executed. But resentment against the British continued and was brought into focus when Hastings Banda revived the Nyasaland African Congress in the early 1950s. He was promptly jailed, only to be released in 1960 to become head of the Malawi Congress Party, which won the election in 1962. Nyasaland was renamed Malawi and became a republic in 1966, with Banda as president. After taking power Banda forced many of his opponents into exile and banned other parties. As a conservative, he refused to condemn apartheid in South Africa and it reciprocated with financial support. Banda maintained his domination until the 1990s. Following public unrest and criticism of him by Catholic bishops, a referendum in 1993 came down heavily in favour of a multiparty system. The 1994 election was won by the United Democratic Front (UDF) under Bakili Muluzi. His government pursued more open policies and initiated a programme of economic reforms that had the effect of inflating the cost of living and increasing unemployment. Despite claims of election rigging and corruption, Muluzi and the UDF remained in power until 2004. The results of the following election were questioned but the UDF's Bingu wa Mutharika was sworn in as president and won a second term in 2009. He died in 2012 and was succeeded by Joyce Banda of the People's Party who lost the 2014 election to Peter Mutharika, Bingu wa's brother. Lilongwe was an important centre during British rule and succeeded Blantyre as the capital in 1975.

OBSERVATIONS

Lilongwe is about an hour's drive from the amazing freshwater Lake Malawi, and is still being built. Due to the relatively low density, its daily life is more discreet than other African cities. The most active streets are in the old town and around the market, where traders protect their stalls with elaborate shade structures.

The market is highly informal in its construction. Timber, card and plastic are used to protect the vendors and their goods and these structures interlock with each other to form a network of spaces that have a unique architectural quality. The market is split between food on one side of the river and goods on the other, and delicate toll bridges, built by construction gangs, span the river with ease.

The houses of the wealthy are very elegant and contribute to the identity of the whole place. They normally employ a rectangular geometry but occasionally it is circular. The poor and informal housing returns to the village vernacular. These settlements are in better shape than examples in other cities. They are organized on a similar basis to traditional villages, with central areas, clusters and different kinds of enclosure.

NATIONAL POPULATION

17,215,000

CITY POPULATION

905,000

ETHNIC GROUPS

Chewa 32.6%, Lomwe 17.6%, Yao 13.5%, Ngoni 11.5%, Tumbuka 8.8%, Nyanja 5.8%, Sena 3.6%, Tonga 2.1%, Ngonde 1%, other 3.5%

RELIGIONS

Christian 82.6%, Muslim 13%, other 1.9%, none 2.5%

LANGUAGES

English (official), Chichewa (common), Chinyanja, Chiyao, Chitumbuka, Chilomwe, Chinkhonde, Chingoni, Chisena, Chitonga, Chinyakyusa, Chilambya

GDP

$19.58 billion

AGRICULTURAL PRODUCTS

tobacco, sugarcane, cotton, tea, corn, potatoes, cassava (manioc, tapioca), sorghum, pulses, groundnuts, macadamia nuts; cattle, goats

INDUSTRIES

tobacco, tea, sugar, sawmill products, cement, consumer goods

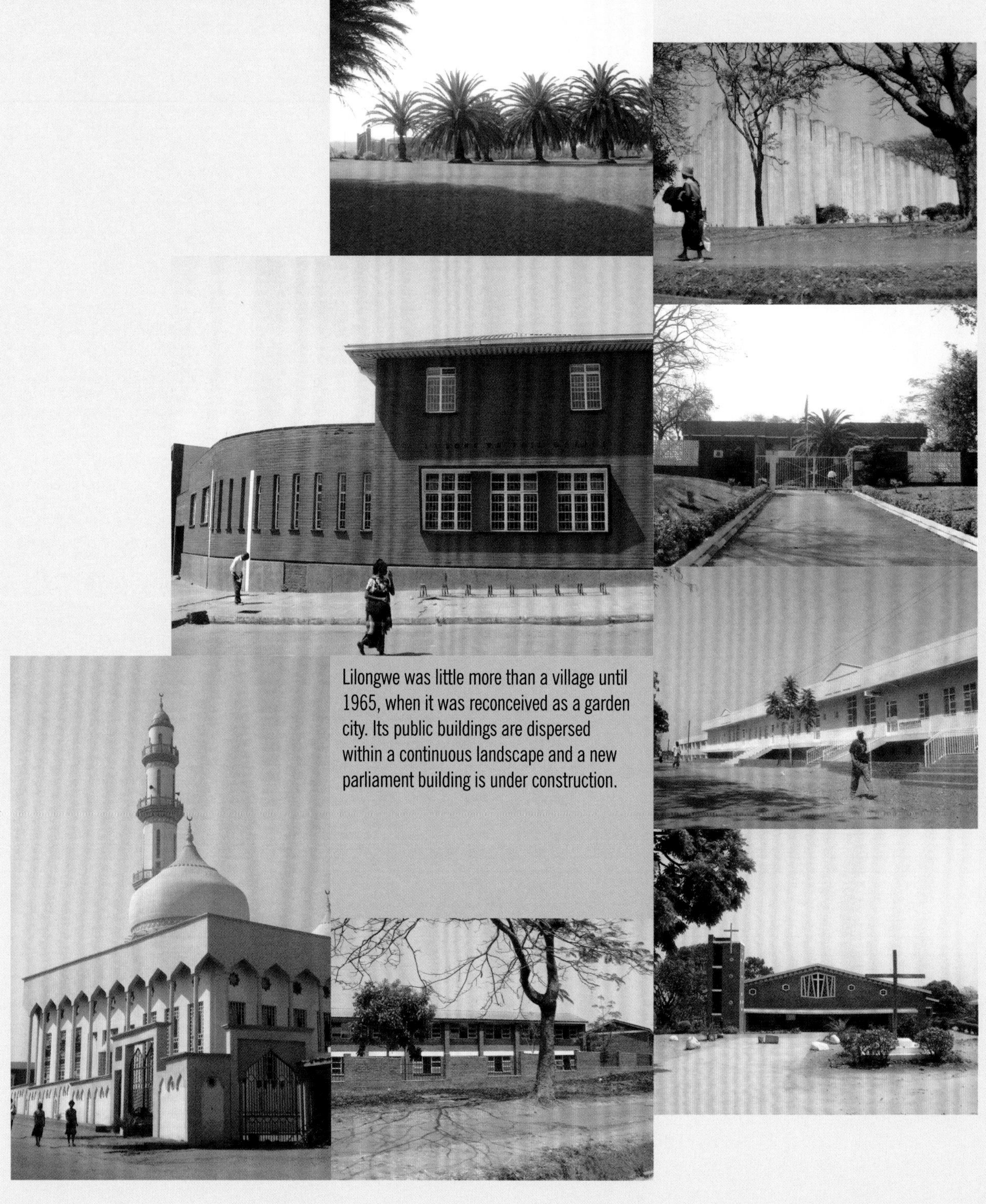

Lilongwe was little more than a village until 1965, when it was reconceived as a garden city. Its public buildings are dispersed within a continuous landscape and a new parliament building is under construction.

LILONGWE / MALAWI / **COMMERCIAL**

There is shopping in the old town, the new malls, or the market on either side of the river. Many of the shops in the old town are single storey with colonnades. Later buildings are painted bright colours and carry advertising.

High walls often screen the homes of the better-off, as if they fear being attacked. The houses of the poor employ traditional materials, such as mud bricks and thatch. They are painted in earth colours, sometimes with white porch areas, and form small hamlets.

LOMÉ / TOGO

OVERVIEW

The Togolese are descendants of the Mina and Guin peoples from the west and the Ewe people from the east, who arrived between the 11th and 16th centuries. The position and shape of the country means that its history has always been closely linked to that of its neighbours. In the medieval period it was on the edge of the Dahomey Kingdom, in future Benin, and on the edge of the Akan–Ashanti Kingdom, in future Ghana. With the development of the slave trade, Togoland, as it was then called, provided a route to inland areas where slaves could be captured. As this trade declined the European powers became interested in exploiting the resources of these countries and Germany laid claim to Togoland in 1884. With the intention of cultivating cash crops, they set about the economic development of the country but were unpopular with the indigenous population because of their taxes and forced labour. The German presence was relatively short-lived due to the First World War, when German troops in Togoland surrendered to French and British troops. After the war the League of Nations divided the country between France, which acquired the eastern section, and Britain. There was considerable discontent at the way in which the Ewe population was arbitrarily split by this arrangement, which became permanent in 1956 when the British section was incorporated into the future Ghana.

French Togoland became the independent Republic of Togo in 1960, with Sylvanus Olympio as the first president, and has the distinction of having the first postindependence coup in Africa. Olympio's time in office was marked by disputes with President Nkrumah of Ghana over the position of their mutual boundary and with Togolese soldiers who had recently served in the French army. One of these, Gnassingbé Eyadéma, was involved in his assassination in 1963. When the border dispute led to civil unrest in 1967, he finally seized power and set out to unify the country through the creation of a single trade union and a single party, the Rassemblement du Peuple Togolais (Rally of the Togolese People). He would remain in power for nearly forty years but after his private plane crashed in 1974 he believed that he had been the target of an attempted assassination and became more isolated and despotic. In the 1990s there was pressure to move towards multiparty government, which Eyadéma resisted. Strikes and demonstrations were severely dealt with by the army and, to draw attention to the repressive regime, twenty-eight bodies were pulled out of the lagoon in Lomé and dumped at the US embassy. At a conference in 1991 Eyadéma was stripped of his powers but the interim government was short-lived as troops loyal to Eyadéma detained his successor and returned him to power. The remainder of the 1990s and the early part of this century were taken up by the continuing power struggle between Eyadéma and the opposition movement. When he died in 2005, the military backed his son Faure Gnassingbé to succeed him and his success in the following election provoked riots; hundreds of people were killed in Lomé and thousands fled to Benin and Ghana. Since then his commitment to open government has won widespread support and he won further elections in 2010 and 2015. Lomé is situated on a narrow strip of land between Lake Togo and the Gulf of Guinea.

OBSERVATIONS

The city is laid out to the north of the coast road, with large avenues that define the different quarters. The older streets are mainly used for commercial purposes and the civic buildings are located in an extension to the central area that was started in the 1960s.

The beach is the city's public promenade. Broad, with good sand, it is separated from the coast road by palm trees. Along its length are various informal markets and it is overlooked by the presidential palace.

NATIONAL POPULATION

7,305,000

CITY POPULATION

956,000

ETHNIC GROUPS

African (37 tribes; largest and most important are Ewe, Mina and Kabye) 99%, European and Syrian-Lebanese less than 1%

RELIGIONS

Christian 29%, Muslim 20%, indigenous beliefs 51%

LANGUAGES

French (official), Ewe and Mina (in the south), Kabye and Dagomba (in the north)

GDP

$10.16 billion

AGRICULTURAL PRODUCTS

coffee, cocoa, cotton, yams, cassava (manioc, tapioca), corn, beans, rice, millet, sorghum; livestock; fish

INDUSTRIES

mining (phosphate), agricultural processing, cement, handicrafts, textiles, beverages

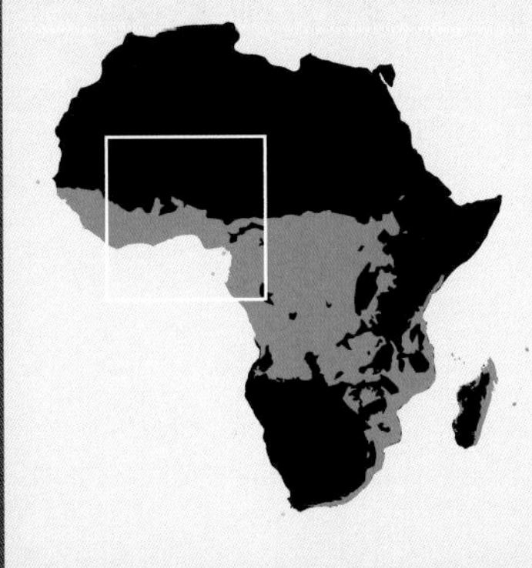

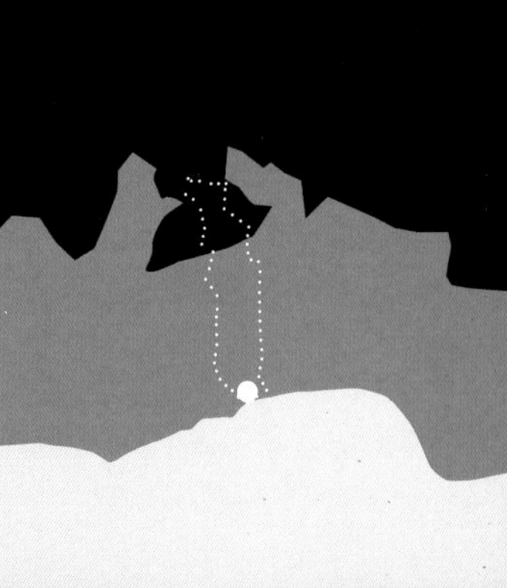

LOMÉ / TOGO / **CIVIC**

In colonial times, this was a waterfront city whose institutions were located on the coast road. Since independence, the centre has moved inland and the public buildings are international style, with a francophone flavour, and stand in manicured landscapes.

MoneyGram
TRANSFERT D'ARGENT INTERNATIONAL

LOMÉ / TOGO / **COMMERCIAL**

Due to its proximity to Ghana, Lomé is a border metropole. While company towers dominate the skyline, the city's gridded plan has different quarters for commerce, market activities and regular shopping.

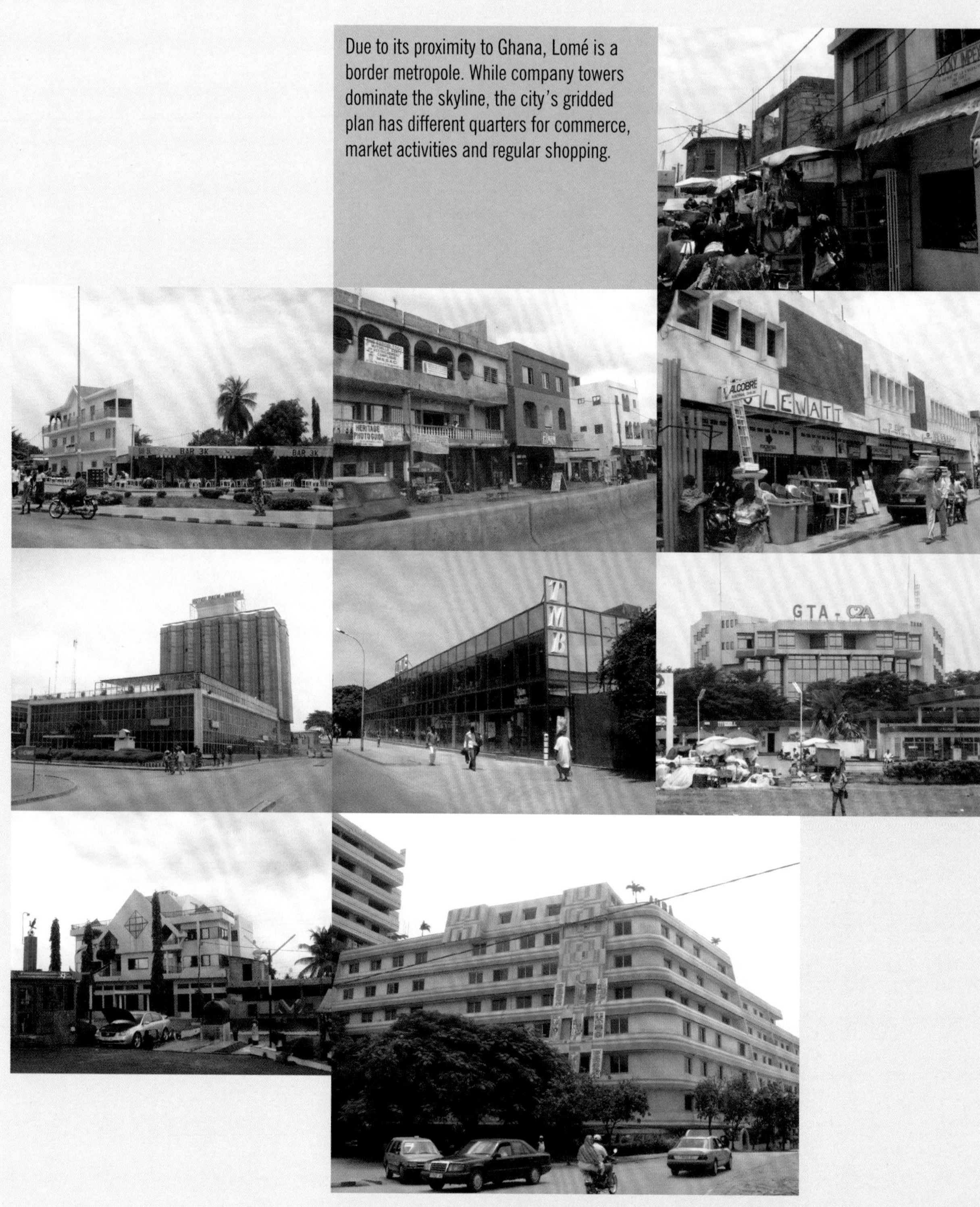

Unlike other African cities, Lomé does not have rich and poor quarters. The homes of football stars are found next to informal housing, making a more equitable environment for everyone. The combination of rich and poor is architecturally interesting.

LUANDA / ANGOLA

OVERVIEW

Vasco da Gama explored the coast of Angola in 1483 but at that stage the Portuguese had little interest in occupying the interior. The Kingdom of Ndongo was an area of subsistence farming dominated by the Mbundu people; it became interesting to the Portuguese only when they noticed that traders from São Tomé were making regular visits to buy slaves from the Ngola, the ruler of the Mbundu. Although Portugal established a base at Luanda in 1575, the colonization of Angola was complicated by a series of disputes: between the settlers and the authorities in Portugal; between the settlers and the Ngolas, especially Ana de Sousa Nzinga, who ruled from 1623 to 1663; and between Portugal and the Dutch. The latter occupied Luanda in 1641, before it was recaptured for the Portuguese by a Brazilian fleet in 1648. Portugal finally gained control of most of Ndongo in 1657. In the 18th century Luanda was exporting more slaves than any other port on the west coast and, by the time of the last shipments early in the 20th century, the total number of slaves to have left Angola was well over three million.

A resistance movement began to take shape after the Second World War but, under the influence of the Salazar dictatorship in Portugal, conditions continued to deteriorate and local rebellions in the early 1960s resulted in massacres by the colonial forces. When the Portuguese administration was finally evacuated in 1975, the government fell into the control of the Movimento Popular de Libertação de Angola (Popular Movement for the Liberation of Angola, MPLA). Based in Luanda, the MPLA was committed to Marxist socialism and enjoyed the support of the USSR, Cuba and ethnic groups in the south of the country. In the north the MPLA was opposed by the Frente Nacional de Libertação de Angola (National Front for the Liberation of Angola, FNLA), which was supported by the Democratic Republic of the Congo and local people. In the central highlands, around Huambo, the União Nacional para la Independência Total de Angola (Union for Total Independence of Angola, UNITA), supported by South Africa, was the dominant force. Over the next fifteen years the country was overtaken by a civil war in which these parties were the main players. When the FNLA surrendered to the MPLA in 1984, UNITA increased the scale of its guerrilla activities, until the collapse of Soviet communism and changes in South Africa provided suitable conditions to resolve the conflict. The elections in 1992 gave a narrow victory to the MPLA and their leader José Eduardo dos Santos but UNITA claimed that there had been irregularities in the voting. Using the income from diamond sales to buy armaments, UNITA returned to guerrilla tactics and set about destroying the country's infrastructure. Their leader was killed in 2002 and, following the amalgamation of UNITA and government forces, a peace plan was signed later that year. Despite his intention to rebuild the country and reconcile conflicting interests, dos Santos's government has been criticized for its record on human rights and its institutional corruption. After bringing in a new constitution in 2010, he won the elections in 2012. Since its days as a colonial capital Luanda has provided a home for many refugees from other parts of the country.

OBSERVATIONS

The city is located on an expansive bay, with a peninsula called 'the Island' stretching 4 miles into the sea. This makes a dramatic setting for a city, providing vantage points and long walks from the island to the mountains behind the city.

The civic architecture of the city forms a garland of neoclassical and modernist buildings along the coast. The commercial area starts immediately behind the seafront and has recently seen a boom in office buildings and towers. The city hall and administrative centre are also located here. Cairo and Tripoli have an amazing apartment culture but Luanda has the most extensive demonstration of this type that I have seen on the continent.

On the edge of the city you encounter the informal settlements resulting from the explosion in the postwar population of the city – five million instead of the half million projected. The government is attempting to replace these settlements with housing estates that take advantage of the city's fine setting. Benfica beach is one of the more popular and people like to spend Sunday there.

NATIONAL POPULATION

25,022,000

CITY POPULATION

5,506,000

ETHNIC GROUPS

Ovimbundu 37%, Kimbundu 25%, Bakongo 13%, mestiço (mixed European and native African) 2%, European 1%, other 22%

RELIGIONS

indigenous beliefs 47%, Roman Catholic 38%, Protestant 15%

LANGUAGES

Portuguese (official), Bantu and other African languages

GDP

$177.3 billion

AGRICULTURAL PRODUCTS

bananas, sugarcane, coffee, sisal, corn, cotton, cassava (manioc, tapioca), tobacco, vegetables, plantains; livestock; forest products; fish

INDUSTRIES

petroleum, mining (diamonds, iron ore, phosphates, feldspar, bauxite, uranium, gold), cement, basic metal products, fish processing, food processing, brewing, tobacco products, sugar, textiles, ship repair

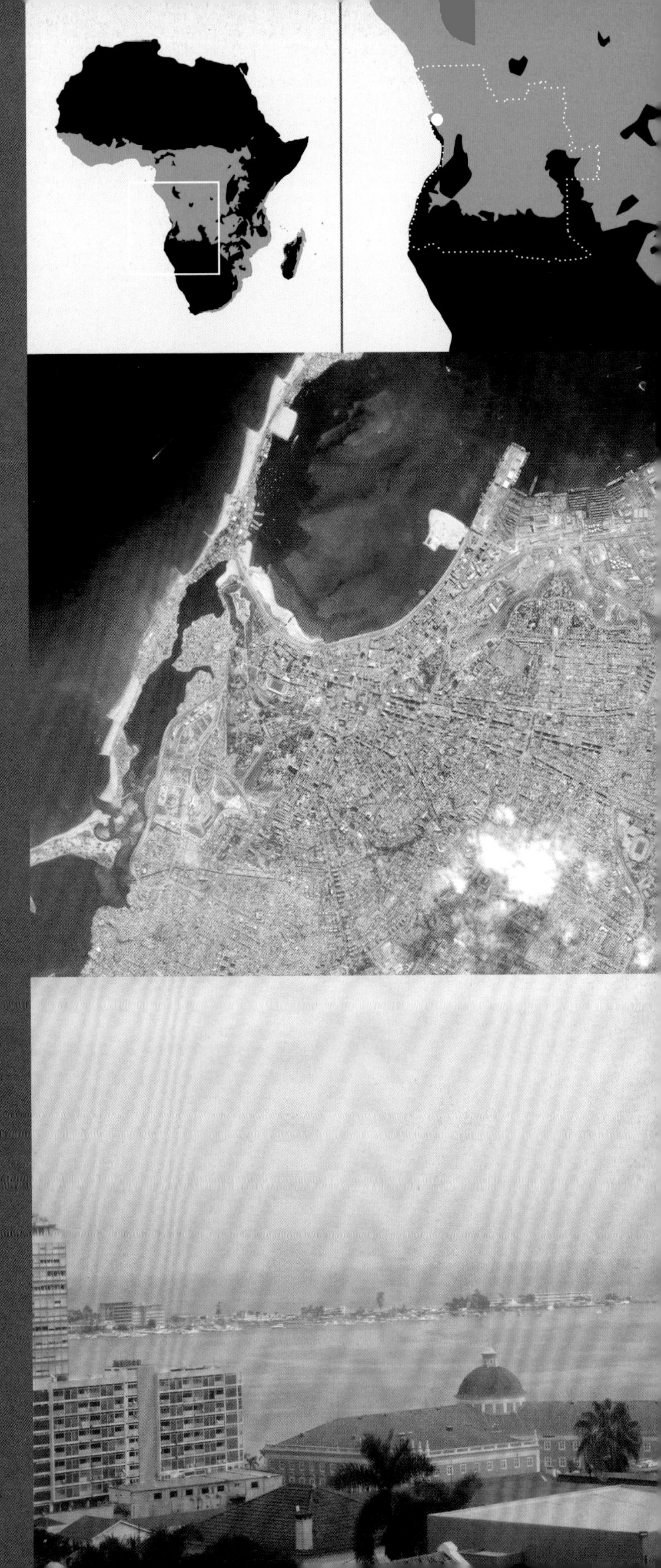

LUANDA / ANGOLA / **CIVIC**

Grand civic structures with elegant proportions, and mid-rise towers on podia, articulate the ground plane and give the city a wonderful architectural heritage. There are beautiful neoclassical and modern churches all over the city.

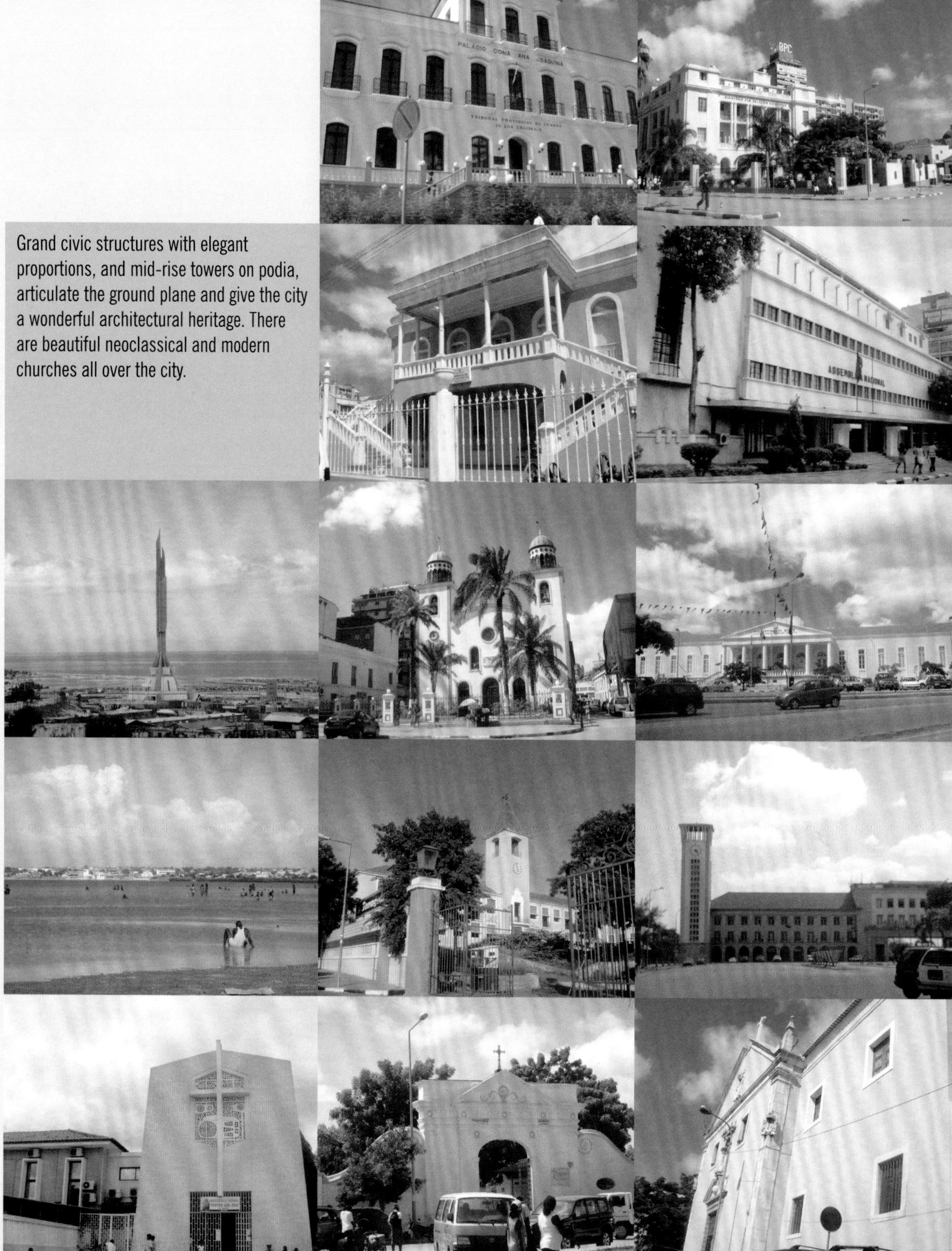

The arcaded streets of the centre have a fine scale and accommodate a variety of uses. They are complemented by an increasing number of higher buildings. With shops and cafes at their base, they make a strong contribution to the streetscape of the city.

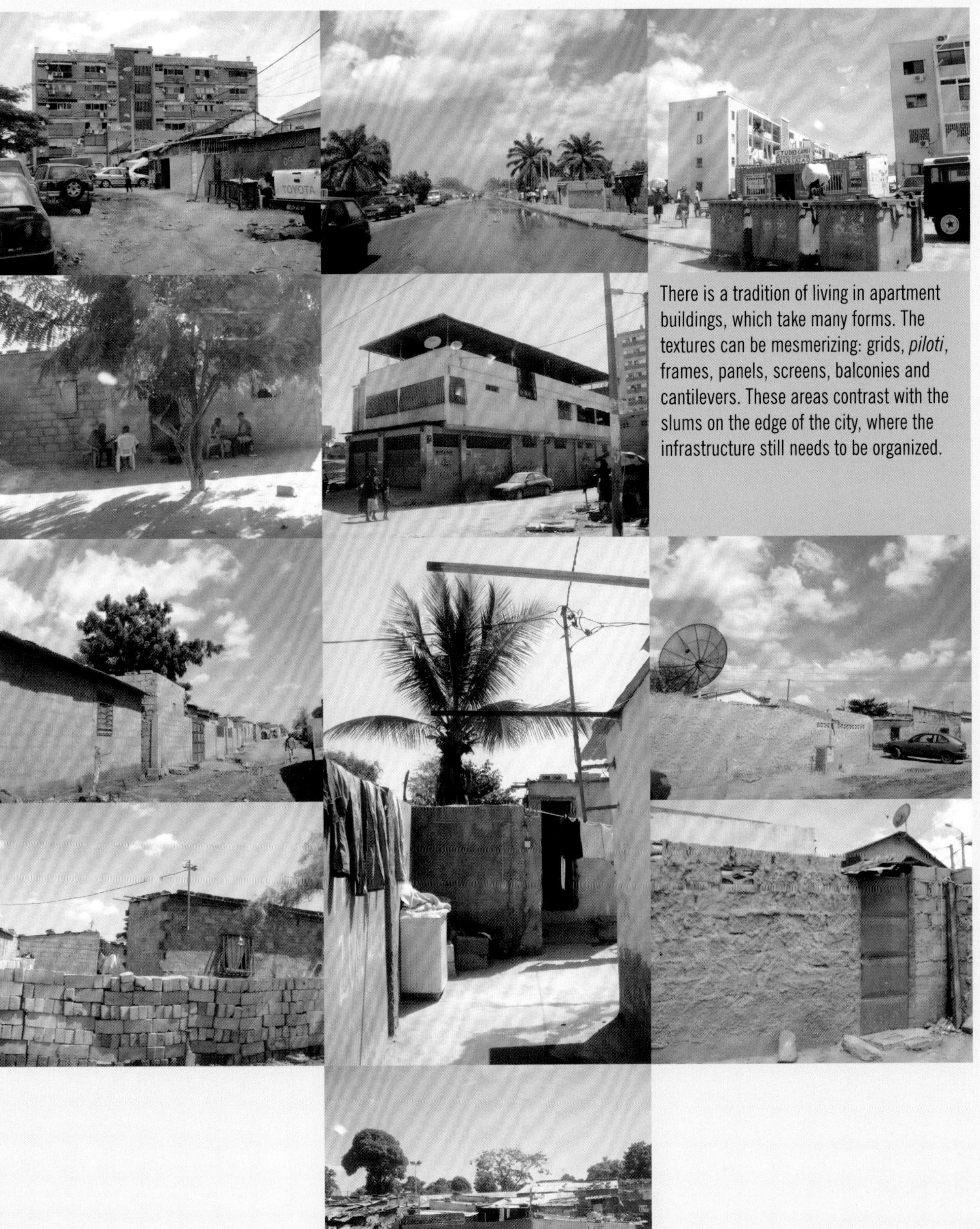

There is a tradition of living in apartment buildings, which take many forms. The textures can be mesmerizing: grids, *piloti*, frames, panels, screens, balconies and cantilevers. These areas contrast with the slums on the edge of the city, where the infrastructure still needs to be organized.

MALABO / EQUATORIAL GUINEA

OVERVIEW

Equatorial Guinea consists of Rio Muni on the mainland and five offshore islands, of which Bioko is the largest and the location of the capital. The Bubi people are indigenous to the area; they colonized Bioko in the 13th century and at that time formed the largest ethnic group on the island, but they have since been partially displaced by several waves of Bantu migrants. Of these, the Fang arrived in the 19th century and now dominate the population. The Portuguese discovered the islands in the early 1470s and occupied Bioko until 1778, when they exchanged their claim to the islands and Rio Muni with Spain for territory in South America. During this period Bioko was an important base for countries involved in the slave trade, a situation that changed only in 1827 when Britain began to use the island for its naval operations against countries that were still trading in slaves. Many of the slaves that were freed in this way settled on the island where, alongside freed slaves from Liberia, they worked in the growing number of cocoa plantations. The Spanish continued to own most of the land on Bioko and in the 1920s they decided to extend their occupation to Rio Muni. The stiff resistance that they encountered from the Fang was symptomatic of the underlying resentment against their regime.

After the Second World War the Spanish took steps to close the gap between their interests and those of the indigenous peoples but could not prevent an independence movement from gathering momentum. Spain finally agreed to independence in 1968 and Francisco Macías Nguema won the elections in 1971 and declared himself president for life. Discovering that the colonial regime had left the country short of resources, the government declared a state of emergency, which created a pretext for the brutal dictatorship that lasted for ten years. Much of the violence was directed at the Bubi people and took place in forced labour camps on the mainland. In 1979 Nguema was deposed by his nephew Teodoro Obiang Nguema Mbasogo and executed a month later. Despite the change of presidency, the country's poor record on human rights continued. Under Obiang all political activity was initially banned. He organized the Democratic Party of Equatorial Guinea in 1987 and changed the constitution to introduce a multiparty system in 1991. Obiang has won all of the subsequent polls but they were boycotted by opposition groups who did not have confidence in their fairness.

The economy has been weak for most of the time since independence. In the 1970s, many Spanish farmers and professionals left the country, leading to a serious contraction in agriculture. In the 1980s, although Spain cancelled two-thirds of Equatorial Guinea's debt, the payments on other debts were increasingly difficult to service and Spain and France stopped their aid programmes in the 1990s due to human rights issues. The discovery of oil in the 1990s should have set the economy on a different course but most of the new wealth remains in Obiang's hands and has not been used to improve the lives of the country's citizens. Although there are still a few colonial buildings in the downtown area, Malabo has become primarily an oil town.

OBSERVATIONS

Located on Bioko Island and surrounded by offshore oil fields, the city faces north to the ocean and turns its back on the volcanic peaks in the south – a dramatic backdrop that contributes to its charm. The waterfront is a working port and oil-handling area.

Due to its its new-found wealth, the old Spanish capital is in a process of transformation. The administrative arm of the government and its ministries are buried in the old part of the city, where the presidential compound, library and cathedral form a civic cluster. Most of the buildings are two to three storeys high, Spanish colonial in style, and make use of bright colours to distinguish themselves from commercial buildings.

The poor housing in the old town is deep within the blocks where clusters of rooms open on to the courts; this is where the lives of the families are played out. Old lanes and grand courts have been skilfully subdivided to accommodate more density, with an additional layer of commerce that springs up to support these new communities. Away from the main streets, there is a second grid of informality only known to the residents.

NATIONAL POPULATION

845,000

CITY POPULATION

187,000

ETHNIC GROUPS

Fang 85.7%, Bubi 6.5%, Mdowe 3.6%, Annobon 1.6%, Bujeba 1.1%, other 1.5%

RELIGIONS

nominally Christian and predominantly Roman Catholic, pagan practices

LANGUAGES

Spanish (official) 67.6%, other 32.4% (includes French (official), Fang, Bubi)

GDP

$28.62 billion

AGRICULTURAL PRODUCTS

coffee, cocoa, rice, yams, cassava (manioc, tapioca), bananas, palm oil nuts; livestock; timber

INDUSTRIES

petroleum, fishing, natural gas, sawmilling

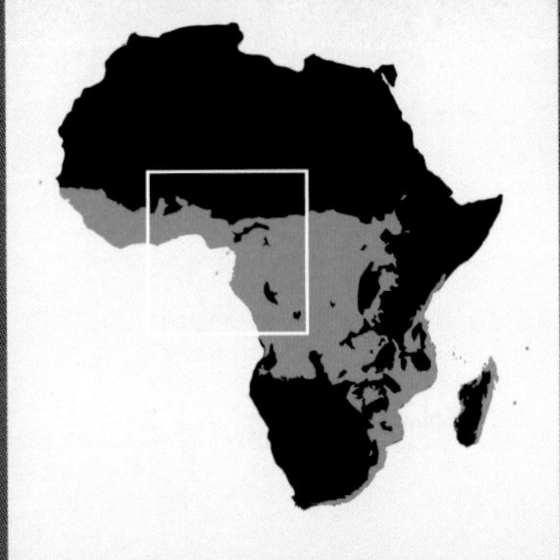

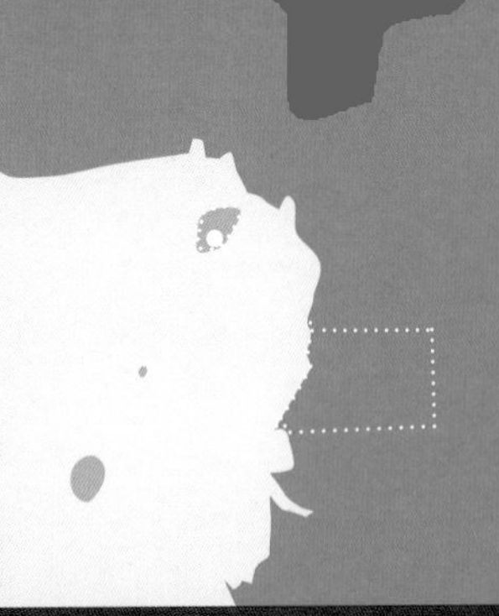

Recent buildings, such as the library and president's offices, are postmodern exercises with a hint of the colonial. A new civic circle, with government offices and an oil tower built by the Chinese, is the symbol of the new Equatorial Guinea.

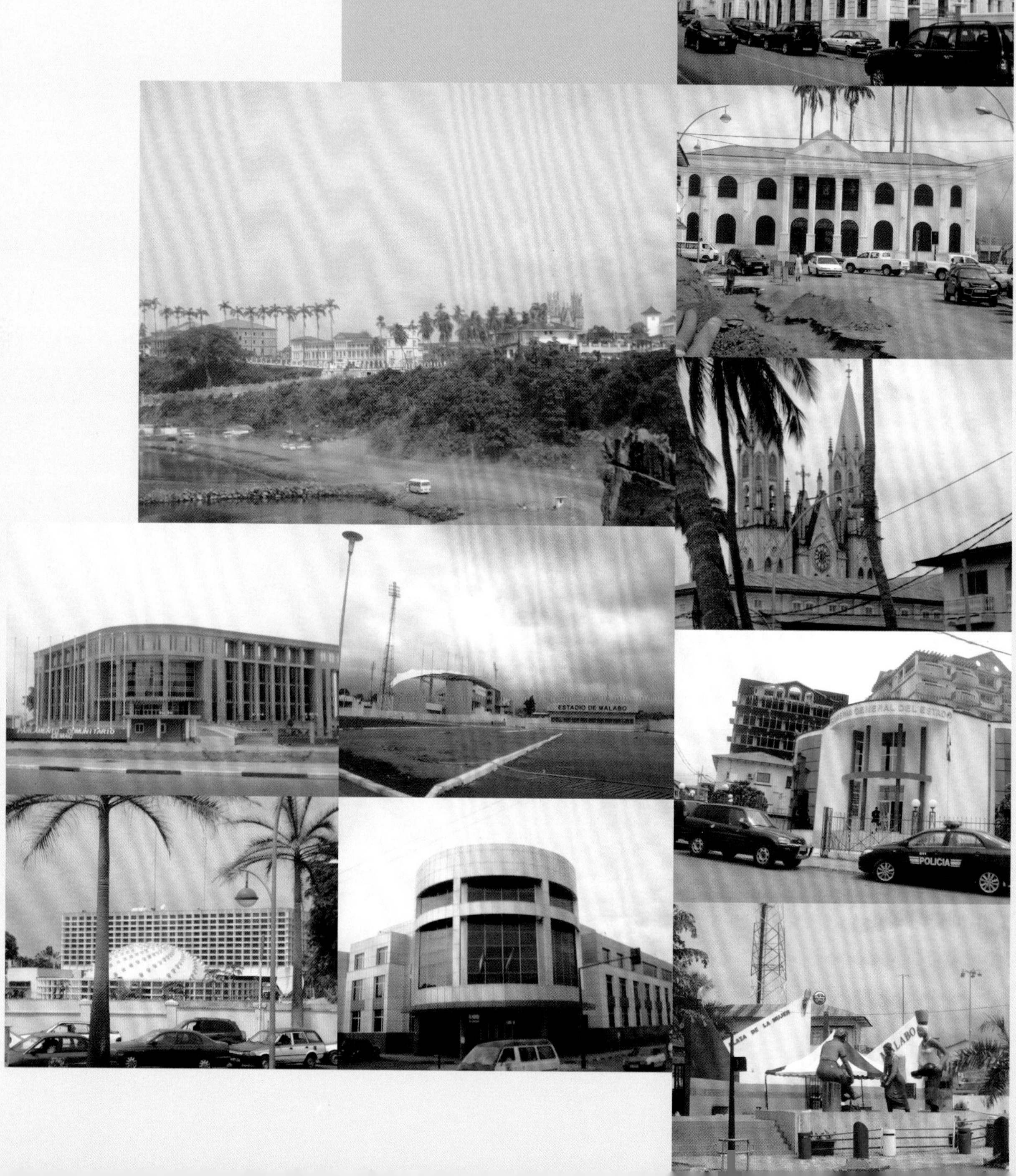

The architecture of the old town, with its projecting bays and balconies, provides plenty of shade for the streets below, whereas the new commercial towers are sealed environments that can only be approached by car.

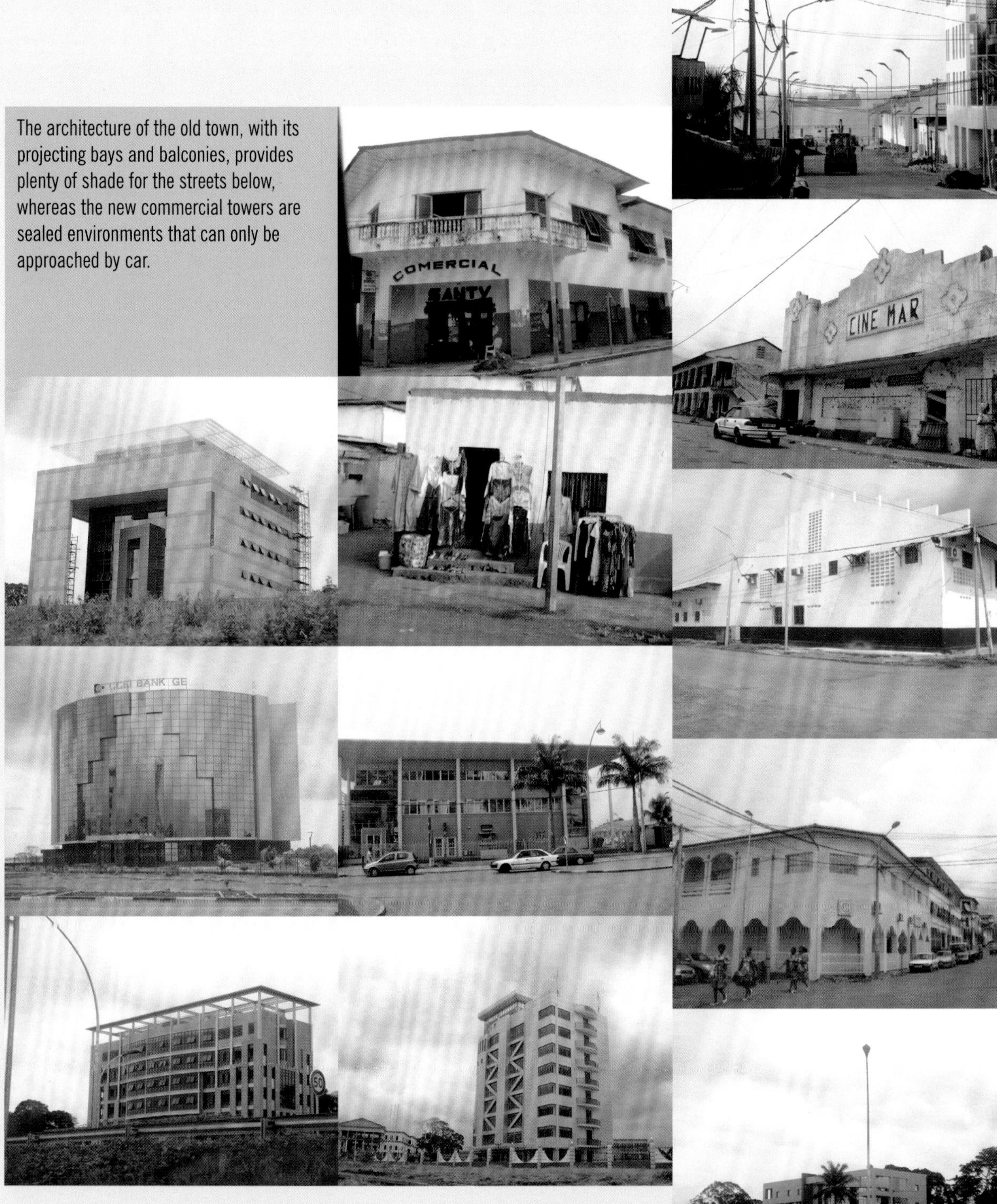

The best colonial houses, facing the ocean, have been taken over by embassies, hotels and clubs. Otherwise, the situation is very polarized with the wealthy in new apartment buildings and gated compounds, and the poor in informal settlements.

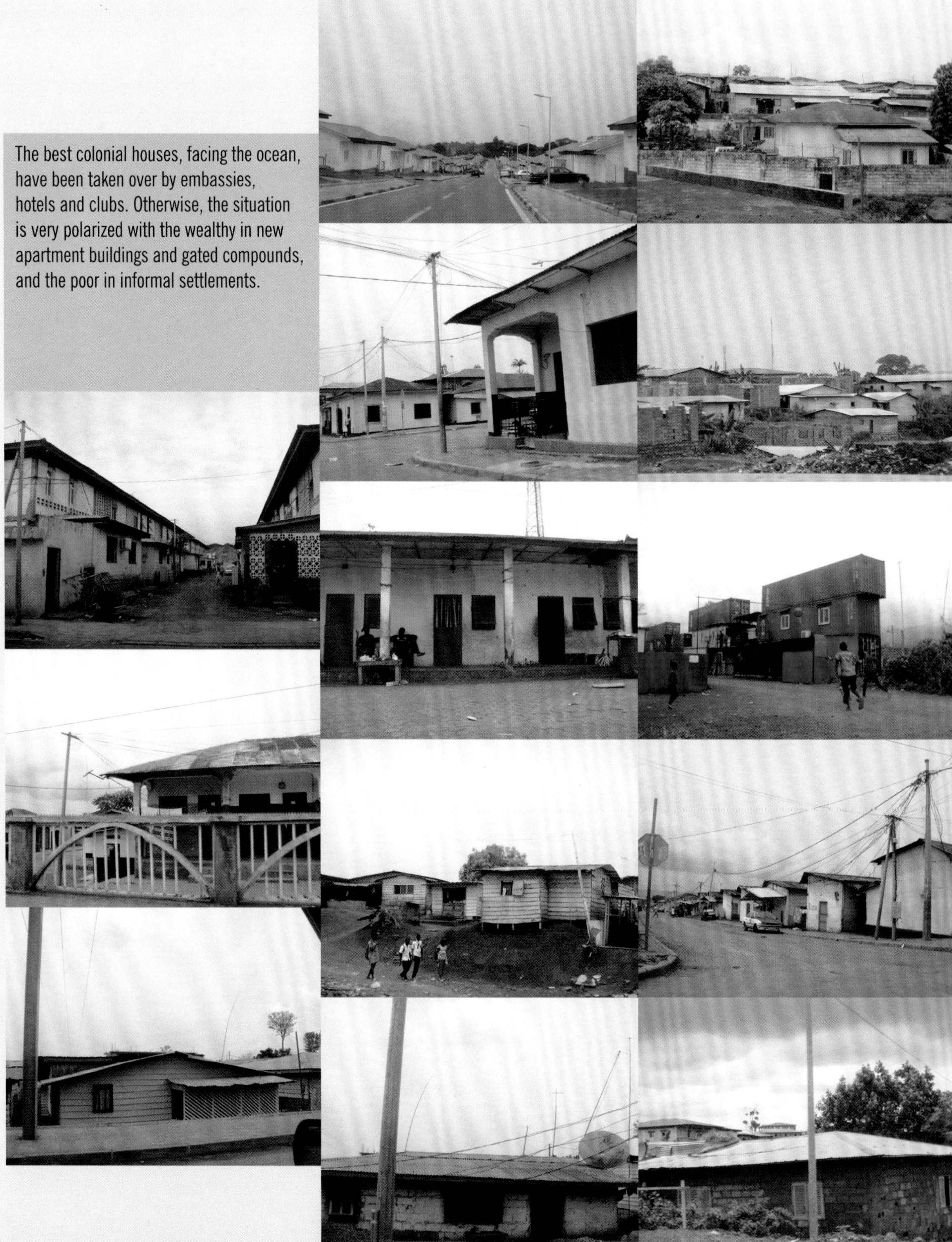

MAPUTO / MOZAMBIQUE

OVERVIEW

The original inhabitants of this part of southern Africa were the San people but they began to be displaced by Bantu people moving into the area from West Africa in the 1st millennium CE. The Bantu traded with the Arabs who sailed up and down the coast, resulting in a shared culture and language known as Swahili. European involvement began in 1498 when the Portuguese explorer Vasco da Gama arrived at the Ilha da Moçambique (Island of Mozambique). Although the Portuguese developed several ports and participated in the slave trade, their impact on the country as a whole was limited. In the 19th century the Bantu and Arabs worked as partners to open up the trade routes to the interior but the Bantu lost their dominant position due to the *Difaqane*, or forced migration, caused by the military success of the Zulu nation. The Portuguese signed an agreement with the British in 1891, which gave them formal control of the country and established its boundaries. But their rule was effective only in the south of the country, where they focused their interests in Maputo, leaving other areas in a state of decline. Mozambique was closed to other investors and from the late 1920s significant numbers of Portuguese arrived in the country to join a repressive and segregated society. The plight of the people in the north was exacerbated by the effects of the Salazar dictatorship in Portugal from the 1930s onwards.

The independence movement was triggered by an incident in the northern village of Mueda in 1960, when several demonstrators were killed by Portuguese troops. In 1962 the Frente de Libertação de Moçambique (Front for the Liberation of Mozambique), known as Frelimo, was founded with the intention of liberating the entire country. With bases in Tanzania, Frelimo had immediate success in the north but after that progress was slow. The Portuguese sought to repress the opposition by destroying crops and restricting movement but international disapproval undermined their position and the repressive regime in Lisbon finally collapsed in 1974. An independent republic of Mozambique was declared in 1975, with the previous leader of Frelimo, Samora Machel, as president. Frelimo adopted a radical socialist programme but the economy did not improve and by the early 1980s the country was in serious financial difficulties. The general situation was made worse by a three-year drought and by the activities of the South African and Rhodesian governments, who wished to destabilize the country because the African National Congress and the Zimbabwe African People's Union had bases there. Both of these countries backed the Resistência Nacional Moçambicana (Mozambique National Resistance, Renamo) and, to cause maximum disruption, Renamo forces indiscriminately attacked individuals, communications infrastructure and public buildings. The chaos that Renamo caused continued for seventeen years but by this stage Frelimo had relinquished much of its socialist programme and sought support from the West. A ceasefire with Renamo was negotiated in 1990 and a peace agreement followed in 1992. Although Frelimo has remained in power since then, Renamo has developed more constructive policies and has attracted substantial support. Filipe Nyusi is the current president.

OBSERVATIONS

Maputo is a major port and, after the restrictions of colonialism and the deprivations of war, it is now enjoying a cultural renaissance.

The city is designed for the car but the pavements are generous and the older buildings have porous ground planes, giving direct access to commerce, retail and culture. The main government buildings are on the coast and are conceived as a series of large palaces.

There is a strong Muslim community with mosques throughout the city but Catholic churches, both old and new, are the most common religious buildings. The coastal strip and its beaches are the focus for leisure and recreation. The restaurants and clubs along its length are often in a simple rustic style.

The special thing about the residential quarters in Maputo is that they are not exclusive to one another. Some of the great residences are in the heart of the city and many of them are modernist experiments in the architecture of the urban villa and are unique to this city. The apartment buildings use distinctive local motifs and patterns.

NATIONAL POPULATION

27,978,000

CITY POPULATION

1,187,000

ETHNIC GROUPS

African 99.66% (Makhuwa, Tsonga, Lomwe, Sena and others), Euro-Africans 0.2%, Indians 0.08%, Europeans 0.06%

RELIGIONS

Roman Catholic 28.4%, Muslim 17.9%, Zionist Christian 15.5%, Protestant 12.2%, other 6.7%, none 18.7%, unspecified 0.6%

LANGUAGES

Emakhuwa 25.3%, Portuguese (official) 10.7%, Xichangana 10.3%, Cisena 7.5%, Elomwe 7%, Echuwabo 5.1%, other Mozambican languages 30.1%, other 4%

GDP

$31.21 billion

AGRICULTURAL PRODUCTS

cotton, cashew nuts, tea sugarcane, cassava (manioc, tapiola), corn, coconuts, sisal, citrus and tropical fruits, sunflowers; beef, poultry

INDUSTRIES

aluminium, petroleum products, chemicals (fertilizer, soap, paints), textiles, cement, glass, asbestos, tobacco

The Portuguese invested heavily in the creation of this capital and constructed an impressive infrastructure of planted boulevards and avenues. The predominant architecture is regional modernism, with cues taken from the climate, place and culture.

Most of the commercial life takes place on the boulevards and in the markets. There is a bustle in the city and the well-planned infrastructure allows business to develop in a variety of locations.

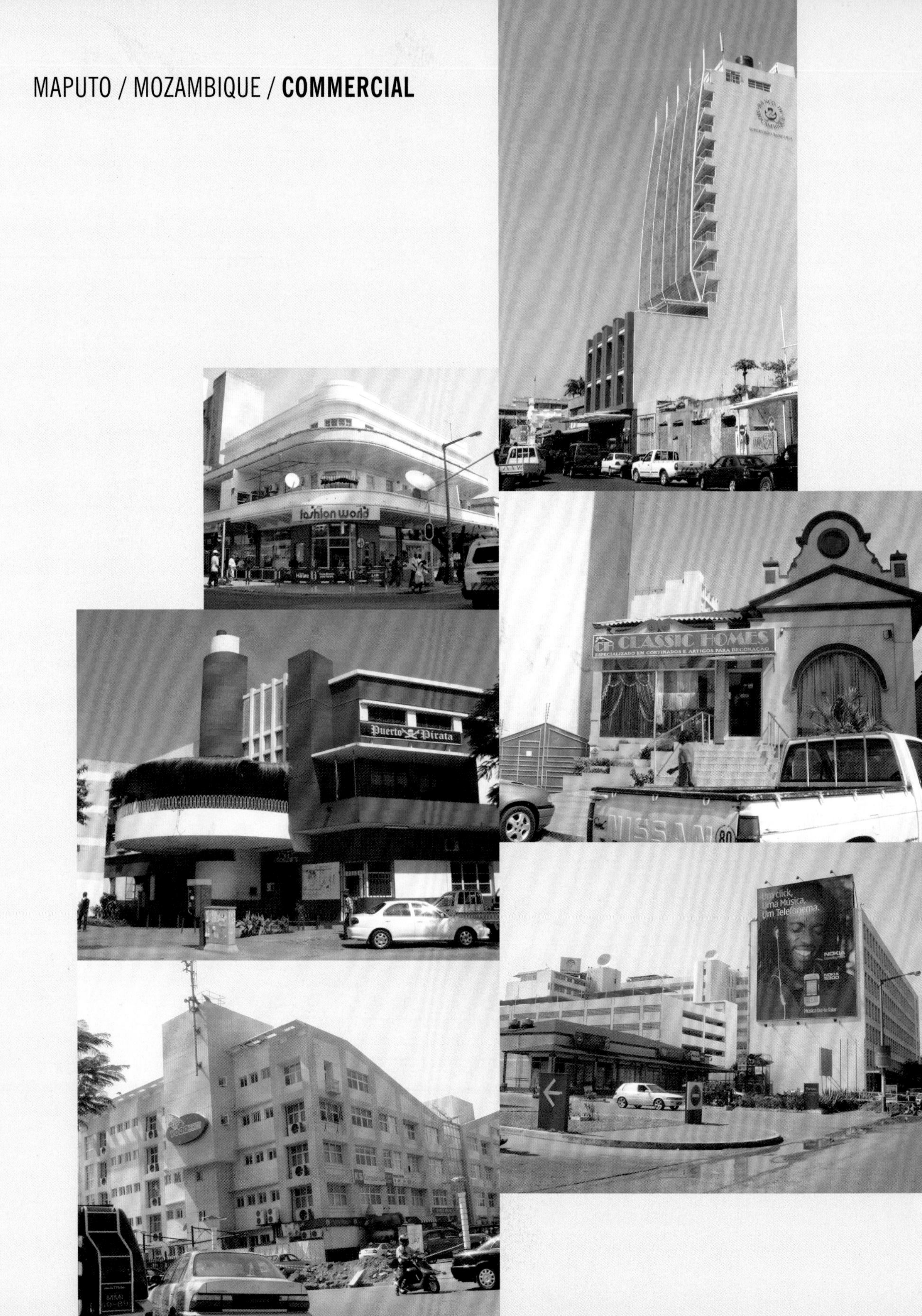
fashion world
Puerto Pirata
CLASSIC HOMES
ESPECIALIZADO EM CORTINADOS E ARTIGOS PARA DECORAÇÃO
NISSAN
Um click,
Uma Música,
Um Telefonema.
NOKIA

MAPUTO / MOZAMBIQUE / **RESIDENTIAL**

City-centre houses and elegant apartment buildings create a sense of metropolitan density. There are many examples of residential typologies for emerging and middle-class groups that explore civic values and inclusion, rather than economy of means.

MONROVIA / LIBERIA

OVERVIEW

Most Liberians are descended from migrants who moved into the area following the collapse of the western part of the Empire of Mali in the 15th century. Portuguese explorers arrived in the 1460s, but it was in the 19th century that abolition groups in the United States, wishing to resettle freed slaves in Africa, developed and named Liberia. Despite some opposition, the American Colonization Society signed a treaty with a local chief and the first black American settlers disembarked at Mesurado Bay in 1821. Further settlements took place at other points on the coast and Thomas Buchanan became the first governor in 1839. His successor Joseph Jenkins Roberts expanded and unified the settlements, and a constitution and declaration of independence were drafted in 1846. Liberia became a republic in 1847 but citizenship was restricted to freed slaves, and every president until 1980 was from this background. Although they comprised a small proportion of the total, the Americo-Liberians completely dominated the indigenous population who were subjected to a system of forced labour. Nevertheless, the country managed to present itself as politically stable and continued to attract international investment in the middle of the 20th century. This increased the inequalities within the population and the president, William Tubman, realized that the indigenous people would need to be given a political and economic stake in the country if conflict was to be avoided. In 1971 he was succeeded by William Tolbert who introduced a number of reforms while keeping control of the government firmly in Americo-Liberian hands.

Anti-government resentment came to a head in 1979, when several people who were demonstrating against an increase in the price of rice were shot and Tolbert was overthrown in a coup led by Samuel Doe in 1980. The coup was not well received by Liberia's previous allies and capital began to leave the country, weakening the economy and leaving many people unemployed. There was growing internal opposition to Doe's government and a failed coup in 1985 led to open hostility between the Krahn people, who supported Doe, and the rival Gio and Mano people. Doe's previous associate Charles Taylor invaded the Nimba area from the Côte d'Ivoire and was joined by government forces in killing local people and burning villages. As Taylor and his men proceeded to take over most of the country, Prince Johnson of the Gio people organized a rebel force that took control of Monrovia. With the country in ruins, Doe refused to surrender and was killed by Johnson's forces. After Taylor attacked Monrovia in 1992, the rivals struggled to reach a peace agreement in 1993. Following a period of transitional government, the armies were disbanded and Taylor's National Patriotic Party won the election in 1997. Any sense of a return to normality was shattered in 1999 when the forces of Liberians United for Reconciliation and Democracy (LURD) attacked the north of the country from Guinea. After more serious fighting in 2002 and 2003 the LURD controlled much of the country and Taylor was forced into exile. The elections in 2005 were won by the economist Ellen Johnson Sirleaf, the first woman president in Africa. She remains in power and her government is working to restore the economy after years of fighting and the Ebola outbreak.

OBSERVATIONS

The city comprises a string of settlements that are connected by one main road. Most of the damage caused by the civil war has been repaired but maintenance is an issue due to the heavy rainfall.

In the old town the density of the buildings sets up specific patterns of use in the streets. Their balconies create areas of shade which become the focus for informal trading and generate lively streetscapes. You sense these activities crisscrossing that part of town.

The wealthier houses are modernist vernacular bungalows, with simple plans, that occupy the higher ground. Despite an increasing number of apartment buildings, the feel of the city is horizontal. Shanty towns have developed around the centre because they have good access to services and infrastructure.

NATIONAL POPULATION

4,503,000

CITY POPULATION

1,264,000

ETHNIC GROUPS

Kpelle 20.3%, Bassa 13.4%, Grebo 10%, Gio 8%, Mano 7.9%, Kru 6%, Lorma 5.1%, Kissi 4.8%, Gola 4.4%, other 20.1%

RELIGIONS

Christian 85.6%, Muslim 12.2%, traditional 0.6%, other 0.2%, none 1.4%

LANGUAGES

English 20% (official), some 20 ethnic group languages few of which can be written or used in correspondence

GDP

$3.71 billion

AGRICULTURAL PRODUCTS

rubber, coffee, cocoa, rice, cassava (manioc, tapioca), palm oil, sugarcane, bananas; sheep, goats; timber

INDUSTRIES

mining (iron ore), rubber processing, palm oil processing, timber, diamonds

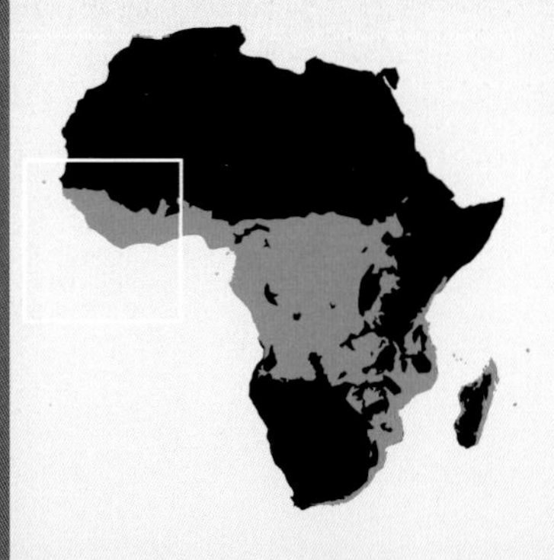

The city is built on a strip of land between the Mesurado River and the sea. Most of the government and administrative buildings are situated on Capitol Hill, at the neck of the peninsula, and their architecture is modernist with neoclassical overtones.

The old town, at the end of the peninsula, is the main commercial area. Many of the four- to five-storey buildings have projecting balconies that protect the pavement below. A large market is situated between these streets and the river.

MONROVIA / LIBERIA / **COMMERCIAL**

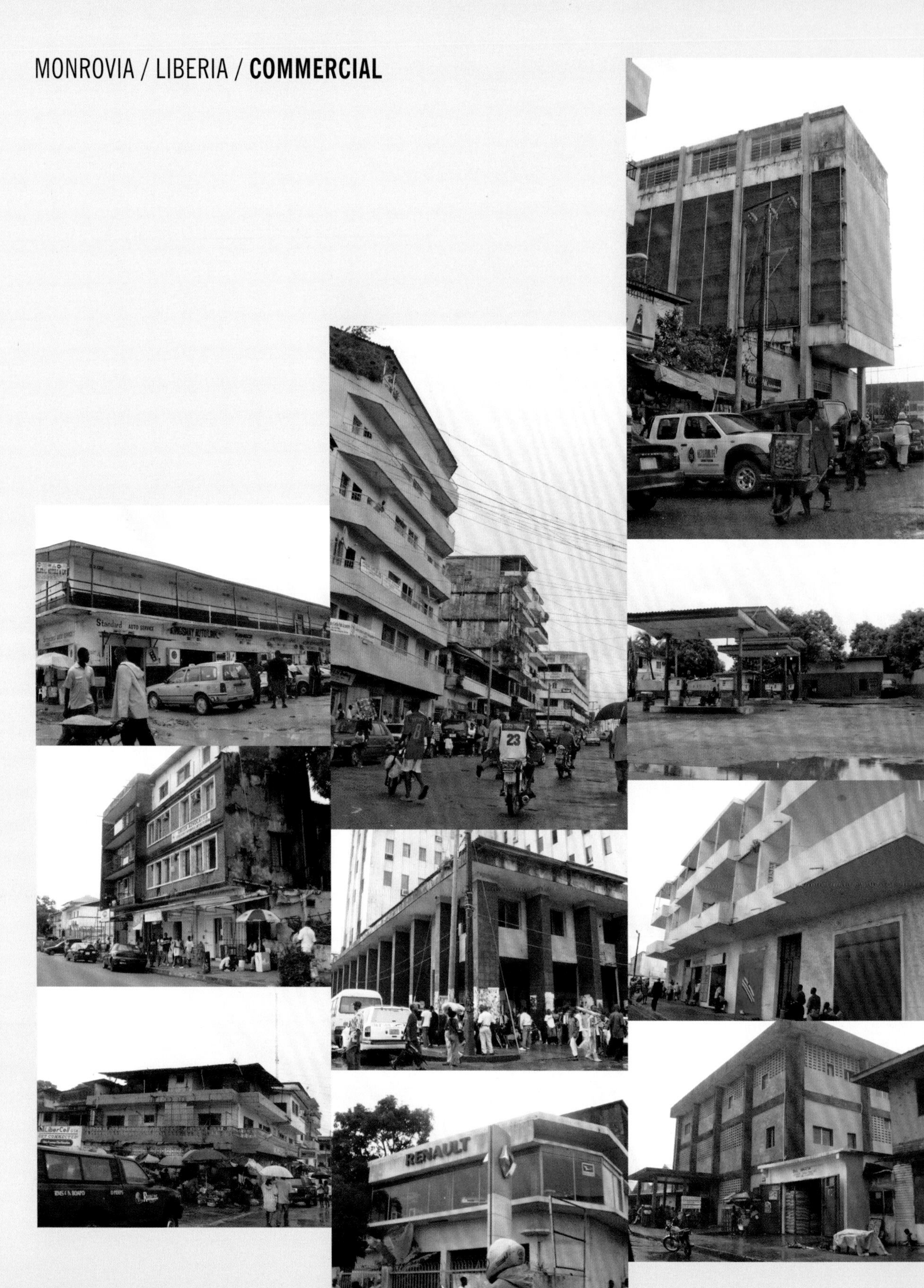

MONROVIA / LIBERIA / **RESIDENTIAL**

Modern Monrovia was conceived as a garden city, but low apartment buildings and areas of informal housing have supplemented the older garden villas. There is also a significant amount of residential accommodation in the old town.

MORONI / COMOROS

OVERVIEW

The Comoros islands are situated to the northwest of Madagascar and their original inhabitants were the same people who emigrated from the Indian subcontinent and settled the larger island two millennia ago. In the middle ages the Comoros were an integral part of the Arab trade network that extended along the east coast of Africa, dealing in a variety of commodities from spices to slaves. Some slaves found their way to freedom and, along with people such as the Persians who arrived in the 15th and 16th centuries, settled in the islands. In the succeeding centuries, rivalry between a number of resident sultans allowed the French to establish a foothold in the 19th century. To change the local balance of power they were invited to play a role on Grande Comore and Mayotte, in a process that drew to a conclusion in 1912 when Anjouan joined the other islands as a French colony. Although the British had an interest in the area, they had a less tolerant attitude to slavery and this was an issue in relation to the plantation culture that had developed in the islands.

In a 1974 referendum Grande Comore, Anjouan and Mohéli were in favour of independence and Mayotte voted to remain French. Before this arrangement was ratified, Ahmed Abdallah Abderemane of Grande Comore declared the unilateral independence of the Federal Islamic Republic of Comoros, which consisted of the three islands that had voted for this option. The status of Mayotte was not affected and France recognized the new republic in 1975. Abderemane was then ousted by mercenaries led by Ali Soilih who, as well as giving lip service to socialism, terrorized the island's population. But Soilih's days were numbered due to the arrival of French mercenaries led by Bob Denard who returned Abderemane to power in 1978. He was reelected in 1987, only to be killed by one of his guards. Said Mohamed Djohar won the election in 1990 but, after a referendum on whether he should stay in power in 1992, Denard's mercenaries reappeared and exiled the president to Réunion. French troops then intervened on behalf of the government but by this stage Mohéli and Anjouan had become disillusioned by the events on Grande Comore and declared themselves separately independent. Forces from Grande Comore launched an unsuccessful attack on Anjouan and the island's president reasserted their independence. Following a military coup in 1999, Azali Assoumani came to power in Grande Comore and, to unite the islands, he organized an election in which each of them would have their own president. After winning the presidential election on Grande Comore in 2002, Assoumani declared himself the president of the Union of the Comoros, comprising the three independent islands. In 2007 the president of Anjouan refused to step down prior to all-island elections, effectively declaring independence. After mediation by the African Union (AU), and with local support, AU and Comoran troops returned the island to the Union in 2008 and Ikililou Dhoinine won the national elections in 2011. Compared with their capital cities in other countries, the French had only a limited influence on the development of Moroni.

OBSERVATIONS

The Comoros Islands constitute one of the six island states in the African Union and Moroni is situated on Grande Comore, the largest island in the cluster. They are of volcanic origin, with black lava stone and soil. The earlier parts of the city were built of this stone but in recent years whitewashed blockwork has become the staple building material.

The city is organized along a north–south coast road that connects the main squares, before doubling back to its commercial quarters. Approaching the city from the north, you arrive at the Place de l'Indépendance, a modern plaza surrounded by government buildings, which is close to the president's palace. From here you wind down to the old city, past the fishing community and the port, until you arrive at an arcaded mosque situated on the waterfront. This is the most visible symbol of the city.

The other public spaces become gradually more commercial as you move back up the hill, a sequence that terminates with the elegant structure of the main market. Beyond this, the residential areas stretch off into the landscape. The fishing community is very poor and remains locked in a ghetto at the heart of the city.

NATIONAL POPULATION

788,000

CITY POPULATION

54,000

ETHNIC GROUPS

Antalote, Cafre, Makoa, Oimatsaha, Sakalava

RELIGIONS

Sunni Muslim 98%, Roman Catholic 2%

LANGUAGES

Arabic (official), French (official), Shikomoro (official: a blend of Swahili and Arabic)

GDP

$1.19 billion

AGRICULTURAL PRODUCTS

vanilla, cloves, ylang-ylang (perfume essence), coconuts, bananas, cassava (manioc)

INDUSTRIES

fishing, tourism, perfume distillation

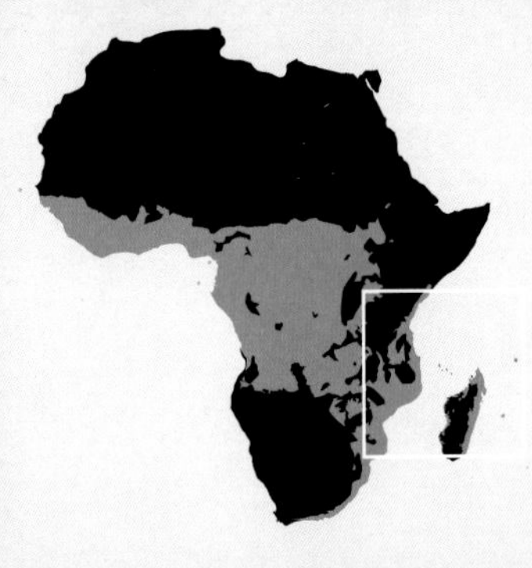

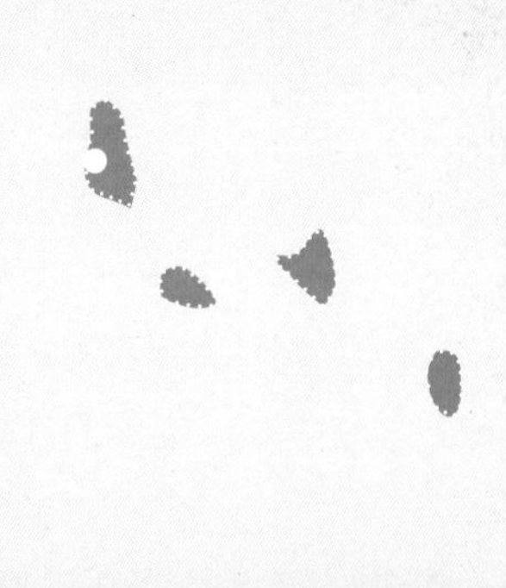

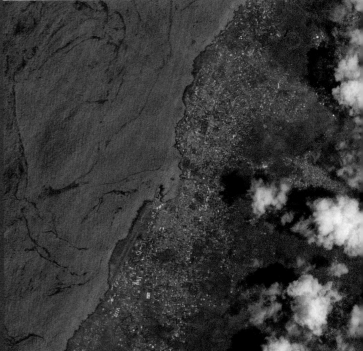

The religious architecture is particularly striking and the mosque with a three-tiered arcade makes a picturesque image for the city. In contrast, due to the islands' turbulent history, some public buildings are hidden from view and guarded. The coast and beaches provide the city's equivalent of parks and landscaped spaces.

Apart from the larger bank buildings, many of the commercial buildings are Swahili in character; they have the sort of style that you see in the south of Kenya or in Tanzania. The informal commercial architecture takes the form of reed and tin structures, or containers that have been converted into shops.

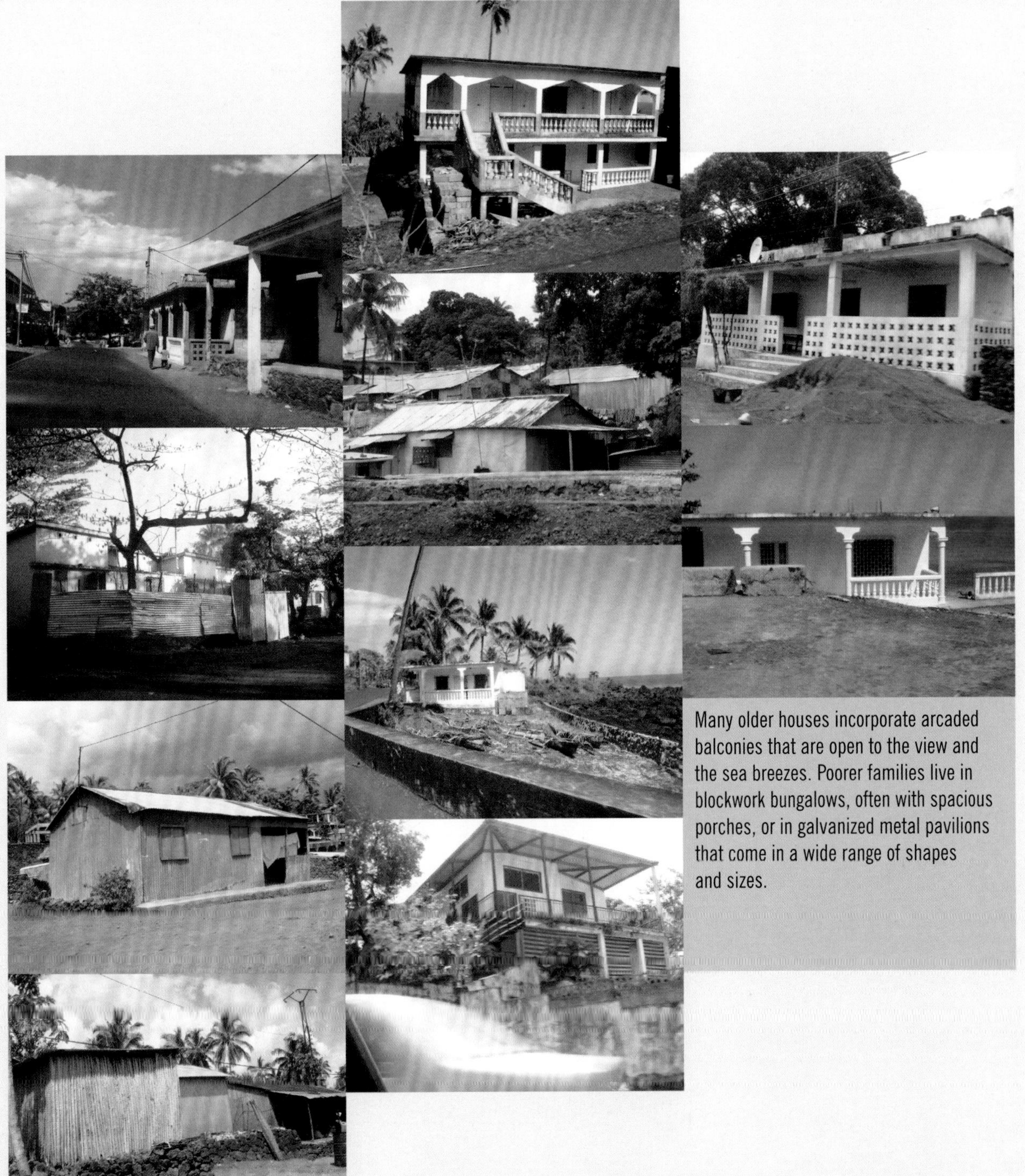

Many older houses incorporate arcaded balconies that are open to the view and the sea breezes. Poorer families live in blockwork bungalows, often with spacious porches, or in galvanized metal pavilions that come in a wide range of shapes and sizes.

PORT LOUIS / MAURITIUS

OVERVIEW

Although no remains of a settlement have been found, Arab sailors may have visited Mauritius and other islands in the 10th century. The Portuguese arrived early in the 16th century but they did not settle. Later in the century the admiral of a visiting Dutch fleet named the island Mauritius and in 1638 the Dutch East India Company established a base there. The population gradually expanded as convicts were brought from Europe, slaves from Africa, and a few free settlers arrived. But the Dutch abandoned Mauritius when they founded a colony on the Cape of Good Hope. After the French East India Company had colonized Réunion they sent Swiss mercenaries, pirates and slaves, as well as members of the company, to occupy Mauritius. Things were difficult in the early days, until the company appointed a young captain, Bertrand-François Mahé de La Bourdonnais, as governor in 1735. He proved to be an inspirational leader, building more ships, improving agriculture and the island's infrastructure, and moving the seat of government from Réunion to Port Louis. In 1764, when the French East India Company went bankrupt, the French government took control of Mauritius. Agriculture was expanded and trade increased, until news of the revolution arrived in 1790. The principles and the trappings of revolutionary government were quickly adopted, including a guillotine (which remained unused), but the islanders did not support the abolition of slavery.

By this stage the British had increased their presence in the Indian Ocean and occupied Rodrigues in 1809, before attacking the Mascarenes. They invaded Mauritius in 1810, the French surrendered and the island became a British colony in 1814. The first British governor Robert Farquhar was quick to appreciate the island's potential, promoting sugarcane plantations and declaring Port Louis a freeport, and allowed the islanders to retain their slaves in spite of British abolition in 1807. Slavery was finally suppressed in 1835, with a scheme that required former slaves to start their new lives by working for very low pay. They often had to live in poverty, as the plantation owners turned to India for their new labourers. Between 1840 and 1870 over 200,000 Indians arrived in Mauritius and became the dominant group in the island's population. They worked on the plantations and became progressively involved in other areas, including politics. When party politics were introduced in 1886, the Indian population did not have a vote and in 1901 Mohandas Gandhi visited Mauritius to campaign for the civil rights of the island's labourers. A socialist party, the Mauritius Labour Party (MLP), was founded in 1936 and the Ralliement Mauricien (Mauritius Rally) represented conservative views. After the Second World War the MLP won the first election with a universal franchise, and independence within the Commonwealth was declared in 1968. Since then the MLP has been superseded by other socialist parties that at different times have governed in a coalition or in opposition to each other. After nine years of Labour government, the 2014 elections were won by the Alliance Lepep, a coalition led by Anerood Jugnauth. Port Louis was founded by the Dutch and renamed by the French in 1722.

OBSERVATIONS

Many of the islanders are of Indian descent and decades of intermarriage have created a Mauritian Indian–African, similar to Trinidad. The vegetation is very green, the people are friendly, and interracial harmony is excellent.

There is great sense of life in the streets, with food sellers, spice traders, and people selling secondhand goods such as clothes. But the atmosphere is gentle, with little targeting of tourists. Mauritians enjoy horse-racing, which takes place on Saturdays at a course above the city.

NATIONAL POPULATION

1,273,000

CITY POPULATION

148,000

ETHNIC GROUPS

Indo-Mauritian 68%, Creole 27%, Sino-Mauritian 3%, Franco-Mauritian 2%

RELIGIONS

Hindu 48.5%, Roman Catholic 26.3%, Muslim 17.3%, other Christian 6.4%, other 0.6%, none 0.7%, unspecified 0.2%

LANGUAGES

Creole 86.5%, Bhojpuri 5.3%, French 4.1%, other 4.1% (includes English, the official language, which is spoken by less than 1% of the population), unspecified 0.1%

GDP

$23.53 billion

AGRICULTURAL PRODUCTS

sugarcane, tea, corn, potatoes, bananas, pulses; cattle, goats; fish

INDUSTRIES

food processing (largely sugar milling), textiles, clothing, mining, chemicals, metal products, transport equipment, nonelectrical machinery, tourism

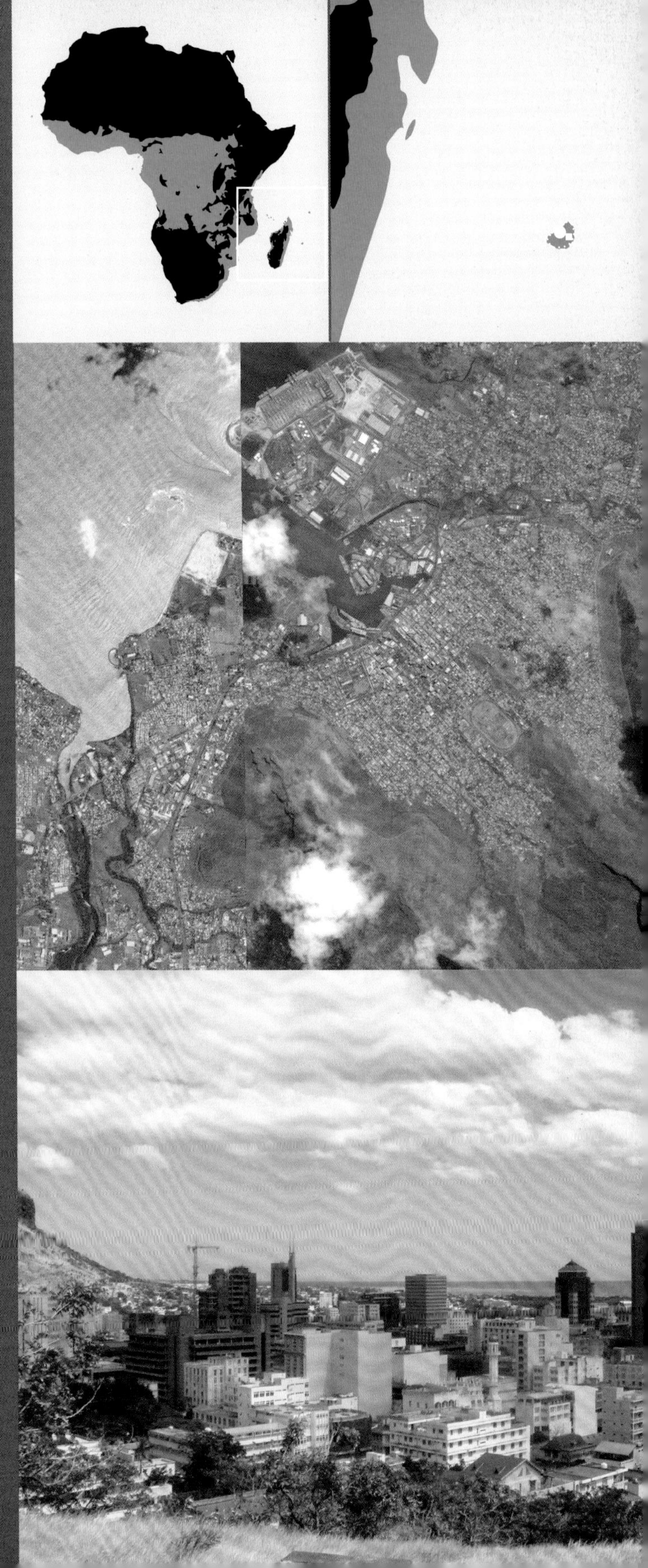

The city occupies a grid of streets between the ocean and the surrounding hills, and the historic centre is close to the harbour. Most of the public buildings are located here, with distinguished examples from colonial times to the recent past.

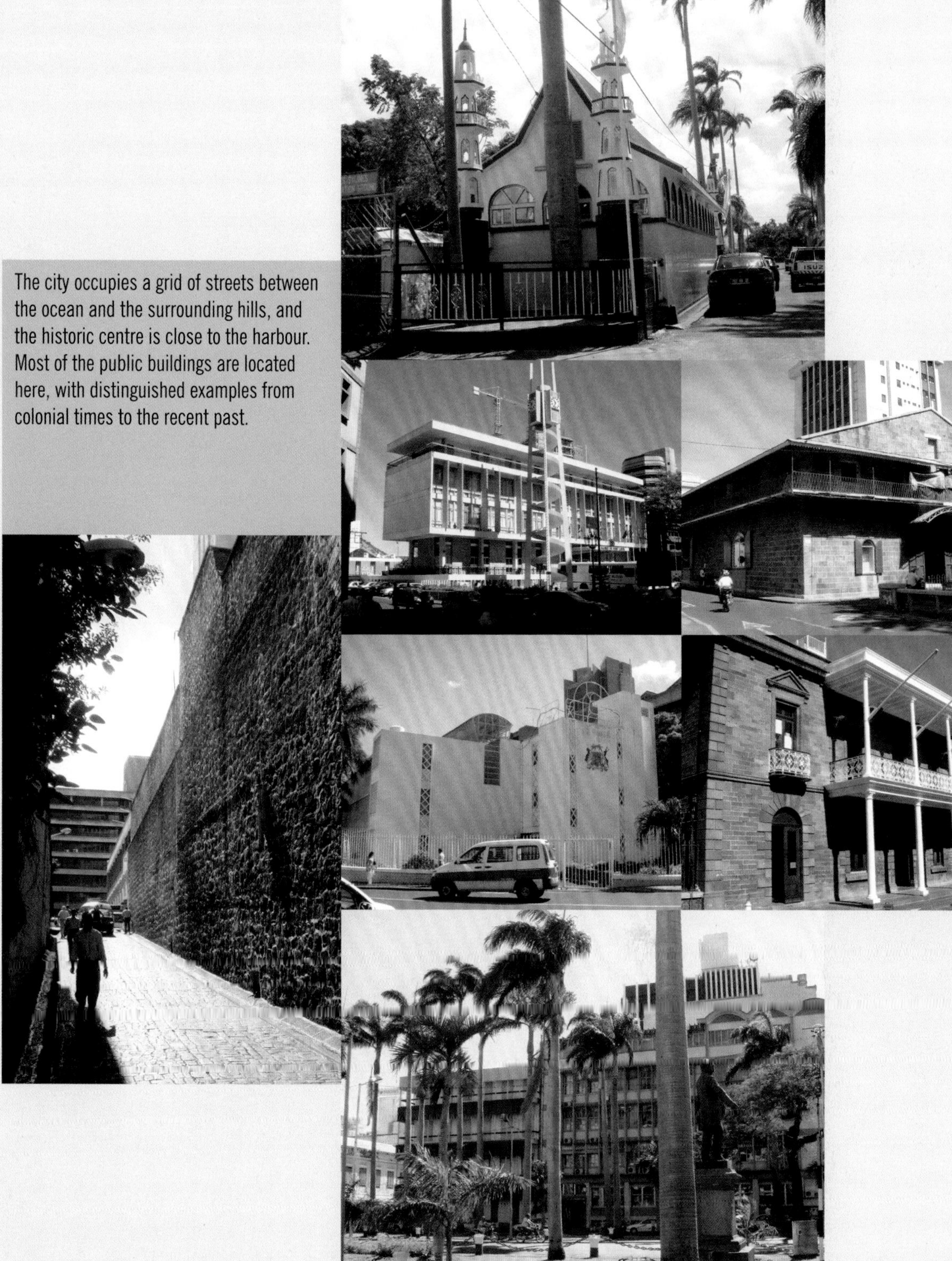

The wealth of the 1990s has led to a boom in high-rise buildings, which has significantly changed the scale of the city and given it a more progressive identity. In contrast, many of the shops in the old town are located in colonial buildings with colonnaded fronts.

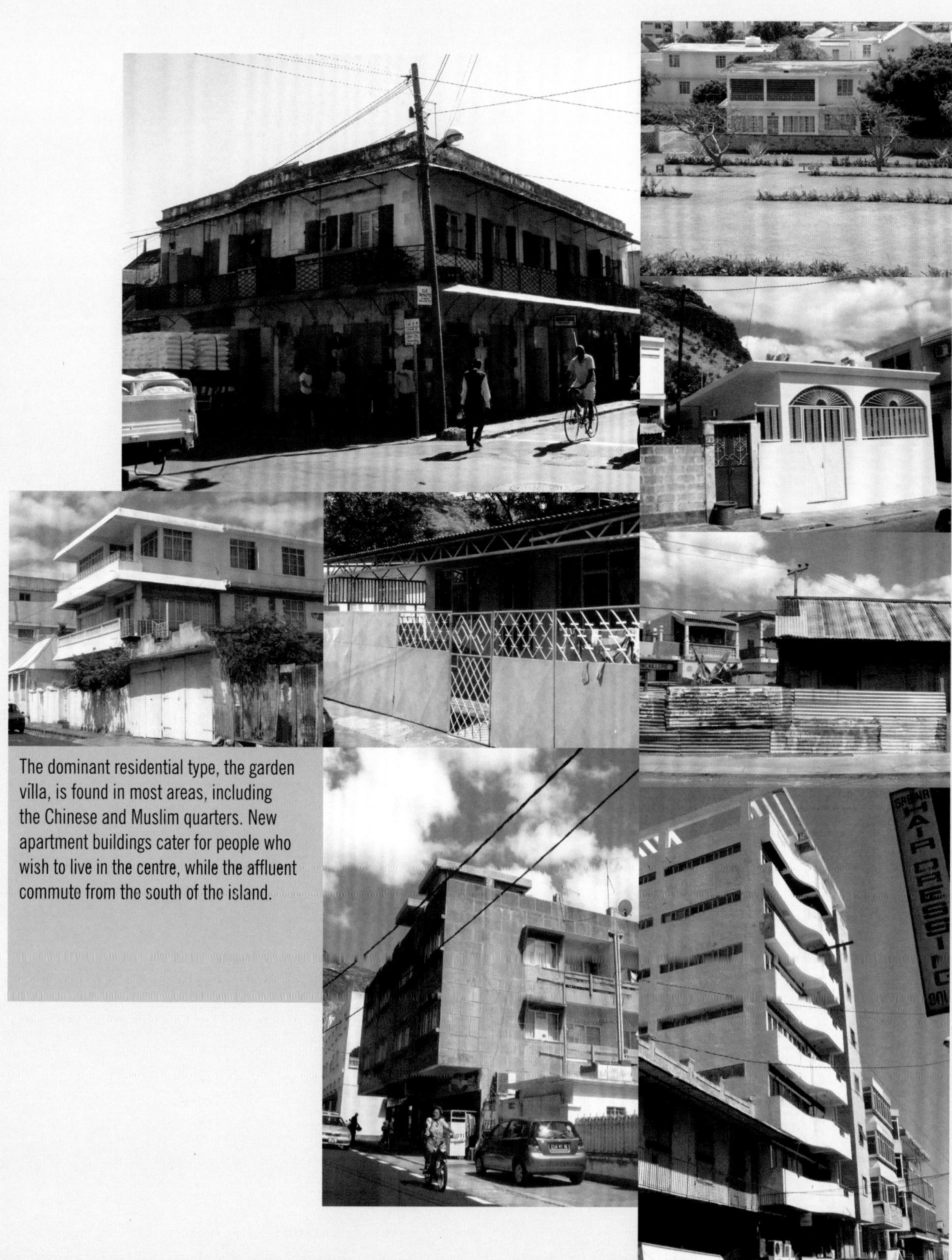

The dominant residential type, the garden villa, is found in most areas, including the Chinese and Muslim quarters. New apartment buildings cater for people who wish to live in the centre, while the affluent commute from the south of the island.

PRAIA / CAPE VERDE

OVERVIEW

The Cape Verde islands were uninhabited when the Portuguese discovered them in 1456, six years before they established the first settlement on the island of São Vicente. With plans to establish sugar plantations, the Portuguese brought slaves to cultivate the land. The plantations were not a success but the position of the islands meant that they were well placed to service the ships involved in the transatlantic slave trade. Based on the wealth that this created, the population grew steadily but droughts in the 18th and 19th centuries resulted in famines that killed over 100,000 islanders. The economy also suffered due to the decline in the slave trade and many of the islands' men had to work on the Atlantic whaling fleets to support their families. At the end of the 19th century, the introduction of transatlantic liners gave the islands a renewed significance. The deepwater harbour at Mindelo became an important fuelling and supply point for these ships and, when their day was over, an international airport was constructed on the island of Sal, performing a similar role for air travel.

Throughout their history, the islands' African-Portuguese population has enjoyed more rights and a higher standard of education than the population of the mainland. This did not interfere with the islanders' understanding of the significance of the independence movement in Africa and in the 1950s they joined the people of Guinea-Bissau in the quest for independence. On Cape Verde Amïlcar Cabral, who had been born in Guinea-Bissau, founded a socialist party that became known as the Partido Africano da Independência da Guiné e Cabo Verde (African Party for the Independence of Guinea and Cape Verde). But the days of the Portuguese colonies were considerably extended by the intransigent views of António Salazar, the dictator who dreamt of a successful colonial role for Portugal long after other European countries had given up such notions. This was reflected in sustained fighting between the Portuguese and the independence movement in Guinea-Bissau, which ended only when there was a change of government in Lisbon in 1974. In the following years there were serious discussions around the possibility of uniting the two countries but Cape Verde withdrew after a coup in Guinea-Bissau in 1980. The Partido Africano da Independência de Cabo Verde (African Party for the Independence of Cape Verde, PAICV), led by prime minister Pedro Pires, organized a socialist economy and developed health and education programmes but its success was undermined by a further drought in 1985, when food relief was supplied by Portugal and the USA. In 1990 the PAICV responded to public pressure for the introduction of democratic government and Carlos Veiga founded the Movimento para a Democracia (Movement for Democracy, MpD) which was in favour of more private enterprise. Although it won the 1991 election, the hoped-for improvements to the economy did not materialize and in 2001 Pires returned to power with a commitment to follow IMF directives. In the 2011 election, the presidency passed to the MpD leader Jorge Carlos Fonseca. Although living standards are higher than in mainland Africa, the economy is constrained by the islands' isolation. Praia was the Portuguese military and administrative base.

OBSERVATIONS

Praia is in a dramatic setting facing the Atlantic with a backdrop of rocky hills. It was a stopping point for slave ships on their way to the New World and became a wealthy citadel in the 18th and 19th centuries. The old city is a network of fine streets, leading to a square that is surrounded by civic buildings.

As the city grew outside the walls, it reoccupied the area around a small inlet, where the earliest settlement took place. This has subsequently become the poor part of town, as the wealthy and middle class have moved to the suburbs.

NATIONAL POPULATION

521,000

CITY POPULATION

130,000

ETHNIC GROUPS

Creole (mulatto) 71%, African 28%, European 1%

RELIGIONS

Roman Catholic 77.3%, Protestant 3.7% (includes Church of the Nazarene 1.7%, Adventist 1.5%, Universal Kingdom of God 0.4%, and God and Love 0.1%), other Christian 4.3%, Muslim 1.8%, other 1.3%, none 10.8%, unspecified 0.8%

LANGUAGES

Portuguese, Crioulo (a blend of Portuguese and West African words)

GDP

$3.33 billion

AGRICULTURAL PRODUCTS

bananas, corn, beans, sweet potatoes, sugarcane, coffee, peanuts; fish

INDUSTRIES

food and beverages, fish processing, shoes and garments, mining (salt), ship repair

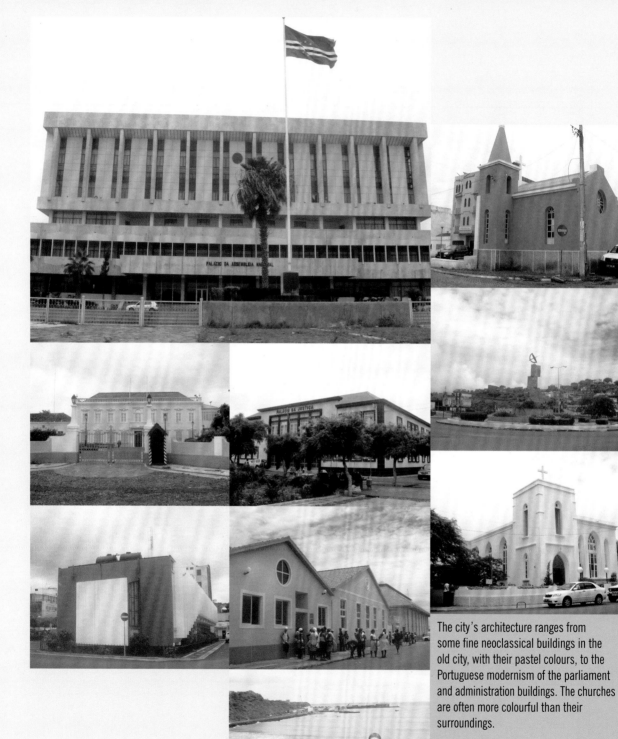

The city's architecture ranges from some fine neoclassical buildings in the old city, with their pastel colours, to the Portuguese modernism of the parliament and administration buildings. The churches are often more colourful than their surroundings.

PRAIA / CAPE VERDE / **COMMERCIAL**

PRAIA / CAPE VERDE / **COMMERCIAL**

Local shops and businesses make the ground plane of the city lively and porous. Some shops are in shed-like structures that are painted in bright colours; a form of commercial signage found in most areas.

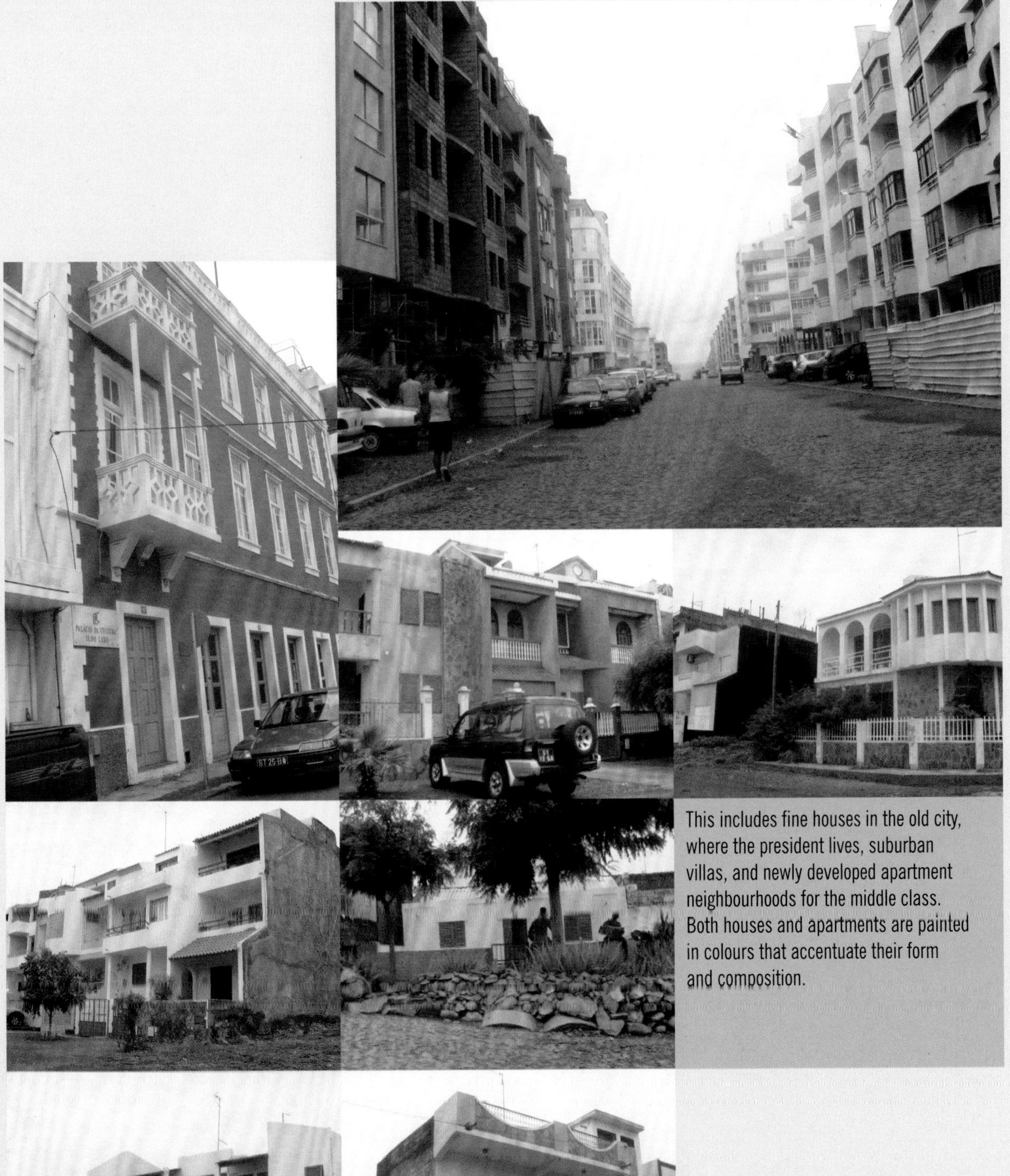

This includes fine houses in the old city, where the president lives, suburban villas, and newly developed apartment neighbourhoods for the middle class. Both houses and apartments are painted in colours that accentuate their form and composition.

SÃO TOMÉ / SÃO TOMÉ AND PRÍNCIPE

OVERVIEW

When the Portuguese located these islands in 1470, they appreciated the rich volcanic soil and, using labour brought from the mainland, began to clear the jungle and plant sugar. By the middle of the 16th century the islands were major sugar exporters and their offshore position gave them a significant role in the transatlantic slave trade. As the production of sugar increased in South America, the islands' economy became more dependent on the slave trade, a situation that began to change with the successful introduction of coffee and cocoa in the 19th century. Portugal abolished slavery in 1869 but this had little effect on the islands as the freed slaves still had to live in the poor conditions on the plantations. And other workers continued to be brought in from the mainland and found themselves in the same predicament. Having recently introduced the cultivation of cocoa to several of their colonies, the British organized a boycott of the islands in 1909 to draw attention to conditions on the plantations. In response, chapels, schools, houses and other facilities were built for the workers and their families but in other ways there was little change and rebellions were common. Portuguese attitudes were especially brutal during the Salazar dictatorship and in 1953 a protest march by contract workers was fired on by Portuguese troops. The country's main nationalist party, the Movimento de Libertação de São Tomé e Príncipe (Movement for the Liberation of São Tomé and Príncipe), was founded in 1960 to oppose colonial rule. It came to power when independence was declared in 1975, following the overthrow of the Portuguese dictatorship in the previous year.

The first president was Manuel Pinto da Costa and, in the economic confusion following the Portuguese evacuation, he nationalized the plantations as part of a socialist programme that was supported by Angola, Cuba and the USSR. But the production of cocoa continued to decline and, with prices falling, this undermined the islands' economy. To encourage new investment, da Costa brought in a new constitution in 1990, which legalized opposition parties and restricted the president to two five-year terms in office, and that was intended to encourage new investment in the plantations. Miguel Trovoada of the Independence Democratic Action party won the presidential election in 1991, to be followed in 2001 by Fradique de Menezes of the Force for Democratic Change – Liberal Party, who remained in power until 2011. The government of his successor, the returning independent Manuel Pinto da Costa, is one of shifting coalitions between opposition parties. Nigeria is collaborating in the continuing exploration of offshore oil fields. The city of São Tomé was founded by the Portuguese in 1485.

OBSERVATIONS

São Tomé is a picturesque colonial town beside Ana Chaves Bay. The civic institutions are along the waterfront, with a commercial core in a central position. As you reach the mountains, the suburbs give way to rural settlements and then you encounter the vast plantations that made this island profitable in the colonial days. It traded in sugar, coffee, cocoa and slaves. The island's history is visible all over the island and makes for an intoxicating cocktail.

The commercial core is a tight grid of streets next to a seafront square. Most of the buildings are no more than three storeys high, with a few modern high-rises – by the island's standards. The residential architecture is a diverse mix of types, from the townhouses in the colonial core to wonderful colonial and modernist villas, nouveau riche estates and apartment buildings, and the timber housing of the poor that spreads in all directions.

In working-class areas, the front garden becomes a living room, with people hanging out their washing, not on trees but on the vegetation outside their houses, making a kind of mosaic of fabric in the sun. Life is generally led outdoors, so all these structures have large porches, generous overhangs and lots of planting. São Tomé is the kind of place where you can grow anything.

NATIONAL POPULATION

190,000

CITY POPULATION

60,000

ETHNIC GROUPS

mestiço, angolares (descendants of Angolan slaves), forros (descendants of freed slaves), servicais (contract labourers from Angola, Mozambique and Cape Verde), tongas (children of servicais born on the islands), Europeans (primarily Portuguese), Asians (mostly Chinese)

RELIGIONS

Catholic 55.7%, Adventist 4.1%, Assembly of God 3.4%, New Apostolic 2.9%, Mana 2.3%, Universal Kingdom of God 2%, Jehovah's Witness 1.2%, other 6.2%, none 21.2%, unspecified 1%

LANGUAGES

Portuguese (official) 98.4%, Forro 36.2%, Cabo Verdian 8.5%, French 6.8%, Angolar 6.6%, English 4.9%, Lunguie 1%, other (including sign language) 2.4%

GDP

$626 million

AGRICULTURAL PRODUCTS

cocoa, coconuts, palm kernels, copra, cinnamon, pepper, coffee, bananas, papayas, beans; poultry; fish

INDUSTRIES

light construction, textiles, soap, beer, fish processing, timber

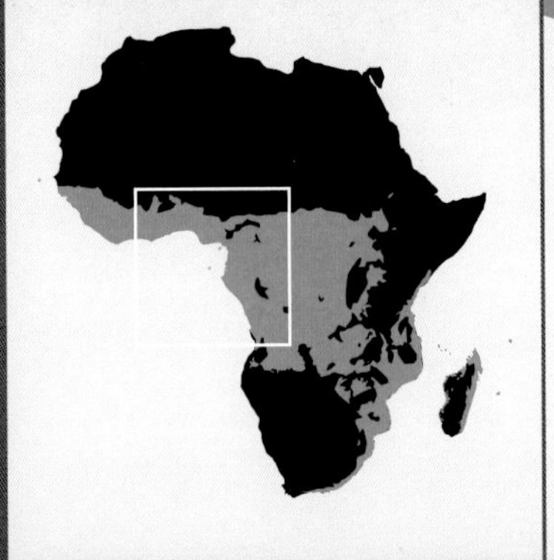

São Tomé was important for its size and the government house, courts and jail are fine neoclassical structures. The 1970s parliament building, on the coast, is an example of regional modernism, along with the central bank and other recent buildings.

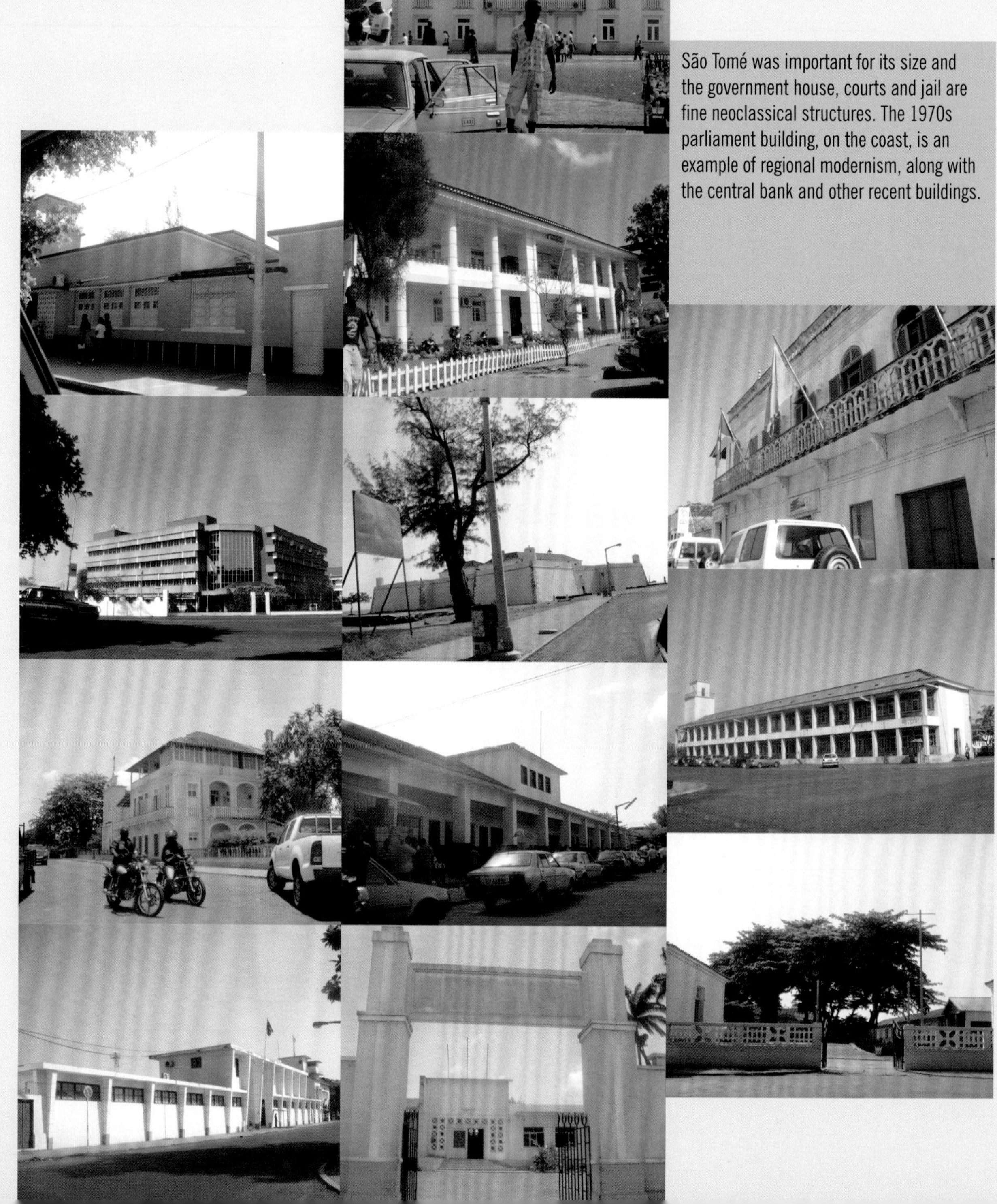

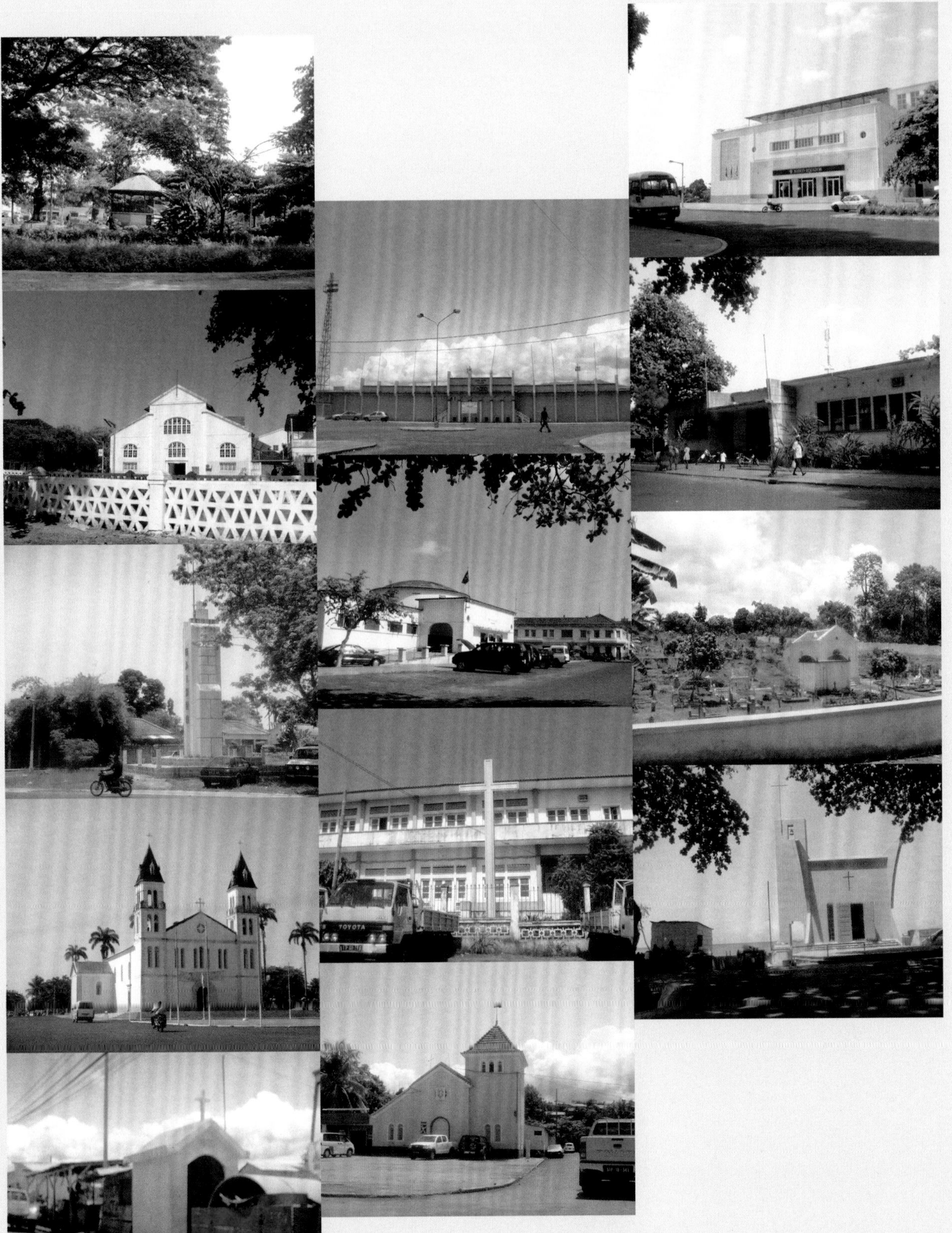

This is found in the arcaded streets of the old town, in the municipal and informal markets, in a scattering of new office blocks, in the hotels overlooking the bay, and in the warehouse area close to the port.

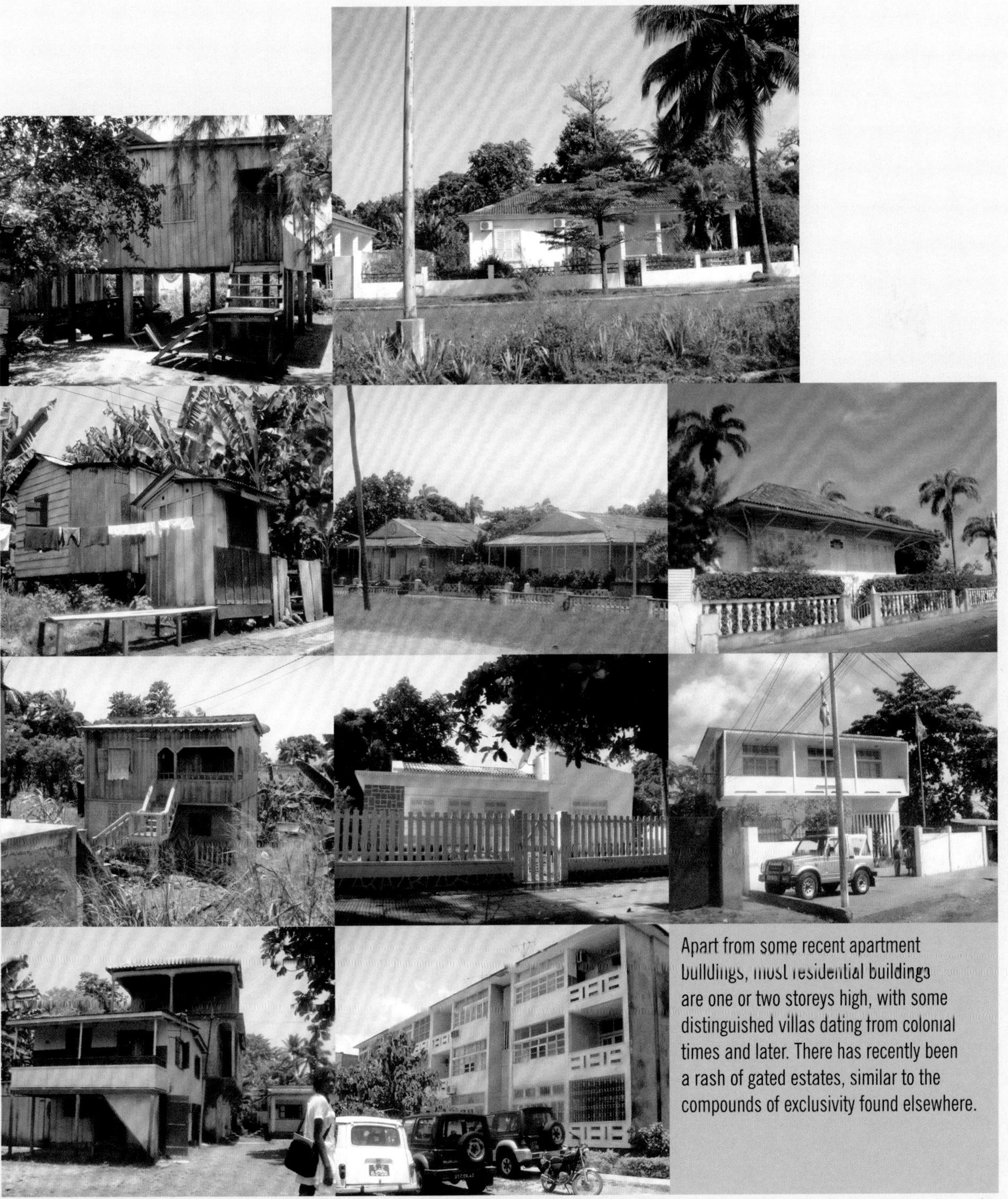

Apart from some recent apartment buildings, most residential buildings are one or two storeys high, with some distinguished villas dating from colonial times and later. There has recently been a rash of gated estates, similar to the compounds of exclusivity found elsewhere.

VICTORIA / SEYCHELLES

OVERVIEW

The Seychelles archipelago consists of 115 islands distributed across a large area of the Indian Ocean in five main groups, with the largest islands in the east. After Portuguese navigators had explored the islands early in the 16th century, the next significant visit was that of a British ship, which anchored off Mahé and noted the ready supply of timber and the abundant sources of food. As the volume of trade between Europe and India increased, the slow-moving ships were exposed to attacks from pirates such as the Frenchman Olivier Levasseur who was based in the Seychelles before being hanged in 1730. The expanding French settlement on Mauritius sent several expeditions to explore Mahé, laid claim to it in 1756 and established a small military base in 1778. Chevalier Jean-Baptiste Quéau de Quincy was made governor in 1793; he was in post during the Napoleonic wars, and had to deal with the British taking an increasing interest in the islands. When Britain took over Mauritius, the Seychelles became a dependent colony and de Quincy continued to administer the islands for the British. At this time the total population was over 7,000, of whom the greater majority were slaves. Their number increased when slaves from ships captured by the British were released here following the abolition of slavery in 1835, and they provided labour for the cultivation of coconuts, which was taking over from cotton.

Britain appointed its first governor in 1903, when the Seychelles became independent of Mauritius. Although English was used in law and business, French remained the everyday language. Both world wars had a detrimental effect on the economy: in 1914–18 the ships that had taken the islands' produce to international markets stopped calling and during the Second World War the islands were used to refuel British ships but there was a similar decline in exports. The first elections were held in 1948, when only property owners were allowed to vote. The two main parties were founded in 1964: the Seychelles People's United Party (SPUP) supported complete independence, while the Seychelles Democratic Party (SDP) was committed to maintaining a connection with Britain. All citizens were entitled to vote from 1967 and, following a constitutional conference, a new legislative assembly was established. In elections in 1970 and 1974 the SDP had a narrow majority but in 1977, when the president was abroad, the SPUP took power in an armed coup. Renaming itself the Seychelles People's Progressive Front (SPPF), the new government operated as a single-party state until 1991, despite several attempted coups. The SPPF has won all the elections since the introduction of a new constitution in 1993, although the opposition has consistently taken a substantial proportion of the vote. James Michel won the presidential election in 2006 and is still in power. By the time of independence in 1976, there was an increasing emphasis on tourism in the islands' economy. Victoria is a transportation hub for reaching the other islands by boat or by helicopter.

OBSERVATIONS

Victoria is a small symbolic and administrative centre on the northwest coast of Mahé Island, although the whole island can also be seen as the capital. The downtown area is Victorian and the architecture has the feeling of an old colonial centre, despite many of the older buildings having been replaced.

The layout of the centre is focused on an English clock that stands on a roundabout, commemorating the island's days as a crown colony. The courthouse and library are close by, and commercial buildings line the streets. It is tempting to picture the island as a southern Creole settlement, like New Orleans where the buildings also have large roofs, wide terraces and porches.

Mahé is predominantly a granite island, with steep and winding roads. There has consequently been a significant amount of land reclamation in order to provide accessible development sites. The islanders generally live in bungalows that nestle into the landscape, with lush gardens and granite boundary walls. Some Creole architecture is made from galvanized tin: standing on granite plinths, their barn-like typology is strikingly archetypal. The newer residential architecture is the usual international vernacular.

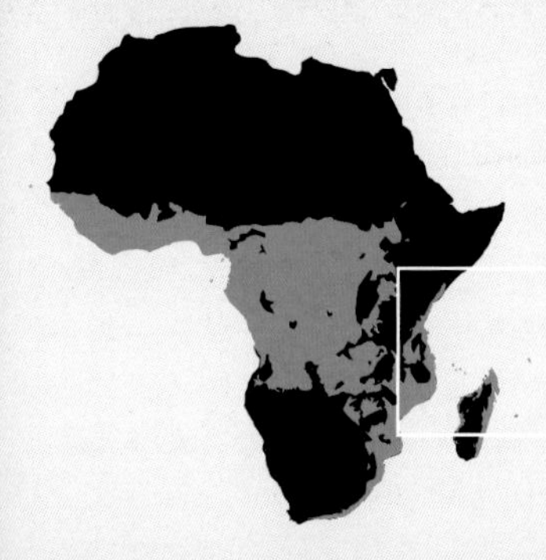

NATIONAL POPULATION

96,000

CITY POPULATION

27,000

ETHNIC GROUPS

mixed French, African, Indian, Chinese and Arab

RELIGIONS

Roman Catholic 76.2%, Protestant 10.6% (Anglican 6.1%, Pentecostal Assembly 1.5%, Seventh-Day Adventist 1.2%, other Protestant 1.8), other Christian 2.4%, Hindu 2.4%, Muslim 1.6%, other non-Christian 1.1%, unspecified 4.8%, none 0.9%

LANGUAGES

Seychellois Creole (official) 89.1%, English (official) 5.1%, French (official) 0.7%, other 3.8%, unspecified 1.3%

GDP

$2.42 billion

AGRICULTURAL PRODUCTS

coconuts, cinnamon, vanilla, sweet potatoes, cassava (manioc, tapioca), copra, bananas; tuna

INDUSTRIES

fishing, tourism, beverages

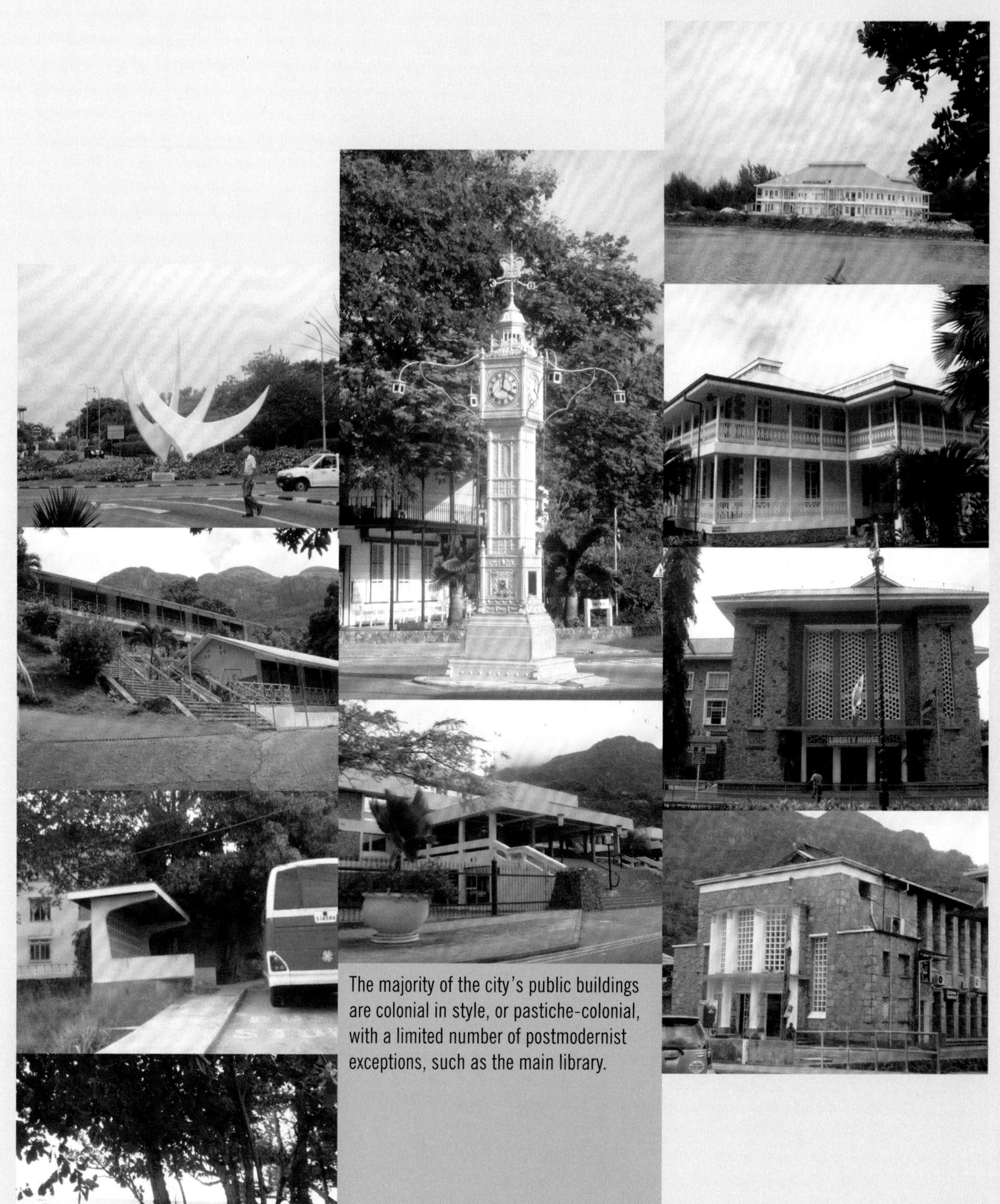

The majority of the city's public buildings are colonial in style, or pastiche-colonial, with a limited number of postmodernist exceptions, such as the main library.

Buildings of this type often repeat the forms of the city's colonial architecture, but on a larger scale. There is a limited number of modernist retail buildings, as well as some postmodernist banks.

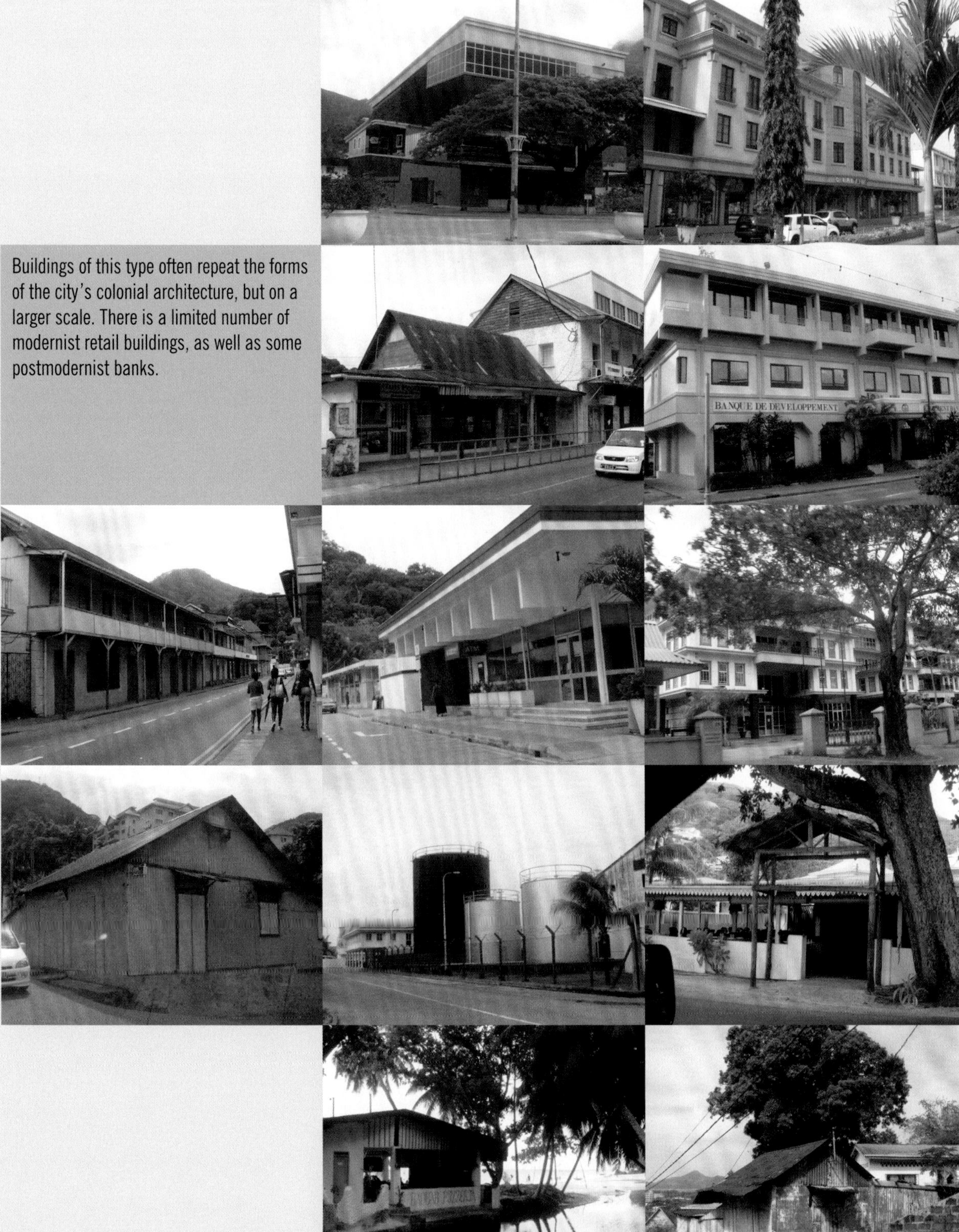

The bungalow type is found in a variety of situations, from flat ground to steep slopes. This is an architecture of roofs and modest enclosures that merge well with the island's flora and enjoy outstanding views. Early examples were built of corrugated tin, with high roofs, large doors and multiple openings for ventilation.

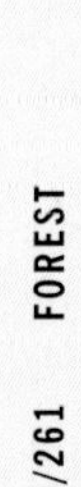

YAOUNDÉ / CAMEROON

OVERVIEW

The south of the country has been occupied for several millennia by ethnic groups such as the Baka, sometimes known as pygmies. Around 2,000 years ago they began to be displaced by Bantu people as they migrated from the north but groups of pygmies continued to coexist with the Bantu. The area around Lake Chad in the far north was settled by Sao people, who had migrated from the Nile valley and were absorbed into the Kanem-Bornu Empire in the 10th century CE. In the 15th and 16th centuries the Fulani people moved eastwards from Senegal and some of them settled in the central area of Cameroon. The name of the country comes from the Portuguese name for the Wouri River, Rio dos Camarões ('River of Prawns'), which they discovered in 1472. Other European countries were frequent visitors during the slave trade but the first permanent settlements did not occur until British missionaries arrived in the 19th century. But it was Germany that developed a more substantial colony after signing a treaty with local leaders. After the First World War the country was divided between France and Britain, who took the areas to the east and west of a diagonal, north–south boundary. The effects of this division still resonate today.

French Cameroon became independent in 1960 and Ahmadou Ahidjo, leader of the Union Camerounaise, was the first president. He ruled in a pragmatic fashion, combining favouritism with repression. As a result of a referendum in 1961 the south of British Cameroon, the area around Bamenda, opted to join a federation with the Republic of Cameroon, while the northern section became part of Nigeria. Ahidjo wished to strengthen the identity of the expanded country and, following a referendum in 1972, the federation became a republic, a change of status that upset the citizens of the previously British area. Ahidjo stepped down in 1982 and was replaced by Paul Biya, who distanced himself from his predecessor by accusing him of involvement in attempted coups. Ahidjo went into exile in France but Biya continued many of Ahidjo's policies and, with good supplies of oil and other resources, the economy expanded and people began to enjoy a higher standard of living. This period came to an abrupt halt in 1985 when, due to an international recession, the economy collapsed. In 1991 Biya responded to public pressure and legalized opposition parties, won the general election in the following year and has remained president ever since. The main opposition party, the Social Democratic Front, based in the area that had previously been British, withdrew from future elections because of suspicions that the Biya victory was the result of ballot rigging. Throughout the 1990s the government struggled with difficult conditions, punctuated by a localized war with Nigeria over the ownership of the Bakassi peninsula and its oil. Despite oil reserves and favourable conditions for agriculture, the economy remains weak. Biya's government is working with international bodies to improve the situation.

OBSERVATIONS

Set in the interior of the country, at an altitude of 750 m, Yaoundé has a refreshing climate and a striking urban scape. In rolling countryside, the city undulates across valleys and hills, offering a multitude of perspectives from many vantage points. The centre is in a valley, close to a small lake that is a pleasure space for the citizens.

The downtown area is centred on the Boulevard du 20 Mai, with the administrative and commercial areas at opposite ends. Many of the government buildings are designed in a striking late-modernist manner that is clearly intended to suggest the aspirations of the country. The service sector, in the form of hotels, is also responsible for several big statements in the city's fabric, while the older commercial buildings climb up the city's dramatic streets.

The architecture of mosques and churches dominates local areas, rather than the city in general. Most of the embassies and wealthier residences are in the north, with less affluent suburbs sprawling to the city limits in other directions. The president's palace and parliament are also situated on hills to the north of the centre. Somewhat inaccessible, they occupy positions that signify their importance to the city.

NATIONAL POPULATION

23,344,000

CITY POPULATION

3,066,000

ETHNIC GROUPS

Cameroon Highlanders 31%, Equatorial Bantu 19%, Kirdi 11%, Fulani 10%, Northwestern Bantu 8%, Eastern Nigritic 7%, other African 13%, non-African less than 1%

RELIGIONS

indigenous beliefs 40%, Christian 40%, Muslim 20%

LANGUAGES

24 major African language groups, English (official), French (official)

GDP

$67.78 billion

AGRICULTURAL PRODUCTS

coffee, cocoa, cotton, rubber, bananas, oilseed, grains, cassava (manioc, tapioca); livestock; timber

INDUSTRIES

petroleum production and refining, aluminium production, food processing, light consumer goods, textiles, lumber, ship repair

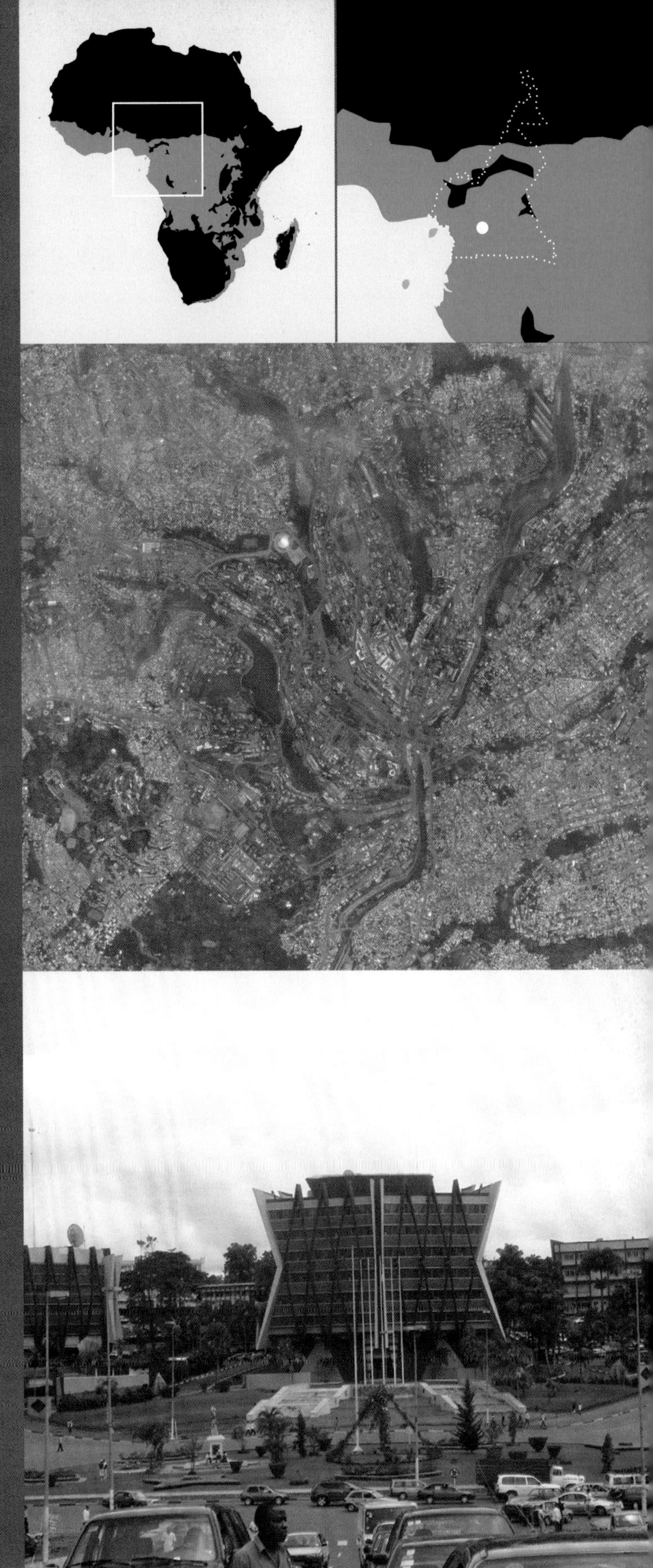

YAOUNDÉ / CAMEROON / **CIVIC**

In a range of styles and colours, these buildings create a distinctive atmosphere in the city. The religious buildings have less impact than in other places, but the city stadium is a dramatic one-sided arena, set on a hill.

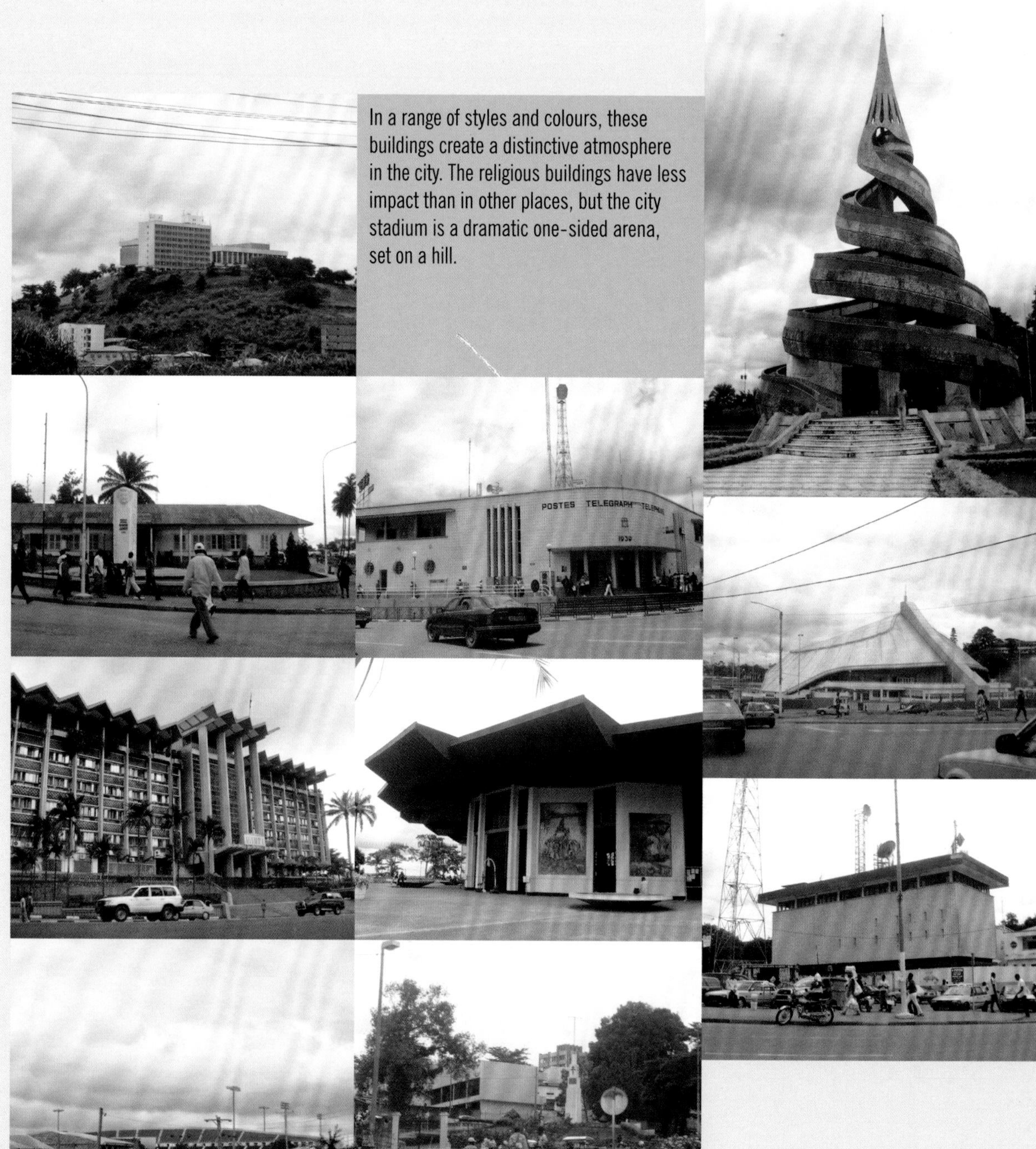

This varies in quality from impressive hotels in late- and postmodernist styles to the more functional type of developments that now typify the continent. The country's main breweries are located here and, with their tanks and storage buildings, dominate the fringes of the city.

SIFFLETS D'OR
LUC'S PRESSING
LUC'S PRESSING
Orange
TIGER ARCADE
PHOTO
SUPER MARCHE
MAHIMA

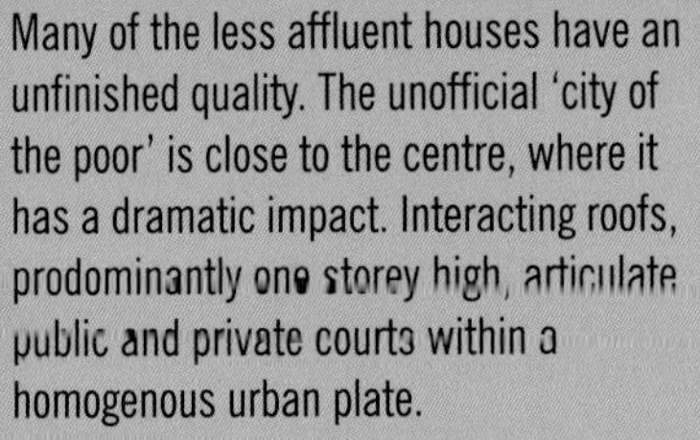

Many of the less affluent houses have an unfinished quality. The unofficial 'city of the poor' is close to the centre, where it has a dramatic impact. Interacting roofs, prodominantly one storey high, articulate public and private courts within a homogenous urban plate.

SAVANNA & GRASSLAND

Savanna grasslands are found between 8 and 20 degrees latitude on either side of the equator. In the north they occupy an area that extends from Senegal in the west to the valley of the Nile in the east, and in the south they extend from Angola to Mozambique. The climate is warm or hot throughout the year, with rainfall occurring in a limited period: April to September in the north, and October to March in the south. Annual rainfall is likely to be in the range of 800–1500 mm but in more continental locations it can be as low as 500 mm. The vegetation consists of grassland with scattered trees forming an open canopy, and the grassland can be divided into three main types, with dry seasons of different lengths. In wet savanna the dry season lasts for 3–5 months and the higher rainfall supports the growth of taller grasses (1.5–4.5 m in height). In dry savanna the dry season lasts for 5–7 months and supports shorter grasses, no more than 30 cm tall. In thornbush savanna the dry season is longer than seven months and the grass turns green only in the rainy season. The distinction between savanna and grassland depends on the number of trees in a given location. In common with other grassland areas, savanna is often the product of human activity, such as the grazing of animals or the cultivation of crops, as well as the climatic conditions.

SAVANNA & GRASSLAND

The rolling out of the landscape, like a carpet, is one of the things that influence the shape of all the cities in this region, and despite the distances between them they have many similarities. In this setting there is a field of architecture that articulates itself to the twists and curves of the topography in Antananarivo and to the soft contours of Gaborone. In Abuja there is an undulating plane with the building pixellated into the landscape, and in Dakar the form of the city addresses the drama of its coastal location. Apart from Antananarivo, with its hills, these cities are short of vantage points and, because of their horizontality, it is difficult to see the edge of them – they just disappear into the wider context. Of the interior cities, two are explicitly colonial – Pretoria and Antananarivo – and two are more recent – Abuja and Gaborone – and represent African modernity. Although the climate is more temperate in this region than others, it is still quite harsh and the architecture has had to come to terms with the strength of the light and the need for shade. This explains the brise-soleil architecture, with its strong horizontals, which articulates Dakar and Pretoria. Abuja uses the technology of tinted glass and in Antananarivo the vernacular roofs and deeply recessed arcades provide a means of controlling the light.

In contrast to some of the other terrains, these cities demonstrate a commitment to public space. This is partly to do with European colonialism – in Dakar, Mogadishu, Pretoria and Antananarivo – but it also figures quite explicitly in the new city of Gaborone, which appears to have accepted the European model for the creation of a forward-looking African city. The fabric of these cities is predominantly horizontal, providing an ideal lining for their civic spaces, and they make use of axes, vistas, imposing facades and formal planting, at a scale that influences their overall organization and development. Towers are more scarce, the most common vertical elements being the minarets and the mid-rise towers of the type you find in Gaborone. The major exception, in terms of architectural space, is Abuja, where the natural landscape continues through the city, due to its relatively low density, and is the primary setting for the country's major institutions.

The original architecture of the colonial cities was very much designed for each place, despite being imposed by foreign powers. Dakar and Antananarivo are genuine experiments in place-making and were organized not just for European settlers, but also to make a relationship with the indigenous communities. I refer to later versions of this architecture as 'tropical modernism'. It is sensitive to climate and terrain and is carefully articulated to reflect a relationship to place, giving each city its own character. At the urban scale, despite the formality of certain elements, the layout of these cities is not something that you would ever find in France. In Dakar, as well as Algiers and the other Maghreb cities, you get a sense of a French-inspired plan but an African city, which is a strange contradiction but the physical, social and climatic conditions demand it. Architecturally speaking, these cities represented a sincere attempt to engage with the needs of the places themselves. I think this is why Dakar and Antananarivo are successful cities and have been easily adopted by the indigenous communities as their own, as an expression of both their identity and their modernity.

Pretoria is the only colonial city that presents a dual phenomenon, as an explicitly European city in the middle of the Savanna that deals with the indigenous context as an afterthought. Colonial Pretoria probably contains more squares overlooked by public buildings than anywhere else on the continent, an arrangement that turns its back on the impressive landscape that surrounds the city. But the recent architecture of the downtown area is emphatically about structure and, although they are quite rigid in character, the commercial buildings are a less expressive version of tropical modernism. There is something very powerful about seeing these distinctive volumes, standing in line on grand boulevards, each employing a different louvre system for solar and humidity control.

ANTANANARIVO / Adjusting to the twists and curves of the topography.

GABORONE / The entrance court to the parliament building.

ABUJA / The rolling landscape.

DAKAR / An example of tropical modernism.

ANTANANARIVO / L'Avenue de l'Indépendance.

ANTANANARIVO / French-inspired but an African city.

Even though this is a generalized architecture of plinths and blocks, its expression is particular to the location. So the contradiction in Pretoria concerns the difference between the emphatic imperial architecture and the modernist buildings that, almost by default, connect with a larger sense of place.

Gaborone is a very bucolic place where the architecture weaves the buildings and the landscape into a single entity. You never have the sense of an overarching urban plan, except when you are on the pedestrian avenue that leads to the parliament building. Apart from that, the entire city is a soft matrix set in the landscape – Abuja is the strong, muscular version of the same thing. The softness comes, in part, from the consistency of the architecture in Gaborone, which is unusual in Africa. You see it in the earlier public buildings but also in several of the recent commercial buildings, which are quite complex. They have a space-making role in the landscape; their scale is limited but there are some very deliberate statements at every level. The population of Gaborone is not that high and, thanks to diamonds, it is very prosperous for its size and that is reflected in the environment, which is very controlled. Abuja is also very affluent and is the city that now represents the whole of Nigeria.

Despite a shared interest in creating public space in their central areas, these cities present a more varied picture when you look at their residential architecture. In Pretoria there is an architectural dialogue between an urban elite, developing increasingly sophisticated models of apartment living, and the cellular architecture of the suburban townships. Gaborone is notable for its courtyard housing. The basic desire here is to be close to the ground and this leads to the simple cubic architecture that dominates many neighbourhoods. There are two-storey versions of these houses in the middle-class areas but single-storey is far more common. In a more metropolitan city like Abuja, you can find everything from shanty towns to grand villas. The houses of the poor are closely related to village architecture in the countryside, which is about enclosed cells and porches. In the prosperous residential areas, the architecture ranges from large villas to the house that is morphing into an aircraft. This type of expression, which sometimes concerns a fantasy about the location of the house, is played out in a more suppressed form in the villas that are wrapped with balconies. Personalized balconies, applied to very large volumes, give these suburbs their grandeur. Dakar and Antananarivo have sophisticated apartment cultures, similar to Algiers and Luanda, where apartment living is very much the norm. Its architectural expression is in cellular modernist buildings where people lead much of their life on the balcony, but this is not typical of Africa.

PRETORIA / The new skyline.

GABORONE / An office building making space in the landscape.

GABORONE / A courtyard house.

ABUJA / A suburban house morphing into an aircraft.

PRETORIA / Emphatic colonial architecture.

GABORONE / The pedestrian avenue.

ABUJA / NIGERIA

OVERVIEW

Following its introduction in 12th century, Islam became the predominant religion of the Kanem-Bornu Empire around Lake Chad and of the Hausa kingdoms in the area around Kano. But Islam was not taken up in the south of the country, which was occupied by a number of independent states that originated in the 12th and 13th centuries, such as the kingdoms of Ife, Benin and Oyo. The organization of these states was based on the central role of a monarch and his court, while the Igbo people in the southeast lived within a more open, federal organization. The people of the south were predominantly Yoruba and were the first to encounter Europeans, when the Portuguese arrived in the 15th century, and became enmeshed in the slave trade as it developed in the following years. In contrast, the people of the north continued to benefit from the trans-Saharan trade routes and had little contact with Europeans until the 19th century. In 1809 an Islamic revival led to the foundation of a caliphate in Sokoto, in the northwest. With the abolition of slavery, the British wished to curtail the Yoruba slavers and took control of Lagos's port. After some competition with the French, they occupied the country early in the 20th century and recognized differences in population and culture by establishing a colony in the south and a protectorate in the north, with Lagos as the capital of both.

As the time for independence approached, it became clear that the main regions had reached different stages of development and that this might lead to a future imbalance of power. A moderate northerner, Abubakar Tafawa Balewa, who had won the elections in 1959, became the first prime minister after independence in 1960 but his government degenerated into favouritism and corruption. When, as a result of ballot rigging, his party won the election in 1965, there was widespread unrest. The country fell into factional infighting, with successive military leaders from different areas displacing each other in quick succession and provoking increasing levels of ethnic violence. Finally, in 1967, the Igbos announced the secession of their homeland, Biafra, around the Niger delta, where oil had been discovered. The civil war over Biafra lasted three years and ended only after a food blockade that resulted in the deaths of many thousands of Igbos. Postwar reconstruction was supported by the growth in the country's oil revenue, and accompanied by widespread corruption. By 1985 there had been six coups since independence, oil revenue was falling, and the country was in serious debt. After a bloodless coup in 1985 the new president, Ibrahim Babangida, declared his aim to return to multiparty elections, which took place in 1993. The results were still not acceptable to some generals and there were two further coups, and a death in office, before Olusegun Obasanjo of the centre-right People's Democratic Party (PDP) was elected president in 1999. He took steps to unify the country and rebuild the economy, and gave Nigeria a significant place in African affairs. Although politics has been largely free of military interference since then, ethnic violence has continued and over 10,000 people were killed in Obasanjo's first term in office. The PDP remained in power until 2015, when they were defeated by Muhammadu Buhari and the centre-left All Progressives Congress. In an ethnically neutral location, Abuja was planned as the future capital in the 1970s and assumed that role in 1991.

OBSERVATIONS

Abuja is in the interior of the country, next to the humped form of Aso Rock, which makes a distinctive backdrop to this modernist city. The main mosque, with its great dome and four towers, is easily recognizable as one enters the city, and the cathedral is a modern rendition of a traditional form, with a striking tower and vaulted interior. These buildings set the scene for the competition between the two religions.

The residential areas are outside the centre and many of the houses represent the fantasies of their owners, making for a potpourri of styles that animates each neighbourhood. An extreme example is the house designed to look like a jet aircraft.

The poor areas are the furthest from the centre. Though better than some cities, they have the same attributes: mud roads, poor infrastructure, informal trading along the main thoroughfares. The houses are built of block, if there is money in the family, or mud and recycled materials.

NATIONAL POPULATION

182,202,000

CITY POPULATION

2,440,000

ETHNIC GROUPS

Over 250 including: Hausa and Fulani 29%, Yoruba 21%, Igbo (Ibo) 18%, Ijaw 10%, Kanuri 4%, Ibibio 3.5%, Tiv 2.5%

RELIGIONS

Muslim 50%, Christian 40%, indigenous beliefs 10%

LANGUAGES

English (official), Hausa, Yoruba, Igbo (Ibo), Fulani, over 500 additional indigenous languages

GDP

$1.05 trillion

AGRICULTURAL PRODUCTS

cocoa, peanuts, cotton, palm oil, corn, rice, sorghum, millet, cassava (manioc, tapioca), yams, rubber, cattle, sheep, goats, pigs, timber, fish

INDUSTRIES

crude oil, mining (coal, tin, columbite), rubber products, wood, hides and skins, textiles, cement and other construction materials, food products, footwear, chemicals, fertilizer, printing, ceramics, steel

The architecture of the public buildings is intended to present Abuja as the country's symbolic centre of power. Key government buildings, the cathedral and the main mosque occupy conspicuous sites in the centre of the city.

ABUJA / NIGERIA / **COMMERCIAL**

This is often found in the suburbs. Major corporations occupy compound buildings, which have become destinations in their own right, and hotels provide an interior world of shopping, eating and conferencing.

The more affluent areas are based on the garden-city model of villas in a landscape. On the edge of the city, the poorer areas are in better shape than other places but still suffer from inadequate infrastructure.

ANTANANARIVO / MADAGASCAR

OVERVIEW

The first inhabitants of Madagascar are thought to have arrived from southeast Asia and to have brought rice cultivation to the island. The existence of Madagascar was known to Arab sailors before it came to the attention of the Portuguese in 1500. Although the British and the Dutch attempted to establish bases at a later date, European colonization did not occur for several centuries. By the beginning of the 19th century the Merina people had become more powerful than their neighbours and, when Radama I assumed power in 1810, he raised an army that subjugated all of the other kingdoms except one. He developed trade with Britain and encouraged Christian missionaries to set up schools. His family remained in power until 1863 when Radama II was assassinated. One of the leaders of the coup became prime minister and married Radama's widow and the two succeeding queens. As Britain became less involved, France was increasingly attracted to Madagascar and, following military intervention, the island became a full colony in 1896 when the queen of the Merina went into exile.

Slavery was abolished in the early years of the 20th century but the tax regime that replaced it was equally harsh and land was seized from local people for coffee plantations. This resulted in an increasing number of demonstrations and strikes; nationalist movements gathered momentum but it was not until the 1930s that a campaign for full independence took shape under the leadership of Jean Ralaimongo. The lingering resentment against the French came to a head in a rebellion of 1947, which was suppressed but provided inspiration for the nationalist parties that were founded in the 1950s. Madagascar became an independent state in 1960, with Philibert Tsiranana of the Parti Social Démocrate (Social Democratic Party) as the first president. Although he retained links with France, the economy declined and an uprising in the capital led to Tsiranana's resignation in 1972. After several coups and attempted coups, the military formed a government under Admiral Didier Ratsiraka who turned away from France with a radical socialist programme. The economy was growing progressively weaker and after his reelection in suspicious circumstances in 1989 riots brought the country to a halt. Although the opposition won the following election, their leader was ineffective and was impeached for money laundering in 1996. Ratsiraka returned to government but the election in 2001 failed to produce a clear result and both candidates, Ratsiraka and Marc Ravalomanana, a businessman and mayor of Antananarivo, claimed victory. After a lengthy power struggle, the military decided to back Ravalomanana who attracted foreign investors and started to repair the country's infrastructure. He won a second term in 2006 but was deposed by the opposition leader, Andry Rajoelina, in 2009. After international mediation, Hery Rajaonarimampianina won the elections in 2013. The Merina founded Antananarivo as a military base in 1610 and made it their capital in the 18th century.

OBSERVATIONS

The city is situated on a plateau in the middle of the island and its centre is surrounded by the hills where people live. Approaching from the airport, you pass paddy fields and signs of an agricultural lifestyle that give some clues about the inhabitants of the city.

There is informal trading on the pavements that makes the city bustle; different areas have markets for food, flowers, medicines and other items. Dramatic staircases are carved into the hillside to give access to the upper parts. Hybridization of the colonial city is everywhere, as new uses are found for every made space.

Unlike other places, the wealthy and the less affluent live side by side in the heart of the city. In very poor areas, some houses have a commercial frontage where people are as entrepreneurial as possible in order to survive. The public spaces in these areas are occupied by informal markets dealing in recycled products.

NATIONAL POPULATION

24,235,000

CITY POPULATION

2,610,000

ETHNIC GROUPS

Malayo-Indonesian (Merina and related Betsileo), Cotiers (mixed African, Malayo-Indonesian and Arab ancestry – Betsimisaraka, Tsimihety, Antaisaka, Sakalava), French, Indian, Creole, Comoran

RELIGIONS

indigenous beliefs 52%, Christian 41%, Muslim 7%

LANGUAGES

French (official), Malagasy (official), English

GDP

$34.05 billion

AGRICULTURAL PRODUCTS

coffee, vanilla, sugarcane, cloves, cocoa, rice, cassava (manioc, tapioca), beans, bananas, peanuts; livestock products

INDUSTRIES

meat processing, seafood, soap, beer, leather, sugar, textiles, glassware, cement, automobile assembly, paper, petroleum, tourism, mining

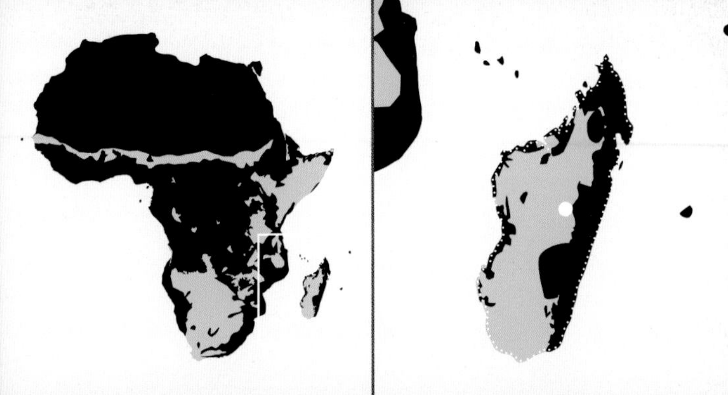

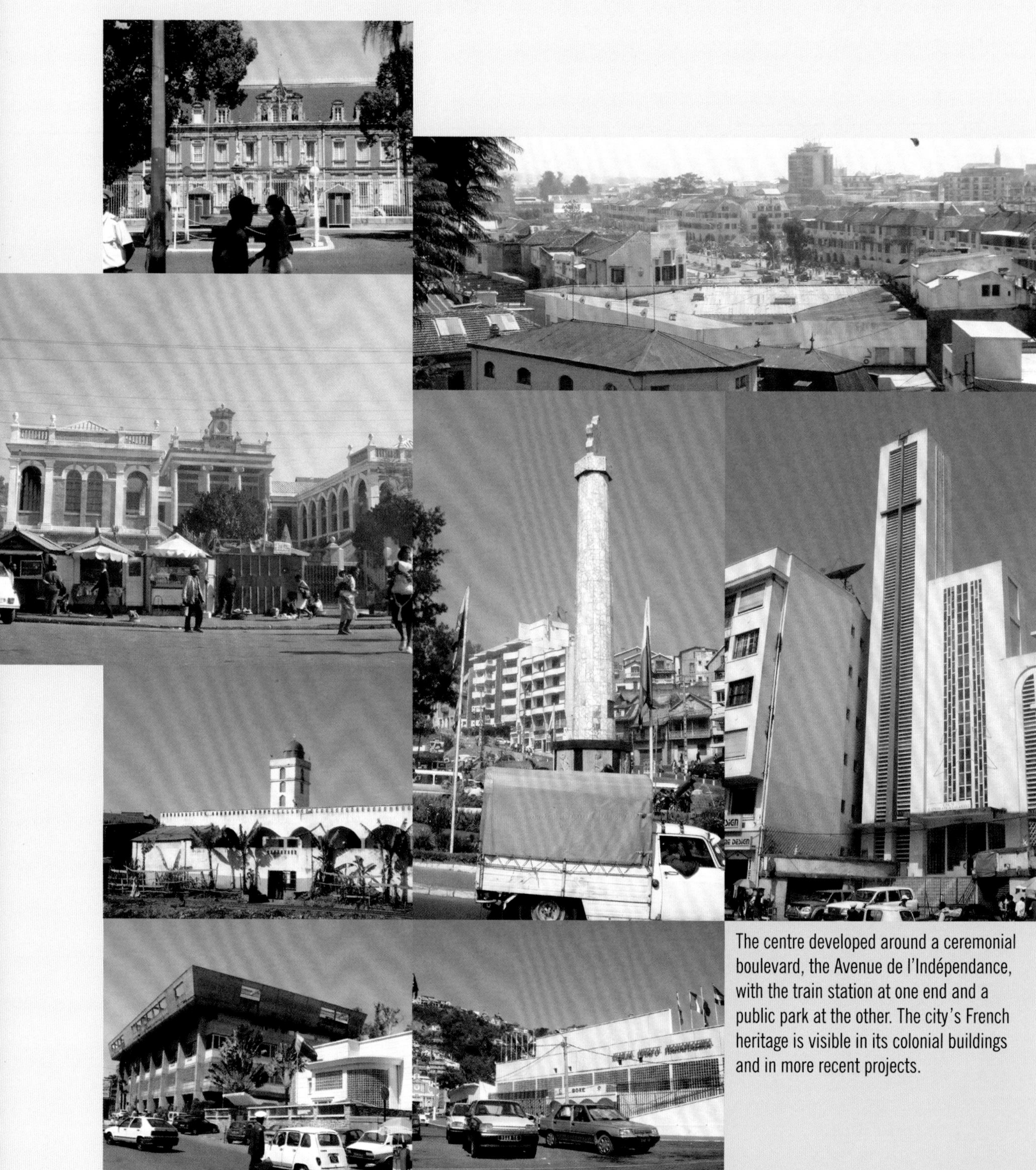

The centre developed around a ceremonial boulevard, the Avenue de l'Indépendance, with the train station at one end and a public park at the other. The city's French heritage is visible in its colonial buildings and in more recent projects.

Most shops are in small- to medium-sized buildings, including some fine examples of art deco. Informal street trading is common in the centre and on the long flights of steps that ascend the hills. More recently, shopping malls have arrived in the suburbs.

The colonial city still provides much of the city's accommodation, and the houses and apartment buildings snake around the hills, making a picturesque landscape. The very poor live on the outer edge of the city.

FID

DAKAR / SENEGAL

OVERVIEW

This area has been occupied since early in the 1st millennium. The Tekrur Empire developed on the Senegal River in the 9th and 10th centuries, and the Jolof Empire flourished in the centre of the future country at a slightly later date. Portuguese explorers reached the Senegal River in 1443 and, starting in the 16th century, the Dutch, British and French struggled for control of the trade in gold, ivory and slaves. After establishing a base at Saint-Louis in the north of the country in 1659, the French occupied the island of Gorée, to the south of the peninsula where the future capital would be sited, and secured access to a large area of French West Africa. The slave trade was banned in 1815 and it was not until Louis Faidherbe was appointed governor in 1854 that the French discovered an economic alternative: the cultivation of groundnuts along the Senegal River. Faidherbe was also responsible for founding the settlement that would become Dakar. The only resistance to the French came from two sources. A Muslim holy man, El-Hajj Umar Tall, established a power base in Mali and his forces repeatedly crossed the border to attack the French in the second half of the 19th century. In this period Islamic brotherhoods were also active within Senegal. From their religious base, the brotherhoods have continued to develop their political and economic power since that time.

In 1887 the residents of Saint-Louis, Gorée, Dakar and Rufisque were given a limited form of French citizenship. The first African was voted onto the French National Assembly in 1914 and Senegalese were able to study in France. One of these students was Léopold Sédar Senghor who, having also represented Senegal in the French National Assembly, became the first president after Senegal's independence in 1960. A popular president, he remained in power until he voluntarily stepped down in 1980. The most serious disruption during this period was caused by student riots in 1968, which were confronted by the army. Senghor's successor was Abdou Diouf and, despite the collapse of a special understanding with Gambia, a dispute with Mauritania, and conflict with a separatist movement in the Casamance area in the south, he continued in power until 2000. The opposition to Diouf was led by Abdoulaye Wade but his Senegalese Democratic Party was defeated in elections in 1983 and 1988. After being arrested in the 1988 election for anti-government activity, Wade was given a suspended sentence and went into exile in France. He returned to Senegal to fight further elections in 1993 and 1998, and was finally successful in 2000. After a peaceful transfer of power, a new constitution was voted through in 2001. Wade was reelected in 2007 but defeated in 2012 by Macky Sall. Due to agreements signed with the rebels in 2001 and 2004, the Casamance area has been more settled, despite an ongoing campaign for independence. Dakar succeeded Saint-Louis as the capital in 1902.

OBSERVATIONS

Dakar is a very lively coastal city and forms the natural border between Arab and black Africa. The old city was built by the French who employed a form of colonial modernism to create the urban landscape. A large part of the population is Muslim, so there is a certain discretion to public life, as well as an air of tolerance.

Although Dakar is a Francophone city, people express an African pride. Other Africans are greeted warmly and French is used – with a local dialect injected, for dialogue and friendship. The predominant ethnic group, the Wolof, still make their presence felt.

The structure and use patterns of this European-type city are so well established that the Senegalese are completely at ease with it. On first impression, you do not notice the obvious signs of mutation but with time you begin to understand that the Senegalese are now the colonizers, bending the city to their culture.

NATIONAL POPULATION

15,129,000

CITY POPULATION

3,520,000

ETHNIC GROUPS

Wolof 38.7%, Fula 26.5%, Serer 15%, Mandinka 4.2%, Jola 4%, Soninke 2.3%, other 9.3% (includes Europeans and persons of Lebanese descent)

RELIGIONS

Muslim 95.4% (most adhere to one of the four main Sufi brotherhoods), Christian 4.2% (mostly Roman Catholic), animist 0.4%

LANGUAGES

French (official), Wolof, Pulaar, Jola, Mandinka

GDP

$34.2 billion

AGRICULTURAL PRODUCTS

peanuts, millet, corn, sorghum, rice, cotton, tomatoes, green vegetables; cattle, poultry, pigs; fish

INDUSTRIES

agricultural and fish processing, mining (gold, phosphate, zircon), fertilizer production, petroleum refining, construction materials, ship construction and repair

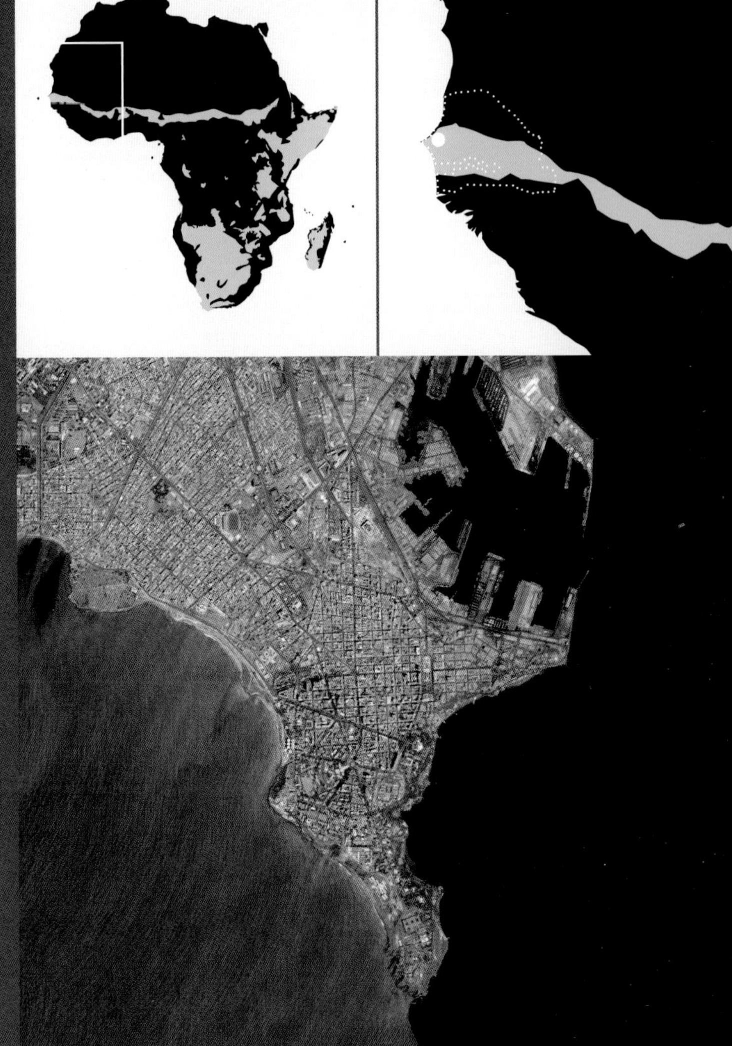

DAKAR / SENEGAL / **CIVIC**

The core of the city, around the Place de l'Indépendance, is located on raised ground above the surrounding waterfront. The city's lively culture, with its Arabic and French influences, is reflected in the diversity of its public buildings.

CREDIT AGRICOLE
CNCAS
EL MANSOUR
MARIZ

DAKAR / SENEGAL / **COMMERCIAL**

A sense of style permeates much of the city's commercial architecture, particularly the sleek modernist buildings whose proportions and light colours are reminiscent of ocean liners.

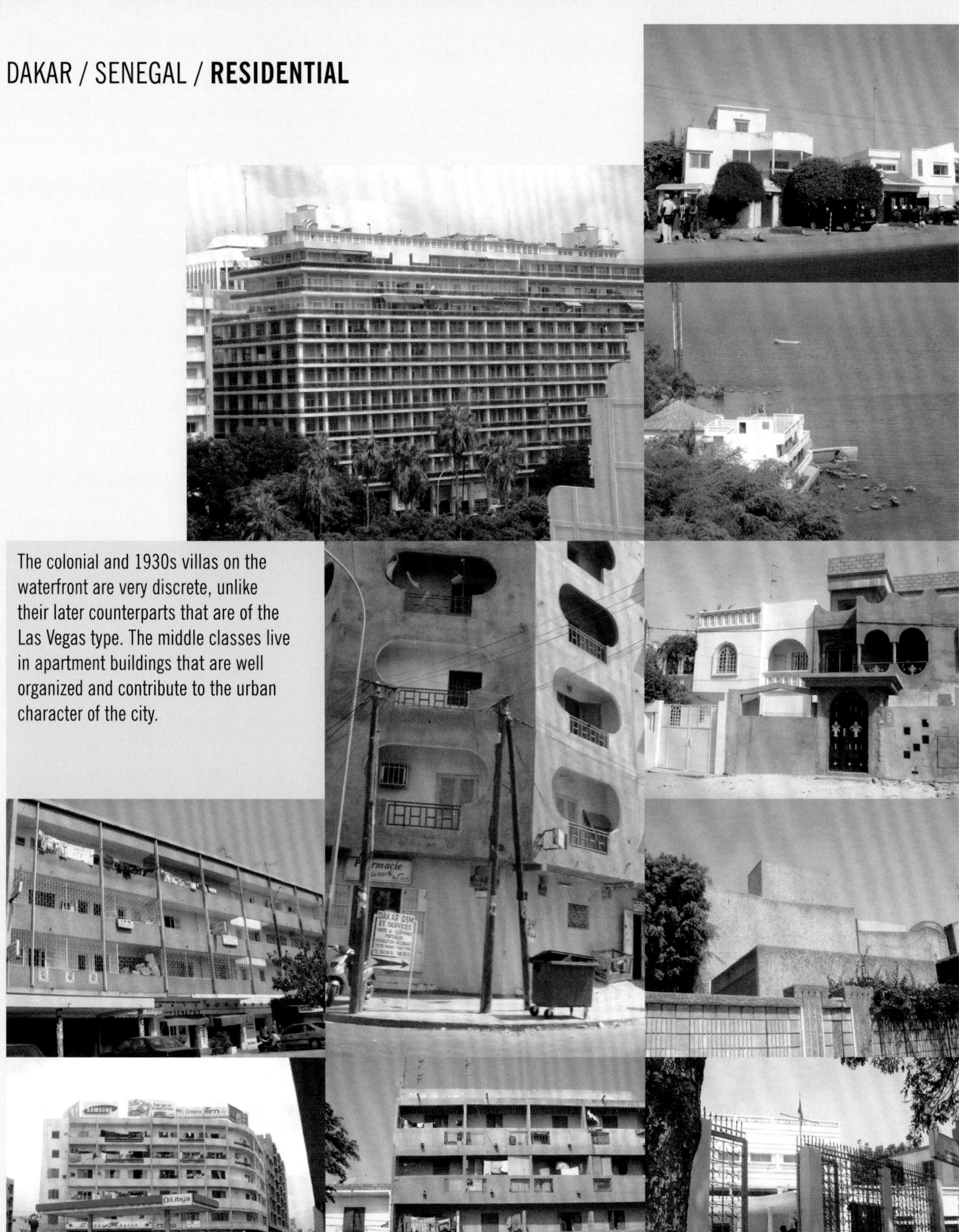

The colonial and 1930s villas on the waterfront are very discrete, unlike their later counterparts that are of the Las Vegas type. The middle classes live in apartment buildings that are well organized and contribute to the urban character of the city.

GABORONE / BOTSWANA

OVERVIEW

Most of Botswana is a 1,000-metre-high plateau that, in the centre and southwest of the country, is occupied by the Kalahari Desert. As in Namibia, the area was originally settled by the San people, who were later joined by the Khoikhoi and, together, they became known as the Khoisan. The first Bantu migration took place in the 1st century CE and was followed by another in the 14th century, when the Tswana people moved into the southeast of the country and eventually dominated the population. During the *Difaqane*, or forced migration, of the 1820s the Zulu pushed the Tswana into the Kalahari before they were able to reorganize themselves in a number of independent settlements. The Tswana were not receptive to the Christianity of the early missionaries, who respected them for their independence. But this was not true of the Boers as they moved into the area from the Cape Colony. When the British recognized the Transvaal in 1852, the Boers informed the Tswana that they were part of the Republic of South Africa. The Tswana were reluctant to accept white rule and repeatedly sought British assistance to maintain their independence. After some delay, the British declared the area to the south of the Molopo River to be the British Crown Colony of Bechuanaland, and the area to the north of the river became the British Protectorate of Bechuanaland. A further threat to the Tswana came in the form of Cecil Rhodes and the British South Africa Company. The company's attempts to take over practical control of the country were resisted by Tswana chiefs, who took their case to London where public pressure forced the government to intervene. The Tswana intended to maintain traditional practices but their rights were heavily circumscribed by the interests of the British. With the rise of more powerful economies in South Africa and Rhodesia, Bechuanaland became increasingly impoverished.

Although there was a growing awareness of nationalist issues in the 1950s, the first independence party was not founded until 1960. In 1961 Seretse Khama, a Tswana chief who had been forced to give up power due to marrying a white Englishwoman while studying in England, founded the more moderate Bechuanaland Democratic Party (BDP) and sought the support of the chiefs and their people in the move towards independence. They organized the transfer of the capital from Mafikeng to Gaborone in 1965, wrote a constitution, and set up a timetable for the new government. After a general election in 1965, Khama became president and the Republic of Botswana declared independence in 1966. Although Khama was well aware of the country's economic links with South Africa and Rhodesia, he disapproved of apartheid and did not exchange ambassadors with South Africa. When he died in 1980 the BDP still had a majority of parliamentary seats and his cofounder, Quett Masire, succeeded him. The elections in 2008 were won by Seretse Khama Ian Khama of the BDP who remains in power. The country's economy was dramatically improved by the discovery of diamonds in 1967. Despite widespread poverty, the country has maintained a relatively high level of growth, and Gaborone now has many more residents than its projected population of 20,000.

OBSERVATIONS

Within the new city, a central boulevard culminates at the parliament and government buildings. The rest of the city is divided into residential and industrial quarters. The village of Gaborone, the original settlement, has become the city's poor neighbourhood.

The informal housing in poor areas is very basic; built of blockwork, with simple roofs, and the windows are often unsealed. The interesting thing is that the houses themselves are arranged in clusters, which have a direct connection to the vernacular typologies in the areas that the inhabitants come from.

NATIONAL POPULATION

2,262,000

CITY POPULATION

232,000

ETHNIC GROUPS

Tswana (or Setswana) 79%, Kalanga 11%, Basarwa 3%, other, including Kgalagadi and white 7%

RELIGIONS

Christian 71.6%, Badimo 6%, other 1.4%, unspecified 0.4%, none 20.6%

LANGUAGES

Setswana 78.2%, Kalanga 7.9%, Sekgalagadi 2.8%, English (official) 2.1%, other 8.6%, unspecified 0.4%

GDP

$35.87 billion

AGRICULTURAL PRODUCTS

livestock, sorghum, maize, millet, beans, sunflowers, groundnuts

INDUSTRIES

mining (diamonds, copper, nickel, salt, coal, iron ore, silver), soda ash, potash, livestock processing, textiles

GABORONE / BOTSWANA / **CIVIC**

Gaborone was planned as a new city in the 1960s. Modernism is the defining style of the public buildings, as demonstrated by the elegant vaulted architecture of the parliament building.

MINISTRY OF LOCAL GOVERNMENT
STOP

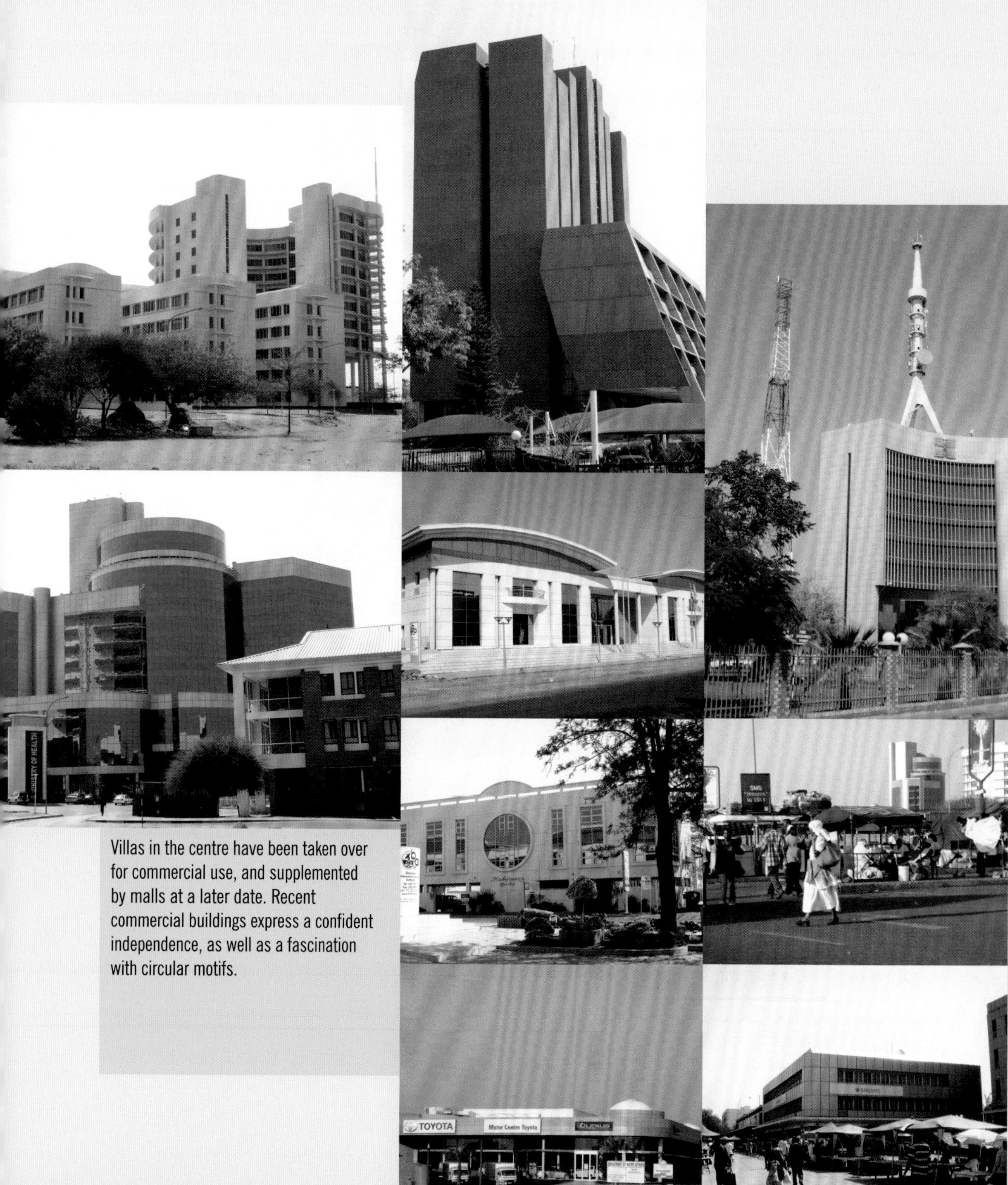

Villas in the centre have been taken over for commercial use, and supplemented by malls at a later date. Recent commercial buildings express a confident independence, as well as a fascination with circular motifs.

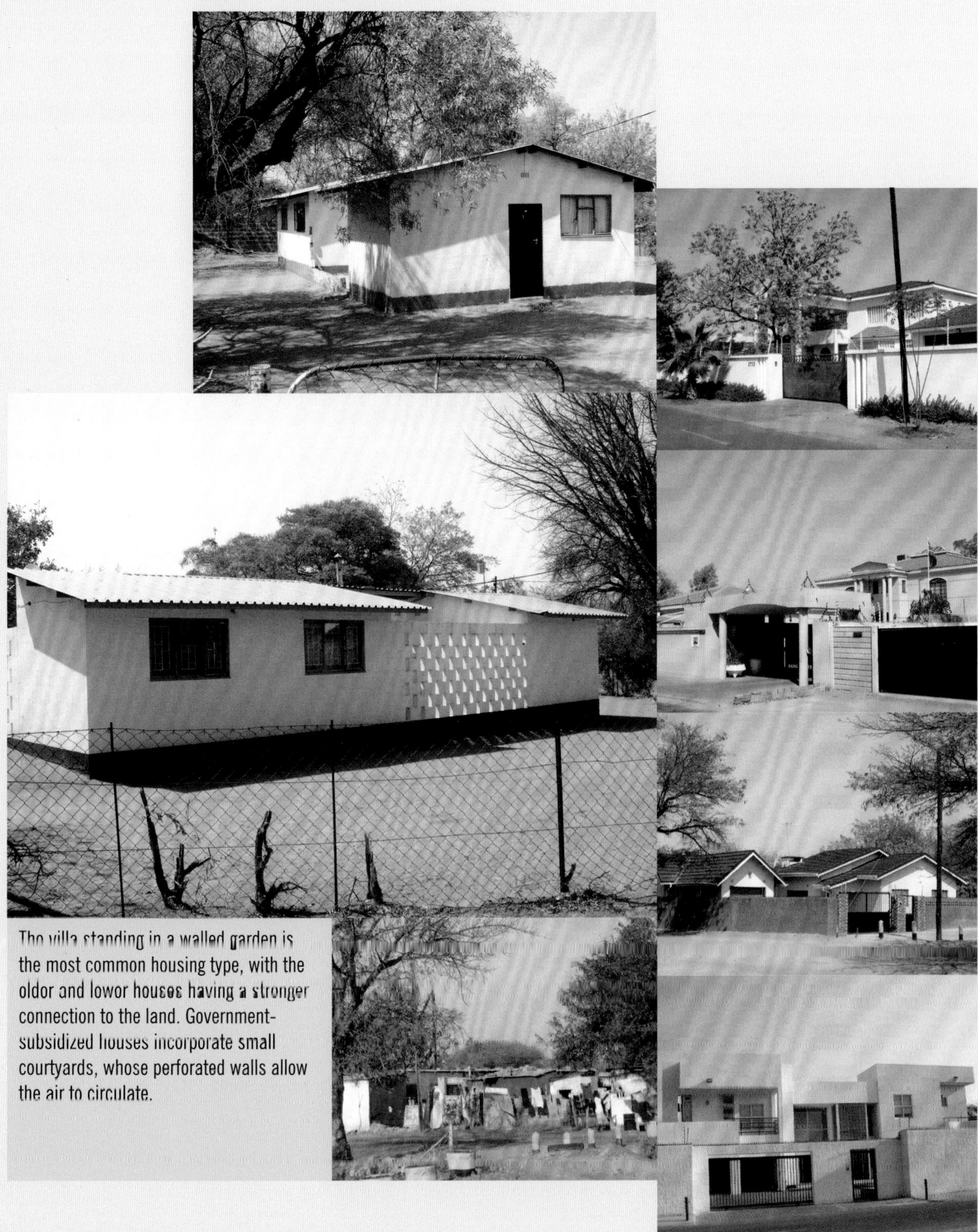

The villa standing in a walled garden is the most common housing type, with the older and lower houses having a stronger connection to the land. Government-subsidized houses incorporate small courtyards, whose perforated walls allow the air to circulate.

MOGADISHU / SOMALIA

OVERVIEW

Arab traders founded Mogadishu in the 10th century as one of a series of ports that connected the Red Sea and the Indian Ocean with the southeast coast of Africa. The Somalis began to settle the north coast at the end of the 1st millennium and gradually occupied more of the country during the 2nd millennium, displacing the Bantu and Galla (or Oromo) people who had lived there previously. As a result, the population is almost exclusively Somalian, united in religion and culture but subject to fierce interclan rivalries. The difficulty of creating a single, unified nation was increased by the effects of colonization in the 19th century. When the French laid claim to Djibouti, the British moved into the north of the country, now known as Somaliland, and the Italians occupied the northeast corner, known as Puntland, as well as the south of the country. Italian attempts to develop the areas in their control met with limited success and Britain did little for the north until 1941, when it took over the Italian areas and tried to unify the country's administration. In 1949 the United Nations put the former territories under Italian administration for a period of ten years in order to prepare for independence.

The Italian and British colonies became the independent Somali Republic in 1960 but, with a weak economy and divisions within the population, the government was indecisive and undermined by corruption. After a coup in 1969 the Supreme Revolutionary Council appointed Mohamed Siad Barre to lead a new socialist state, the Somali Democratic Republic, which was to be allied to the USSR. In 1977 Barre invaded an area of the Ogaden Desert, which had previously been annexed by Ethiopia, with the intention of reuniting the Somali population who lived there. As Ethiopia enjoyed military support from the USSR, it was able to repulse the attack, which subsequently degenerated into interclan violence within Somalia. Siad Barre, the last national leader, left Somalia in 1991 when troops of the Somali National Alliance under Mohamed Farrah Aidid took control of Mogadishu. In 1992 a United Nations peace force led by the United States attempted to separate the warring factions and to distribute food in areas suffering from drought. The UN's efforts were only partly successful and, following the killing of twenty-four Pakistani peacekeepers by Aidid's troops, the force withdrew. After Barre's departure, Mohamed Haji Ibrahim Egal had led the former British zone into a peaceful, but largely unrecognized, independence as the Somaliland Republic. Puntland in the northeast also enjoyed some stability on a semi-autonomous basis but in the remainder of the country there was continuing conflict between Aidid's followers and those of Ali Mahdi Mohamed, leader of the Somali Salvation Alliance, with both men claiming to be president. Following peace talks in the late 1990s a transitional national government was set up in 2000, which proved to be ineffectual in controlling the militia. In 2009 a unity government was given responsibility for introducing a new constitution and moving to representative government. This process concluded in 2012, when Hassan Sheikh Mohamud was elected president. Mogadishu was probably at its most prosperous in the medieval period. It is now recovering from the destructive effects of armed conflict.

OBSERVATIONS

The historic images on the following pages show something of the city before the damage resulting from the conflict between government forces and various terrorist groups. In the period when I was photographing other African cities, I was not able to visit Mogadishu due to safety concerns.

The old city is located directly on the coast, with defensive walls and Arabic architecture. After the Italians arrived, the city developed more slowly than Asmara, the other Italian centre, due to a form of indirect rule in which the administration of the country was entrusted to Italian companies.

At a later stage Rome took direct control and a small group of officials were responsible for developing the city's political and administrative organization as a regional centre. This resulted in improvements to the infrastructure and the construction of public buildings, starting around 1910.

Many of the buildings that defined the city's appearance dated from the 1930s onwards and were colonial, modernist or Arabic in appearance. These styles continued to influence built form until the 1980s, before many buildings were destroyed in the civil conflict that continued from the 1990s to 2011.

NATIONAL POPULATION

10,787,000

CITY POPULATION

2,138,000

ETHNIC GROUPS

Somali 85%, Bantu and other non-Somali 15% (including Arabs 30,000)

RELIGIONS

Sunni Muslim (official)

LANGUAGES

Somali (official), Arabic (official), Italian, English

GDP

$5.9 billion

AGRICULTURAL PRODUCTS

bananas, sorghum, corn, coconuts, rice, sugarcane, mangoes, sesame seeds, beans; cattle, sheep, goats; fish

INDUSTRIES

light industries including sugar refining, textiles, wireless communication

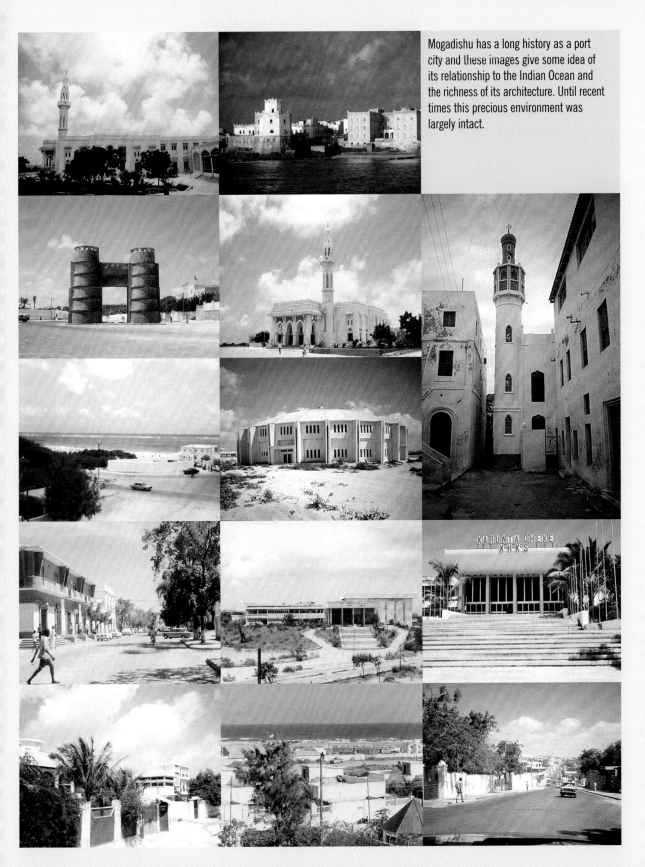

Mogadishu has a long history as a port city and these images give some idea of its relationship to the Indian Ocean and the richness of its architecture. Until recent times this precious environment was largely intact.

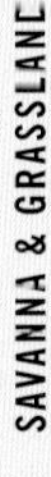

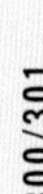

PRETORIA / SOUTH AFRICA

OVERVIEW

San people first occupied this area in 40,000 BCE but in the 3rd century BCE Bantu migrants began to arrive from the north. The Bantu remained dominant until the 19th century, when there was a sharp increase in European settlers and an expansion of the Zulu nation. European settlement was complicated by tension between the British Cape Colony and the Dutch in the Boer area to the west, following which the Boers expressed their dissatisfaction by migrating to the interior in the Great Trek of the 1830s. This caused conflict with local ethnic groups and with the British over voting rights for non-Boer migrants. After the second Anglo-Boer war of 1899–1902 the Boer republics became British colonies. The Union of South Africa was founded in 1910 and the first elections were won by a Boer coalition that legislated against the interests of black people. In the following decades white attitudes became more extreme until the formal adoption of apartheid in 1948. At this point the African National Congress (ANC), which had been founded in 1912, started a campaign of civil disobedience. Their difficulties in advocating a nonracial society were made clear by the Sharpeville massacre in 1960, in which sixty-nine protesters were shot dead by police, and by the life sentence given to their leader Nelson Mandela in 1963.

In 1966 the prime minister, Hendrik Verwoerd, was assassinated and was succeeded by John Vorster, and by P. W. Botha in 1978. The latter two were committed to policies under which blacks were to occupy separate 'homelands' and this resulted in seventy-five per cent of the population living on thirteen per cent of the available land. But two events in the 1970s drew worldwide attention to this untenable arrangement. In Soweto in 1976, at a student demonstration against the use of the Afrikaans language in schools, the police opened fire, beginning a cycle of demonstrations and police crackdowns that would result in over 1,000 deaths. And in 1977 police killed the leader of the Black Consciousness Movement, Steve Biko, while he was in custody and no one was held responsible. After changes to the constitution in 1983 token roles in government were given to mixed-race and Indian residents, but not blacks. Protests continued for the next two years and the government declared a state of emergency that would remain in force until 1990. Although Botha took steps to repeal the so-called 'pass laws', this did not satisfy the protesters or the international community, whose sanctions were starting to undermine the country's economy. To avoid things getting worse, Botha was replaced by F. W. de Klerk in 1989 and apartheid was abolished in the following year, opposition parties were legalized, and Mandela was finally released from jail. In 1991 the Convention for a Democratic South Africa opened discussions on the organization of a multiracial government. At the election in 1994 the ANC won with a comfortable majority but the National Party, representing white interests, secured enough votes to be represented at cabinet level. For the election in 1999 Thabo Mbeki succeeded Nelson Mandela as leader of the ANC and the party won an increased share of the votes at that election and in 2003. After an internal power struggle, Jacob Zuma won the elections in 2009 and 2014. Pretoria was founded as the capital of the Boer Republics in 1855 and was involved in the Boer Civil War of 1863–69.

OBSERVATIONS

This prosperous and stable city developed from uncertain beginnings. In the 1850s the Boers purchased land on the Apies River as a site for a future capital, despite ongoing wars with local people and with the British in the 1860s.

As a result of earlier policies, the population of the city remains predominantly white. Together with the European character of its squares and public buildings, this contributes to the period character of Pretoria compared with the contemporary metropolis of Johannesburg, which is not far away.

NATIONAL POPULATION

54,490,000

CITY POPULATION

2,059,000

ETHNIC GROUPS

black African 80.3%, coloured 8.8%, white 8.4%, Indian/Asian 2.5%

RELIGIONS

Zion Christian 11.1%, Pentecostal/Charismatic 8.2%, Catholic 7.1%, Methodist 6.8%, Dutch Reformed 6.7%, Anglican 3.8%, Muslim 1.5%, other Christian 36%, other 2.3%, none 15.1%, unspecified 1.4%

LANGUAGES

IsiZulu 22.7%, isiXhosa 16%, Afrikaans 13.5%, English 9.6%, Sepedi 9.1%, Setswana 8%, Sesotho 7.6%, Xitsonga 4.5%, siSwati 2.5%, Tshivenda 2.4%, isiNdebele 2.1%, sign language 0.5%, other 1.5%

GDP

$707.1 billion

AGRICULTURAL PRODUCTS

corn, wheat, sugarcane, fruits, vegetables; beef, poultry, mutton, wool, dairy products

INDUSTRIES

mining (world's largest producer of platinum, gold, chromium), automobile assembly, metalworking, machinery, textiles, iron and steel, chemicals, fertilizer, foodstuffs, commercial ship repair

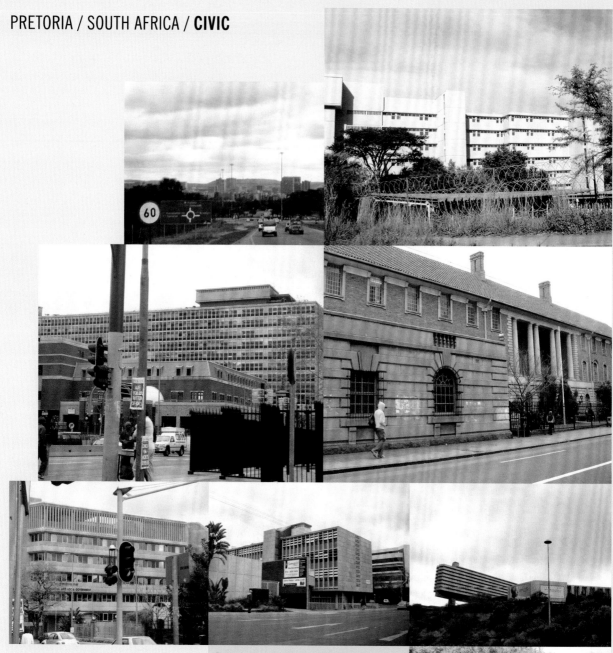

Pretoria has an intensely gridded centre, with several squares that are overlooked by classical-style public buildings. The parliament buildings and university occupy prominent sites on the sides of the valley overlooking the centre.

The business area has been redeveloped with high- and medium-rise buildings whose lower floors address the street. Their facades employ a variety of devices to protect the glazing from the sun. There is no informal trading on the streets.

PRETORIA / SOUTH AFRICA / **RESIDENTIAL**

There is a tradition of apartment living here. In the centre people live above the retail spaces that line the streets, while the residential buildings on the surrounding hills enjoy wide views and catch the breeze.

MOUNTAIN & HIGHVELD

The mountains in East Africa are a southerly continuation of the Ethiopian highlands. They include the Imatong Mountains in the south of Sudan, Mount Elgon (4,321 m) in Uganda, Mount Kenya (5,199 m), and Kilimanjaro (5,895 m) in the north of Tanzania. The climate of this extensive area is temperate, although the temperature decreases and the precipitation increases at higher elevations – normal cultivation is not possible above 2,750 m. The temperature falls below 10°C in winter and rises to 30°C in summer, and rainfall varies between 1,200 mm and 2,000 mm per year. The area was previously a patchwork of forest and grassland at higher levels, with savanna and woodland at lower levels. These landscapes are still to be seen in protected areas; otherwise agriculture and other human activities have had a decisive effect, especially at lower levels where there is extensive cultivation of tea and coffee. South of the Congo basin these mountainous uplands merge with the elevated area that occupies much of the continent. The highveld is an extensive grassland area situated on a high plateau to the west of the Drakensberg range in South Africa. It has an annual rainfall of 1,000 mm or more and is intensively farmed. A rich heritage of indigenous wildlife still survives despite a growing number of threats to its habitat. The landscape and climatic conditions in the mountains and highveld attracted European homesteaders in the 19th and 20th centuries.

MOUNTAIN & HIGHVELD

This terrain includes ten cities, from Asmara in the north to the mountain cities of Mbabane and Maseru in the south. The general environment of the region is comparatively permissive, in the sense that the architecture does not need to take account of the extreme climatic conditions found in other parts of Africa. Because of the elevation, precipitation is high, the vegetation is lush, and the landscape is often bucolic. This is reflected in the picturesque, suburb-like quality that you find in most of these cities, with the exception of Asmara, Harare and Nairobi, the last being the most metropolitan city in the group. I have known about Nairobi since I was a child and heard my parents discussing its high buildings and their contribution to 'the skyline of Africa'. It was already one of the most developed cities in East Africa in terms of its modernity and its politics, and seemed like a model that other places might emulate. Since then the grid of streets at its heart has become even more dense, with the Aga Khan adding to the buildings of the 1960s and 1970s that impressed my parents. But as you move away from the centre the suburbs roll out over the surrounding plateau and it becomes a landscape city where the vegetation is dominant.

Asmara is on the northerly edge of the same mountainous plateau as Addis Ababa but is a very different kind of city because of the art deco and rationalist architecture that was constructed when it was the capital of an Italian colony. With its dispersed Coptic churches, it is a city that is at once classical, modernist and African. It is not planned on a grid but on a boulevard that runs through the heart of the city, and all the secondary functions are related to that: the squares, cathedral and public buildings that punctuate one's sense of space. In Asmara, the architecture of the centre is the dominant image of the city, but in Addis Ababa it is the relationship between the centre and the suburbs that informs the overall character. The downtown area is in a hollow and the residential areas take advantage of their elevated position on the surrounding hills to enjoy the breeze. Addis is not a city that is about looking at a dominant skyline but is about the individual's orientation to nature. This could explain why it can sometimes seem fragmented, when it is actually a strongly formed city that is about enjoying the landscape in a particular way.

Moving further south, the landscape theme is equally strong. In Kigali, where the architecture has no particular quality, the atmosphere is especially bucolic. The usual image of Rwandan architecture is of a house buried in a landscape, and in a similar way Kigali appears to be part of the hill that it stands on. There is no architectural skyline; the city's composition fits the profile of the hill exactly. Compared with Kigali, Lusaka does have some exquisite buildings that are well crafted and suited to the site. But the climate supports an incredible profusion of ornamental plants and the dominant image of the city is of nature creating architectural space – as architecture recedes, the garden begins to dominate. Standing besides Lake Tanganyika, Bujumbura is somewhat different from the other cities in this group. The landscape is equally lush but the proximity of such a large body of water has a direct impact on the life of the city and gives it a special orientation.

The second metropolis in this terrain is Harare, a modernist British city that is also situated on a plateau. The downtown area has a fine grid and the scale of the buildings rises to a peak in the centre. There is a good balance of buildings to open space, including a beautiful park, and you have the sense that this is a really habitable city – well organized and not too big. Most of the buildings are elegant and have an integrity and rigour of construction that relates to the whole place. Moving away from the centre, you discover a beautiful landscape where everything seems to grow very easily but, unlike the cities in the Forest region, it is not too humid. The villas and housing estates blend with the groves of trees, so that the architecture and the landscape are in balance. The poor settlements are furthest from the centre but benefit from being in a more rural location. This arrangement is in line with the way that

ASMARA / A bucolic landscape near the city.

KIGALI / The city fits the profile of the hill.

LUSAKA / A well-crafted church.

ASMARA / Italian rationalist architecture.

ADDIS ABABA / A suburban road.

NAIROBI / 'The skyline of Africa'.

Okwui Enwezor describes the African city: the centre being where the power is and, the poorer you are, the further you live from the centre.

Mbabane and Maseru, even though they are capitals, are quite small towns, where you arrive only after a long journey up the mountain. In both cases the centre is very compact and, once you leave it, you are part of the surrounding landscape. Mbabane is more lush, greener, whereas Lesotho seems higher, more remote, and the sparse vegetation is broken up by the rocky terrain. In Namibia, Windhoek really is the landscape city on a hill. It was a German colony and, in a similar way to Asmara, you notice buildings that remind you of Frankfurt or Cologne and the main avenues have a vaguely Germanic character. Apart from these fragments, Windhoek is a garden city where the manicured landscape, rather than the buildings, tells the story. Socially it is a city of extremes but even the township architecture has a kind of flair to it, due to the amount of government-sponsored housing. In these areas, people do much of their living outside and the houses have a vibrant coastal-like expression.

In each of the cities in this region, the landscape is significant for the way in which it allows different types of architectural expression to sit comfortably side by side. In Nairobi, for instance, there are examples of Victorian, Sikh and Hindu architecture, and you have the modernism of different periods, as well as the postmodernism of the circular towers. These cities all have the capacity to absorb many different expressions without any sense of conflict. This is significant in view of their relative isolation, especially compared with West Africa where the capitals are not that far apart. Travelling to Addis Ababa, you fly across a vast landscape with very little physical development, before you rise up to the plateau where Addis stands and realize just how unique its location is. So the distances people may have travelled to reach these cities, and the baggage they bring, is part of their culture and is reflected in the architecture. Instead of the hybridization that you find in the Sahel, you have singular architectural statements standing next to one another. Hybridization is not necessary as it is included in the composition as a whole. In this region the type of cellular architecture that is the traditional response to the warmer climate in other areas is largely restricted to parts of Addis Ababa and Asmara.

Whether in the form of apartment buildings standing in their own grounds or villas set in beautiful gardens, the highland cities have an abundance of residential architecture that takes full advantage of the cultivated landscape. But the most exceptional residential example in this region is that of Kibera, in the heart of Nairobi. It forms a mat-like plate that follows the profile of the site and accommodates all the needs of the community. It is a special scenario, which I do not wish to overglamorize, where a number of intersecting roofs make a series of courtyards and organize the settlement pattern of the entire community. This 'community mat', as I call it, seems to fold and work with the landscape in a way that is quite profound. This is an architecture of the poor that is a direct expression of the people who live there: instead of closely knit individual houses, a single unit subdivides to meet all the needs of the community. The roof is the key element: driving the articulation of space and replacing the dominance of the wall in other regions, it is a response to the heavy rainfall that occurs at certain times. You find similar roofs on some of the poorer houses in Bujumbura but here the sites are very steep, the roofs are discontinuous, and the houses define family courtyards, as you would find in a village.

With the exception of Asmara, all of these cities take advantage of the climate and vegetation in their elevated positions, as they reach out into the surrounding landscape. At the same time there are major differences in their history and culture and these are reflected in the scale and pattern of their development.

HARARE / Looking towards the centre.

MBABANE / Looking from the centre to the suburbs.

NAIROBI / A public building behind a screen of palm trees.

WINDHOEK / A manicured landscape.

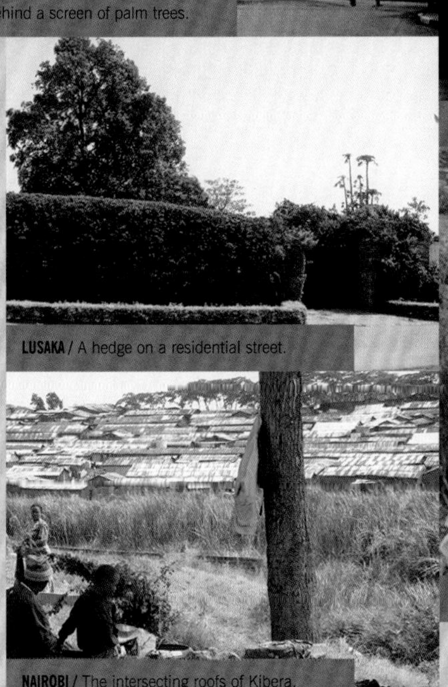

LUSAKA / A hedge on a residential street.

NAIROBI / The intersecting roofs of Kibera.

BUJUMBURA / Hillside houses forming courts.

ADDIS ABABA / ETHIOPIA

OVERVIEW

There are many strands to Ethiopia's rich history. Several of the earliest hominid remains, dating back millions of years, have been found in the Danakil Depression. In 3500–2000 BCE, the coastal region of what is now Ethiopia and Eritrea was part of the Land of the Punt, an area that had a strong export trade with Egypt. Further links developed with southern Arabia and the meeting of two great cultures led to the pre-Aksumite civilization in northern Ethiopia from 1500 to 400 BCE. Occupying a similar area, the Aksumite Kingdom flourished in the early centuries CE. Its wealth was based on agriculture and trade, and the foundations of the future country were laid in this period, including the dominance of Christianity. Islam, the second religion, was introduced by Arab traders who settled on the Red Sea coast in the 7th century. The Ethiopian middle ages lasted for 500 years, starting in the 13th century. During this period there was a series of bloody conflicts between Christians and Muslims, and continuing instability caused by the migration of Oromo people from Kenya into the south of the country.

The political unification of the country was encouraged by successive emperors in the 19th century. Tewodros II is credited with starting this process but, after imprisoning some British visitors to his court, he died under siege by the British in 1868. Yohannes IV was an astute politician and soldier who allowed local chiefs to stay in power on condition that they paid taxes to the state, but was killed fighting the Sudanese in 1889. In exchange for recognition of his claim to power, Emperor Menelik II signed a treaty with Italy that would eventually lead to the creation of Eritrea. He had founded Addis Ababa in 1886 and pursued an ambitious building programme in the city, introducing electricity and a telephone system. He was responsible for starting the construction of the national railway, before his death in 1913. After serving as prince regent, Ras (or Prince) Tafari Makonnen became His Imperial Majesty Haile Selassie in 1930 and remained in power until he was deposed in 1974. Opposition to his reign had grown since the Italian occupation from 1936 to 1941, when he left the country, and was not deflected when Addis Ababa was chosen as the location for the headquarters of the Organization of African Unity in 1963. Selassie was finally ousted in a military coup by the Derg, a short-lived group that was replaced by a socialist military dictatorship under Colonel Mengistu Haile Mariam. Its early idealism was quickly replaced by brutal suppression of any opposition. A period of great hardship followed, with conflict between the government and armed opposition and widespread famine in the 1980s. With the withdrawal of aid following the collapse of the USSR in 1990, Mariam was unable to resist the forces ranged against him and fled the country. After a military campaign the Ethiopian People's Revolutionary Democratic Movement, led by Meles Zenawi, established a new government and the country was divided into eleven electoral regions in 1994. Eritrea declared independence from Ethiopia in 1993 and withdrew from their common currency in 1997, which resulted in growing tension between the two countries and armed conflict over the position of their mutual boundary. Following a peace settlement in 2000, a joint commission ruled on the position of the border in 2007 but their findings were disputed by Ethiopia. Zenawi died in office in 2012 and was succeeded by his deputy, Hailemariam Desalegn who won the 2015 election.

OBSERVATIONS

Addis Ababa is in a lush valley, surrounded by eucalyptus trees and hills that are used as places of respite and relaxation. It is all very green, with small hamlets dotted around, and the air is fragrant. The city sits comfortably within this setting and there is a natural order to its layout.

The roads are not exclusively for cars: carts, donkeys and people use them with the same intensity. Everything from recycled sandals to camels is available in the market, and its life and trade extend to other streets. Ancient and new melt into a single reality. Religious buildings punctuate the urban vista, whether Orthodox churches, mosques or other religions, and their grounds are important public spaces.

The people really contribute to the sense of the city. It is not an aggressive place, but helpful to visitors. They are very beautiful people from many ethnic groups, speaking a large number of languages.

NATIONAL POPULATION

99,391,000

CITY POPULATION

3,238,000

ETHNIC GROUPS

Oromo 34.4%, Amhara (Amara) 27%, Somali (Somalie) 6.2%, Tigray (Tigrinya) 6.1%, Sidama 4%, Gurage 2.5%, Welaita 2.3%, Hadiya 1.7%, Afar (Affar) 1.7%, Gamo 1.5%, Gedeo 1.3%, Silte 1.3%, Keffiho 1.2%, other 8.8%

RELIGIONS

Orthodox 43.5%, Muslim 33.9%, Protestant 18.6%, traditional 2.7%, Catholic 0.7%, other 0.6%

LANGUAGES

Oromo 33.8%, Amharic (official national language) 29.3%, Somali 6.2%, Tigrigna 5.9%, Sidamo 4%, Wolaytta 2.2%, Gurage 2%, Afar 1.7%, Hadiyya 1.7%, Gamo 1.5%, Gedeo 1.3%, Opuuo 1.2%, Kafa 1.1%, other 8.1% (includes English and Arabic)

GDP

$145.1 billion

AGRICULTURAL PRODUCTS

cereals, pulses, coffee, oilseed, cotton, sugarcane, vegetables, khat, cut flowers; hides, cattle, sheep, goats; fish

INDUSTRIES

food processing, beverages, textiles, leather, chemicals, metals processing, cement

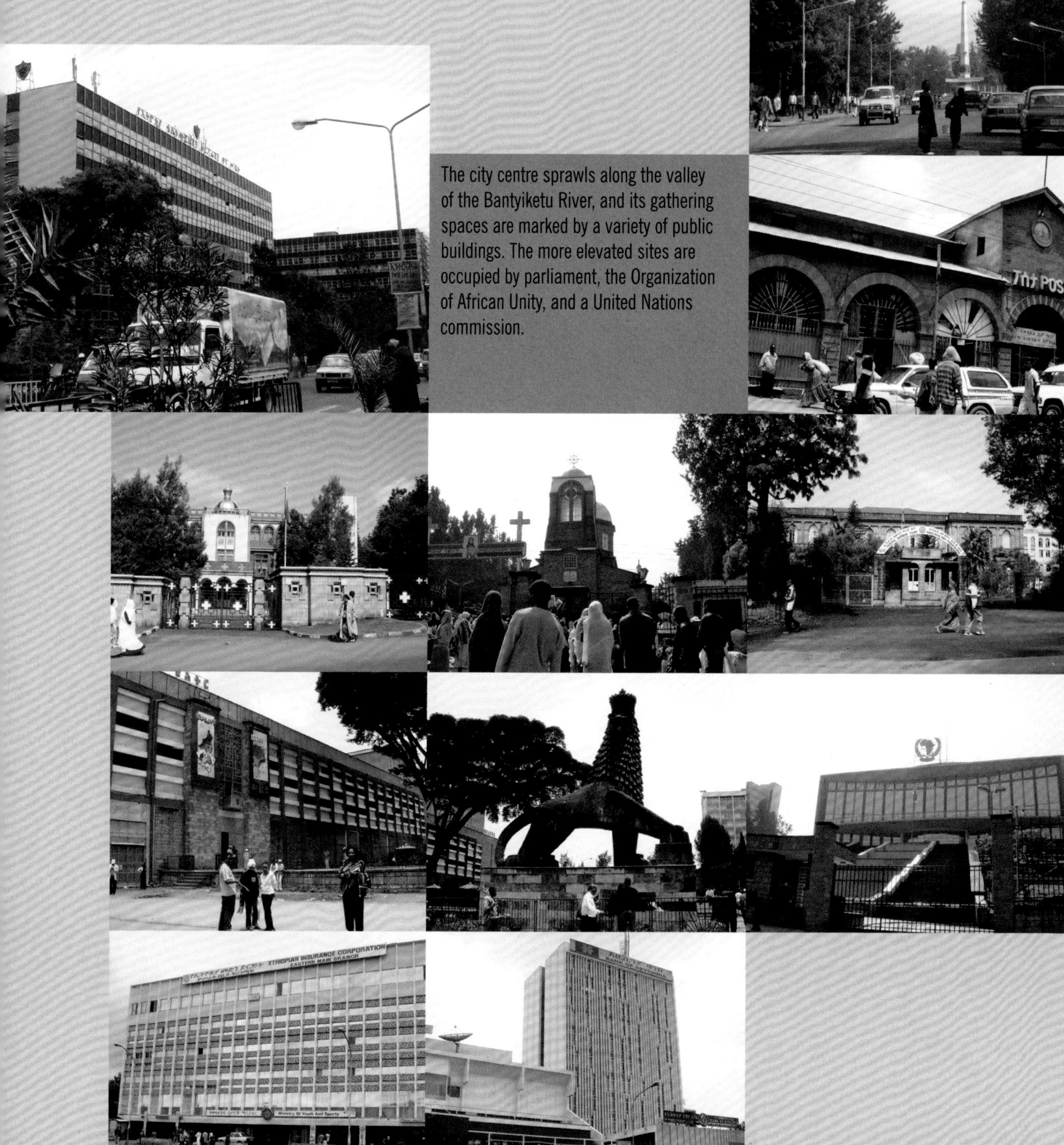

The city centre sprawls along the valley of the Bantyiketu River, and its gathering spaces are marked by a variety of public buildings. The more elevated sites are occupied by parliament, the Organization of African Unity, and a United Nations commission.

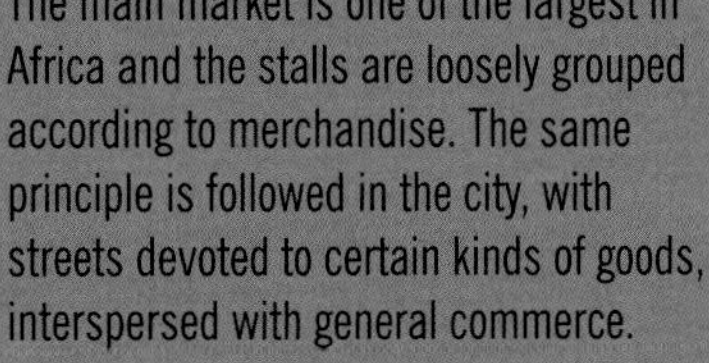

The main market is one of the largest in Africa and the stalls are loosely grouped according to merchandise. The same principle is followed in the city, with streets devoted to certain kinds of goods, interspersed with general commerce.

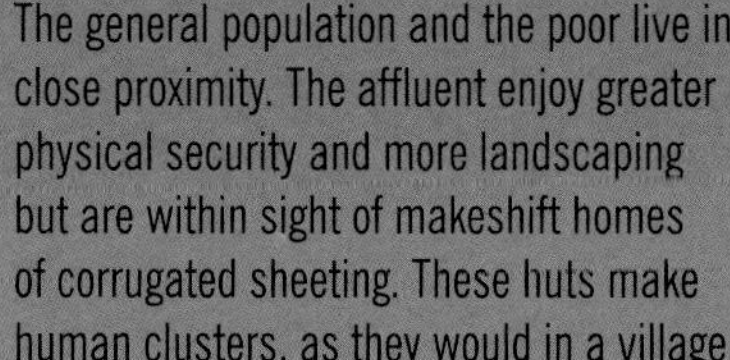

The general population and the poor live in close proximity. The affluent enjoy greater physical security and more landscaping but are within sight of makeshift homes of corrugated sheeting. These huts make human clusters, as they would in a village.

ASMARA / ERITREA

OVERVIEW

Until the second half of the 19th century, Eritrea was an integral part of Ethiopia but its history was strongly influenced by proximity to the Red Sea. In the 1st millennium the wealth of the Aksumite Kingdom was based on trade, much of which was handled by the Eritrean ports. This coast probably saw the arrival of Christianity in Africa and the introduction of Islam in the 7th century was due to Arab traders settling in the Dahlak Islands and the port of Massawa. From the 16th century until the Italians began to occupy the coastal strip, Turkey was the major trading power in the Red Sea. They took formal control of the area that would become Eritrea in 1880 and selected Asmara as the national capital in 1897. Having established a colonial administration, they set about modernizing the country's infrastructure and industry in order to exploit its natural resources. In 1936, under Mussolini, the Italians invaded Ethiopia but their occupation was short-lived due to their declaration of war against Britain in 1940. As the British already had forces in Sudan, they were able to drive the Italians out of Ethiopia and occupied Asmara.

In 1950, when a postwar commission decided that it should become part of Ethiopia, Eritrea ceased to exist as an independent country. As political power shifted to Addis Ababa, Eritrea lost its autonomy and its economy became increasingly enfeebled. This state of affairs was especially difficult to tolerate in view of Eritrea's cultural diversity, and this was reflected in the number of resistance movements that emerged in the 1960s: the Eritrean Liberation Movement, the (Christian) People's Liberation Front, and the (Muslim) Eritrean Liberation Front. After periods of civil war, the last two organizations joined forces as the Eritrean People's Liberation Front (EPLF) and were increasingly successful in defying Ethiopia's communist-backed forces. Between 1978 and 1986 the EPLF successfully resisted eight major offensives before taking control of several towns in the north. By this stage internal resistance to Ethiopia's military dictatorship had led to civil war and in 1991 the EPLF occupied Asmara without meeting any resistance. After a national referendum, independence was declared in 1993 with Isaias Afewerki as president. The EPLF became the People's Front for Democracy and Justice and, in government, moved quickly to rebuild the country and improve the daily lives of its citizens. These much needed developments were severely interrupted by the border dispute with Ethiopia that resulted in armed conflict between 1998 and 2000. Since then there has been an uneasy truce between the two countries. Ethiopia has refused to withdraw its troops in line with the 2007 findings of the boundary commission and Eritrea has been accused of arming rebel groups in the disputed area. There have been no elections since independence and Afewerki remains in power. During the period of their occupation the Italians rebuilt Asmara and most of the buildings survived the conflict with Ethiopia.

OBSERVATIONS

Asmara is a dramatic, high-altitude city – an agreeable and balmy citadel. Of largely Italian origin, it was constructed as the jewel in Mussolini's African outpost.

The architecture is a mix of religious buildings and Italian modernism, sometimes with Fascist overtones. There is not much new building because of the country's political situation.

The main road through the city is Harnet Avenue. Many public spaces and buildings are close to this boulevard, simplifying navigation. The citizens still follow the Italian custom of taking an early evening promenade, when the atmosphere is especially convivial.

NATIONAL POPULATION

5,228,000

CITY POPULATION

804,000

ETHNIC GROUPS

Tigrinya 55%, Tigre 30%, Saho 4%, Kunama 2%, Rashaida 2%, Bilen 2%, other (Afar, Beni Amir, Nera) 5%

RELIGIONS

Muslim, Coptic Christian, Roman Catholic, Protestant

LANGUAGES

Tigrinya (official), Arabic (official), English (official), Tigre, Kunama, Afar, other Cushitic languages

GDP

$7.84 billion

AGRICULTURAL PRODUCTS

sorghum, lentils, vegetables, corn, cotton, tobacco, sisal; livestock, goats; fish

INDUSTRIES

food processing, beverages, clothing and textiles, light manufacturing, salt, cement

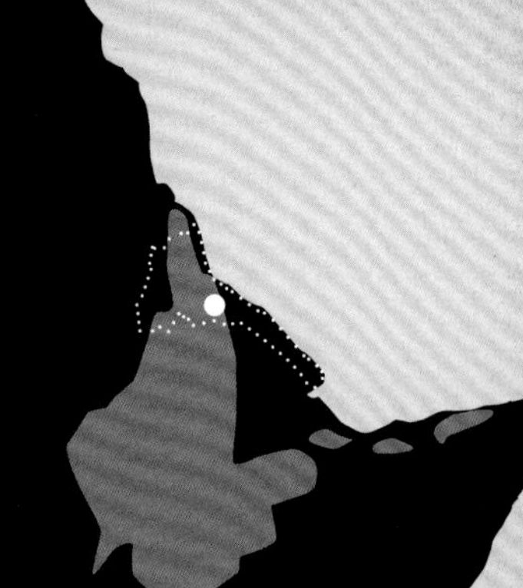

Italian modernist and Fascist buildings house the city's institutions. Most buildings are only two to three storeys high, so many churches and mosques break the skyline.

Activity lines the main boulevards, and there are many cafes, bars and restaurants. The main market occupies several urban blocks and informal trading is widespread. Most of the Italian buildings are still in use, but not the Fiat garage.

TAGLIERO
TOYOTA

When the Italians built the city, they segregated themselves from the locals, who now live in its modernist houses and apartment buildings. There are new suburbs of garden villas and areas of poor housing on the edge of the city.

BUJUMBURA / BURUNDI

OVERVIEW

The first people to occupy this area were the Twa pygmies, who were displaced by the Hutu at the end of the 1st millennium CE and by Tutsi from Ethiopia and Uganda in the 16th and 17th centuries. At the end of the 19th century both Burundi and Rwanda were colonized by Germany but after the First World War the League of Nations mandated both countries to Belgium. It established coffee plantations and ruled through Tutsi chiefs, an arrangement that led to tension with the Hutu who comprised the majority of the population. In the 1950s the independence movement had the support of both groups and was led by the son of the *mwami*, or king, who was assassinated before independence was declared in 1962. After the elections in 1964 the *mwami* declined to appoint a Hutu prime minister, when it was clear that they had won the majority of the votes. In their frustration, Hutu politicians and military leaders staged an unsuccessful coup, which was followed by the expulsion of Hutu from the army and from government positions. Further ethnic tension led to a Hutu rebellion in 1972 in which 1,000 Tutsi were killed. The Tutsi military responded with a programme of targeted genocide and any Hutu who had any kind of position or standing was likely to be murdered. It is thought that 200,000 Hutu met their death in this way and another 100,000 left the country.

When Jean-Baptiste Bagaza came to power in 1976 he intended to remove some of the causes of ethnic conflict but in practice the situation remained largely unchanged. His successor, Pierre Buyoya, brought more Hutu into the government and in 1993 he responded to international pressure and agreed to multiparty elections that resulted in a Hutu-led government. But the new leader was assassinated in an unsuccessful coup that precipitated ethnic violence in which thousands of people lost their lives. In 1994 the new Hutu president, Cyprien Ntaryamira, lost his life in a plane crash near Kigali, which also killed the president of Rwanda. Although the cause of the crash was never confirmed, it resulted in genocide in Rwanda and two years of violent conflict between Hutu militia and the Tutsi-led army in Burundi. Over 100,000 people had been killed by 1996, when former president Buyoya returned to power in a military coup. The conflict continued alongside peace talks that were conducted by Julius Nyerere, former president of Tanzania and, at a later stage, by Nelson Mandela. An agreement was finally reached in 2003; Buyoya stood down in favour of a Hutu leader, Domitien Ndayizeye, and they agreed to collaborate on the planning of elections. By this stage about 300,000 people are thought to have lost their lives in the conflict. In 2004 the United Nations sent peacekeeping troops and elections were held in 2005. A former rebel group and now political party, the Forces for the Defence of Democracy, won a majority of votes and their leader, Pierre Nkurunziza, became president. After months of protest he was reelected for a third term in 2015. There is now a legal requirement that parliament includes sixty per cent Hutu and forty per cent Tutsi, of whom thirty per cent must be women. Although one rebel group remains active, the country is more stable than previously.

OBSERVATIONS

The city was wealthy and an important port for the Belgians. Architecture makes a substantial contribution to the quality of the environment and gives a fine grain to the centre.

Bujumbura is a heady mix of colonial town planning, wide boulevards, parks and prominent public buildings. It is laid out from Lake Tanganyika to the mountains, with the civic buildings close to the waterfront, then the commercial area. Overlooking the centre from a nearby hill, the university is a masterpiece of Belgium modernism.

There are several parks with monuments to the struggles that have marked the country's turbulent history. The wealthy areas stretch along the lakefront, on either side of the centre, and the wonderful beaches are served by numerous cafes and clubs. The poor areas are on the edge of the city, in ravines and on hilltops.

NATIONAL POPULATION

11,179,000

CITY POPULATION

751,000

ETHNIC GROUPS

Hutu (Bantu) 85%, Tutsi (Hamitic) 14%, Twa (Pygmy) 1%, Europeans 3,000, South Asians 2,000

RELIGIONS

Catholic 62.1%, Protestant 23.9% (includes Adventist 2.3% and other Protestant 21.6%), Muslim 2.5%, other 3.6%, unspecified 7.9%

LANGUAGES

Kirundi 29.7% (official), Kirundi and other language 9.1%, French (official) and French and other language 0.3%, Swahili and Swahili and other language 0.2%, English and English and other language 0.06%, more than 2 languages 3.7%, unspecified 56.94%

GDP

$8.41 billion

AGRICULTURAL PRODUCTS

coffee, cotton, tea, corn, sorghum, sweet potatoes, bananas, cassava (manioc, tapioca); beef, milk, hides

INDUSTRIES

light consumer (blankets, shoes, soap), assembly of imported components, public works construction, food processing

The civic buildings are on the main boulevards, in various styles but normally standing within a secure compound. Their secular architecture is complemented by the strong forms of the city's mosques and churches.

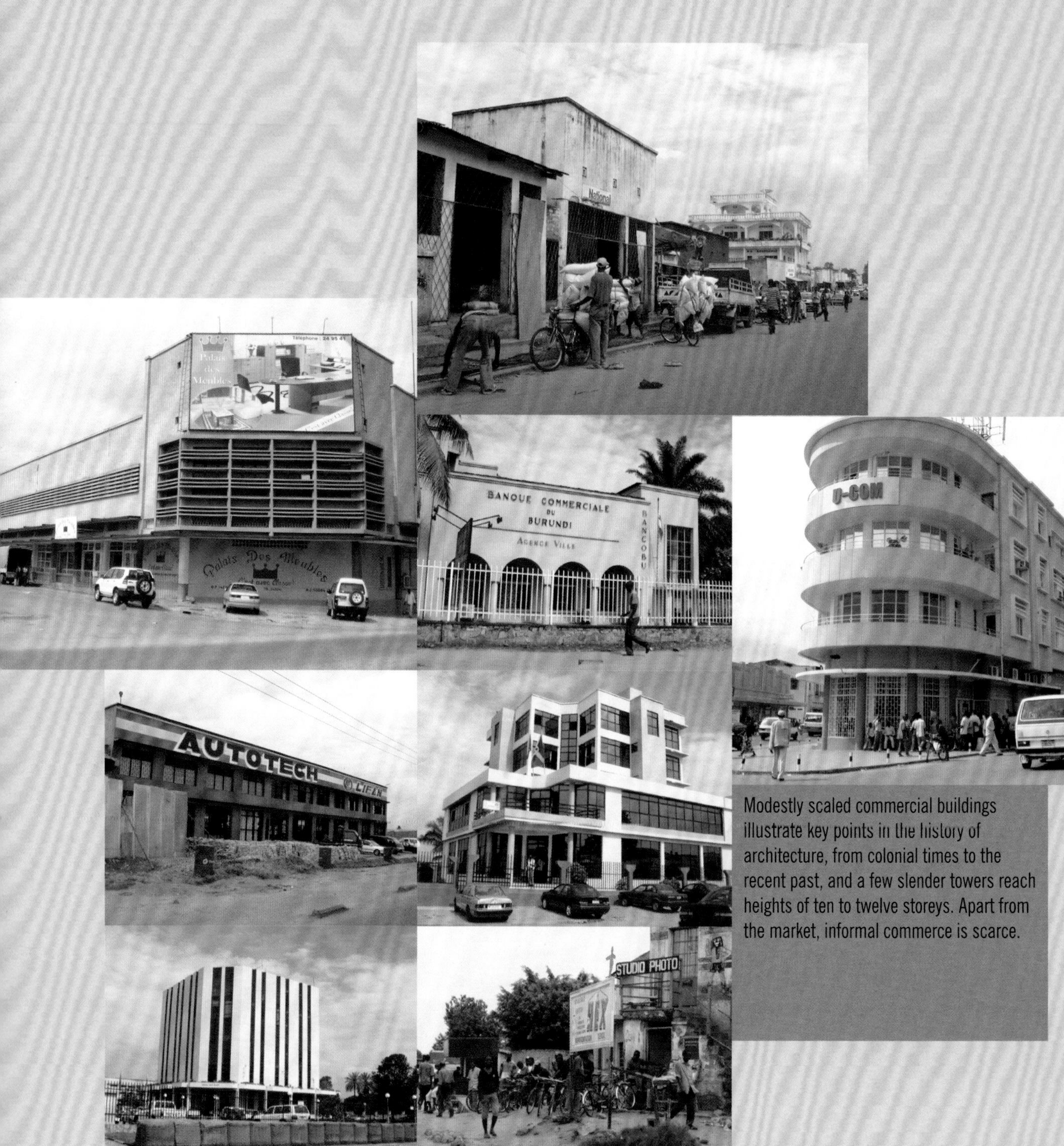

Modestly scaled commercial buildings illustrate key points in the history of architecture, from colonial times to the recent past, and a few slender towers reach heights of ten to twelve storeys. Apart from the market, informal commerce is scarce.

The most desirable areas are close to shore, with views of the lake, while the poor live in the hills where access is difficult. Their homes are made of mud and tin, and clustered together to form courtyards and private spaces for the family. They turn their backs to the street and embrace the inner life of the block.

HARARE / ZIMBABWE

OVERVIEW

During the 1st millennium CE Bantu people from West Africa migrated to the south and to the east, and one of these groups eventually developed into the Kingdom of Zimbabwe, with a capital at Great Zimbabwe, near modern Masvingo. They prospered through contact with Swahili traders but in the 15th century their society began to fragment and was replaced by an alliance of Shona ethnic groups. Known as the Rozwi Empire, it included a large part of the future country. In the 19th century the Rozwi Empire was overrun by Ndebele raiders from the south who at a later stage encountered Cecil Rhodes of the British South Africa Company (BSAC). In the Rudd Concession of 1888 the Ndebele handed over mineral rights to the BSAC in exchange for armaments. When they did not find gold, the colonists began to appropriate farmland and in 1895 the country was named Rhodesia. As the government was concerned only with white interests, the Shona and Ndebele joined forces to drive the settlers out, a rebellion that was halted when the leaders were hanged. The government continued to disenfranchise the black population and commandeer the best farmland until the 1950s, when two political parties were founded to represent African interests: the Zimbabwe African People's Union (ZAPU) and the Zimbabwe African National Union (ZANU). In 1964 a newly elected president, Ian Smith, sought independence from the British and, when they insisted on racial equality and majority rule, his government signed the Unilateral Declaration of Independence (UDI).

Britain responded to UDI by imposing trade sanctions but these were ignored by Western countries and by some British companies. ZAPU and ZANU responded with guerrilla raids that began to drive the whites off the land. In 1974, under the aegis of South Africa and Zambia, a ceasefire was called as a prelude to peace talks. When the talks foundered, ZAPU and ZANU formed an alliance known as the Patriotic Front (PF) and Smith attempted an 'internal settlement' based on selective representation from opposition groups and a fixed proportion of government seats for whites. This resulted in an intensification of the guerrilla war, to such an extent that Smith was left with no alternative but to negotiate with all parties at a peace conference in London in 1979. The resulting Lancaster House Agreement guaranteed majority rule while reserving a number of government seats for whites. In the first election in 1980 Robert Mugabe's ZANU party won comfortably but initial optimism was soured by renewed rivalry between ZAPU and ZANU, who had a majority of Ndebele and Shona supporters respectively. This led to armed conflict and in 1982 troops sent into Matabeleland by Mugabe are estimated to have killed 20,000 people. Fearing civil war, Mugabe opened talks with ZAPU that resulted in merging of the two parties as ZANU-PF. The 1990s were marked by a decline in the economy and an increase in personal taxation but Mugabe continued to win elections. Public dissatisfaction finally expressed itself in a two-day strike in 1998, and the following year the trade unions organized a rally to launch a new party, the Movement for Democratic Change under the leadership of Morgan Tsvangirai. Although Mugabe won the 2008 election, he was forced into a power-sharing agreement with Tsvangirai due to the severity of the country's problems. Mugabe was reelected in 2013.

OBSERVATIONS

Harare is a beautiful southern African city. It is planned on a grid, with Samora Machel Avenue forming a classical east–west axis. The height of the buildings gradually rises towards the commercial centre that clusters around Harare Gardens.

You have these high modernist buildings, so there is a balance between the vertical composition of the core and the horizontality of the suburbs. Different architects have clearly been aware of this distinction and it represents a popular way of thinking about the city's need to mark its position in the wider landscape.

Because of its grid and orderly layout, you get a strong sense of the layering of history in Harare. In its heyday, it was a modern and prosperous city.

NATIONAL POPULATION

15,603,000

CITY POPULATION

1,501,000

ETHNIC GROUPS

African 99.4% (predominantly Shona; Ndebele is the second largest ethnic group), other 0.4%, unspecified 0.2%

RELIGIONS

Protestant 75.9% (includes Apostolic 38%, Pentecostal 21.1%, other 16.8%), Roman Catholic 8.4%, other Christian 8.4%, other 1.2% (includes traditional, Muslim), none 6.1%

LANGUAGES

Shona (official), Ndebele (official), English (official), 13 minority languages (official; includes Chewa, Chibarwe, Kalanga, Koisan, Nambya, Ndau, Shangani, sign language, Sotho, Tonga, Tswana, Venda and Xhosa)

GDP

$27.26 billion

AGRICULTURAL PRODUCTS

corn, cotton, tobacco, wheat, coffee, sugarcane, peanuts; sheep, goats, pigs

INDUSTRIES

mining (coal, gold, platinum, copper, nickel, tin, clay, numerous metallic and nonmetallic ores), steel, wood products, cement, chemicals, fertilizer, clothing and footwear, foodstuffs, beverages

HARARE / ZIMBABWE / **CIVIC**

The city's architecture is dominated by its colonial heritage, including some later buildings with finely proportioned facades and elegant concrete sunshades. They are located in a compact area around Harare Gardens, which mark the centre of the city.

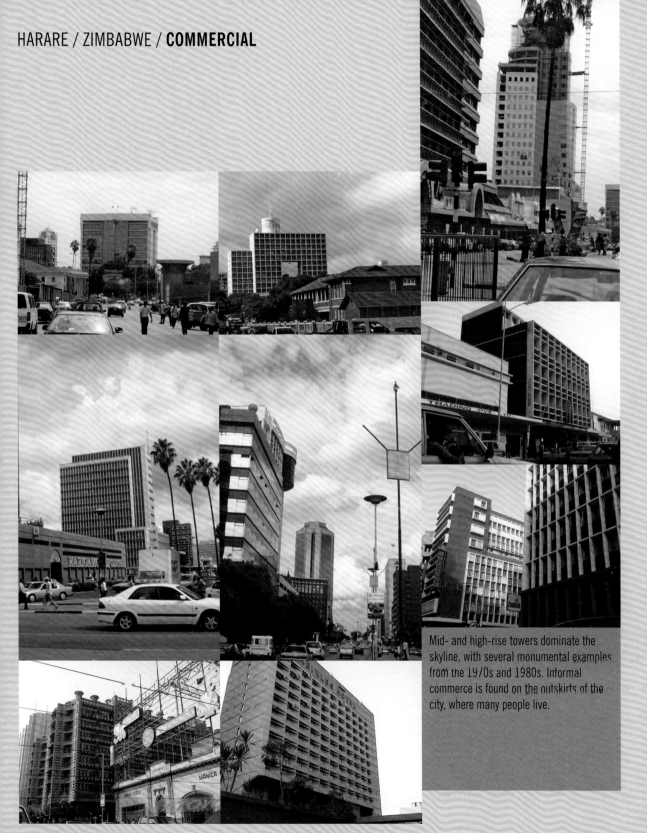

HARARE / ZIMBABWE / **COMMERCIAL**

Mid- and high-rise towers dominate the skyline, with several monumental examples from the 1970s and 1980s. Informal commerce is found on the outskirts of the city, where many people live.

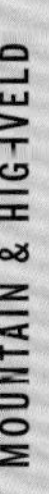

HARARE / ZIMBABWE / **COMMERCIAL**

The affluent areas are close to the centre, and two- and three-storey government housing lines the main roads out of the city. Many people live in the countryside, in thatched hamlets and low-cost bungalows, and commute to the city by bus.

OVERVIEW

The ancient history of Rwanda is closely linked to that of neighbouring countries such as Uganda. Following an agreement between Britain and Germany in 1890, Rwanda became a German colony until the aftermath of the First World War, when it was ceded to Belgium. Both colonial powers favoured the Tutsi people, choosing to impose their rule through Tutsi chiefs and allowing the Tutsi to monopolize missionary education. This inevitably led to tensions with the majority ethnic group, the Hutu. But the balance of power was abruptly changed in 1956, when the Tutsi *mwami*, or king, sought independence from Belgium, which reacted by taking up negotiations with the Hutu. Compared with the Tutsi, the Hutu were in favour of introducing democracy as a preliminary step towards independence. The inherent conflict in this situation led to the first serious violence between the Tutsi and the Hutu, following the death of the *mwami* in 1959. As a result many Tutsi left Rwanda and settled in neighbouring countries. With independence in 1962, the Hutu assumed power and educational and employment opportunities for the Tutsi were reduced, provoking guerrilla raids from Tutsi exiles. In reprisal, thousands of resident Tutsi were killed and many more left the country. Further violence erupted in 1972, leading the head of the army, Juvénal Habyarimana, to assume power in 1973 with the intention of resolving the deep-seated divisions within Rwandan society.

Following disturbances in the 1980s, ethnic conflict was reignited in 1990 when the Rwandan Patriotic Front (RPF), a Tutsi army led by Paul Kagame, invaded the country from Uganda. France, Belgium and the Democratic Republic of the Congo sent troops to support Habyarimana, and the Rwandan army went on a killing spree directed against the Tutsi and their supporters. Undeterred, the RPF regrouped and on their second invasion in 1991 they were better prepared and advanced towards Kigali. A peace conference was called in 1993 and this was followed by a conference of neighbouring heads of state in 1994. But as Habyarimana was returning to Kigali with the possibility of a power- sharing agreement, his aircraft crashed as it approached the airport.

In the aftermath, elements of the government and army decided to take steps to terminate what they saw as the Tutsi problem. In one of the worst cases of genocide in the last century the army and a Hutu militia, known as the Interahamwe, roamed the country and killed people indiscriminately.

At the same time the RPF continued its military campaign and finally expelled the remnants of the Rwandan army and the Interahamwe into the Democratic Republic of the Congo and Burundi. By this stage there were two million refugees living in camps in the surrounding countries, under the control of the Interahamwe. This situation changed only in 1996, when a guerrilla army supported by Rwanda and Uganda moved into the Congo, dispersing both the remnants of the Congolese army and the Interahamwe. Refugees began to return to Rwanda and, following local elections in 1999, Kagame won the presidential election in 2003. Since then government has continued to make progress with uniting the population and in 2009 conducted joint operations with the Democratic Republic of the Congo against Hutu extremists in that country. Kagame remains president. When the RPF forces arrived in 1994, Kigali was in a seriously wrecked condition but since then it has made a remarkable recovery.

OBSERVATIONS

Kigali is surrounded by hills that stretch out into the landscape. Rwanda is the garden country of Africa and its landscape informs the experience of the city.

Many of the city's commercial buildings are connected by arcades that protect people from the sun in the middle of the day. This comparatively dense area is surrounded by extensive suburbs. The main park is close to the genocide museum, the Kigali Memorial Centre.

The government has tried to introduce row houses, to increase the density, but Rwandans dislike living too close to their neighbours. This can be seen in the courtyard hamlets where, if you do not look carefully, there appears to be nobody in the landscape. These bungalows are built from rendered and painted block, with tin roofs.

NATIONAL POPULATION

11,610,000

CITY POPULATION

1,257,000

ETHNIC GROUPS

Hutu (Bantu) 84%, Tutsi (Hamitic) 15%, Twa (Pygmy) 1%

RELIGIONS

Roman Catholic 49.5%, Protestant 27.2%, Adventist 12.2%, other Christian 4.5%, Muslim 1.8%, animist 0.1%, other 0.6%, none 3.6%, unspecified 0.5%

LANGUAGES

Kinyarwanda only (official, universal Bantu vernacular) 93.2%, Kinyarwanda 6.2%, French (official) 0.1%, English (official) 0.1%, Swahili (or Kiswahili, used in commercial centres) 0.02%, other 0.03%, unspecified 0.35%

GDP

$18.9 billion

AGRICULTURAL PRODUCTS

coffee, tea, pyrethrum (insecticide made from chrysanthemums), bananas, beans, sorghum, potatoes; livestock

INDUSTRIES

cement, agricultural products, small-scale beverages, soap, furniture, shoes, plastic goods, textiles, cigarettes

Most public buildings are south of the commercial downtown and consist of neoclassical or late-modernist villas behind walls or fences. Mosques and churches are plentiful but do not dominate the skyline. The many parks and gardens are ornamental, rather than places for the citizens to use.

STADE REGIONAL
DE
KIGALI

AMUR
EPIB

KIGALI / RWANDA / **COMMERCIAL**

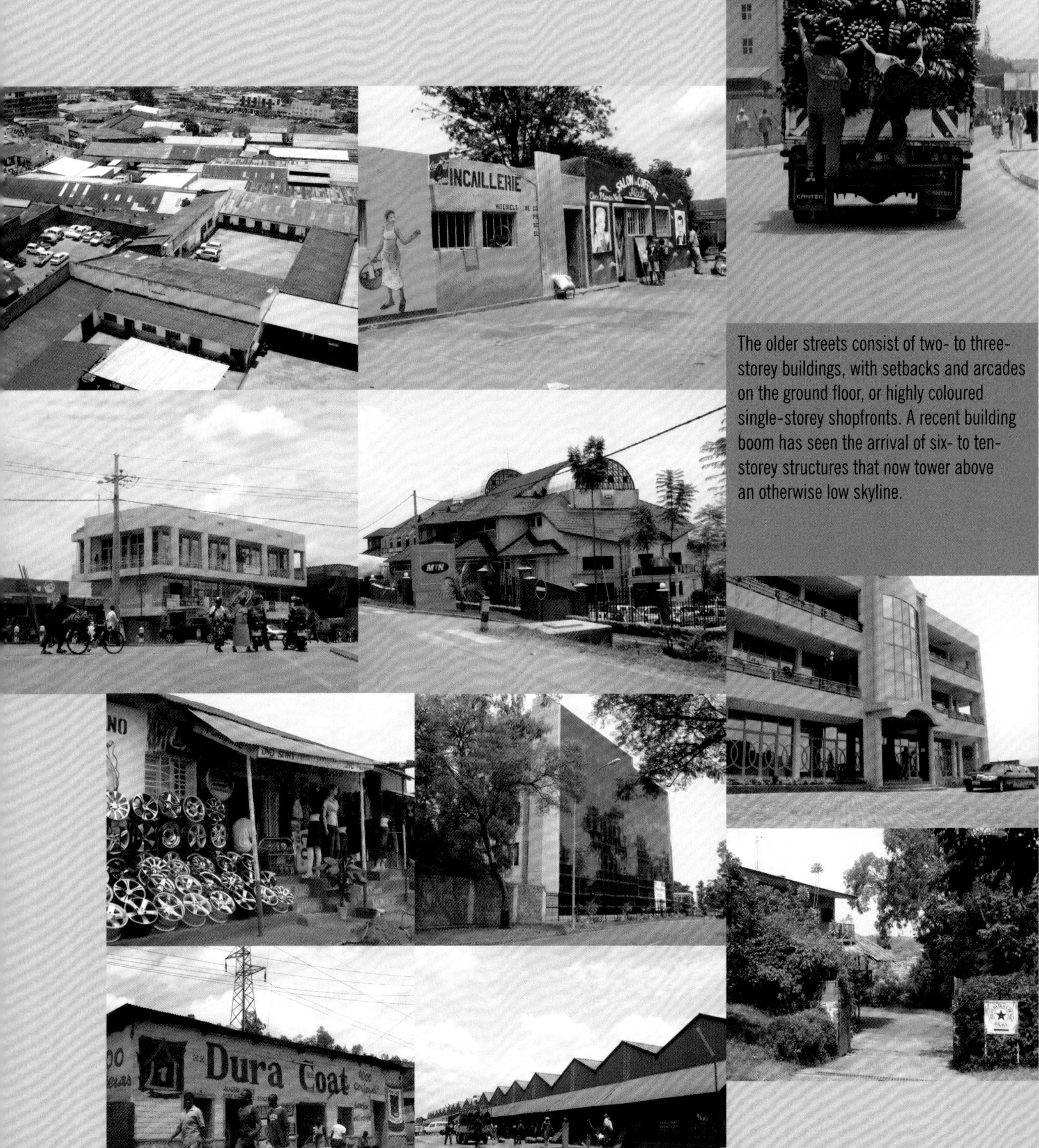

The older streets consist of two- to three-storey buildings, with setbacks and arcades on the ground floor, or highly coloured single-storey shopfronts. A recent building boom has seen the arrival of six- to ten-storey structures that now tower above an otherwise low skyline.

Luxury villas come in a variety of styles, but always with large gardens. In other areas, the plots are smaller and the urban grain is more sinuous. Off the main arteries, small lanes lead to the houses. Despite the high density, these areas have a great deal of charm.

LUSAKA / ZAMBIA

OVERVIEW

As in other parts of southern Africa, the Bantu people had become the dominant ethnic group by the 2nd millennium CE. During the *Difaqane*, or forced migration, in the early 19th century the Zulu drove out some local ethnic groups and in the south the Makololo people displaced the Tonga. The Portuguese had been the first Europeans to arrive, in two different groups. One party had travelled from the west coast and the other had followed the Zambezi River through Mozambique, the latter following the route of Swahili-Arab traders operating on the east coast. With the intention of undermining the slave trade and introducing Christianity, the Scottish explorer David Livingstone travelled up the Zambezi River in the 1850s, reaching what he named Victoria Falls in 1855. He was followed by other adventurers, including Cecil Rhodes, whose British South Africa Company (BSAC) took control of the area in 1895. The company had the support of the British government who wished to counter Portuguese influence and stop the slave trade. The BSAC dominated the next twenty years of Zambia's history. Large deposits of copper were found around the turn of the century and Livingstone was made the capital in 1907. In 1924 the country, which was then known as Northern Rhodesia, became a full British colony and the capital was moved to Lusaka in 1935.

As a basis for greater independence, the British settlers entered into a federation with Southern Rhodesia and Nyasaland in 1953. In representing the interests of colonials over African people, the federation was criticized by Kenneth Kaunda and his United National Independence Party, founded in the late 1950s. Following a campaign of civil disobedience against it, the federation was disbanded and the country became independent in 1964, changing its name to Zambia. As leader of the majority party, Kaunda was the first president and inherited a situation where most of the profits of colonization had not been invested in the country. He disbanded opposition parties in 1972 and, declaring himself the only presidential candidate, remained in power for another nineteen years. He combined Marxist principles with traditional African values but with falling copper prices, the economy was seriously depressed by the end of the 1970s. Conditions in the 1980s improved slightly when Zimbabwe became independent and a direct railway line from Lusaka to Dar es Salaam was completed. In 1986 the International Monetary Fund sponsored economic reforms that involved the withdrawal of food subsidies and this resulted in soaring prices and food riots. Further unrest in 1990 led to a demand for the legalization of other political parties, which Kaunda accepted. In the 1991 elections he lost to Frederick Chiluba, leader of the Movement for Multiparty Democracy (MMD). Chiluba embarked on a further programme of economic reform, the consequences of which for ordinary people were catastrophic. Kaunda made a brief return to politics in the mid 1990s but despite the failing economy the MMD remained in power until the elections in 2011, won by Michael Sata and the Patriotic Front. After further economic difficulties, Sata died in 2014. Edgar Lungu has replaced him until the next full elections in 2016.

OBSERVATIONS

Lusaka is the garden-city capital of Zambia, which is landlocked by other African countries. It inherited an administration and several institutions from its time as a British colony. The recent revival in its economy is due to its huge copper reserves.

Most commercial architecture consists of low-rise buildings with shopfronts or houses that have been converted to business compounds. Due to the city's relative wealth, the informal economy does not play a significant role here.

It is very difficult to see the most affluent homes as they are inside gated enclosures. In these areas, you are mainly presented with lush planting and security guards. And the few houses you can see cannot be photographed as they belong to ministers and generals.

The informal housing tends to be made from materials salvaged from building sites and is arranged as cottages within family compounds. The poor infrastructure in these areas makes them unhygienic and difficult to negotiate.

Lusaka is a city that is very much forming and crafting its identity. As the economy improves, there is an opportunity to diversify the city and hopefully avoid it being completely taken over by gated communities.

NATIONAL POPULATION

16,212,000

CITY POPULATION

2,179,000

ETHNIC GROUPS

Bemba 21%, Tonga 13.6%, Chewa 7.4%, Lozi 5.7%, Nsenga 5.3%, Tumbuka 4.4%, Ngoni 4%, Lala 3.1%, Kaonde 2.9%, Namwanga 2.8%, Lunda 2.6%, Mambwe 2.5%, other/unspecified 24.7%

RELIGIONS

Protestant 75.3%, Roman Catholic 20.2%, other 2.7% (includes Muslim Buddhist, Hindu and Baha'i), none 1.8%

LANGUAGES

Bembe 33.4%, Nyanja 14.7%, Tonga 11.4%, Lozi 5.5%, Chewa 4.5%, Nsenga 2.9%, Tumbuka 2.5%, Lunda 1.9%, English (official) 1.7%, other/unspecified 21.5%

GDP

$61.39 billion

AGRICULTURAL PRODUCTS

corn, sorghum, rice, peanuts, sunflower seed, vegetables, cotton, flowers, tobacco, cotton, sugarcane, cassava (manioc, tapioca), coffee; cattle, goats, pigs, poultry, milk, eggs, hides

INDUSTRIES

mining (copper, emeralds), construction, foodstuffs, beverages, chemicals, textiles, fertilizer, horticulture

The assembly building is a copper-clad volume, making a direct connection between the source of the city's wealth and its architecture. Other institutions are housed in elegant modernist buildings from the 1960s.

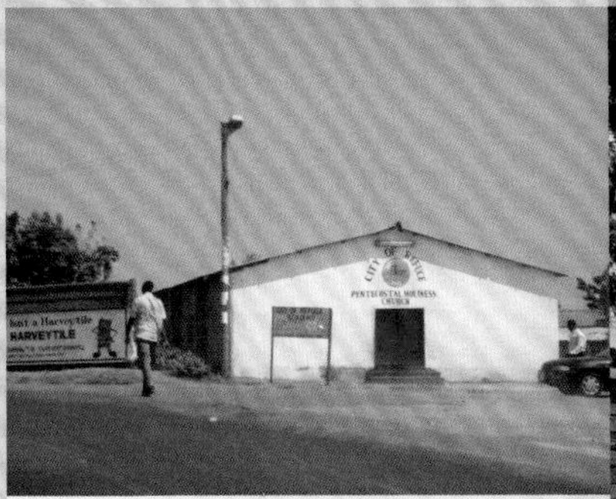

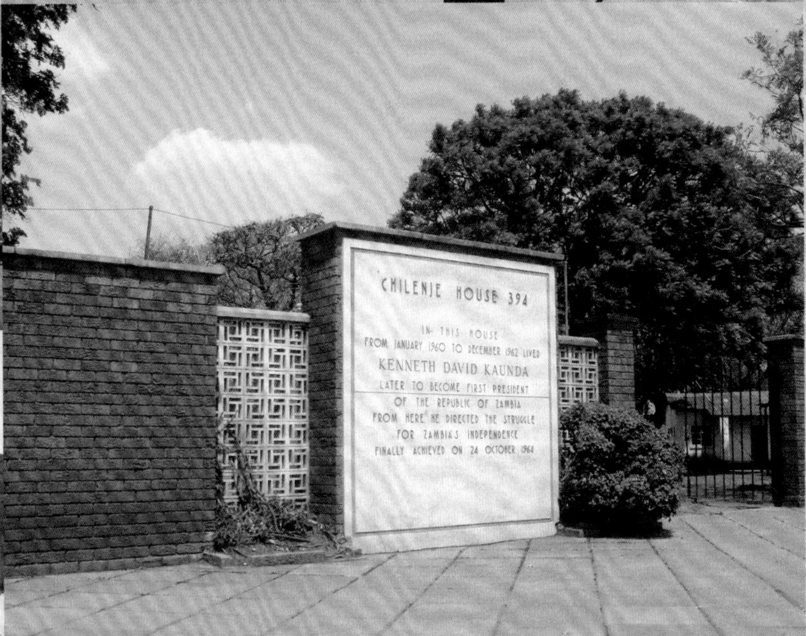

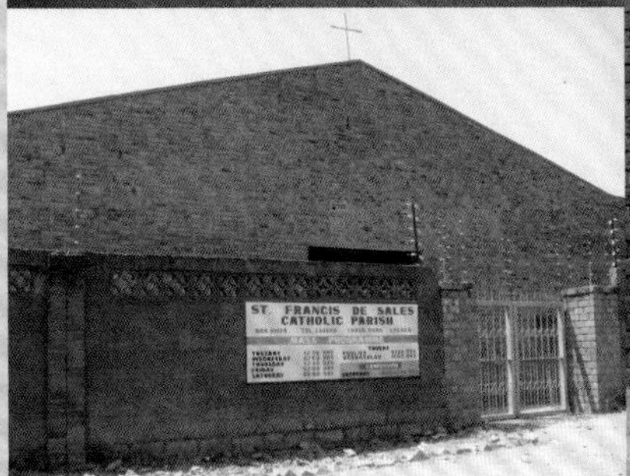

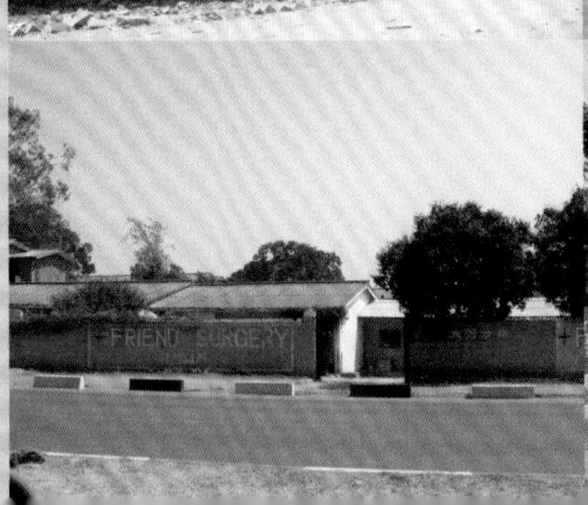

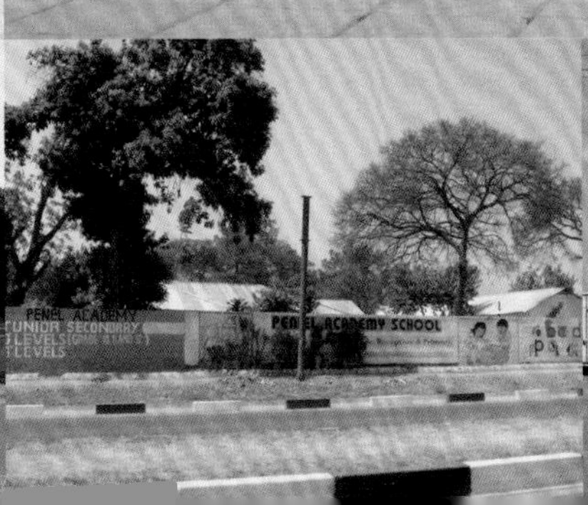

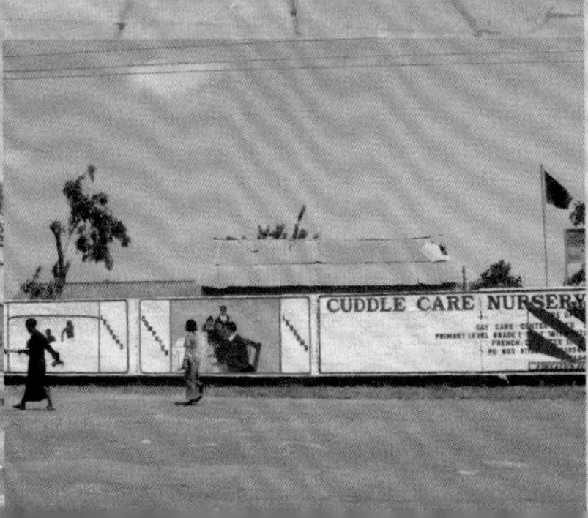

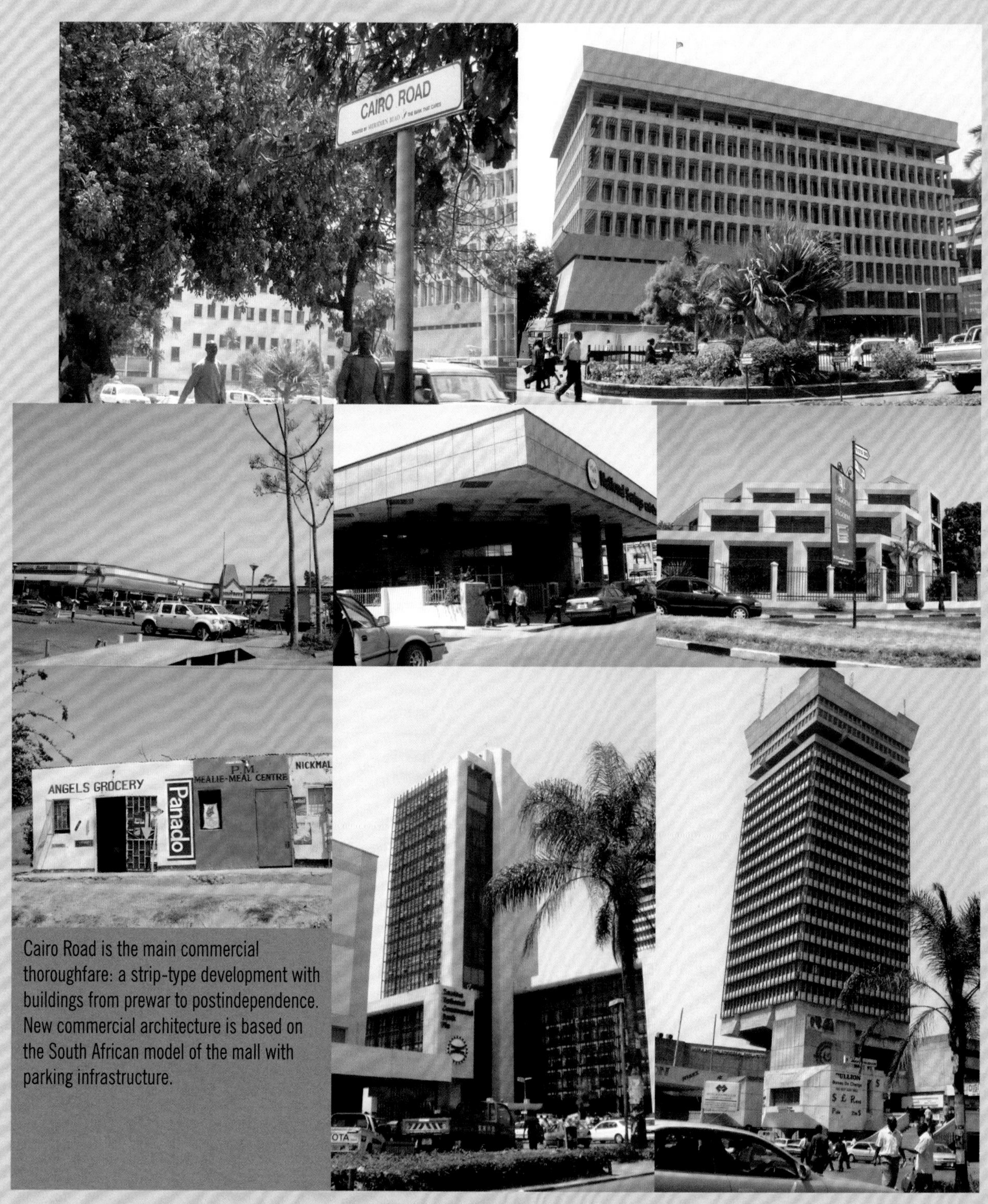

Cairo Road is the main commercial thoroughfare: a strip-type development with buildings from prewar to postindependence. New commercial architecture is based on the South African model of the mall with parking infrastructure.

The most affluent housing is in gated communities and therefore difficult to see. Elsewhere the villa and compound model is employed at a variety of scales, with public and company housing in apartment bulldings.

MASERU / LESOTHO

OVERVIEW

The Sotho people have occupied Lesotho since the 16th century. By the beginning of the 19th century they had settled most of the land that could be grazed or cultivated, before coming under pressure from two very different sources: the *Difaqane*, the forced migration of Bantu peoples by the Zulu nation, and the arrival of Boer settlers. Due to a powerful leader, Moshoeshoe I, Lesotho was one of the few places that successfully resisted the Zulu wars of the 19th century. He led his people to a mountainous area in the north and moved his base to a more defensive stronghold to the east of Maseru in 1824. He strengthened his position by developing relations with other leaders and by offering land and protection to refugees who could contribute to the resistance. By the time of his death in 1870 his expanded kingdom, Basutoland, had laid the foundations for the country's future. In an attempt to control the Boer incursions, Moshoeshoe had allied himself with the Cape Colony but the British had been reluctant to become involved. They intervened, to annex Basutoland to the Cape Colony in 1871, only after the Free State–Basotho Wars of 1858 and 1865. After Moshoeshoe's death, Basutoland became a British protectorate and was not included in the Union of South Africa when it was founded in 1910.

The Basutoland National Council was formed in 1910, with representatives nominated by local chiefs. A more democratic basis for choosing representatives was introduced in the 1940s, when the council requested the right to self-government. By 1960 a new constitution had been written and there were elections for a legislative council. The two main parties were the Basutoland Congress Party (BCP), which had similar aims to the African National Congress (ANC) in South Africa, and the more conservative Basutoland National Party (BNP, later the Basotho National Party) led by Chief Leabua Jonathan. The BCP won the elections in 1960 and sought full independence from Britain but before it was achieved, they lost a second election to the BNP in 1965. Chief Jonathan therefore became the first prime minister of the Kingdom of Lesotho. But his attempt to divest the king, Moshoeshoe II, of his remaining powers was not popular and the BNP lost the election in 1970. Jonathan suspended the constitution, banned opposition parties and exiled the king, before calling for a government of national unity. Having previously supported the apartheid policies of South Africa, Jonathan became more critical and was suspected of harbouring ANC guerrillas. South Africa then crippled the country by closing the borders, the Lesotho military seized power and the monarchy was restored. Although the BCP won the elections in 1993, the incumbent prime minister formed a breakaway party, the Lesotho Congress for Democracy (LCD), and continued in power. After the LCD won the elections in 1998 suspicions about the fairness of the ballot lead to serious divisions between the government, civil service and military. The government requested external assistance to restore order but when South African troops entered the country there was fierce resistance from sections of the Lesotho army and Maseru suffered considerable destruction. With the return of order, the LCD won the next two elections; the third in 2012 resulted in a coalition government, and the 2015 election was won by the Democratic Congress party led by Pakalitha Mosisili. Maseru has been largely restored after the damage caused in 1998.

OBSERVATIONS

Maseru is in the high hills of Lesotho, a beautiful country of mountain plateaus reaching 3,000 m above sea level. The city is very modern. It was a base for Anglican missionaries in the 19th century and has recently started to flourish due to new wealth and tourism.

High-end residential architecture is represented by the royal palace of the king and by the prime minister's house. Ironically, the palace is a modernist complex on the side of a hill, while the prime minister's house is a neoclassical villa on top of a hill.

NATIONAL POPULATION

2,135,000

CITY POPULATION

431,998

ETHNIC GROUPS

Sotho 99.7%, Europeans, Asians and other 0.3%

RELIGIONS

Christian 80%, indigenous beliefs 20%

LANGUAGES

Sesotho (southern Sotho), English (official), Zulu, Xhosa

GDP

$5.56 billion

AGRICULTURAL PRODUCTS

corn, wheat, pulses, sorghum, barley; livestock

INDUSTRIES

food, beverages, textiles, clothing, handicrafts, construction, tourism

The main street, Kingsway, was paved only in 1947, and the royal palace and administrative buildings are close by. The cathedral employs a fine sandstone, and the parliament building is a 1970s monolith whose facade was designed for solar shading.

The commercial architecture is pretty haphazard, mainly one- and two-storey structures. A few mall buildings break the high street, bold but not very big. Informal trading is found around the main market, with its metal roof, and the transport hubs.

The residential areas consist of detached bungalows and houses on the hillsides around the centre. There are two types of poor housing: government-built, with a tin roof, one door and two windows, and the indigenous stone-built one-room shed.

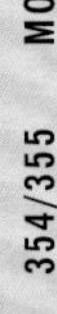

MBABANE / SWAZILAND

OVERVIEW

The earliest human remains found in Swaziland are over 100,000 years old but the current inhabitants have lived here only since the 18th century. King Ngwane III was the head of a Nguni clan that was part of the Bantu migration into southern Africa and, due to pressure from other groups, he led his people from a location near Maputo and settled in the south of Swaziland. His successor, Sobhuza I, was in power during the *Difaqane* of the 1820s and moved his base to the Ezulwini Valley, south of Mbabane. King Mswati, who died in 1868, is credited with uniting the kingdom and the country is named after him. The Zulu expansion during the *Difaqane* was partly curtailed by Europeans beginning to move into the area. The Boers were interested in extending the South African Republic to include Swaziland and the area around Maputo but this was prevented when the British annexed the South African Republic in 1877. When Swaziland's boundaries were fixed at the Pretoria Convention in 1881, its independence was undermined by an understanding that the British and the Boers would both have the freedom to pursue their interests within the country. This arrangement continued until the Second Anglo-Boer War resulted in the collapse of the Boer administration in 1902, when Swaziland became a British protectorate. As the then king, Sobhuza II, was still a child, his grandmother and uncle ran the country until 1921. They were also the people behind a scheme to buy back Swaziland from foreigners and two-thirds of the country was eventually returned to Swazi ownership.

After Sobhuza II had resisted British moves to unite the country with South Africa, Britain put forward the constitution for an independent Swaziland in 1963 and the first elections for the Legislative Council took place the following year. A newly formed party, the Imbokodvo National Movement, won the elections in 1967 and 1972, after independence had been declared in 1968. But in 1973 the Legislative Council was suspended by the king because it did not accord with the principles of Swazi culture. The new constitution vested all power in the king and, when Sobhuza II died in 1982, Mswati III succeeded him and continues to uphold Swazi traditions. The lack of democratic rights led to student and worker protests in the 1990s, a new constitution was introduced in 2005 and elections followed in 2008. Following a period of economic difficulty that led to further protests, elections took place in 2013, resulting in the reappointment of Sibusiso Dlamini as prime minister. Mbabane has been the capital since the British moved here from Manzini in 1902.

OBSERVATIONS

Mbabane is located in the lush hills of Swaziland and stands above a river that runs through the city. It is a small town with large residential suburbs. There are two important streets that cross at a high point and the river makes the third side of a triangle. The administration is close to the crossing of the main streets.

The early 1990s brought mall architecture to this tiny kingdom and its key permutations are found here: the internal arcade and the off-street, open-air mall. Informal trading takes place around the transport hubs and busy intersections, the vendor usually sitting on the ground next to their goods.

The homes of the poor are limited to one or two rooms. Some are built of mud in the traditional vernacular. Others salvage metal or timber to make intriguing patchwork constructions. The more substantial examples approach the style of government houses. Their settings are always interesting, forming clusters and intimate spaces.

NATIONAL POPULATION

1,287,000

CITY POPULATION

94,874

ETHNIC GROUPS

African 97%, European 3%

RELIGIONS

Zionist 40% (a blend of Christianity and indigenous ancestral worship), Roman Catholic 20%, Muslim 10%, other (includes Anglican, Bahai, Methodist, Mormon, Jewish) 30%

LANGUAGES

English (official, government business conducted in English), siSwati (official)

GDP

$10.56 billion

AGRICULTURAL PRODUCTS

sugarcane, cotton, corn, tobacco, rice, citrus, pineapples, sorghum, peanuts; cattle, goats, sheep

INDUSTRIES

coal, forestry, sugar, soft drink concentrates, textiles and clothing

The main administration buildings, dating from independence, form an elevated cluster, with good views of the surrounding hills. The city has beautiful parks, sports fields and children's play areas.

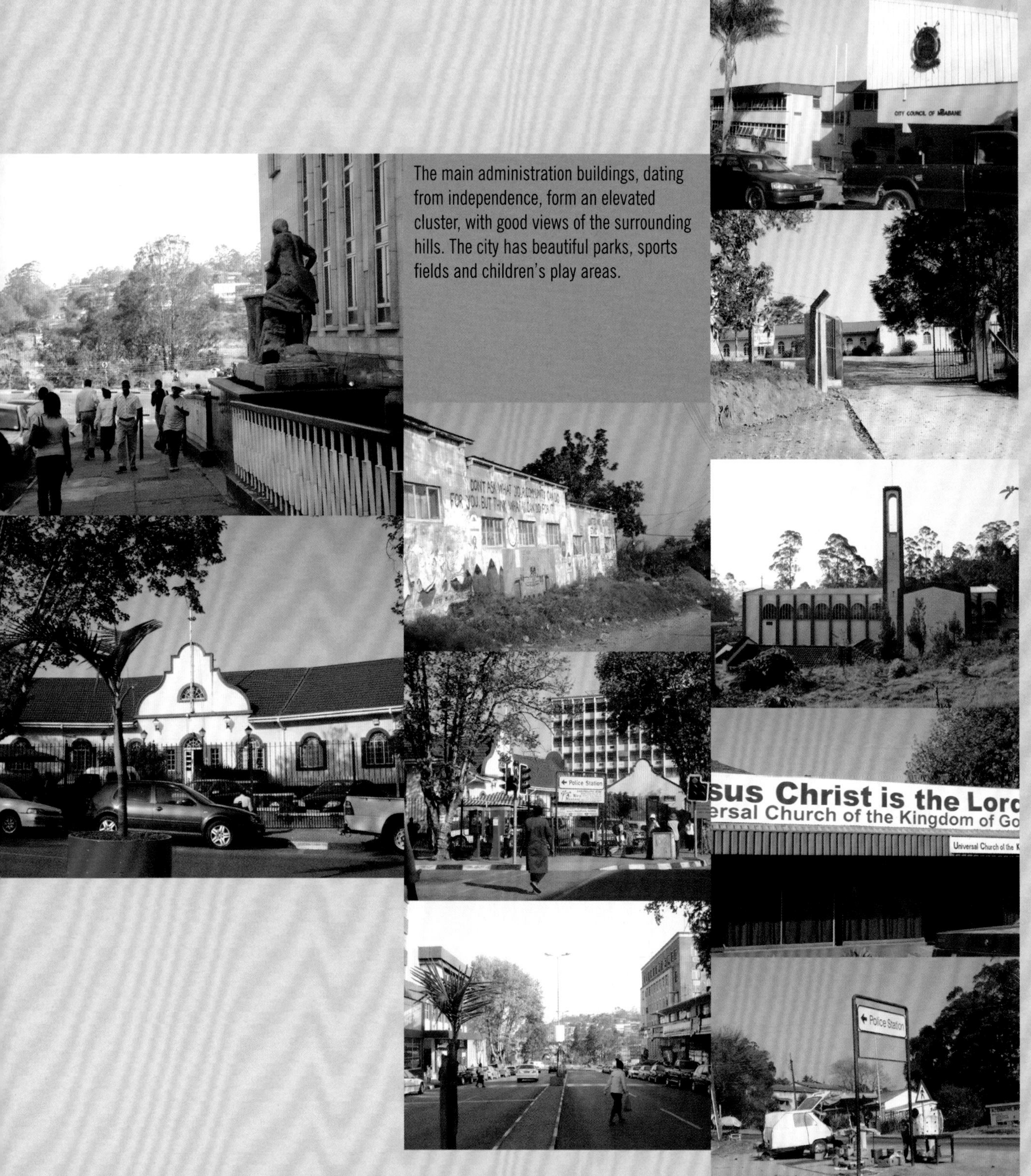

The commercial architecture is very mixed. The earliest examples are quite modest; the concrete frame arrived in the 1960s, and there are some higher buildings from the end of the century.

NEW WELCOME SUPERMARKET
Standard Bank
Vivi Fashions

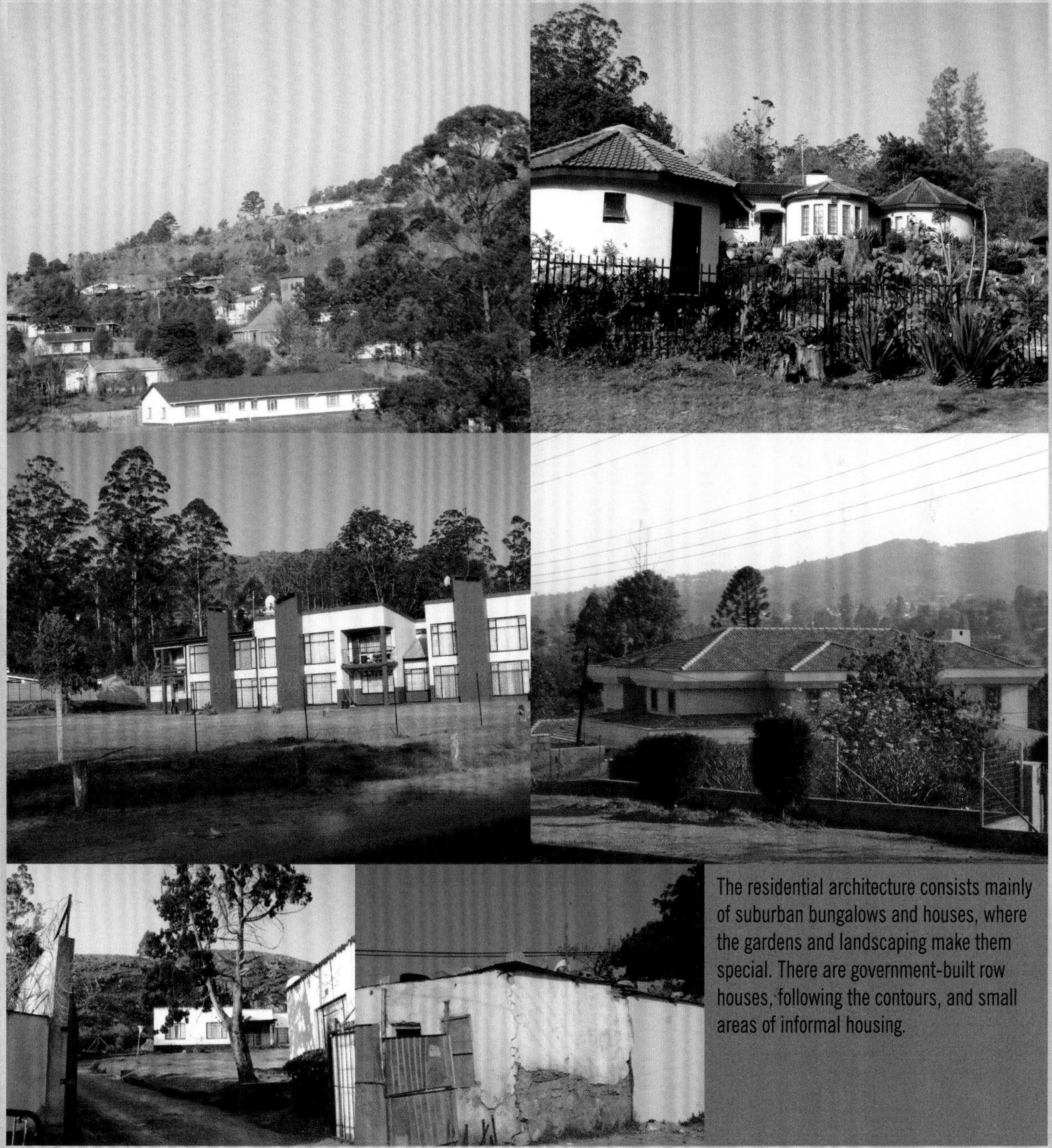

The residential architecture consists mainly of suburban bungalows and houses, where the gardens and landscaping make them special. There are government-built row houses, following the contours, and small areas of informal housing.

NAIROBI / KENYA

OVERVIEW

Hominid remains from over three million years ago have been found in the Rift Valley south of Lake Turkana, often referred to as the 'cradle of humanity'. The ethnic groups that now inhabit the country began to arrive from different directions in the 1st century BCE, in a process that continued until the 18th century. During the 1st millennium the coast was settled by Arab traders who introduced Islam. In the 18th and 19th centuries they participated in the East African slave trade. Of the colonial powers, the Portuguese were the first to arrive but, in an agreement with Germany, Britain took formal control of Kenya in 1890. The farms of the 80,000 settlers who had arrived by 1950 were often on land previously occupied by the Kikuyu people. They started an opposition movement in 1920 that climaxed in the Mau Mau uprising of the 1950s, when farms and government buildings were attacked. In 1960 the British government recognized the case for independence and the land rights of the Kikuyu, and a leader of the rebellion, Jomo Kenyatta, was elected as the first prime minister in 1963. He was soon made president and his fifteen years in office were relatively stable.

Kenyatta was leader of the Kenya African National Union (KANU) and after his death in 1978 he was succeeded by Daniel Arap Moi. He banned all other parties in 1982 and, as the 1987 election approached, he imprisoned opposition leaders without trial to ensure that there was only one possible result. In the 1990s such disregard for democratic rights became increasingly unacceptable to international organizations working in Kenya. This encouraged the pro-democracy movement but their rallies were still regularly disrupted by the youth section of KANU. The worst incident of this kind took place at an opposition rally in Nairobi in 1990 when activists were arrested and twenty people were killed. In response, the Forum for the Restoration of Democracy was founded. Its leader was promptly arrested but after a public outcry he was released and the constitution was amended to permit alternative political parties. But the elections of 1992 and 1997 were characterized by the harassment of opposition politicians and outbreaks of violence. The results of the 1997 election were finely balanced between KANU and several opposition parties but Moi avoided a potentially difficult situation by organizing a coalition government. In the 2002 election he had planned to hand power to Uhuru Kenyatta, one of Jomo Kenyatta's sons, but KANU was defeated by an alliance of twelve opposition parties known as the National Rainbow Coalition. The elections in 2007 were followed by allegations of vote rigging, and widespread violence, resulting in a coalition government. After the introduction of a new constitution in 2010, the 2013 election was won outright by Uhuru Kenyatta. The British relocated their capital from Mombasa to Nairobi in 1905 but most of the colonial buildings were demolished when the city was redeveloped after independence.

OBSERVATIONS

Nairobi is nearly 2,000 m above sea level and is surrounded by low hills. Its location means that the city is free of insects like mosquitoes and has very green suburbs. There are no views apart from those of the city itself. Downtown is a densely developed grid, with the civic centre on the edge.

The circular towers here were probably inspired by the cylindrical towers that punctuated the historic settlement of Greater Zimbabwe – they look so deliberate. I think that the intention to establish a balance between a low field of development and a central place is the correct reading in both places.

The extremes of wealth and poverty are constantly visible. The office building or suburban villa comes into sight at the same time as the interlocking roofscape of Kibera, an extensive area of informal housing 3 miles from the city centre. This double image occurs throughout the city, and constantly alters one's perception of place. It equalizes the environment, as poor people are not out of sight and their architecture is in full view.

Kibera represents an explosion of urban building that has found its own rules and morphology. Its character is somewhere between a castle and a village. This city within a city has access roads that tie it into the surrounding area but, due to the poor infrastructure, they turn into rivers of detritus when it rains.

NATIONAL POPULATION

46,050,000

CITY POPULATION

3,915,000

ETHNIC GROUPS

Kikuyu 22%, Luhya 14%, Luo 13%, Kalenjin 12%, Kamba 11%, Kisii 6%, Meru 6%, other African 15%, Asian, European and Arab 1%

RELIGIONS

Christian 82.5% (Protestant 47.4%, Catholic 23.3%, other 11.8%), Muslim 11.1%, traditional 1.6%, other 1.7%, none 2.4%, unspecified 0.7%

LANGUAGES

English (official), Kiswahili (official), numerous indigenous languages

GDP

$133 billion

AGRICULTURAL PRODUCTS

tea, coffee, corn, wheat, sugarcane, fruit, vegetables; dairy products, beef, fish, pork, poultry, eggs

INDUSTRIES

small-scale consumer goods (plastic, furniture, batteries, textiles, clothing, soap, cigarettes, flour), agricultural products, horticulture, oil refining, aluminium, steel, lead, cement, commercial ship repair, tourism

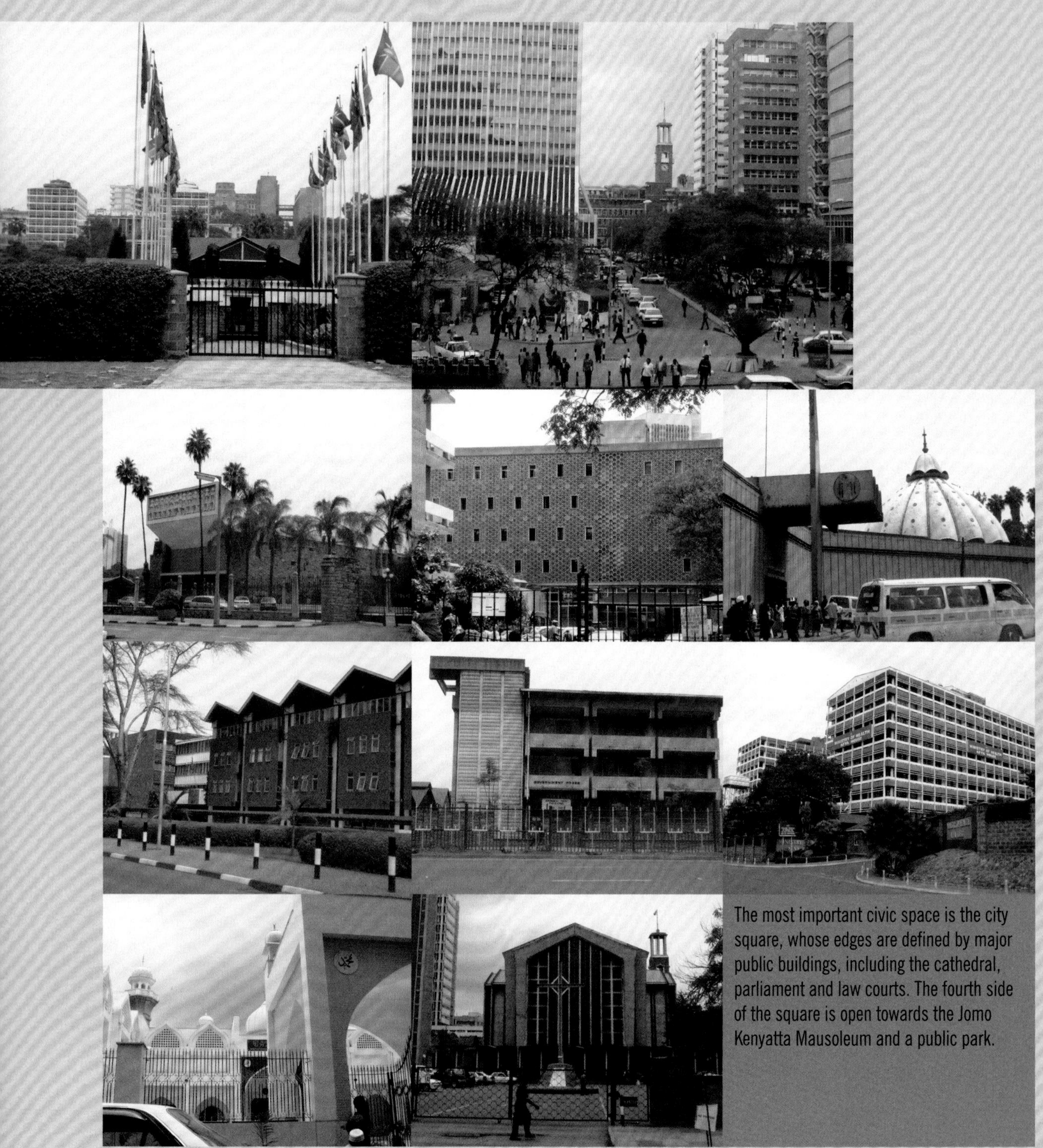

The most important civic space is the city square, whose edges are defined by major public buildings, including the cathedral, parliament and law courts. The fourth side of the square is open towards the Jomo Kenyatta Mausoleum and a public park.

These buildings represent the boom that Nairobi has experienced since independence. The most iconic is a conference and retail centre, with a circular tower and viewing platform. Built in the 1970s, this was one of the first of the high-rise buildings that now dominate the skyline.

The more wealthy suburbs are on the hillsides that overlook the centre. The middle classes live in neighbourhoods of more modest houses and the poor live on the fringes of the city in four- to six-storey blocks.

This is a large shanty town in a prominent position. With its makeshift construction and informal economy, it is an alternative city for the very poor. Due to the limited space available, public and private are constantly redefined here.

WINDHOEK / NAMIBIA

OVERVIEW

The country's first settlers were the San people who merged with later Bantu immigrants. In the 17th century the Herero migrated into the north and west of the country and their numbers grew until they dominated the population. The Nama inhabit other areas and are the descendants of Khoikhoi who were driven north by Europeans arriving in the Cape Colony. Portuguese sailors explored the coast in the late 15th century but it was not until the end of the 19th century that the area was annexed by Germany and named South West Africa. The Herero and the Nama rebelled against the Germans in 1904 but were brutally subdued. The German colony survived only until 1914, when it was successfully invaded by South African forces as a consequence of the European war. After the war the League of Nations gave South Africa a mandate over South West Africa and this arrangement was renewed by the United Nations after the Second World War. Although South Africa did not have the right to annex the country, much of the land was given to white settlers and pass laws restricted the movement of blacks to designated areas. South Africa's interest was motivated by the country's extensive reserves of copper, lead, zinc and uranium. Namibia is also a major source of diamonds.

From the days of the German colony the country had been run on the basis of forced labour and this fuelled the mass demonstrations and the independence movement that began in the 1950s. Several political parties were formed but over time the majority of them joined the South West African People's Organization (SWAPO), which took the question of South Africa's ongoing occupation to the International Court of Justice in 1966. Although the court did not come to a clear decision, the United Nations General Assembly took up the issue and voted to end South Africa's mandate. It also set up a new commission to administer Namibia. South Africa responded by imprisoning activists and shooting demonstrators, driving SWAPO into a campaign of guerrilla warfare. On the political front, there were several attempts to negotiate a more satisfactory arrangement with South Africa but they had little effect on the overall situation. SWAPO intensified its guerrilla warfare with increasing effect, preventing free movement in the north, pressurizing the South African military, and generally undermining the economy. Only then was South Africa drawn into international negotiations that resulted in the withdrawal of its troops from Namibia, in exchange for the removal of Cuban troops from Angola. The first elections took place in 1989 and, with the majority of votes, SWAPO's leader, Sam Nujoma, became president when independence was declared in 1990. He served three terms and pursued a programme of reconstruction and reconciliation to make good the destructive effects of the previous twenty-five years. SWAPO remains in power and Hage Geingob won the elections in 2014. Windhoek came to significance as the centre of the German administration; it is 1,728 metres above sea level and occupies a key position in the country's infrastructure.

OBSERVATIONS

Windhoek is a city on a mountain in the south of the country. The German colonial past seems to have left its mark on the infrastructure and city planning. Most of the shops, banking, commerce and administration are located around Independence Avenue, whose street life animates the heart of the city.

The civic architecture is mainly colonial or modernist, signifying inheritance and a search for the new. The parliament building is in the form of a large colonial palace, similar to other colonial parliaments in this region.

Houses are brightly coloured in both the well-to-do and less well off areas. The light is very special in this part of the world – naked, sharp and revealing.

The architecture of the wealthy residential areas is of the compound and villa type. These areas are well served in terms of infrastructure and landscaping, and the security is not as manic as other cities. Walls are lower, so the houses can be seen from the street.

Housing for the poor is further from the centre. Unless you know where to go, you could be forgiven for thinking there are no poor people here. Their state-built housing consists of simple sheds made from blockwork and corrugated sheet. These can be customized by painting and adding extensions.

NATIONAL POPULATION

2,459,000

CITY POPULATION

368,000

ETHNIC GROUPS

black 87.5% (Ovambo 50%, Kavango 9%, Herero 7%, Damara 7%, Nama 5%, Caprivian 4%, Bushmen 3%, Baster 2%, Tswana 0.5%), white 6%, mixed 6.5%

RELIGIONS

Christian 80% to 90% (Lutheran over 50%), indigenous beliefs 10% to 20%

LANGUAGES

Oshiwambo languages 48.9%, Nama/Damara 11.3%, Afrikaans 10.4% (common to most of population), Otjiherero languages 8.6%, Kavango languages 8.5%, Caprivi languages 4.8%, English (official) 3.4%, other African languages 2.3%, other 1.8%

GDP

$23.48 billion

AGRICULTURAL PRODUCTS

millet, sorghum, peanuts, grapes; livestock; fish

INDUSTRIES

meatpacking, fish processing, dairy products, mining (diamonds, lead, zinc, tin, silver, tungsten, uranium, copper)

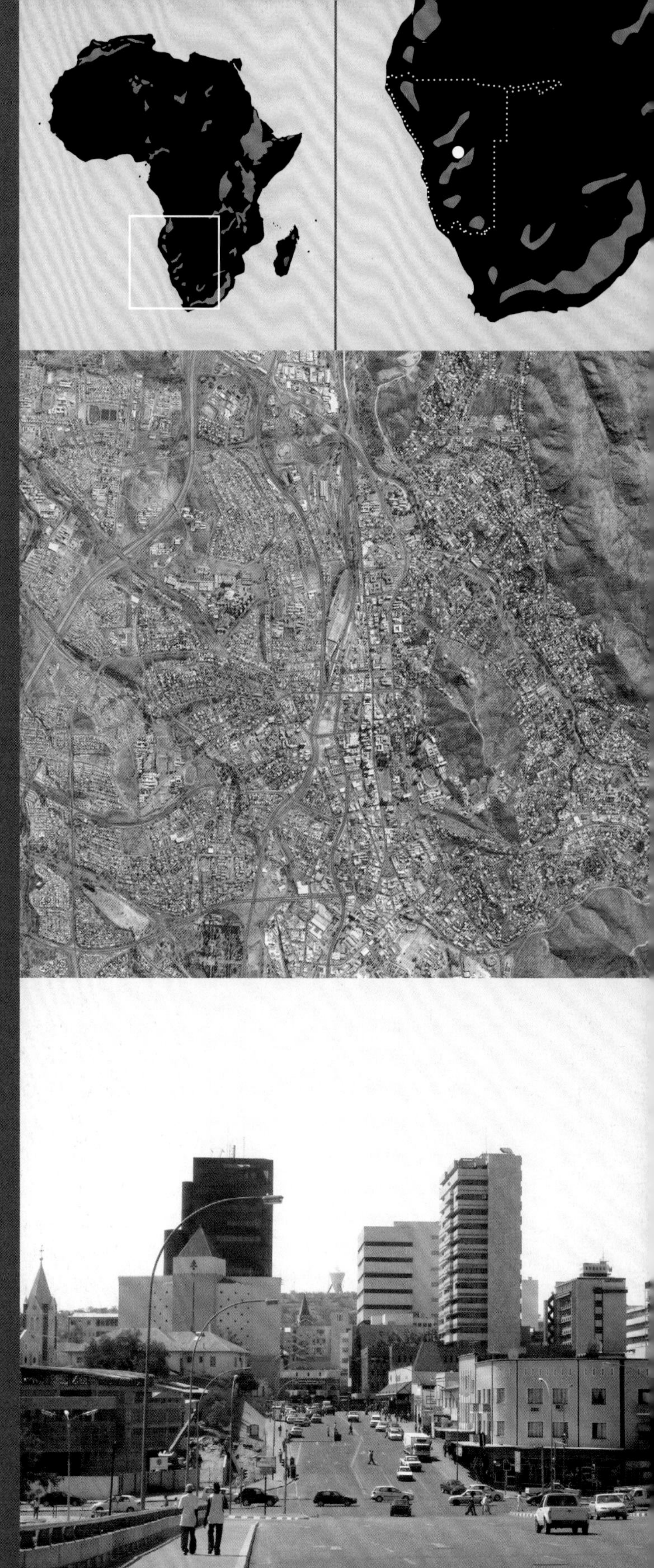

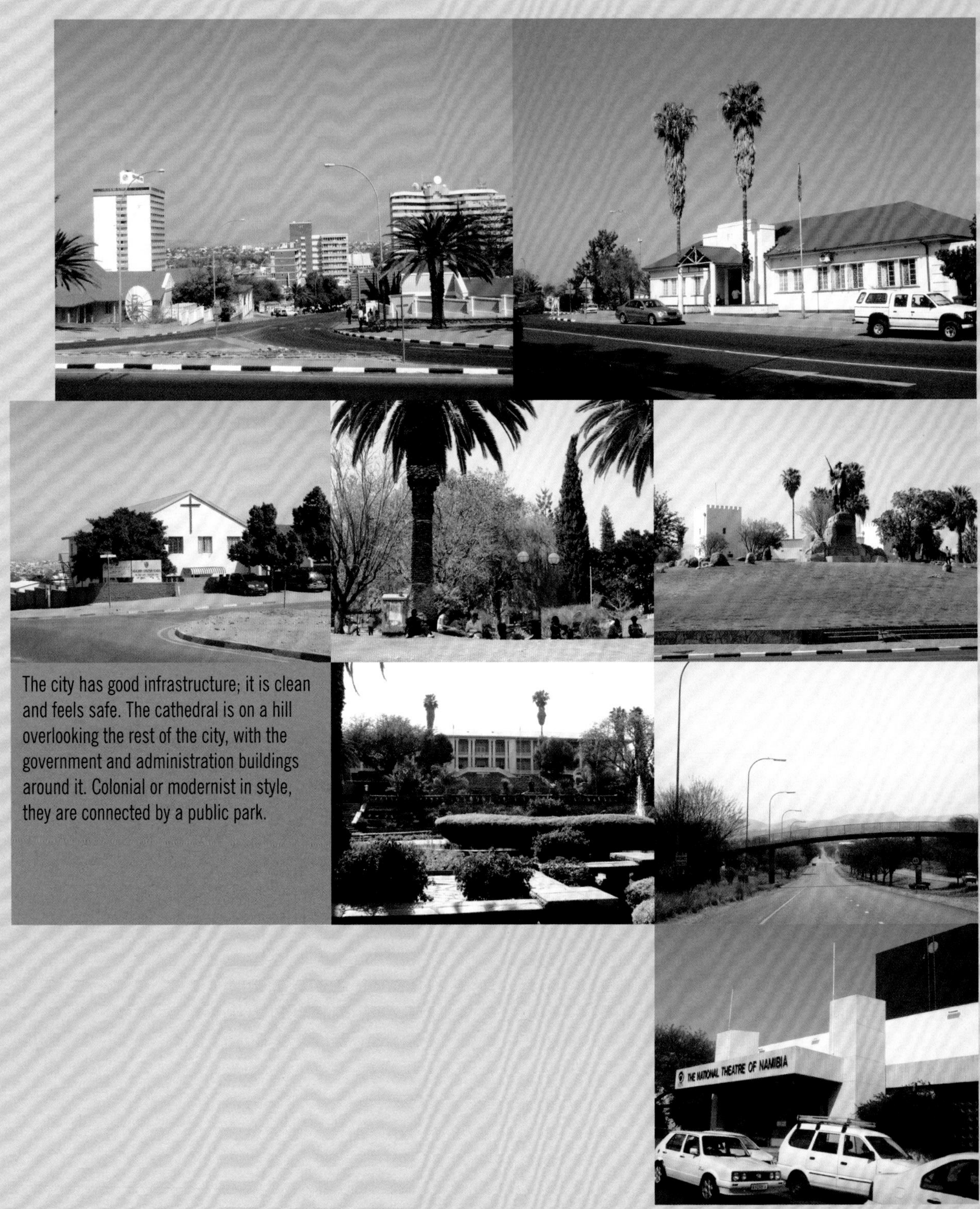

The city has good infrastructure; it is clean and feels safe. The cathedral is on a hill overlooking the rest of the city, with the government and administration buildings around it. Colonial or modernist in style, they are connected by a public park.

Windhoek
Gobabis
Reiterdenkmal
Alte Feste
Parliament Building

BIBLIOTEEK
LIBRARY
BÜCHEREI

Windhoek

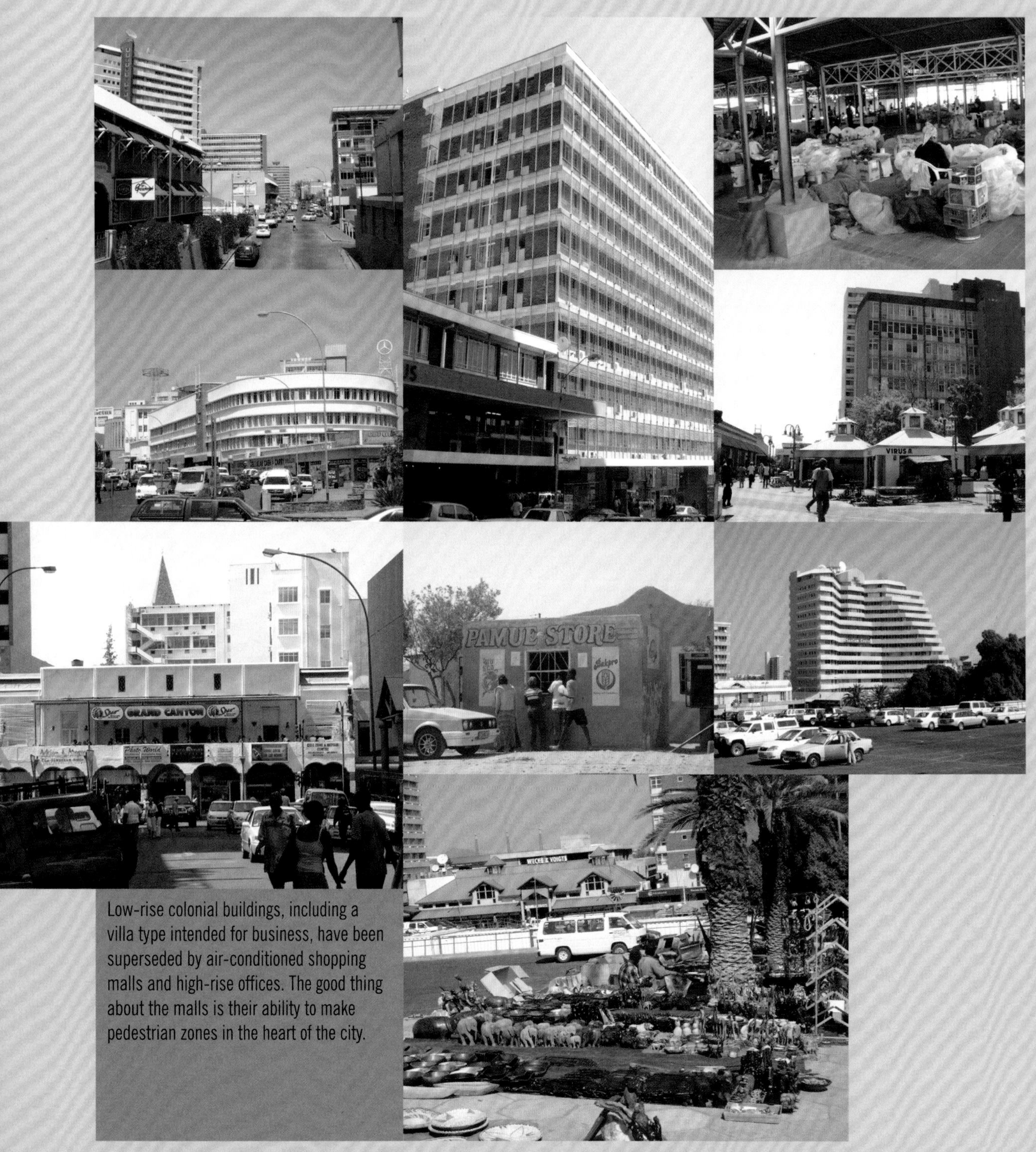

Low-rise colonial buildings, including a villa type intended for business, have been superseded by air-conditioned shopping malls and high-rise offices. The good thing about the malls is their ability to make pedestrian zones in the heart of the city.

The villa standing within a garden enclosure is the predominant type. Housing for the poor is found on the edge of the city and is a utilitarian version of the homes of the affluent. Residents try to customize these sheds by adding porches or using colour.

"The Africa study allowed me to develop a particular overview and to improve my understanding of other cities and of how architecture could be made. I wanted to look at the fundamentals of the African city, to understand the issues that are currently in play, beyond the continent's historical and architectural traditions. The climate and landscape of Africa are so varied that there you can really feel how powerfully geography and culture shape place."

ESSAYS

DAVID ADJAYE
AFRICAN METROPOLITAN ARCHITECTURE

This book involves a return to some of the formative experiences of my childhood. I was born in Dar es Salaam, Tanzania, and my parents took me to other cities in East Africa, such as Kampala and Nairobi. But my family is from Ghana, and later we returned there and my father was given one of the estates that the government was then building. The country had embarked on a programme of modernization, following the Nkrumah era, and we witnessed the transformation of Accra from being a colonial city into the modern metropolis that it is today. My father was then posted to Beirut, a French colonial city with a glamour that I had never seen before. It was very international and cosmopolitan, and the lifestyle by the sea was a new experience. With Beirut as a base, we began to explore North Africa and Cairo, where I saw the Muslim city with all its commerce. The places that I visited during this period made an incredibly strong impression: the colours and light in East, West and North Africa are very different, as are their languages and culture. As I travelled with my parents, I began to understand the incredible diversity that existed on this continent, and the kind of internationalism that it represented. It was my first experience of such things.

As an architect in London, I became interested in the effects that my early experience of Africa may have had on me and I conceived a project that would reconnect with the landscapes I had previously visited. Africa has always been a point of reference for me. When I was a young kid, it was an anchor in the very mobile world that I was living in and, during my upbringing and education in Europe, it was a reference point for understanding my identity. As a student, and specifically after spending some time in Japan, it became a source for me to make structures, to articulate things that I knew and felt were important. It provided a basis for taking a strategic view and moving forward even though Africa was still, in many respects, shrouded in darkness.

My plan, when it finally took shape, was to complete the journey I had started in my early life. Africa is an entire continent, and I would need to travel from north to south, east to west, taking in many different terrains, to record the diversity of its fifty-four countries and their capitals. While there is a considerable amount of research about developmental and sociological issues in Africa, there is a lack of information for architects, urban designers and planners, so this book aims to add something to the cultural and visual history of the continent.

It is over fifty years since the first African countries gained independence – and South Africa has recently emerged as the continent's superpower. Since then nations have been built, and we are now in a position to reflect on the significance of these changes for communities that, prior to colonization, were essentially rural. The colonial city existed primarily for purposes of trade and administration but, after independence, the same cities have become symbols of modernity, nationhood and emancipation. For Africans, this involves a complex negotiation as the identity of place is transferred from local to national significance, and becomes a more artificial construct in the process. Quiet colonial cities have been transformed into metropolitan capitals, and the speed with which this has happened is fundamental to understanding how the African perceives the city.

I felt that this aspect of the continent's urbanism was not fully understood, so this book is an attempt to narrate some of these stories visually. It is not intended to be an archive of types to be copied, but an attempt to understand African urbanism by looking at certain kinds of building in each city. I hope that the reader will compare different places and see emerging conditions and patterns of development. I see this as a new area of study, an exploration of the opportunities and drawbacks connected with the urban environment as it emerges.

METROPOLITAN

In Africa, the concept of the 'metropolitan' has had a different history and trajectory from other continents and carries a distinct meaning. Africa has always been a continent of kingdoms and empires, each with its own centre of power and administration: Meroë in modern Sudan, capital of the Kushite kingdom; Great Zimbabwe, near modern Masvingo, capital of the Shona trading empire; al-Ghaba, near modern Koumbi Saleh in Mauritania, capital of the Empire of Ghana (not to be confused with the country); Jenne, possible site of the Empire of Mali's capital; Gao in modern Mali, capital of the Songhai Empire. There are many other examples but, in all of these places, the idea of difference and of negotiating difference was an integral part of their reality. For me, this history has immediate relevance as it gives strong clues to what the concept of a metropolitan identity might be in Africa.

Different people coming together in a metropolitan situation is not new. In Africa it was originally associated with the consolidation of these empires – unlike the Western idea that concerned mercantile, industrial or capitalist centres. In this context, the African city is a construction to organize power and make identity, and many families have both urban and rural homes. This is not part of a flight from the countryside, which happened in the West, but a side-by-side existence of urban and rural communities, which feed one another and reinforce each other's identity. Although you are in the city, your identity is still very much derived from the country; I have found that most Africans derive their identity from their rural and pastoral beginnings.

The idea of the metropolitan in Africa is not just about the density of people coming together but includes the parallel layering of many conditions: from the modernity of the city, and its embrace of development and commerce, back to its function as a heroic symbol of emancipation from a colonial past. And, as we have seen, it may include an imperial past that goes back through the centuries. This complex notion of the metropolitan is further conditioned by the geography of the continent because, although their histories have much in common, the character of each city is unique to its location. My purpose was to understand the interplay between shared themes and special circumstances and, in order to do this, I needed to look at each city on a similar basis.

The continent encompasses a range of climatic zones (the Maghreb, desert, the Sahel, forest, savanna and grassland, mountain and highveld) which, with the rural culture of the hinterland, inflect the identity of each city. Addis Ababa is very much a mountain city with a close relationship to the rolling highlands that surround it, as is Antananarivo, the inland capital of Madagascar. In Addis, I saw a culture of the bucolic, and the sense of well-being that it brings, affecting how the city organizes itself. Housing areas are situated where it is cool, and as far from where the mosquitoes gather as possible, with civic and administrative areas positioned on the flat lands. In Antananarivo, the power of the market and the mercantile culture, derived from the countryside, is not just located in one area but laces itself, like fingers, through the city.

I talk about geographical inflection as a way of focusing on the particularities of a place: it might be a hill town in a forest or a coastal city on the edge of a bay. Dar es Salaam, Accra and Dakar all demonstrate the way the city is distorted as it develops from its historic core towards a leisure quarter. In Dar, you have the old town overlooking the harbour, while the main residential areas follow the coastline to the north. In Accra, the British settlement, Jamestown, is at the western end of the coast road, and Nungua, where the Ga people live and several hotels are located, is several miles to the east. In Dakar, the historic core occupies a narrow peninsula, while a new residential city, which has become the most desirable neighbourhood, has developed on another peninsula further up the coast. These kinds of geographical relationship can be seen in almost any city; their significance here concerns the part that the continental geography plays in determining the metropolitan identity of African cities.

A surprise, even to me, is the common misunderstanding that Africans do not have a concept of the metropolitan, or of what it means to be a citizen of such a place; there is somehow a tendency to see Africans as rural. But you do this at your own peril, as you may well be dealing with someone who – even if they are having to relearn a set of codes – is actually very familiar with the urban script. Contrary to popular belief, the African immigrant is extremely comfortable in most metropolitan conditions. The city is a mechanism that is well understood, mainly due to the vast urbanization that took place very early in the history of the continent – far earlier than on other continents. This has always fascinated me.

ARCHITECTURE

When I talk about architecture in Africa, I am not referring to the traditional role of architecture: the creation of symbolic objects – or icons – that are the synthesis of a culture going back over several centuries. I am looking at the architecture of habitation, of humanity in general: the city as an inclusive conglomerate. It is a way of looking at architecture in terms of its collective identity, not as a series of freestanding icons.

When photographing each of the cities, I had in mind the interpretation of 'metropolitan' and the definition of 'architecture' outlined above. I was looking at the layering of the city and how that plays out. At first glance these cities might appear to be modernist, colonial or even medieval, but that is a misreading of the complexity and the layering of types that are always present, always in play. I was curious to understand what had been built and whether it came from expedience, a relationship to colonial power, economics, self-belief or self-identity. I have tried to reexamine familiar tropes and typologies and, by documenting the fifty-four capitals, to provide a nuanced view of building activity across Africa. Although architecture can absorb ideas and influences from many sources, African architecture is ultimately very specific. It has a particular power and influence that organizes more than a billion people and contributes to their psyche, their identity, and the way they inhabit the city today.

Some of modernism's greatest experiments have been played out in African cities, but in the context of a climate and people who coopted modernity from being a form of universal construction to something local. In the different terrains, it is very powerful to see this kind of nuance. In cities such as Abuja, Accra, Kinshasa and Maputo, I see ways of constructing architecture that combine the science and technology of our age with their own identity and cultural inflections. As I see it, identity is no longer a theme to be applied to the surface of things but grows out of the actual work of a place, and how that generates distinctive readings of economic, cultural, religious and secular activities.

It is important to respect the subject and to trust direct observation. The identity of a place, and of Africa itself, is not the result of applying theories or teasing out narratives. For this reason, I have tried to engage directly with the specifics of each place and to apply minimal constraints on my experiences there. The real idea of newness comes from establishing a position based on understanding and close study, and then moving forward. I find this fascinating because it offers a methodology that can avoid the repetitive internationalization of cities. Working more closely with different geographies in a variety of continental locations, modernism is no longer universal but nuanced across localized landscapes. The identity of each modernity can supply incredible richness.

The process behind this project is based on a way of understanding how to make a language when the starting point is looking. From looking to language, we can construct specific narratives that apply to those cities: what they might be, how they might grow and develop in their future. As we progress, we can move beyond international modernism towards a localized and specific modernity, aided by science, technology and culture.

Some of modernism's greatest experiments have been played out in African cities, but in the context of a climate and people who coopted modernity from a form of universal construction to something local. In the different terrains, it is very powerful to see this kind of nuance. In cities such as Abuja, Accra, Kinshasa and Maputo, I see ways of constructing architecture that combine the science and technology of our age with their own identity and cultural inflections.

David Adjaye

GARTH MYERS & JENNY ROBINSON

CITIES, CONNECTIONS AND CIRCULATIONS IN AFRICA

Despite their great diversity, cities in Africa have much in common. Similar building designs and city forms reflect shared historical processes, especially those associated with colonialism, and since most African city governments are resource-poor, many cities show signs of physical neglect and decay. Economic decline has caused architectural and infrastructural deterioration, even as globalization has led to renewal in certain parts of the city and has fragmented the urban experience.

These sometimes banal but widespread commonalities indicate how ideas and practices circulate to link the forms and fortunes of African cities. These circulations – often outside the frame in which cities are pictured – help to make sense of features across Africa that in isolation are often quite puzzling: something that may appear to be an idiosyncrasy of one city landscape emerges in another, perhaps with a different meaning altogether. The circulations and connections that stretch across and beyond cities, in Africa as elsewhere, often produce strangely familiar, even uncanny, urban forms and are an important source of the dynamism and generativity of city life. What AbdouMaliq Simone calls the 'worlding' of cities in Africa proceeds apace on the ground, affecting formal and informal activities, and observers are increasingly aware of it in their thinking about cities.[1]

A GENEALOGY OF CIRCULATION

Circulations across the continent predate European colonialism and shaped cities in myriad ways. Major historical polities, such as Buganda and Abyssinia, even circulated their capital city or seat of power between settlements, distinctively symbolizing the geography of power. Other precolonial urban capitals soon established a dualism that is characteristic of many African cities, of having separate quarters for strangers and outsiders, most commonly traders who brought goods, as well as new religious ideas and different cultures. Such early circulations established the now familiar pattern in which connections beyond the city produce the internal diversity that continues to characterize them.

Colonial-era connectivities are well known and documented. New forms of urbanism and many new cities were initiated, as were global-scale flows of goods and people. But even here we suggest that the links among African cities were more extensive and complex than many historical analyses would lead one to think. Circulars – called just that – issued in London, for instance, suggested or set policies and plans for cities across Britain's colonies. And the mundane modernisms of architects, engineering firms, town planners or housing officers, who often worked in one city after another in different colonies or visited on study tours, set in place the familiar physical form and feel of many of Africa's cities founded during this period. These colonial circulations were ubiquitous and multidirectional, and yet have only recently attracted attention in studies of colonialism generally, and then very little in relation to cities.

Conversations about how best to manage colonial cities crossed imperial boundaries as well, especially in relation to questions of racial segregation, which has been an important influence shaping the many fragmented and quartered cities which have emerged across Africa. Belgian, British, French, Portuguese or Italian colonialists regularly intersected in Europe and across the continent, observing one another's tactics and strategies for segregating and managing cities. They often travelled to view 'models' of urban development, such as McNamee Village in Port Elizabeth, South Africa. It was built around 1936, along the lines of a 'garden village', which accounts for the arrangement of roads radiating from a central common area, and the cul-de-sacs which enclose neighbourhoods of small houses. McNamee Village (named after the local township administrator) attracted official visitors from across the country and from as far afield as Kenya, Northern Rhodesia and Tanzania.

There is some way to go before we really understand the meaning of the astonishingly similar colonial histories – and thus present forms – of some of Africa's cities. The historical narratives of the growth of cities like Dar es Salaam, Lusaka and Johannesburg are strikingly similar, especially in relation to issues of segregation, housing, planning, youth, crime, prostitution and law. Closer attention to how ideas and practices moved across the continent could put these now familiar narratives in a new light.

CONTEMPORARY CIRCULATIONS

Connections and circulations continue to be significant in shaping both physical forms of cities in Africa and the trajectories of their development. It is commonly asserted that many cities across the continent are disconnected from contemporary globalization and its related flows of investment, goods and ideas about urbanism. The limited role that many cities here play in the global circulation of direct investment in the world, in global stock-market transactions or in airline traffic, is often cited as evidence, though too often this data is heavily biased towards processes coming from the West. As new kinds of international investors – notably South African and Chinese – come to dominate economic development in some African countries, the limitations of these analyses will become increasingly apparent.

Some transformations in the era of globalization certainly do cut off African cities from certain kinds of circulation. Filip De Boeck has talked about the 'growing ruralization of Kinshasa' that is in part a result of the breakdown of many of its traditional ties to wider economic and political processes, and its dislocation from global development.[2] But at the same time new modes of connection and flow are also emerging.

Informal trade, migration, displacements of people from areas of conflict, circuits of weapons and unregulated commodity trade and even highly speculative investment in property developments: there are many kinds of flow connecting and shaping cities like Kinshasa. Certainly the circulations that matter to some cities may be primarily imaginary, as anthropologists have documented the important role that imagining and planning for migration, for example, can play in shaping urban identities and practices.[3] But more material flows abound and are essential for maintaining city life. Mining regions draw temporary migrants to and from cities; transnational informal trade draws city-dwellers to establish connections to cities further afield, often following tracks of earlier colonial relationships, or heading to emerging centres of economic prosperity. In the case of Kinshasa these links might be to Belgium, but also increasingly to South African cities, where an infrastructure to support migrants from the Democratic Republic of the Congo is emerging. For example, at the same time as migrants are keeping their ties back home alive through their use of internet cafes in Yeoville, an inner-city suburb of Johannesburg, they are also using these venues to create distinctive new local associations of fellow migrants from the same regions of the Democratic Republic of the Congo.

In the last thirty years or so a great many urban Africans have migrated to Europe and North America, and to a lesser extent Asia, creating a transnational diaspora that now generates development initiatives 'back home':[4] money sent 'home' from wealthy countries to Africa is having a strong impact on the continent's cities as remittance flows directly transform the built environment. Richard Grant has, for example, documented the dozens of gated communities of Accra that cater to the diaspora Ghanaians who build million-dollar homes from remittance wealth.[5] Migrations, journeys, diasporas and transnationality also cause other things, such as cultural ideas, to circulate and connect cities in more ephemeral ways. This is part of the 'worlding' of African cities that Simone has discussed. Dominique Malaquais offers a detailed analysis of a suggestive skyline painting in Douala, Cameroon, that depicts New York in ways that speak of a distant imaginative engagement on the part of Douala's residents with that city and its potential. But in its detail, she suggests, the painting also shows that the artist had crafted the image based on careful, local observations in New York, revealing both the material and imaginative links between those two cities.[6]

If it is important to understand the range of wider connections shaping Africa's cities, it is also necessary to question the ways in which these links work on the ground. James Ferguson, for example, has suggested that globalization does not flow in many African contexts, rather it 'hops'.[7] This is an image of a neoliberal capitalism that flits here and there, lands a bit, moves on, staying only as long as profits attained balance out the negatives and the margin for instability. Actual investments remain thin, though, having little impact on the infrastructure or the wider development needs of the country. This globe-hopping nature of capitalism across Africa can help to explain why, in Ferguson's example of Angola, most of the country remains poor despite its staggering resource base and the growing role of the West – and now China – in exploiting it in these selected enclaves.

For quite a few cities in Africa, then, this 'thin globalization', with its distinctive spatiality and frequently corrupt local management, can mean that global links and resource development have few of the anticipated consequences for urban economic expansion. Globalization may result in less adequate shelter, or even serviced land, for those who move into cities in search of some kind of livelihood, despite substantial resource exploitation across the country. Of course the effects can just as well be seen in the wealthier urban quarters and consumption lifestyles of those who do reap a personal benefit from this kind of globalization and governance. Experiences across Africa are very diverse though. In places economic growth and state formation have resulted in broad investment in productive infrastructure, housing and service delivery. Cities like Alexandria, Cairo, Tripoli, Gaborone, Port Louis and

Johannesburg have benefited from expanded investment, growing exports and moderate economic growth to make significant improvements in housing and infrastructure for poorer residents.

In a range of different ways, then, cities across Africa are profoundly connected, both with one another and with much more distant places. As we have seen, some of these connections are purely imaginative and some quite conventional, involving flows of money, goods, people and ideas; others are, perhaps, more surprising.

Two examples here exemplify and perhaps stretch our sense of how circulations have shaped cities in Africa. We start, within the photographic frame, from familiar, perhaps iconic, elements of many cities – modernist high-rise apartment blocks and public statues commemorating great political leaders – and track their connections to distant places. The links we have chosen to focus on are not commonly discussed in an age absorbed with Western-centric globalization: these ties are to the former Soviet bloc, although as we will see there are similarities and associations with more Western urban idioms. The historical layers of different connections which have shaped cities in Africa can, we suggest, provoke us to think about their pasts and futures in more imaginative ways.

RESIDUAL CONNECTIONS

Postindependence Zanzibar had strong links to socialist East German planning, and they are littered across Zanzibar Town: high-rise apartments, new spatial segmentations, and a residential landscape designed for surveillance. What might seem to be banal international-style apartments carry a specific set of socialist connections and ambitions.

After the 1964 revolution in Zanzibar, the new regime under Abeid Karume began rebuilding the city, with assistance from the German Democratic Republic. Everyone in urban and rural Zanzibar was to be organized into ten new towns. In the city phase of the project, New Zanzibar, Karume turned to a team of East German planners, architects and engineers. Their 1968 plan concentrated on Ng'ambo, the historically African 'other side', because the East Germans considered the city's elite central area, known as Stone Town, to be well serviced, and thought Ng'ambo could become a shining example of socialism.

The East Germans' proposal for Ng'ambo consisted of building flats for nearly all residents, a new road system, a sewage system, schools and a new industrial area. Had they been built to the original plan, the new flats would have been the town's tallest buildings. This plan used techniques and concepts of monumental socialist architecture. Throughout Eastern Europe in the mid to late 1960s Soviet model projects consisted of rational distribution, order and control, and a conception of the city as an ideological instrument. Yet the scheme, despite its very different ideology, replicated and indeed entrenched British colonialism's spatial ordering and enframing tactics, as Timothy Mitchell has outlined.[8] It relied on a segmented plan in which the city was broken down into parts. Although in this case the segments were identified less with race than with class and ideology, the zoning strategies of the city's colonial town plan of 1958 were left intact. The southern zone of British colonial seaside villas was now used as the residential area of party and state leaders. Police roadblocks at the boundaries of areas of elite villas both north and south of the city continue to containerize the city forty-five years after the revolution, and the arrangement of apartments, corridors and stairwells was notorious for enabling close surveillance of residents' activities.

PROPAGANDA BY MONUMENTS

As with Soviet-era monuments in postsocialist cities, monuments from the apartheid era disturb the postapartheid cities they inhabit. In former socialist countries many Soviet-era monuments have been dismantled and relocated to museum-like outdoor statue parks. In Strijdom Square, Pretoria, there was a huge brutalist bust of Johannes Strijdom, one-time president of the apartheid Republic of South Africa. In an uncanny moment in 2001, on the fortieth anniversary of South Africa's unilateral declaration of independence from the Commonwealth, the statue collapsed suddenly without any apparent explanation.[9] Elsewhere, apartheid and colonial-era statues have been removed, creatively reimagined or replaced by new icons, as South Africa's cities have slowly transformed themselves during the postapartheid era.[10]

Picking up on these often traumatic changes in South Africa's urban public spaces, and observing that postsocialist cities were also divesting themselves of their familiar but unwanted public monuments, one of South Africa's foremost novelists, Ivan Vladislavić, created a short story, 'Propaganda by monuments'.[11] He exposes how urban experiences are reframed in the wake of these now ghostly absences.

In exploring this process Vladislavić also draws on some other urban dynamics familiar across Africa, such as an urban informality which often involves the creative reuse and recirculation of objects – what AbdouMaliq Simone calls 'pirate urbanism'.[12] In the story the owner of a *shebeen* (an illicit liquor store and public house) in a Pretoria township corresponds with a Russian government translator about the possibility of buying one of the busts of Lenin being removed from Russia's public places. He hopes the bust will give his shebeen – the V. I. Lenin Bar and Grill – the distinction it needs for business success. The story evokes the intense historical links between South African politics and former socialist countries – antiapartheid movements, trade unions, the ANC (African National Congress) and Communist Party all had strong networks with and received much practical support from governments in these countries. The language and practice of contemporary postapartheid South African politics carry memories of these connections. However, since for long periods these movements were banned and operated underground, South Africa's cities bear very few traces of these connections. Only some informal settlement names, and now some street names, reflect this socialist heritage. To track these largely invisible connections, Vladislavić uses the anachronistic – and stylistically similar – statues from South Africa and the Soviet bloc countries to draw attention to their parallel transitional experiences, and imaginatively to insert these invisible historical links into the physical space of the city.

'Propaganda by monuments' begins in Moscow with the translator dealing with the Pretoria-based shebeen owner Boniface Khumalo's request for a bust of Lenin. He is heading off to watch workmen dismantle just such a statue in one of Moscow's neighbourhoods. As he watches, he rereads and reflects on this unusual letter from Atteridgeville, Pretoria. He has been safeguarding a copy of the letter in his coat pocket together with the original envelope. After the statue has been removed, he walks over to examine the pedestal:

> A single thread of iron, a severed spine twisting from the concrete, marked the spot where the head had stood. The head of Lenin. It was hard to imagine something else in its place. But that's the one certainty we have, he thought. There will be something in its place.[13]

The owner of the shebeen in Pretoria expects that a Lenin bust would appeal to his working-class customers, especially on the national May Day holiday. Through the letters, substantially mistranslated between the two continents, we are alerted to the power of imaginative associations to bring distant places together and potentially to transform the cityscape. For example, Khumalo visits the stylistically similar Strijdom bust in Pretoria and ponders how his Lenin statue will fit into his yard, and Vladislavić evokes the bizarre image of a huge (7 m by 17 m) bust of Lenin peeking out above the small dwellings of an apartheid-era township:

> At the Church Street intersection he waited for the robot [traffic light] to change even though there was no traffic. He looked right, and left, and right again towards Strijdom Square, and caught a glimpse of the dome like a swollen canvas over the head of J. G. Strijdom [...] Then he looked at the head. His heart sank. According to his calculations, the head of V. I. Lenin promised to him in the letter from Grekov was at least three times larger than the head of J. G. Strijdom! The pedestal would hardly fit in his yard. Perhaps if he knocked down the outside toilet and the Zozo [...] but surely it would cost a fortune to build a pedestal that size. And who would pay for the installation?

Nonetheless, he considers that the impossible might yet come to pass, and as he does so he manages to decipher the mystery of how the Strijdom monument, which appears to be floating in the air, is able to defy the laws of gravity. Vladislavić's magical-realist style shows the possibility of disrupting the here and now of the physical spaces of the city with the sometimes extraordinary potential of elsewheres.

In a literary register, the idea of translation – and the surplus and excess involved in mistranslation – helps to catch the generative quality of these strange proximities.[14] In terms of physical spaces, though, the often uncanny nature of such proximities might incline one to delve into figures of ghostliness or psychodynamics.[15] In this perspective, connections can be forged not only through physical flows and connections, but also through imaginative and emotional associations, drawing distant places together in sometimes unanticipated ways. For some cities in Africa today, then, where connections and circulations may be much prefigured, hoped for and planned, but perhaps not often actually put into motion, such imaginative links, like the ephemeral public spaces that Simone discusses,[16] have to be attended to as an integral part of the making and worlding of cities. Of course, and as we discussed in the first part of this essay, the physical landscape of the city – past and present – is also replete with the products of actually moving ideas, people and resources. In our view the diversity of these circulations, both physical and ephemeral, is increasing, and scholars, observers and inhabitants of these cities will have to be looking in many different directions, within and beyond the city, to comprehend their present forms and future trajectories.

NOTES

1. AbdouMaliq Simone, *For the city yet to come: Changing African life in four cities*, Durham: Duke University Press, 2004; Sarah Nuttall and Achille Mbembe, eds, 'Johannesburg: The elusive metropolis', *Public Culture*, vol. 44 (Fall 2004) (special edition).

2. Filip De Boeck and Marie-Françoise Plissart, *Kinshasa: Tales of the invisible city*, Ghent: Ludion Press, 2004.

3. De Boeck and Plissart, *Kinshasa*; Simone, *For the city yet to come*.

4. Claire Mercer, Ben Page and Martin Evans, *Development and the African diaspora: Place and the politics of home*, London and New York: Zed Press, 2008.

5. Richard Grant, *Globalizing city: The urban and economic transformation of Accra, Ghana*, Syracuse, NY: Syracuse University Press, 2009.

6. Dominique Malaquais, 'Douala/Johannesburg/New York: Cityscapes imagined', in Martin J. Murray and Garth A. Myers, eds, *Cities in contemporary Africa*, London and New York: Palgrave Macmillan, 2007.

7. James Ferguson, 'Global disconnect: Abjection and the aftermath of modernism', in Peter Geschiere, Birgit Meyer and Peter Pels, eds, *Readings in modernity in Africa*, Oxford: James Currey; Bloomington, IN: Indiana University Press, 2008, pp. 8–16.

8. Timothy Mitchell, *Colonising Egypt*, Cambridge and New York: Cambridge University Press, 1988.

9. Derek Hook, 'Monumental space and the uncanny', *Geoforum*, vol. 36 (2005), pp. 688–704.

10. Zayd Minty, 'Post-apartheid public art in Cape Town: Symbolic reparations and public space', *Urban Studies*, vol. 43, no. 2 (February 2006), pp. 421–40.

11. Ivan Vladislavić, 'Propaganda by monuments', in *Propaganda by monuments and other stories*, Cape Town: David Philip, 1996.

12. AbdouMaliq Simone, 'Pirate towns: Reworking social and symbolic infrastructures in Johannesburg and Douala', *Urban Studies*, vol. 43, no. 2 (February 2006), pp. 357–70.

13. Vladislavić, 'Propaganda', p. 31.

14. Monica Popescu, 'Translations: Lenin's statues, post-communism, and post-apartheid', *Yale Journal of Criticism*, vol. 16, no. 2 (Fall 2003), pp. 406–23.

15. Hook, 'Monumental space'; Steve Pile, 'A haunted world: The unsettling demands of a globalised past', in Clive Barnett, Jennifer Robinson and Gillian Rose, eds, *Geographies of globalisation: A demanding world*, London: Sage and The Open University, 2008, pp. 237–89.

16. Simone, *For the city yet to come*.

There is some way to go before we really understand the meaning of the astonishingly similar colonial histories – and thus present forms – of some of Africa's cities. The historical narratives of the growth of cities like Dar es Salaam, Lusaka and Johannesburg are strikingly similar, especially in relation to issues of segregation, housing, planning, youth, crime, prostitution and law. Closer attention to how ideas and practices moved across the continent could put these now familiar narratives in a new light.

Garth Myers & Jenny Robinson

OKWUI ENWEZOR

FRIEND, ENEMY, NEIGHBOUR, STRANGER: PROXIMITY AND THE CRISIS OF HOSPITALITY IN AN AFRICAN CITY

> The zone where the natives live is not complementary to the zone inhabited by the settlers. The two zones are opposed, but not in the service of a higher unity. Obedient to the rules of Aristotelian logic, they both follow the principle of reciprocal exclusivity. No conciliation is possible, for of the two terms, one is superfluous.
>
> FRANTZ FANON, *The wretched of the earth.*

How is space produced? Modern rationality would respond to this question with a panoply of planning concepts, from the grid to cellular models of spatial organization. Such planning methods employ disciplining apparatuses to conceal and smooth over potential antagonisms between users of space, through the bureaucratization of everyday life. However, in the most atavistic sense, all spaces are produced through conflict. Acts of boundary-making, formations of national frontiers, the marking of city lines, defining the outlines of neighbourhoods, all have a sense of latent conflict inscribed in their production.

If space is a product, a priori, of concealed conflict, it raises the question of who the neighbour is, and lays bare the fundamental contradiction that governs all relations associated with what Michel de Certeau calls 'spatial practices'.[1] Such practices can be observed at a more ad hoc and molecular level in the division between the first-class and economy compartments of an airplane or in more disciplinary, juridical, formal societal levels, such as in the separation of the kasbah from *la ville européenne*, the segregation of social amenities between the native quarter and the settler area, the boundary lines of the apartheid regulation of space and social amenities, as well as the Jim Crow ordinances in the old American South. The rules of space-making are not based just on forms of planning and organizing of space. As a consequence of the production of space in which common inhabitants are separated, either by racial or ethnic, religious or gendered lines, hierarchies are introduced. Thus acknowledged, the conflictual relations between social classes and race relations become superimposed on the outline of space.

RULES OF SEPARATION

The rules that govern these demarcations are fundamentally based on exclusion and separation, and thus are anti-neighbourliness. It is that fundamental apartness, the anticipation of the conflict inherent in all spatial practices, that Leviticus 19:18 ('Thou shalt love thy neighbour as thyself') sought to abrogate. But, as we know, the biblical edict which calls for the recognition and incorporation of the stranger into the community of common inhabitants, as a neighbour who requires protection, bears no relation whatsoever to the way that the violence of spatial practices marks the separation between human beings in cities and countries across the world. As recent history in many cities has proven, the tension between the neighbour and stranger continues to bedevil contemporary politics. In the introduction to their book *The neighbour: Three inquiries in political theology*, Slavoj Žižek, Eric Santner and Kenneth Reinhard assess the concept and ontology of the neighbour by considering Freud's antipathy, in *Civilization and its discontents*, to the notion that a neighbour is someone to whom unreserved love should be directed. For Freud the neighbour is not someone to love unconditionally, but someone to be kept at bay, at a distance, and if possible to be subjected to, and placed under the spotlight of, hostile scrutiny. A neighbour for Freud is not the friend we suppose him to be, but a stranger, an object of suspicion, understood only as someone whose sole interest is to usurp his neighbour's place, and because of such suspicion, 'I must honestly confess that he has more claim to my hostility and even my hatred'.[2]

If the neighbour is someone whom we must abhor, by the necessity of our instinctual drive for survival, why then has the concept of the neighbourhood – as the place where we share meals together, raise kids, build social consciousness – acquired such a sentimental sense of intimacy, when the history of neighbourly living together is such a checkered one? Many of the pogroms of the 20th century bear out this uneasy relation between the neighbour and stranger, and the distinction between friend and foe, in unsettling ways.

But what of the moment when the stranger is dominant, such as in the context of colonial regimes that discipline and subordinate the majority native populations? Frantz Fanon's analysis of colonial spatial practices (quoted above) reveals another level of this issue in contradistinction to the biblical injunction in Leviticus.[3] For instance, at the height of the struggle against apartheid in South Africa, there was a familiar antiapartheid refrain (sung by black resistance fighters) that amplifies the hostility between blacks and whites in the starkest possible term: 'one settler, one bullet'. If apartheid by definition is the juridical order par excellence of the latency of conflict in the production of space, then the establishment of racial boundaries admits of the noncomplementary relationship between the native and settler. The upheaval into which the settler throws the native destabilizes the concept of neighbourly relations. In fact, it exacerbates the conflict between friend and enemy, between neighbour and stranger. Here Freud's notion that the neighbour is the one who must be held in suspicion no longer proves merely suggestive and philosophical, but, fundamentally, is an existential reality in which the native must live within the colonial regime.

In this case then, 'one settler, one bullet' goes further by radicalizing the very nonbelonging of the settler within the African community. If the native was the nonperson in the colonial regimes and apartheid's racialized spatial laws, to the native, the settler's space is that which must remain under the spotlight of hostility. The settler and native cannot share space, they are strangers to one another; their desires for the autonomy of each of their communities from the other ensures the conflictual discourse that connects them. Freud writes of this situation: 'But if he is a stranger to me and if he cannot attract me by any worth of his own or any significance that he may already have acquired for my emotional life, it would be hard for me to love him. Indeed, I should be wrong to do so, for my love is valued by all my own people as a sign of preferring them, and it is an injustice to them if I put a stranger on a par with them.'[4] Surely the racial ideologue who crafts the laws of apartheid – which by definition from the Dutch means separateness of neighbourhoods – obviously sees his job as an act of love for his people (whites), but not for strangers (blacks). Frantz Fanon examines the inverse of this logic from the vantage point of the colonized native: 'The colonized man is an envious man. And this the settler knows very well; when their glances meet he ascertains bitterly, always on the defensive, "they want to take our place." It is true, for there is no native who does not dream at least once a day of setting himself up in the settler's place.'[5]

The operating principle of these two forms of antagonism lies in the critique of proximity, which is supposedly inherent in the virtue of living together. Whites interpreted their fear of proximity to blacks as a case of deep estrangement and antipathy to the uncivilized, unworthy other, by imposing a spatial and cultural cordon sanitaire around them and imposing political and juridical inferiority on their lives. Much of the twentieth century is replete with such antagonism towards classes of people and communities who are placed beyond the edge of the city. It is on such terms that the Jim Crow laws in the American South, like apartheid laws in South Africa, were made, and the Nuremberg edicts were created by Hitler and the Nazis in Germany. In Lebanon, during its fifteen-year civil war, different communities – Shias, Sunnis, Christians, Druze, Maronites, Armenians, among others – all accepted the principle of self-enclosure that sealed off each community from the other. Cyprus is still today divided between Turkish and Greek sides; Bosnia-Herzegovina is separated in religious enclaves after the wars of the 1990s; Berlin was divided between East and West, and so on. On a religious level, the city of Mecca is completely sealed off from non-Muslims.

DWELLING AND NEAR-DWELLING

Our own cities are commonly divided according to economic rationales between affluent and less affluent areas, between ghettos accommodating different races. Each of these distinctive manifestations reveals cracks in the idyll of city life as a zone of belonging together. Living together – neighbourliness – establishes proximity, which in turn imposes, according to ancient customs of all human societies, certain obligations, responsibilities, and duties. To love thy neighbour as thyself, even if you actually wish him ill and may loathe his very existence, is an imposition produced by proximity. Thus proximity commands hospitality, while imposing neighbourliness. It is perhaps in response to the irresolvable multiple schisms that appear at the centre of living together that the philosopher Martin Heidegger was led to explore the metaphysical relationship between the concepts of building and dwelling. His classic essay on the concept of building and dwelling as two interconnected principles of bridging the gap of separation, provides a contemporary interpretation that examines the antinomies contained in both Freud's and Fanon's writings on the unresolved antagonism between the native and settler, or the neighbour and stranger. Heidegger tells us that 'we attain to dwelling, so it seems, only by means of building.'[6] Here, he sets up clearly the idea that any act of living or dwelling together is not in itself an ontological concept, but constructed. The dwelling, in a place that may call forth the vision of living next to a stranger who is then transformed into a neighbour, is a means of building. It is like a bridge that spans a body of water linking two severed spaces: 'The space allowed by the bridge contains many places variously near or far from the bridge. These places, however, may be treated as mere positions between which there lies a measurable distance; a distance – in Greek, *stadion* – always has room made for it, and indeed by bare positions.'[7]

All of these relationships exist on the dimension of nearness. *Nachbar*, 'neighbour' in German, Heidegger tells us, when extended to *Nachgebauer* signifies near-dweller, someone who not only lives nearby, but next to another, thus establishes a form of radical proximity. Perhaps we can explore the condition of the African city today by considering the issue of proximity and the near-dweller not as a neighbour but as an unwanted stranger. We examine this relationship in the context of this analysis along with the concomitant problems that have been produced dating from colonial rule which have exacerbated the practices of spatial production. If the *Nachgebauer* is merely a near-dweller for whom some sort of bridge is required in order to incorporate his state of dwelling to already existing conditions of dwelling, then to belong together (which Freud makes explicit in the choice one makes in choosing one's own people over the stranger of neighbour) is not the same as living together.

But when that difference becomes amplified, when proximity becomes disturbing nearness, a threat to the cohesion of those who see themselves as belonging together by those who live amongst them, what emerges is a zone where the line between friend and enemy, neighbour and stranger gains incredible vividness and spatial disorientation. What such a situation makes possible is ethical and communitarian violence. In February and March 2010, the city of Jos, in the central region, the so-called Middle Belt, of Nigeria, was plunged into an abyss of despair when neighbours were transformed into strangers and friends became enemies. During this period the city experienced a wave of communal violence, with killings and reprisals that left nearly 1,000 people dead, and houses and entire neighbourhoods burned to the ground. These killings and counterkillings were not new to the city and the surrounding area. As far as anyone can remember, they have been a part of the pattern for the attempt to realize a cosmopolitan space where strangers and neighbours, settlers and natives, the *Nachgebaueren*, can coexist.

Most news reports and social analyses tended to look at the violence through the prism of religious conflict between the 'indigenous' (natives), the predominantly Christian Berom, Anaguta and Afisare groups, and the 'migrant' (settler) Hausa-Fulani communities who are Muslim. The analyses also explored the communal violence from the perspective of economic competition between the two groups, and resentments built up against the 'migrants' by the 'indigenes' over the relative prosperity of the settlers to the disadvantage of the natives. In this economic competition, the successful Hausa-Fulani friend or *Nachgebauer* had become the enemy, a former neighbour transformed into a stranger. In this conflict there is neither dwelling nor building. Only conflict commands the processes of identification, be it around ethnicity or religion. As Nigerians, the Hausa-Fulani migrants perhaps resented being considered as settlers, as not belonging within the city. While there are far more complex issues underlying the conflict, we should be interested in how forms of city-making and modes of living together in the contemporary African city can be conceived around the internalized differences that are partly products of colonialism, on one hand, and on the other, the heritage of the myth of a cohesive community that fears pollution from outside.

NEIGHBOURLINESS BY DESIGN

In the predominantly Muslim north of Nigeria, there is a tradition of city-planning that offers an object lesson in the conceptualization of degrees of proximity and distance. While most modern cities are planned along the rationalist principle of the grid, the Hausa-Fulani city is formulated as a series of circles that moves from the innermost, where the indigenous natives dwell and are governed by separate laws, to the outermost, where the strangers and settlers live. Each circle represents a degree of proximity and familiarity to the privileges of indigenity or lack of access to them. The closer you are to the innermost circle the greater your proximity to its privileges and familiarity with customs, and therefore the more visible your neighbourliness is to this central zone from which power and authenticity radiate outwards. Those who inhabit the outer circles, and even beyond the edge of the circle, lose the privileges of proximity and familiarity. In other words they are more strangers than neighbours, neither *Nachgebaueren* nor friends. Understanding this basic rule of spatial organization is what makes one a good neighbour, not by belonging or living together, but by existing adjacent to the city, by knowing your place, and admitting to the status to which your inhabitation of one of the circles consigns you.

The traditional northern Nigerian cities inhabited by Hausa-Fulani formally acknowledge the inherent separateness, not nearness, between 'indigenes' and 'non-indigenes,' between neighbours and strangers. It is a distinction further clarified by Islam through the laws of Sharia that is applied only to Muslims, non-Muslims being governed by either secular laws or so-called traditional laws. But never was this separateness understood as a line between friend and enemy. In the circular plan of the cities, there are three basic rings. The first and innermost ring, Birni, is the city of the town's people. It is occupied by indigenes of the city or town who are understood to be Muslims. The second ring, Tudun Wada, is occupied by Hausa-Fulani Muslims who are not indigenes. The third ring, Sabon Gari, is the neighbourhood of non-indigenes. It is the quarter of strangers: *la ville fantôme*, the city of phantoms and foreigners. Under British colonial rule, this outline of traditional spatial mapping was surmounted by a fourth ring, the European Reservation Area, or as it is referred to in Nigeria, Government Reserved Area (GRA), which was off limits to all non-Europeans (both northern Muslim indigenes and non-Muslim strangers from the south). Colonial rule thus imposed a second spatial order which further refined the distinction between colonizer and colonized, ruler and the ruled, or as Mahmood Mamdani made us aware in his study of late colonialism in Africa, between citizens and subjects.[8]

NEIGHBOURLINESS IN CRISIS

The killings in Jos exposed the fault-line of proximity in the city that had long been divided between natives and settlers, neighbours and strangers. In so doing, they revealed a crisis in neighbourliness, and the concept of hospitality normally accorded to strangers. But Jos is hardly the only case of its kind in recent memory in Africa in which proximity between neighbours and strangers has devolved into open conflict. One can certainly add Abidjan, Kano, Kigali, Harare, Nairobi, Johannesburg and Kinshasa to the long list of African cities where competition for space has degenerated and severed the bonds linking various social bodies, reducing them to the level of the tribe. This prompts the question: What does it mean to live in a city today? This question gains a sharper edge when we consider the basic fact that most inhabitants of cities across the world were recent arrivals, not born in those cities. They come from elsewhere. They do not have roots in those places. In a sense, the city today is essentially an elsewhere, an anomalous, non-ontological space. In most cities, it is so conditioned by dynamic shifts organized by employment, capital, tourism, technology, media and transience, that it is impossible to distinguish between the native-born, migrants, and transients. So what form does a city take today beyond its spatial dimension and symbolic civic amenities? What we find today in cities are temporary *Nachgebaueren*. Despite the flourishing of architecture, the rise in new schemes of urban renewal, the revitalization of downtown as a hub of activities unifying the desire for citizens to engage one another, or the recent novelty-promoting localism – consider for example, the modish notion of eating locally grown food – the city still remains a community of strangers, an elsewhere, a place of transience. Architecture, strangely enough, has found no convincing response to this conundrum, no conceptual articulation of what it means to be a citizen beyond the restatement of the obvious idylls of community based on city squares, parks, playgrounds, 'public' buildings.

Though the classical Greek notion of the city denotes a community of citizens who share a common bond through belonging to a place, in the global world that most people live in today, the city is more a community of strangers bound not by one common bond, but by multiple allegiances that require accommodation with one another. To live in a city today is to belong to a temporary community where individual identity and subjectivity subtend the collective. Since the majority of people hardly remain in the cities of their birth, the contemporary city has become an experiment in forms of proximity that are fundamentally beyond the scope of rules and laws around which institutional formations are developed. This is the lesson of Jos. To make sense of its violence, and the future competition between the different factions that would surely follow the recovery from the horrific acts of killing, any analysis must come to terms with the idea that the city is a place of strangers, not a Manichean zone separating natives and settlers. The violence that inflamed the city and consumed so many lives and property, destroying the goodwill of the indigenes, fracturing the fragile bond that held the settlers and natives together as common inhabitants, must make room for the fact that Nigerian cities, like all African cities, have multiple claims on them. This simple reality is affirmed every day. That is why the production of space is often accompanied by conflict, since no one wants to be consigned to the outskirts of the city to the Sabon Gari of inferiority. The diverse social bodies that constitute the boisterous, diverse, multicultural and multiethnic cosmopolitanism we find in contemporary African cities, as in other parts of the world, make clear that there can be no natives but only strangers to the city. It is only through mutual estrangement that proximity can be developed beyond the concept of the neighbour.

POSTSCRIPT

Throughout this essay, we have focused primarily on the tension between the stranger and the neighbour in spatial practices. What have not been addressed are the specific urgencies that lie beneath David Adjaye's African metropolitan architecture project. The outline of the project was to travel and photograph every African capital city and, in so doing, compose a compendium of architectural, spatial and symbolic forms that lend each capital its unique identity. Through nearly ten years of relentless travel, all fifty-four capital cities were to be visited and photographed. The visual impact of the collection reveals the remarkable richness of architectural diversity, as well as vast ecological, geographic and spatial differences: from the arid Sahara and Kalahari deserts to the semiarid Sahel regions of West Africa, coastline to savanna, mountain ranges to equatorial forests, all attest to the continent's biodiversity. Peering closer at the urban forms, what constantly leaps out from the density of the collected material, which appears less programmatic than is initially suggested by the scope of the project, is not a unified vision of African city forms, but rather a sense of discontinuity between various capitals. Closer scrutiny of this epic project reveals a *punctum*: of the fifty-four cities, contemporary photographs accompany only fifty-two. Due to civil war and the current state of conflict in both Mogadishu, the capital city of Somalia, that *ur*-nation which lies on the Horn of Africa between the Gulf of Aden and the Indian Ocean, and Juba, capital of the recently formed South Sudan, Adjaye has been unable to photograph examples of their architectural typologies.

Mogadishu's predicament, which since the early 1990s has been engulfed in conflict, exposes again the concept of *Nachgebauer*, a concept which now has been further radicalized by Islamist insurgents seeking to impose not only new political rule but also new spatial paradigms on the city. The contest for the control of Mogadishu between the nominal government and the insurgents reveals the fundamental fact that the civic discontinuity which the destruction of the city has produced would require not merely a new type of postwar reconstruction scheme, but the creation of new concepts of building and dwelling that could transform the city into a zone of hospitality between friend and enemy, neighbour and stranger.

Fifty years ago, as multiple African countries gained independence, the utopian postcolonial dream of liberation gave way to fantasies of ritual unity. The capital city was at the centre of this new fantasy as a symbol of two things: first, as showcase of arrival into the modern scene through modernization schemes; and second, as the heart of national unity, to be exploited by the ruling elites in order to quell ethnic competition. The capital city was simultaneously the site of ritual power and national cohesion. As well as modernizing cities, several countries set about fashioning, *tabula rasa* style, entirely new cities. The creation of new capital cities in Nigeria (Abuja), Côte d'Ivoire (Yamasoukrou), Malawi (Lilongwe), and the changing of names of the capital cities from the previous colonial names (Léopoldville was changed by Mobutu to Kinshasa in his *authenticité* programme), represented attempts at reclaiming an African identity for that most symbolic of centres of power: the capital city. In Nigeria, the plan for Abuja was based on an attempt not simply to relocate the capital from the coastal city of Lagos to the so-called geographic centre of the country, which would symbolize the neutrality of the political power in relation to all the states that make up the federal republic, but also to dramatize the unity of the nation after the devastating three-year civil war that claimed the lives of more than a million Nigerians.

The Nigerian capital city was designed to project the image of unity between the fractious members of the nation and to heal the scars of the conflict that highlighted the paradigmatic problem of proximity as a cause of social and ethnic conflict. Thus, Abuja represented not simply a spatial but also an ethical concept. It is a city built to project the ritual power of a benevolent state, but also a symbolic site in which to explore the conditions of the *Nachgebauer*. Mogadishu's absence in this compendium, however, anticipates issues that must be raised when the guns become silent again. Its current state of conflict marks not only the incompleteness of the African Metropolitan Architecture project, it also reveals the various forms of discontinuity and the crisis of hospitality still bedevilling African cities: between natives and settlers, indigenes and migrants, neighbours and strangers, governments and insurgents.

NOTES

1. Michel de Certeau, *The practice of everyday life*, trans. Steven Rendall, Berkeley: University of California Press, 1988.

2. Sigmund Freud, quoted in Slavoj Žižek, Eric L. Santner and Kenneth Reinhard, *The neighbour: Three inquiries in political theology*, Chicago: University of Chicago Press, 2005, p. 2.

3. Frantz Fanon, *The wretched of the earth*, trans. Constance Farrington, New York: Grove Press, 1963, p. 38.

4. Žižek et al., *The neighbour*, p. 2.

5. Fanon, *The wretched of the earth*, p. 39.

6. Martin Heidegger, 'Building, dwelling, thinking', in *Poetry, language, thought*, trans. Albert Hofstadter, New York and London: Harper and Row, 1971, p. 145; quoted in Okwui Enwezor, ed., *The unhomely: Phantom scenes in global society*, Seville: BIACS, 2006, p. 18.

7. Heidegger, 'Building, dwelling, thinking', p. 155; quoted in Enwezor, *The unhomely*, p. 23.

8. See Mahmood Mamdani, *Citizen and subject: Contemporary Africa and the legacy of late colonialism*, Princeton: Princeton University Press, 1996.

The upheaval into which the settler throws the native destabilizes the concept of neighbourly relations. In fact, it exacerbates the conflict between friend and enemy, between neighbour and stranger. Here Freud's notion that the neighbour is the one who must be held in suspicion no longer proves merely suggestive and philosophical, but, fundamentally, is an existential reality in which the native must live within the colonial regime.

Okwui Enwezor

NAIGZY GEBREMEDHIN

A TALE OF THREE HIGHLAND CITIES: PERSONAL OBSERVATIONS OF AN OCTOGENARIAN AFRICAN ARCHITECT

I was born in Addis Ababa, spent most of my adult life in Nairobi and now consider Asmara as my permanent home, having moved there soon after Eritrea's independence in 1993. All three cities are located at the rim of Africa's canyon system, the Great Rift Valley: Asmara in the north, at a height of 2,350 m, Addis Ababa in the middle at 2,326 m, and Nairobi slightly south of the equator, at 1,661 m.

ADDIS ABABA, THE NEW FLOWER

Our home in Addis Ababa, where I grew up, was some distance from Emperor Haile Selassie's Ghenete Leul Palace, a building for which I retain a bit of nostalgia because in the 1930s, my father worked on it as the chief mason. Haile Selassie's ascent to the throne of Ethiopia's Solomonic dynasty was just around the corner. For that auspicious occasion, the Emperor wished to welcome his guests, including the Swedish crown prince, in style: hence Ghenete Leul Palace. My father often talked of how he and his co-workers were forced to work long hours, even during heavy downpours. Father was sure that was when he developed asthma, a malady that plagued him in later life.

Ghenete Leul Palace became notorious in 1960 when the abortive *coup d'état* against the emperor led by General Mengistu Neway, the chief of the palace guard, executed cabinet members and other dignitaries close to Haile Selassie. Soon afterwards the emperor donated the palace to the university named after him. Decades later, as lecturer and dean of the faculty of architecture of that university, I sat in the baroque-style hall of the palace attending meetings of the academic council, my mind occasionally flitting back to my father's asthma and the dozens of dignitaries who bled to death in this very hall in 1960. Considering those circumstances the name Ghenete Leul, which means 'high paradise' in Amharic, sometimes seemed a misnomer.

Addis Ababa is, with Asmara, one of Africa's highest capitals. Its thin but refreshing air challenges the newcomer. A first-time visitor is advised to take it easy until he or she is sufficiently acclimatized. Ethiopian capitals had moved progressively from north to south as firewood was depleted. A few years after the Emperor Menelik and his energetic Queen Taytu had settled in Addis Ababa, scouts were sent out to reconnoitre a new location for the next capital. And indeed a site was identified some 40 km westward, with plenty of trees for firewood.

But the innovative emperor had also been supporting a fast-growing, renewable tree named *baher zaf* in Amharic, meaning 'the tree from abroad'. Eucalyptus from Australia must be given the credit for fixing Addis Ababa to its current site. Thanks to *baher zaf*, the practice of moving capitals in search of firewood came to an end.

Addis Ababa started essentially as a collection of encampments or *sefer* of Menelik's military commanders. Even today neighbourhoods retain the names of those same commanders. Any visitor wishing to get to an address in Addis Ababa need only mention the name of the military commander and any taxi driver will get him there. The numbered street address is unknown here.

Addis Ababa evolved from the spontaneous and relatively uncoordinated decisions of military commanders. Their main concern was to ensure enough grazing land and water around each of their *sefer*. As the *sefer* matured a church was built, each *sefer* competing for the most imposing church building. A common market area, *arada*, was set aside for the exchange of goods and services. During the brief Italian occupation of 1936–41, *arada* developed into the *merkato,* from the Italian word for market place. Nowadays the *merkato* is described as Africa's largest open market place.

The Amharic word *arada* has both a physical and a sociological meaning. As a physical phenomenon it refers to a place where goods and services are exchanged. *Arada* is also perceived as the den of iniquity, the haunt of cheats and double-dealers. As a young man I remember hearing a popular singer lamenting the loss of his innocent lover in that den of iniquity with the words, 'she passed the night in *arada*, my rose, and my orange'.

I am convinced that in the traditional Ethiopian mind *arada,* and by extension all urbanization, *is* associated with decadence and rootlessness, in contrast with the upright lifestyle of rural areas, or *geter*. In Ethiopia in the late 1950s one working definition of an urban area was, 'a place where a stranger can rent a bed for the night'. The conceptual distance between *arada* and *geter*, between the urban and the rural, has always been stark and wide.

The first town plan for Addis Ababa was commissioned by the Fascist dictator Benito Mussolini in 1936. His ambition was to make Addis Ababa the capital of his Eastern Africa Empire, Africa Orientale Italiana. Le Corbusier, apparently an admirer of Mussolini, offered the leader architectural advice. The monumental route from the old palace down to the new one, discernible even today, was actually sketched by Le Corbusier. But the definitive town-planning effort for Addis Ababa was carried out from 1936 to 1939 by the Italian architects Gio Ponti, Enrico Del Debbio and Giuseppe Vaccaro, and the engineers Cesare Valle and Ignazio Guidi.

In the 1950s Emperor Haile Selassie invited the British town planner Sir Patrick Abercrombie to propose a development plan. One of Abercrombie's intriguing proposals was to create a series of linear parks or green reserves along the several streams that flowed from the hills surrounding the city. This proposal was unfortunately not realized. Nowadays a great deal of waste is dumped along these stream beds.

The Addis Ababa I grew up in has now spread beyond the green hills of Entoto, sprawling in all directions. And despite many Chinese-built ring roads and some imposing high-rise buildings, it remains a city of small houses made of mud walls and corrugated iron sheet roofing.

Unlike Nairobi, Addis Ababa does not have clearly defined slums or squatter settlements. Its neighbourhoods do not reveal whether they house the poor or the well-to-do. Modest huts coexist with sumptuous villas. Addis Ababa is one of the rare cities that has tacitly done away with zoning, that overrated tool of modern town-planning. Some of Addis Ababa's enthusiasts refer to it as 'Africa's capital city' because the African Union has its headquarters there, in buildings originally designed for the National Police College by the French architect Henri Chomette.

The devout probably continue to curse *arada,* as do the new political commissars in the government palace anxious to ensure that *arada*'s quarrelsome nature does not get out of hand and threaten their leadership. Unfortunately for them *arada* seems to persist in fomenting trouble. But as for people like me, born in *arada,* it continues to embrace us all, the rich or poor, the rogue or angel, the mendicant or the almsgiver.

NAIROBI, THE PLACE OF COOL WATERS

Enkare Nyirobe, the Massai words meaning 'the place of cool waters', describe Nairobi perfectly. Of the three highland cities where I have lived, Nairobi combines sun and rain perfectly. Nairobi, the green city in the sun, is a veritable garden of delight. Kenya was still a colony under siege when I first visited the city in 1959. In those days the Mau Mau emergency was in full swing and security was tight. I had driven down all the way from Addis Ababa with a Swedish architect and his family, on an arduous journey of nine days. Tired and looking for a meal and a bath, we proceeded to the heart of the city, to the Queens Hotel.

The white proprietors promptly chased me out because I was African but welcomed my Swedish companions. Curfew was approaching and I was advised not to be wandering around after dark. Eventually I found a hotel run by an Indian at Tom Mboya Street. It was called Princess Hotel, an apt name given that my more respected Swedish companions were staying at the Queens. I was reminded of E. A. T. Dutton's statement in 1919 about the city of Nairobi: 'a slatternly creature, unfit to queen it over so lovely a country'.[1] Four decades after Dutton's comments, not much had changed. It was not the city, but Africans like me who were considered unfit to 'queen' it at Queens Hotel in Nairobi, however thoroughly we were educated to practise a creative and exacting profession such as architecture. Queens Hotel was still out of reach for this young African architect.

Nairobi, founded in 1899, had taken over its capital status from Mombasa in 1905. The site was chosen because it had plenty of fresh water and it was also midpoint between the Mombasa and Kampala rail-line, then under construction.

In 1975, sixteen years after my first visit, I came back to Nairobi, this time to stay. Ethiopia, where I was born, was in the throes of revolutionary fervour. I had established a reasonably successful private practice in planning and construction in Addis Ababa, and that sort of thing was regarded with jaundiced eyes. That year, I left behind all I had and came to Nairobi to start afresh.

Since then I have had a home in Lavington, one of the leafy neighbourhoods of Nairobi and once exclusively reserved for whites, the sort that chased me out of Queens Hotel in 1959. In some ways my story is a metaphor, albeit an incomplete one, for changes that have taken place in Nairobi over the years. The Duttons have gone and Africans have taken over, queen and all, for good or bad. My home is about 6 km from the centre. When I first came I used to drive there in less than ten minutes. Parking was plentiful and safe. Now it is a major challenge to get there and parking is expensive, if you can find it. And when your car has been broken into three times, as mine has been, you begin to avoid downtown. I have completely given up going there unless it is absolutely necessary.

Nairobi's population has grown tenfold without a commensurate increase in housing and infrastructure. Eastleigh was a solid, working-class neighbourhood with excellent roads. Now the roads are potted quagmires deep enough to hide small vehicles.

In 1975 the city council of Nairobi used to pick up waste regularly from our neighbourhood. The last time they did so was in 1982. Eventually we had to retain a private contractor to collect waste. However, the city council continues to collect garbage collection fees as part of land rent.

Crime, always a concern, has risen dramatically. In 1975 the cost of security was a tiny fraction of monthly income. Now the same services cost significantly more.

But the most dramatic development of the past thirty years is the rise of slums and squatter settlements, some whose size and extent defy imagination. Kibera, with more than one million people, is now recognized as the largest slum area in the world. While life continues comfortably in the suburbs like Lavington, the same cannot be said about slum areas. These areas seem to be beyond recovery. When the discussion on slums and squatter settlements was full-blown in the early 1970s, planners and urban sociologists had introduced the concept 'slums of hope' – that is, slum areas where families and individuals had a fighting chance to 'make it' – and their opposite, 'slums of despair'. While definitive evidence might still be lacking, the current trend seems to indicate that as slums of hope retreat, slums of despair expand.

In 2007 there was a wave of violent unrest in Kenya, following the disputed elections. Almost all death and destruction was concentrated to the slum areas. I employ two workers, and both live in slums and squatter settlements not far from the leafy suburb of Lavington. During that wave of unrest both workers were unable to go to their rooms in the slum areas. When the unrest subsided, my gardener went back to his room in the Kawangware slums, only to discover he had lost everything. He was forced to move to makeshift quarters in Lavington. He also had to send his wife to her parents in the rural areas to wait for peace and security. This was not an isolated example. Hundreds of slum dwellers had been forced to return to their rural tribal enclaves for safety, albeit temporarily, as slums and squatter settlements burned.

For generations, urban planners have argued that there are two 'factors' that propel urbanization: the 'push factor' that pushes people out of their rural misery, and the 'pull factor' that attracts them towards the promises of cities. The example above seems to indicate the 'push' and 'pull' factors governing urbanization may be reversing. If that is truly the case, urban planning in Africa faces a paradigm shift. African architects and urban planners may have to return to their drawing boards, and seek new directions.

In all fairness, Nairobi's image should not be formed only by what its slums and squatter settlements convey. As a regional hub, Nairobi attracts thousands of young professionals engaged in business, finance, insurance and information technology. The city's sophisticated private health service system draws hundreds of people from the region seeking medical care. Nairobi is the preferred location for the corporate headquarters of a number of regional banks and insurance companies as well as major international and regional organizations and research institutions. Landlocked countries and regions such as Uganda, Rwanda, Burundi, Eastern Congo and Southern Sudan depend on Nairobi to coordinate import and export services. While the challenges Nairobi faces in its huge slums and squatter settlements are daunting, its future will be determined by its role as a hub for service and commerce. Research and information technology are also likely to play a significant role.

ASMARA, AFRICA'S SECRET MODERNIST CITY

In Tigrigna, the official language of Eritrea, *asmara* means 'they made peace'. The pronoun 'they' refers to women. Asmara, founded around the 14th century, consisted of four bickering villages, periodically threatened by slave-traders preying on citizens. According to legend, the women threatened to deny their menfolk all rights, including conjugal rights, until they united against this heinous crime. But Asmara came into its own in the early 1930s, after the ascendance of Italian Fascism and Mussolini's ambitions to enlarge his colonial empire with the conquest of Ethiopia. Asmara served as the logistical base for that ambition, and one of the most amazing feats of urban development in Africa took place here, at the dizzying altitude of Hamassien, the comparatively well-watered central plateau of Eritrea.

Asmara is a few metres higher than Addis Ababa, and like Addis Ababa it is located at the rim of the East African Rift Valley, that remarkable canyon system that runs all the way from the Dead Sea to the shores of Lake Victoria and beyond. Between 1936 and 1941 Mussolini's government created a modernist city of unparalleled beauty and serenity. Asmara has survived unscathed from years of war and has one of the most extensive and well-kept examples of modernist architecture. The 1938 Asmara masterplan authored by Vittorio Cafiero continues to guide the city's development even today. Present-day Asmara is a faithful implementation of Cafiero's intentions.

After independence in 1993 the government of Eritrea decided to preserve Asmara's colonial architecture. A bold decision because it questioned old assumptions. First, a public consensus emerged that correctly recognized Asmara's architecture not only as the work of Italian colonialists but also as the work of hundreds of Eritreans, many of whom laboured under duress. Eritreans, especially the citizens of Asmara, had no difficulty in identifying with and appropriating the architecture created during Italian colonialism. Second, there was a recognition of the need to take immediate action to preserve Asmara. With the establishment of the Cultural Assets Rehabilitation Program (CARP), the institutional basis for conservation was quickly put in place. Third, to the surprise of Eritreans, the expectation that Italy would collaborate enthusiastically in preserving Asmara's architecture was not satisfied and Eritreans had to proceed alone without Italian participation. In 1998 the government sought and received a modest loan from the World Bank to set in motion a number of actions to preserve Asmara's modernist architecture.

UNESCO has been invited to ensure that Asmara is on its modern heritage list, a process that is now underway. Asmara has survived years of war with very little damage. But the intention is not to retain Asmara as an architectural museum. It is a vibrant, living city providing its citizens an admirably high quality of life. The government argues that the costs incurred in preserving the architecture can be recovered as tourism begins to bring much needed foreign exchange. Asmara's numerous cafes and restaurants serve excellent *caffè macchiato* and other Italian delicacies, and still bear unabashedly Italian names: Bar Torino, Bar Roma, Pasticceria Moderna, even Bar Crispi, named after the Fascist minister of foreign affairs who argued Italy's case for colonial possessions at the League of Nations in Geneva. The city's sidewalks are immaculately maintained, an army of women workers reinstalling the original cement tiles decorated with the fleur-de-lis motif. It is a sheer joy to walk the streets of Asmara late in the afternoon, when the sun's rays have softened and the thin mountain air is still delicately warm. In Asmara the simple walk becomes a form of relaxation, an African version of the *passeggiata*.

But Asmara, like other cities in Africa, faces difficult problems. For one, it is running out of water fast and the prospects for finding more for its rising population are daunting. Forty per cent of the historic buildings are privately owned. Owners do not always see why they should not be allowed to tear down their old buildings and build higher and bigger. 'Why all the obstacles?' they ask. Holding the course of preservation will not be easy.

CITIES IN THE RIFT VALLEY: ANY LOCATION ADVANTAGES?

The three cities have some things in common. Their location at high altitude made them cool for residential purpose, especially for the Europeans who came to colonize. The fact that the ambient temperature was too low for malaria to survive was an added bonus, although new evidence seems to suggest that nowadays the *anopheles* mosquito is beginning to survive at higher altitudes as the climate warms up.

Are there any inherent advantages in siting cities in or at the edge of the Rift Valley or canyon system, as with the three cities we have reviewed? It should be noted that while Asmara and Nairobi are located at the edge, Addis Ababa is nestled at the base of the Rift Valley. From Addis Ababa proper it is difficult to discern the edges of the Rift or canyon and equally difficult to visualize it as a city at the bottom of a canyon. After all, Addis Ababa's elevation is more than 2,500 m. But place around it the chain of the Entoto mountains, and it can be reasonably described as a city at the base of the Rift Valley. In contrast Asmara and Nairobi are at the periphery of the canyon. Asmara in particular hangs on dramatically at the edge of a precipice, looking down to the base from its dizzying height of 2,350 m. The base of the valley, that is the Red Sea, is only 45 km away as the crow flies. The road between Massawa and Asmara is reputed to be the steepest between two significant urban centres. When the Italians built a narrow-gauge rail-line between the two centres, they had to install thirty-nine tunnels, one for every 2 km, in order to maintain a manageable gradient for the locomotives. The situation to the northwest of Nairobi is equally dramatic as the road through Limuru, at almost 3,000 m, traces its way to the base of the Rift Valley at 700 m.

Are these locations ideal for city growth and development? The answer may not be unequivocal. There are some pros and cons to consider. These locations have placed major challenges on planners and developers. As far as Asmara is concerned the early governors like General Baldissera were satisfied that Asmara's location at the edge of an impregnable canyon system provided an excellent assurance against insurrection from the eastern and southeastern lowlands. In the case of Addis Ababa, its founder Emperor Menelik was never worried about insurrection from the north or northeast as the Entoto Mountains served as bulwarks. The southwestern aspect, however, had to be guarded carefully. Other advantages can be summarized as follows: a natural system of reservoirs for water, with lakes and rivers abounding in the valley; a varied ecosystem, incorporating both highland and lowland regimes, which is rich in plant biodiversity; and a deep soil profile, especially in the valley, which is the single most important indicator of agricultural potential.

Despite the other factors and the relative abundance of water in the valleys of the Rift system, water seems to be a decisive factor in the growth of all three cities. But as demand grows and rainfall and run-off patterns change with urbanization, all three cities seem to be approaching limits to orderly growth. Addis Ababa, Asmara and Nairobi have survived because water and energy for households is imported from the rural hinterland, in some cases from beyond the Rift Valley. Can the rural hinterland continue to subsidize slums and squatter settlements indefinitely? Even in the case of Asmara, with a much smaller population, providing water and energy for households is becoming increasingly challenging.

The colonial footprint is deeply set in Asmara and Nairobi, but not so much in Addis Ababa. As a result, is urban life any better in Asmara or Nairobi than it is in Addis Ababa? Having lived in all three cities, I find it difficult to draw any clear conclusions. Addis Ababa is no less habitable than Nairobi or Asmara, with their deep colonial imprints. Nairobi is vibrant and productive. So is Addis Ababa. Nairobi is crime-ridden and Kenya's legendary state corruption erodes the hard work of the poor and the middle class. Addis Ababa has much less crime, but its streets are home to thousands of beggars. The prime minister of Ethiopia nonetheless admits that the national effort to reduce poverty is much more successful in rural areas than it is in urban areas. Asmara conveys a rather different image, possibly because its population is much smaller than the other two. The size of the urban population could be a telling clue to the future success of cities in Africa.

NOTES

1. E. A. T. Dutton, *Kenya Mountain*, London: Jonathan Cape, 1929, pp. 1–2.

The Amharic word arada has both a physical and a sociological meaning. As a physical phenomenon it refers to a place where goods and services are exchanged. Arada is also perceived as the den of iniquity, the haunt of cheats and double-dealers. As a young man I remember hearing a popular singer lamenting the loss of his innocent lover in that den of iniquity with the words, 'she passed the night in arada, my rose, and my orange.'

Naigzy Gebremedhin

SUZANNE PRESTON BLIER
THE AFRICAN URBAN PAST: HISTORICAL PERSPECTIVES ON THE METROPOLIS

Cities, as sites of human aggregation, are different from rural settlements, and size and scale have little to do with this. I grew up near Vergennes, in Vermont, the smallest city in the US, with a population of 2,741 in the 2000 census. Some of my seminal urban experiences, however, were in three West African cities: Savé in Benin, and Ile-Ife and Lagos in Nigeria – all centres of the long-established Yoruba people. There are many definitions of what constitutes a city, but normally the label refers to a well-populated centre, inhabited by a relatively heterogeneous population, marked by complex sociopolitical institutions and distinctive forms of planning and architecture.[1] In the West urbanism has been viewed historically as a mark of civilization, an attribute that, falsely, precolonial Africa was once seen to lack. In Africa, urbanism has long figured prominently. Most early African cities, like historic urban centres elsewhere, developed in relationship to local conditions (soils, water sources, minerals, trade potential) and various sociopolitical factors.[2] Agriculture and the neolithic revolution are assumed to have been vital to early urban development, allowing not only for greater population density, but also requisite surpluses, trade goods, new forms of specialization, and attendant administrative and organizational developments.

PATTERNS OF URBAN DEVELOPMENT

Three historic patterns of urban settlement are found in Africa. Monumental urbanism is characterized by substantial permanent structures in stone, and was especially prominent in north, eastern and southern Africa, from Egypt and Eritrea to Zimbabwe. Satellite urbanism is characterized, in both early and later contexts, by collaboration between interlinked community clusters that together create an urban settlement structure. This type of settlement, which is normally identified with earthen structures, is found especially in West Africa, from Mali to northern and southern areas of Nigeria. Migratory or peripatetic urban settlements characteristically prevailed in central Africa, these cities sharing a relatively nomadic identity. Related cities were often reestablished on a new site following the death of a ruler or a sequence of traumatic events. Many peripatetic cities were built of more ephemeral materials, such as raffia and bamboo, but were also associated with more permanent ritual sites, such as cemeteries. In some African urban contexts, several of these design attributes were at play, with local building materials providing unique possibilities for creativity.

MONUMENTAL URBANISM: NORTH, EASTERN AND SOUTHERN AFRICA

Metropolitan centres in Egypt were among the largest and most durable in urban global history. These cities featured an array of monumental building forms serving multiple functions, some dating back to the predynastic and early dynastic period.[3] Abydos in southern Egypt (4000 BCE to 641 CE) long served as a royal burial ground, Osiris cult site and pilgrimage destination. Memphis, near modern Cairo, which became the administrative, religious and trade centre of lower Egypt, was founded around 3100 BCE, purportedly after King Menes conquered the Nile Delta. Estimates of the size of Memphis's diverse population range from 6,000 to 30,000 occupants, making it possibly the largest world metropolis around 2250 BCE and again from 1557 to 1400 BCE.[4] Luxor, Egypt's New Kingdom capital from 2134 to 1191 BCE, served at once as a political, religious, learning and art centre, its diverse population coming from as far away as Syria, Phoenicia, Canaan and Kush (the latter in modern Sudan). Abydos, the Kushite capital of Meroë from 800 to 350 CE, was a royal burial site and a manufacturing hub for prestige goods.

Aksum (400 BCE to 619 CE), situated in modern Eritrea, was also an important early urban centre, known for its grouping of seven large scale stone menhirs, a broken one now weighing 500 tons.[5] Similar in style, these monuments include images of windows and portals, as if to suggest the portals found in this area. Aksum is thought to have been a compact city inhabited by political and trade elites, with producers at the centre's outskirts. Its rulers also controlled several Red Sea ports, as well as nearby lands in Yemen, and its population was diverse, in keeping with its role in a trading empire that circulated goods from India to the Mediterranean. Aksum's conversion to Christianity was among the earliest in Africa, and it was eventually taken over by Ethiopian rulers.

To the south, the stone remains of the elaborate Shona capital of Great Zimbabwe, which flourished in the 11th–14th centuries CE, covered some 722 hectares and as many as 18,000 people may have lived here. Similar stone walls are found at distances several hundred kilometres away. An oracle site and trading depot were among this centre's possible draws, the latter dealing with goods from as far away as China. Other cities rose along the East African coast from the 8th to the 19th centuries CE, some with richly decorated, stone-like, coral edifices. These Swahili coastal sites, such as Kilwa and Mombasa, also benefited from the Indian Ocean trade in gold, ivory, slaves and other goods.

SATELLITE URBANISM: WEST AFRICA

Numerous metropolitan centres emerged in West Africa in regions south of the Sahara. One of the most important of these was Jenne-Jeno, a grouping of urban settlements established along the inner Niger River floodplain of Mali, within a few kilometres of Jenne (Djenne). Roderick McIntosh describes Jenne-Jeno as a composite or clustered city marked by the aggregation of semispecialized settlements with coordinated activities.[6] The excellent rice-farming conditions, good pasturage and adjacent Niger River communication were central to Jenne-Jeno's development in the 3rd century BCE, after herding populations moved there during the Sahara desiccation that began around 1000 BCE. In 450 BCE Jenne-Jeno covered some 25 hectares; by 450 CE, 33 hectares; by 850 CE, 41 hectares. Between 450 and 850 CE Jenne-Jeno functioned as a single urban complex. The city had walls that were 3.7 m wide at the base and which employed cylindrical brick building forms. There were common urn burials, and Roman or Greek beads, as well as those made of iron, were found at the earliest levels, evidence of regional and trans-Sahara trade.

Jenne, I have argued, may also have been the site of the Empire of Mali's famous 14th-century royal capital.[7] Al-'Umari (died 1349) notes that Mali's capital was called Bny or Bani, suggesting its early identity with the Bani River. This tributary merges with Niger River at Jenne. Al-'Umari's description of Mali's capital as having an island-like setting is also consistent with modern Jenne, its watery surround serving as a natural protective moat for this wealthy trading city.[8]

The Tellem (11th–16th century CE), and the Dogon populations that merged with and replaced them (14th century onwards) in Mali's Bandiagara Escarpment, created a number of urban settlements as well. These densely populated centres were ethnically diverse: the Dogon arrived in waves as they escaped from the reach of Islam, dynastic expansion and slavery. They created a new culture here based on agricultural innovation (irrigated onion farming), technological and ritual specialization (iron working and so on), and various forms of external trade. Related architecture suggests not only Mande architectural sources, but forms of symbolic organization consistent with utopian idioms, defined by flexible anthropomorphic design referents, which is a feature of other populations in the West African savanna area.[9]

Clustered or satellite cities also appear to have distinguished the densely populated Igbo communities in southeast Nigeria. By the end of the 1st millennium CE the Igbo area was in trade contact with regions as far away as southwest Asia, creating works of extraordinary complexity in bronze and elaborate burial forms at Igbo Ukwu sites. While little is known about early settlement plans or domestic architecture at Igbo Ukwu, more recent Igbo plans suggest a system of clustering defined by relative egalitarianism, and an economy based on agriculture and trade.

In Yoruba oral traditions, a complementary satellite-style urbanism is said to have characterized the city-state of Ife (Ile-Ife), a polity rising to power in southwest Nigeria by the end of the 1st millennium.[10] Strategically located near the headwaters of the Oni River, which flows into the Atlantic, and at the juncture of forest and savanna, Ife sits on high ground that is surrounded by wetlands, a fertile savanna plain and hills. The settlements in the hills collaborated in trade and other areas, and they eventually came together to form a single urban centre.[11] Economic activities, such as the hunting of elephants for their ivory, may have been part of this satellite urbanism, as the larger Ife area functioned as a natural elephant-trapping area where local groups could block escape routes from the Ife valley wetlands. This communal hunting appears to have been a key factor in West African state development.[12]

During Ife's fluorescence in the 12th–15th centuries CE this metropolitan area may have covered 30 square kilometres, with a population of about 130,000. Iron that had been mined, smelted and smithed locally and various agricultural goods (yam, sorghum, palm oil, kola nuts) formed part of a local exchange system, along with ivory, slaves and locally manufactured glass beads and cloth. Ife's proximity to the Niger–Benue River confluence provided access to distant trade centres in all directions. Oral traditions suggest that by the early 15th century, under the patronage of King Obalufon II, the city of Ile-Ife was reconfigured around a central plan defined by a circumscribing moat-wall, broad avenues leading to a central palace and adjacent market, as well as wards extending radially from the centre. Ife ward chiefs fulfilled key political and juridical functions. Obalufon also appears to have had diplomatic and trade treaties with several other Yoruba cities, along with military and tribute agreements with affiliated crown cities, to provide certain goods based on their location and history. These affiliated polities were legitimated by oral tradition that identified their founders as offspring of the mythic founder, Odudua. Other, later-established, Yoruba cities, such as Ibadan and Lagos, began as military camps. Whatever the origins, Yoruba metropolitan centres grew to enormous scale and featured unique craft specialization (from metal- and glassworking to weaving and dyeing), marked population diversity (though trade and war) and major population shifts throughout the year (many inhabitants moving to distant agricultural fields for part of the rainy season).

In Ife, as in most other Yoruba cities, roads, tracks and paths led ultimately to the palace and nearby market, widening into large squares at the centre, where festivals and political events took place. The earthen fabric of residences and walls provided urban planning flexibility through time, allowing even densely populated communities to grow easily and change. Frequently sited on hills, where the palaces are the most prominent architectural feature, Yoruba cities incorporated striking axes and sightlines, along with a grid-style radial form, in keeping with urban planning in the grand manner. Characteristically, the palace was the largest, tallest, most ornate structure in city, with surrounding walls that were exceptionally high. Geographic information system (GIS) analysis of Ife reveals the strategic ways in which religious and other structures were sited to underscore broader calendrical, political and historic themes.[13] In both mythic and spatial terms the city of Ile-Ife complements at once the mounded pregnant body of the mother goddess Yemoja, the watery surround where the culture hero Odudua is said to have first sprinkled sand to create earth, and the image of a tortoise in reference to Obatala, the head of the opposing deity's pantheon. The city is also divided ritually into quadrants, which are traversed yearly by ceremonial paths that crisscross the city (and the year), dividing the centre between competing families and deities.

In the Edo royal capital, Benin City, southwest of Ife, European travellers who began reaching this area in the middle of the 15th century describe an impressive urban centre distinguished by broad avenues and well-constructed residences. The massive palace, located in the middle of this walled metropolis, was graced in later centuries by several large portico structures with massive turrets decorated with cast bronze birds and serpents, visible from many parts of the city. As at Ife, Benin was notable for its historic potsherd mosaic pavements and a new palace and plan that date to the early 14th century. A complex system of earthworks honeycombed the larger urban area to mark the lands of court-affiliated families.

To the west, in the Fon Kingdom of Benin Republic, early urban centres were planned with a centralized palace, market, temple complex, and circumscribing moat-wall system, similar to Yoruba examples. The plan for Abomey, the Fon capital, is said in local oral traditions to have been established by King Agaja (1708–40), the son of Abomey's first king, Hwegbaja. The city was also defined, in important ways, by the strategic positioning of palaces for the crown princes. Placed in a spiral pattern that extended outwards from the central palace, they provided a basis for urban growth and renewal over time. Each crown prince built his own palace in an area of the city along the outward spiral, appropriating adjacent lands from earlier residents to create structures for family members and retainers. The spiralling design of this urban renewal idiom is said to reference the powerful local rainbow python god, identified with life, wealth and well-being.[14] The first mosque also is said to have been built in the city during Agaja's reign. The square, rather than circular, shape of Abomey's circumscribing wall suggests complements with early Hausa cities to the northwest, centres that were Islamicized in the 16th century.

Hausa cities, in northern Nigeria and adjacent regions of Niger and Cameroon, have their precursors in the preIslamic, Kanem (Bornu) urban centres of the late 8th to 10th centuries CE that developed in the Lake Chad area around the time of Jenne-Jeno and Igbo Ukwu. Like these other polities, Kanem figured prominently in short- and long-distance trade. In the 11th or 12th century, Kanem's ruler converted to Islam and, in the 14th century, the capital was moved westward into Bornu. At this time, Kanuri agriculturalists in the new Kanem-Bornu state were creating centres featuring baked earth bricks for central edifices and unbaked *tubali* for the city walls. These changes, along with an array of Coptic pottery sherds, suggest possible ties with Christian monasteries in areas west of the Nile valley.[15] Kanuri city planning, as in later Hausa and Yoruba examples, positioned the palace at the middle of the city, within a larger walled area. This centralized plan reinforced the primacy of ruler within the capital, and the latter within the state.

Hausa cities emerged in locations close to the intersections of major trade routes, valued resources, especially iron, and powerful spirit locales. Many developed, in part, around the need for protected cattle corrals of Fulani pastoralists who were seeking more settled lives, a feature that Hausa cities share with Timbuktu, which also had a well at its centre. The Kano chronicle dates the first permanent market in Kano to the 15th century, crediting Bornu refugees with this institution. Later that century, the Hausa ruler Muhammad Rumfa constructed, or extended, the Kano city walls and built a centralized palace and a new market, and introduced new forms of pomp and a state council. The Hausa walled city, like other walled cities in this area, also served the protective needs of refugees from neighbouring communities. As with Yoruba, Fon and other African city-wall systems, it also played a role in the control of merchants and goods for purposes of taxes, tolls and the reduction of smuggling.

Hausa cities were also linked to a system of satellite urban settlements, the six main Hausa cities furnishing key goods or services within the larger network: textiles from Kano, markets in Katsina and Daura, militias from Gobir and slaves from Zaria, the most southern Hausa city. While certain technical developments, such as the use of domes, distinguished Hausa urban architecture, decorative features varied from one urban locale to another, with palaces, merchant residences and mosques being particularly ornamental. In symbolic terms, Hausa urban settings carried varied cosmological significance, based in part on orientation toward the cardinal directions and the positioning of special gates.

CENTRAL AFRICAN MIGRATORY CITIES

Congo, Angola, Cameroon, Rwanda and other countries in Central Africa also saw the development of urban settlements. These were often characterized by historic patterns of migratory or peripatetic identity. Characteristically, moving capitals of this sort were created at the beginning of each king's reign, or after difficult circumstance. Some migratory cities reached populations of 15,000–20,000 inhabitants and were identified, like early West African cities, by cluster-like relationships with nearby communities. Rather than emphasizing attributes of permanence and monumentality, as in northeast and southern Africa, significant manpower was committed to the creation and maintenance of large-scale, richly decorated architecture, employing ephemeral materials, such as bamboo and raffia, very little of which would remain for archaeologists to discover. Such centres suggest an emphasis on idioms of dynastic innovation, conveying the unique power of kings to impress through their control of resources and labour, for both the initial construction and upkeep over time.

In the Angola–Congo border area near the Luezi River, M'banza Kongo, the capital of the Kingdom of Kongo (1400–1914), was establish prior to the Portuguese arrival in 1483. Sited on high ground, it was already a sizable city, comparable in scale to Evora, the then thriving Avis dynastic seat in Portugal. The Kongo practice of assimilating the conquered inhabitants of other regions meant that this urban centre had a diverse population, and it was an important location for royal rituals that continued here over the centuries. While Kongo rulers rebuilt their capital cities on coming to the throne, taking up a previously inhabited site in many cases, the existence of the royal cemeteries gave spiritual vitality when a site was reoccupied. In the thickly forested areas where related raffia fibre buildings and walled compounds were constructed, many of these heavily populated centres were difficult to discern by travellers.[16]

In the nearby Kuba Kingdom (1625–1900), in the Zaire River basin forests northeast of Kongo, a grouping of ethnically diverse principalities coalesced, following migrations in the 16th century. A local leader, Shyaam a-bul a Ngoong-Shyaam, is credited with creating a new Kuba capital city and administrative centre, drawing on Kongo and Pende models. Here a rich court life developed based on the use of local and new-world crops, craft manufacturing, wealth from trade, and tribute revenue from satellite communities. Shyaam is said to have greatly increased the size of the capital city by encouraging artists, traders and warriors to take up residence here; the Kuba monarchs provided residence with relative ease, since food and other needs derived largely from surrounding peasant communities. Joseph Cornet documented the extensive work that went into the creation of new Kuba capital cities, and the unique roles of supervising architects and designers within this process.[17] A caravan system linked Bushong, the Kuba royal capital, to centres of Kongo trade activity on the coast, such as Luanda and Luango, and other places. Located, like Ife, near the juncture of forest and savanna, and in proximity to important rivers, the Kuba capital offered an array of resources and trade opportunities that, when coupled with taxes, tribute, craft specialization and status competition focused on the arts, encouraged local productivity.

The Luba Kingdom (1585–1889), situated in the marshy grasslands of the Upemba depression, with the source of the Zaire River to the southeast, was one of many Kuba trading allies. Thomas Q. Reefe has suggested that the Luba setting was critical to its political development, encouraging shared communal activities and cooperation in the creation of dams and drainage systems to counter seasonal flooding, which impacted everything from housing to agriculture and fishing.[18] Archaeological evidence identifies human occupation here from at least the 5th century CE, with urban settlements emerging around the 10th century. Their wealth was based on agriculture, specialized metalwork, and trade in salt, iron, charcoal and copper, from the Zambian copper belt, as well as cowrie shells and glass beads from the Indian Ocean. Two Luba leaders, Nkongolo and Kalala Ilunga, are identified in local oral traditions with salt and iron, as well as better government. If they were historical figures, it is not clear when they lived but suggestions have been made ranging from the 15th to the early 18th century.[19] Mary Nooter and Allen Roberts have discussed the enduring importance of Luba capital cities that, once abandoned by rulers when new centres are founded, became key ritual sites.[20]

The migratory urban centres of Kongo, Kuba and Luba, as well as those of the Lunda Kingdom (*c.* 1600–1887) – and of the Cameroon grasslands – take an array of symbolic forms, linked to internal positioning in relation to nearby rivers or mountains, central axis plans with bilateral siting of key structures (suggesting in some cases spiders or tortoises), and maze-like spatial confirmation within some palace complexes. Other important urban forms associated with migratory settlements include Ethiopian royal capitals and Buganda dynastic capitals, as well as Zulu war centres, the latter evoking Assyrian and Roman war cities.[21]

Taken together, these diverse African settlements convey the early and enduring importance of ancient cities in Africa, as focal points of political and artistic engagement, complex administrative organization and trade affiliations with centres near and far. The communal need to address larger environmental and other issues (floods, the hunt, protection, manufacturing, trade control) seems to have been important to their success. Whatever the reasons for their development, Africa's urban centres show broad appreciation for the benefits of social aggregation. The more ephemeral materials that often distinguish many African cities and towns offer unique advantages to growth and change over time, providing ready flexibility in response to changing needs. If architectural durability is less important in many historic Africa cities than in the West or Asia, this feature is often replaced by concomitant interest in creativity and innovation on the part of local leaders, as well as a larger interest in more egalitarian political approaches: perspectives that, even within royal contexts, preclude the descendants of a single ruling line from assuming political and resource control through many generations. African cities are also creative, in many different ways, in terms of providing new opportunities for their residents.

NOTES

1. The differences between towns and cities are in truth little defined, with many cultures using the same term for both.

2. For the most part they did not begin as a result of outside Islamic or European intervention. On African historic cities more generally, see David M. Anderson and Richard Rathbone, eds, *Africa's urban past*, Oxford: Oxford University Press; Portsmouth, NH: Heinemann, 2000; Peter Garlake, *Early art and architecture of Africa*, Oxford: Oxford University Press, 2002; Bill Freund, *The African city: A history*, London and New York: Cambridge University Press, 2007; Toyin Falola and Steven J. Salm, eds, *Nigerian cities*, Trenton, NJ: Africa World Press, 2004; Kolawole Adekola, 'Early urban centres in West Africa', *African Diaspora Archaeology Network* (March 2009), http://www.diaspora.uiuc.edu/news0309/news0309.html, accessed 8 November 2010.

3. This also reflects the frequent association of cities (and societies associated with them) as 'civilizations', and those regions lacking such centres as 'uncivilized'.

4. Mohenjo-daro in Pakistan (2600–1900 BCE) was one of the largest ancient cities (with a population of perhaps more than 40,000) and one of the first to incorporate a grid plan (Jonathan Mark Kenoyer, *Ancient cities of the Indus Valley civilization*, Karachi, Oxford and New York: Oxford University Press, 1998).

5. Other early African trading centres include Tripoli in Libya and Carthage in Tunisia, which were both founded by Phoenician traders and became popular merchant destinations and early European rivals for east–west Mediterranean trade. With the fall of Carthage to Rome in 146 BCE, Tripoli became a protectorate of Kush (Nubia).

6. Roderick J. McIntosh, 'Clustered cities of the Middle Niger: Alternative routes to authority in prehistory', in Anderson and Rathbone, eds., *Africa's urban past*, pp. 19–36, and *Ancient Middle Niger: Urbanism and the self-organizing landscape*, Cambridge and New York: Cambridge University Press, 2005; Roderick J. McIntosh and Susan Keech McIntosh, 'The inland Niger Delta before the Empire of Mali: Evidence from Jenne-Jeno', *Journal of African History*, vol. 22, no. 1 (1981), pp. 1–22.

7. James Morris and Suzanne Preston Blier, *Butabu: Adobe architecture of West Africa*, Princeton, NJ: Princeton Architectural Press, 2003.

8. As he notes: 'A branch of the Nil [Niger] encircles the city on all four sides. In places this may be crossed by wading when the water is low but in others it may be traversed only by a boat' (in J. F. P. Hopkins and Nehemia Levtzion, eds, *Corpus of early Arabic sources for West African history*, New York: Markus Weiner, 1981, p. 262).

9. On Tellem and Dogon architecture, see also Rita Bolland, *Tellem textiles; Archaeological finds from burial caves in Mali's Bandiagara Cliff*, Amsterdam: Royal Tropical Institute; Leiden, Rijksmuseum voor Volkenkunde; Bamako: Institut des Sciences Humaines; Bamako: Musée National, 1991; Jean-Christophe Huet, *Villages perchés des Dogon du Mali: Habitat, espace et société*, Paris: L'Harmattan, 1994. On architectural anthropomorphism, see among others, Suzanne Preston Blier, *The anatomy of architecture: Ontology and metaphor in Batammaliba architectural expression*, Chicago: University of Chicago Press, 1994.

10. Early Yoruba cities were sometimes discounted by Western theorists because they were assumed to be lineage-based (rather than heterogeneous). In Yoruba urban centres, however, 'lineage' is used to define a wide array of non-kin social relationships as well, among these prisoners of war and strangers who were integrated into lineage like units for socio-political-religious reasons.

11. On Yoruba cities more generally, see Akin L. Mabogunje, *Yoruba towns*, Ibadan: Ibadan University Press, 1962; G. J. Afolabi Ojo, *Yoruba palaces: A study of Afins of Yorubaland*, London: University of London Press, 1966; Robert Smith, *Kingdoms of the Yoruba*, London: Methuen, 1969. On Ife area archaeological traditions, see Akinwumi Ogundiran, 'Chronology, material culture, and pathways to the cultural history of Yoruba-Edo region, 500 BC–AD 1800', in Toyin Falola and Christian Jennings, eds, *Sources and methods in African history: Spoken, written, unearthed*, Rochester, NY: University of Rochester Press; Woodbridge, Suffolk: Boydell & Brewer, 2003, pp. 33–78.

12. On the elephant hunt and state formation, see Humphrey J. Fisher, 'The Eastern Maghrib and the Central Sudan', in Roland Oliver, ed., *The Cambridge history of Africa*, vol. 3, Cambridge: Cambridge University Press, 1977, pp. 232–312.

13. On cosmological dimensions of city planning more generally, see Amos Rapoport, *The meaning of the built environment: A nonverbal communication approach*, rev. edn, Tucson: University of Arizona Press, 1990.

14. On Fon, Savi and Ouidah architecture, see Michael Houseman, Blandine Legonou, Christiane Massy and Xavier Crepin, 'Note sur la structure évolutive d'une ville

historique: L'exemple d'Abomey (République populaire du Bénin)', *Cahiers d'Etudes Africaines*, vol. 26, no. 104 (1986), pp. 527–46; Robin Law, 'Ouidah: A pre-colonial urban centre in coastal Africa, 1727–1892', in Anderson and Rathbone, eds, *Africa's urban past*, pp. 85–96; Neil L. Norman and Kenneth G. Kelly, 'Landscape politics: The serpent ditch and the rainbow in West Africa', *American Anthropologist*, vol. 106, no. 1 (2004), pp. 98–110; Suzanne Preston Blier, 'Razing the roof: The architecture of destruction in Dahomey', in Tony Atkin, ed., *Structure and Meaning in Human Settlements*, Philadelphia: University of Pennsylvania, 2005.

15. A. D. H. Bivar and P. L. Shinnie, 'Old Kanuri capitals', *Journal of African History*, vol. 3, no. 1 (1962), pp. 1–10.

16. Georges Balandier in Suzanne Preston Blier, *Royal arts of Africa: The majesty of form*, New York: Prentice Hall, 1998.

17. Joseph Cornet, *Art Royal Kuba*, Milan: Sipiel, 1992.

18. Thomas Q. Reefe, *The rainbow and the kings: A history of the Luba Empire to 1891*, Berkeley: University of California Press, 1981.

19. Bassey Andah, 'Genesis and development of settlements in the Guinea and savanna regions', in *The development of urbanism from a global perspective*, Uppsala Universitet, 2002. On urban development in the eastern lakes area more generally, see Andrew Reid, 'The character of urbanism in inter-Lacustrine Eastern Africa', in *The development of urbanism from a global perspective*, Uppsala: Uppsala Universitet, 2002.

20. Mary Nooter and Allen F. Roberts, *Memory: Luba art and the making of history*, New York: Center for African Art, 1996.

21. Beginning in the later half of the 15th century, Europeans created trading and replenishment centres as well as later forts along the African coast that grew in time into important cities, among them Dakar (Senegal), Accra (Ghana) and Luanda (Angola). By the late 19th century Europeans were also creating inland cities to serve as new colonial capitals, among these Niamey (Niger), Nairobi (Kenya), Harare (Zimbabwe) and Johannesburg (South Africa). Each had its own colonial importance, Nairobi as an East African railway midpoint, Harare as a military-protected settler town (organized by Cecil Rhodes) and Johannesburg as a gold-rush town.

Three historic patterns of urban settlement are found in Africa. Monumental urbanism is characterized by substantial permanent structures in stone. Satellite urbanism is characterized, in both early and later contexts, by collaboration between interlinked community clusters that together create an urban settlement structure. Migratory or peripatetic urban settlements characteristically prevailed in central Africa, these cities sharing a relatively nomadic identity. In some African urban contexts, several of these design attributes were at play, with local building materials providing unique possibilities for creativity.

Suzanne Preston Blier

NANA OFORIATTA AYIM
IMAGINED TOPOGRAPHIES

We live in a world where technology and access have created overlapping realities, ethnicities, languages and religions, some of which are culturally determined. Africa's pluralities and relativities of life are its greatest source of conflict as well its greatest strength. Its polysidedness has a parallel in the polyrhythms found throughout the continent, where time overlaps through the simultaneous beating of two or more rhythms and where a sonic space is created that gives equal weight to both sides of the rhythmic boundary, the silent offbeat as well as the sounded onbeat. Musically, this layering results not in discordance, but in harmony. In reality, it often does the opposite.

The legacy of colonialism, especially the forced deportation of so many Africans, is doubtless a crucial chapter in the continent's history, but it is often seen as Africa's defining chapter, calcifying the continent into being the impassive object rather than the subject of its own definition. Africa and Africans have continuously redefined themselves and their place in the wider history and context of the formation of nations from centralized and pastoral states. The transition to a global world order calls for us to define ourselves again, not in a vacuum, but by building on and renegotiating the terms of the past.

Artists can harmonize chaos, to present new topographies of past-present-future so that we can imagine what is not yet possible and, by imagining it, bring it into being.

ABOUDRAMANE

The Ivorian sculptor Aboudramane, in creating models of churches, mosques and ritual buildings in wood, clay and straw, accentuates their different iconographies and at the same time creates an artistic space in which vernacular buildings are not flattened by zealous conversion but subsumed into an architectural pidgin. In his vision, different spatial dialects can coexist without cancelling each other out. He creates an imagined polyphonic past that echoes that of the Akans of Côte d'Ivoire, Ghana and Togo. The Akan religions were inclusive, in that they regularly created new demiurges for new exigencies, and evolutionary, in that they discarded old ones that became obsolete. When the singular, linear, grand narrative religions of Islam and Christianity arrived, they sought to swallow the old religions whole. The Akan peoples in their modernity adopted these new religions, but also adapted them with elements of the old. Even today, in many states, the Akan calendar, the Adaduanan, itself a multiple calendrical system that combines seven- and six-day cycles, is used side-by-side with the Gregorian one. This calendar marks the sacred days on which citizens pay allegiance to their kings and founding fathers. When nation-builders attempted to encourage citizens to singular loyalties, they fought to hold onto those multiple allegiances that in the past were made to king, clan, age-set and professional guild; and today are made to king and country.

Aboudramane's *sculptures-mémoires* pay homage to these pluralities and, by creating a space in which they exist side by side, remind us that they are not mutually exclusive.

SUSAN HEFUNA

Through her photographs, drawings and videos, Egyptian-German artist Susan Hefuna similarly displaces the linear Western notion of time, as in her video *Life in the Delta 1423 / 2002* (2002). A hidden camera sits on the roof her family home in the Nile Delta, showing us a street that at first glance seems static, like life has been lived for centuries, until it is displaced with an appearance by the artist in Western clothes. As the title implies, different time frames are encapsulated at once, whether the past lives on in the continuous present, or through the duality of the Christian and Islamic calendars.

Hefuna draws on her dual heritage, repeatedly using the metaphor of the *mashrabiya* or window screens in her work. She is aware that to Western observers *mashrabiya* present abstract patterns while for Egyptians they hold a deeper meaning. They were used in the past to screen women from the outsider's gaze as they looked out. To the outside world they may have seemed like prisons of femininity, but on the inside they provided freedom to observe unobserved. She plays on the ambiguity of interpretation, questions it, creating a tension of the gap in which she stands somewhere in the middle.

Her drawings of the lattices are layered on papers of different thickness and translucence, patterned with indistinct shadows, deliberately obscured. Obscured too are the blurred and scratched images of Egypt taken with a pinhole camera, or the photographs of herself in seemingly exotic places, such as on a sphinx that turns out actually to be situated on

London's Embankment. She turns the idea of the exotic on its head by fictionalizing it, taking control of the myth of the past as exoticizing subject rather than exoticized object.

This ambiguity is inherent in the classical designs of the strip-woven Akan Kente cloth, which depends on cultural knowledge for understanding its layers. As with Kente cloth, in Hefuna's work the whole is not necessarily apparent, so that we are urged to go deeper and think harder about what we perceive.

JULIE MEHRETU

Ethiopian-born painter Julie Mehretu similarly layers but, instead of obscuring, she unearths our recurring commonalities, the order under the seeming chaos, by piling supposedly unconnected built environments, such as those of Lagos onto those of the Upper West Side of New York. She alchemizes influences from all over the world in her large-scale paintings. Traces of European abstraction, Chinese calligraphy and Ethiopian illuminated manuscripts, as well as cartoons, maps and graffiti, are built up through layers of clashing, staccatoed pen and pencil marks and rushing, controlled swirls of paint.

In *Transcending: The new international* (2003), urban plans for Africa are superimposed on aerial maps of actual economic and political capitals of the continent, as well as photographs of cityscapes clashing with those urban plans. Abstract marks act as characters, the subjects and social agents of the spaces they inhabit.

Like the Ayan – the classical drum poems of the Akan that speak of 'the I of the past as the I of the present', overlapping the subjects' present and past in one continuous time frame – Mehretu's paintings eloquently collapse the spatial structures that define our modern lives into one artistic space and reveal their complexities and juxtapositions.

BODYS ISEK KINGELEZ

The Democratic Republic of the Congo artist Bodys Isek Kingelez, through curves, circles and lines, patterned with green, red, yellow, blue abstractions and inspired by Gothic, Egyptian, Soviet, Congolese and Japanese idioms, creates a supra-Bodysian sculptural language. As with his design model for l'Hôpital pour le Sida (AIDS hospital), Kingelez is by turns hopeful and playful, challenging the French developer Francis Bouygues to realize his upside-down pyramid-shaped sculpture *Stars Palms Bouygues*. Sometimes his models have a symbolic pathos, like *Bel Atlas* (1989), which reimagines the Arche de la Défense in Soviet style, complete with revolutionary symbols – a sculptural dirge, perhaps, to the now crumbling ideals of what was the ultimate socialist experiment.

Sometimes the works are aggressive in their futurism, like those on the subject of the Democratic Republic of the Congo's capital Kinshasa: *Projet pour le Kinshasa du troisième millénaire* ('Project for the Kinshasa of the third millennium', 1997), *La ville fantôme* ('Ghost town', 1996) or *Kinshasa Label* (1989), a pun on 'Kinshasa la Belle' ('Kinshasa the beautiful'; a further work of 1991 was called *Kinshasa la Belle*). Using bottle caps, corrugated cardboard, tinfoil and paper, Kingelez infuses waste with life, creates a utopian ideal, a fantastical city replete with its own multicoloured skyscrapers and Empire State Building, an African city at the forefront of tomorrow. His work expands the realms of possibility and in that is reminiscent of the classical sculptures of the Fang that once inspired the likes of Picasso and Matisse. Like their sculpture, which presented the impossibly many angles and planes of human existence at once, rather than from the single fixed eye of the beholder, his models break down the boundaries of our imaginations.

Globalization has allowed us access to countless cultures and traditions. The basis of these artists' work is plural; it traces multiple trajectories from various sources, one of which is the polyvocality found in classical aesthetics throughout Africa.

These trajectories of modernity, or polymodernities, some of which are conscious or direct and some of which exist implicitly, do not have to break with the past in order to recreate themselves. They open up new avenues of understanding by elevating various and multiple traditions rather than one dominant one.

By using metaphors of the built environment in their works, Aboudramane, Hefuna, Mehretu and Kingelez reconfigure the old perceptions of Africa. They do not present these new interpretations in isolation, an Africa alone in and distinct from the rest of the world, but in the context of the global, allowing us as citizens of the world to redefine ourselves within it, and to imagine more clearly how we stand in relation to each other.

Meroe Pyramids, Sudan.

BIOGRAPHICAL NOTES / DAVID ADJAYE

David Adjaye OBE is recognized as a leading architect of his generation. Adjaye was born in Tanzania to Ghanaian parents and his influences range from contemporary art, music and science to African art forms and the civic life of cities. In 1994 he set up his first office, where his ingenious use of materials and his sculptural ability established him as an architect with an artist's sensibility and vision.

He reformed his studio as Adjaye Associates in 2000 and immediately won several prestigious commissions. In Oslo he designed the Nobel Peace Centre in the shell of a disused railway station (completed in 2005). In London his design for the Whitechapel Idea Store pioneered a new approach to the provision of information services (2005). Later projects in London included the Stephen Lawrence Centre, with teaching and community spaces (2007), Rivington Place, an exhibition venue and resource centre (2007), and the Bernie Grant Arts Centre (2007). He is currently working on two major redevelopment projects in the city: 70–73 Piccadilly, a £600 million scheme in the prestigious Piccadilly area, and the Hackney Fashion Hub, a masterplan to renew a significant central area in the Borough of Hackney. Adjaye Associates's largest completed project to date is the £160 million Moscow School of Management Skolkovo (2010).

In the United States Adjaye was the designer of a new home for the Museum of Contemporary Art in Denver (2007), two public libraries in Washington DC (2012), as well as of several innovative residential projects. In 2009 a team led by Adjaye was selected to design the new $360 million Smithsonian National Museum of African American History and Culture on the National Mall in Washington DC. The practice has also completed a social housing scheme in New York's Sugar Hill (2014) and the Ethelbert Cooper Gallery of African & African American Art at Harvard's Hutchins Center (2014). Adjaye is currently working on the new home for the Studio Museum in Harlem, the Ruby City building for the Linda Pace Foundation in San Antonio, and a condominium development for Four Seasons in Washington DC.

Adjaye Associates now has offices in London, New York, and Accra, with projects throughout the world. These include the Aishti Foundation shopping and cultural complex in Beirut (2015), the Alara concept store in Lagos (2014), and a new headquarters building for the International Finance Corporation in Dakar (ongoing).

Adjaye frequently collaborates with contemporary artists on art and installation projects. Examples include *The upper room*, with thirteen paintings by Chris Ofili (2002), *Within reach*, a second installation with Ofili in the British pavilion at the Venice Biennale (2003), and the Thyssen-Bornemisza Art for the 21st Century Pavilion that was designed to show a projection work by Olafur Eliasson, *Your black horizon*, at the 2005 Venice Biennale. *The upper room* is now in the permanent collection of Tate Britain. Adjaye recently collaborated with Okwui Enwezor on the design of the 56th Venice Art Biennale (2015).

Adjaye has taught at the Royal College of Art, where he had previously studied, and at the Architectural Association School in London, and has held distinguished professorships at the universities of Pennsylvania, Yale and Princeton. He is currently the John C. Portman Design Critic in Architecture at Harvard. He was awarded the OBE for services to architecture in 2007, received the Design Miami/Year of the Artist title in 2011 and the *Wall Street Journal* Innovator Award in 2013.

The material from Adjaye's ten-year study of the capital cities of Africa was shown in *Urban Africa,* an exhibition at the Design Museum, London (2010), and published as *African Metropolitan Architecture* (New York, 2011) and as *Adjaye Africa Architecture* (London, 2011). He was the artistic director of *GEO-graphics: A map of art practices in Africa, past and present*, a major exhibition at the Centre for Fine Arts, Brussels (2010). An exhibition of his architectural work, *David Adjaye: Output*, was held at Gallery MA, Tokyo (2010). In 2015 a comprehensive retrospective exhibition of his work to date was held at Haus der Kunst in Munich and the Art Institute of Chicago.

BIOGRAPHICAL NOTES / CONTRIBUTORS

PETER ALLISON is an architectural writer based in London. He has contributed widely to exhibition catalogues and international publications on architecture and edited *David Adjaye: Houses* and *David Adjaye: Making public buildings*, both published by Thames & Hudson.

KWAME ANTHONY APPIAH is Professor of Philosophy and Law at New York University. His major current work concerns the relationships between philosophical ethics and other disciplines. Recent books include *Thinking it through: An introduction to contemporary philosophy*, *The ethics of identity*, *Cosmopolitanism: Ethics in a world of strangers*, *Experiments in ethics*, *The honor code: How moral revolutions happen* and *Lines of descent: W. E. B. Du Bois and the emergence of identity*.

NANA OFORIATTA AYIM is a writer, filmmaker and cultural historian. She is the founder of the research initiative ANO (http://anoghana.org). She has written for publications, such as *Frieze* magazine and the *National Geographic*; shown her films in institutions like the New Museum and on Channel 4; and curated for venues such as KNUST, Kumasi and the Liverpool Biennial. She recently received the Art & Technology Award from LACMA for her pan-African *Cultural Encyclopaedia*, and was named one of fifty African trailblazers by *The Africa Report*.

OKWUI ENWEZOR is a curator, writer and critic. He is the director of the Haus der Kunst, Munich, editor of *Nka: Journal of Contemporary African Art*, and previously served as the artistic director of Documenta 11 and as dean of academic affairs and senior vice president of the San Francisco Art Institute. In 2015 he was director of the Venice Biennale and co-curator of a major travelling exhibition on the work of David Adjaye.

NAIGZY GEBREMEDHIN is an architect born in Addis Ababa in 1934. He studied at Kansas University and MIT. He served as Dean of the Faculty of Architecture and Building at the former Haile-Selassie University. Between 1975 and 1994 he served as a member of the staff of the United Nations Environment Programme. Naigzy was coordinator of the study of the modernist architecture of Asmara, Eritrea, and is coauthor of the book, *Asmara, Africa's secret modernist city*.

GARTH MYERS is Distinguished Professor of Urban International Studies at Trinity College Hartford, CT, USA. Myers has authored four books: *Verandahs of power: Colonialism and space in urban Africa*, *Disposable cities: Garbage, governance and sustainable development in urban Africa*, *African cities: Alternative visions of urban theory and practice* and *Urban environments in Africa: A critical analysis of environmental politics*. He has coedited two further books, along with more than fifty articles on African development.

SUZANNE PRESTON BLIER is the Allen Whitehill Clowes Professor of Fine Arts and of African and African American Studies at Harvard University. Her books include *The anatomy of architecture: Ontology and metaphor in Batammaliba architectural expression*, *African vodun: Art, psychology and power*, *Royal arts of Africa: The majesty of form*, and *Butabu: Adobe architecture of West Africa* (with photographer James Morris). She has served as a museum consultant and curated several exhibitions of African art.

JENNY ROBINSON is Professor of Human Geography at University College London and Honorary Visiting Professor in the African Centre for Cities at the University of Cape Town. She has also worked at the Open University in the UK and the University of Natal, South Africa. Her book *Ordinary cities: Between modernity and development* offers a postcolonial critique of urban studies, explaining and contesting urban theory's neglect of cities of the global South.

SPECIAL THANKS

Special thanks to the fifty-two drivers whom I encountered on this journey and whose insights into their cities and communities I have relied on while mapping this project.

CREDITS

CITY DATA

With the exception of the population figures, the statistical data on the introductory pages to each city were sourced from the CIA *World factbook*, https://www.cia.gov/library/publications/resources/the-world-factbook/ accessed on 11 January 2016.
The country population figures were sourced from the United Nations *World population prospects, key findings and advanced tables, 2015 revision*, http://esa.un.org/unpd/wpp/publications/files/key _ findings _ wpp _ 2015.pdf.
The city population figures were sourced from the United Nations *World urbanization prospects, 2014 revision,* http://esa.un.org/unpd/wup/Publications/Files/WUP2014-Report.pdf.

IMAGES

All images by David Adjaye unless otherwise indicated.
Images of Mogadishu, Somalia, provided by Rashid Ali and Kudu Arts.
All satellite images courtesy of TerraServer.com, with the exceptions of Yaoundé, Cameroon, copyright © DigitalGlobe, image provided by European Space Imaging, 2011, and Juba, South Sudan © Alamy.
Title images for 'The Maghreb', 'Desert', 'The Sahel', 'Forest', 'Savanna & Grassland' and 'Mountain & Highveld' sections © Alamy.

TEXT

Essays 'The Maghreb', 'Desert', 'The Sahel', 'Forest', 'Savanna & Grassland' and 'Mountain & Highveld' by David Adjaye and Peter Allison.
City overviews by Peter Allison.
City observations and captions by David Adjaye.
Copyright of the foreword and the contributors' essays is retained by the respective authors.

PUBLICATION

Editing: Peter Allison
Concept and design: Adjaye Associates
Design: Zoe Simpson and Ama Ofeibea Amponsah

With special thanks to:

Doreen Kibuka-Musoke for her encouragement in starting this project.

Wanja Michuki and Ikena Carreira for their support and generosity.

Professor Ray Harris, Dr Ben Page and Mathew Tyburski of the Geography Department, University College London, for advice on the geographic terrains.

James McComish of Pearce McComish Architects, Harare, for assistance with images of Harare.

Rashid Ali and Kudu Arts, London, for assistance with images and information on Mogadishu.

Joe Adjekum, for advice on Malabo.

The Adjaye family, wherever they are in the world, and all those who patiently supported me on this long journey.

First published in 2011 in paperback in the United States of America by Rizzoli International Publications, 300 Park Avenue South, New York, NY 10010-5399

This compact edition first published in 2016 in the United States of America by Thames & Hudson Inc., 500 Fifth Avenue, New York, New York 10110

thamesandhudsonusa.com

Library of Congress Catalog Card Number: 2016932434

ISBN 978-0-500-34316-6

Printed and bound in China by C & C Offset Printing Co. Ltd

ABIDJAN / CÔTE D'IVOIRE ABUJA / NIGERIA ACCRA / GHANA ADDIS ABABA / ETHIOPIA ALGIERS / ALGERIA ANTANANARIVO / MADAGASCAR ASMARA / ERITREA BAMAKO / MALI BANGUI / CENTRAL AFRICAN REPUBLIC BANJUL / GAMBIA BISSAU / GUINEA-BISSAU BRAZZAVILLE / REPUBLIC OF CONGO BUJUMBURA / BURUNDI CAIRO / EGYPT CONAKRY / GUINEA COTONOU / BENIN DAKAR / SENEGAL DAR ES SALAAM / TANZANIA DJIBOUTI / DJIBOUTI FREETOWN / SIERRA LEONE GABORONE / BOTSWANA HARARE / ZIMBABWE JUBA / SOUTH SUDAN KAMPALA / UGANDA KHARTOUM / SUDAN KIGALI / RWANDA KINSHASA / DEMOCRATIC REPUBLIC OF CONGO LIBREVILLE / GABON LILONGWE / MALAWI LOMÉ / TOGO LUANDA / ANGOLA LUSAKA / ZAMBIA MALABO / EQUATORIAL GUINEA MAPUTO / MOZAMBIQUE MASERU / LESOTHO MBABANE / SWAZILAND MOGADISHU / SOMALIA MONROVIA / LIBERIA MORONI / COMOROS NAIROBI / KENYA N'DJAMENA / CHAD NIAMEY / NIGER NOUAKCHOTT / MAURITANIA OUAGADOUGOU / BURKINA FASO PORT LOUIS / MAURITIUS PRAIA / CAPE VERDE PRETORIA / SOUTH AFRICA RABAT / MOROCCO SÃO TOMÉ / SÃO TOMÉ AND PRÍNCIPE TRIPOLI / LIBYA TUNIS / TUNISIA VICTORIA / SEYCHELLES WINDHOEK / NAMIBIA YAOUNDÉ / CAMEROON